OUR "REGULAR" READERS RAVE!

"Your books are the greatest I have ever read. The eternal struggle for reading material has finally been quenched!"

—Tucker J.

"Thank you for the *Bathroom Readers*. I no longer have to read the backs of my shampoo bottles. My husband and I read so much in the bathroom that we refer to it as 'the study'."

—Charissa A.

"I've constructed a special shrine for my *Bathroom Readers*. I heard that people spend about ten months in the throne room during their lifetime. I'm sure, thanks to you, I'll spend a couple of years."

—William F.

"I want to thank you for the reply to my email. Even though I feel that my life is as exciting as they come, I was tremendously pleased when I checked my email and found that it was a personal reply. It makes me love the BRI even more."

—Steve S.

"I found your website very commodious—quite easy to get a handle on. Frankly, I was bowled over, flushed actually, and almost fell off my stool when I discovered that Vol. 6 was not the end of your roll. I could barely keep the lid down! And the new books seem to have twice as many sheets as the prior ones—a seemingly endless supply of two-ply reading if ever there was one! Thank God there's Uncle John to float us through tough times."

—Uncle Harry Jr.

"I love the *Bathroom Readers*...I take them everywhere I go. Before I found the BRI, I was unpopular with the ladies; now that I'm a walking font of knowledge, they can't keep their hands off me. Thanks!"

—Dwayne R.

"I was shopping and saw your book for the first time. I love trivia so I just threw one in the basket and continued shopping. I thought it would look good in the bathroom.

"Well, I started to read it and found myself looking forward to going there. Then I started taking it with me to the den. Now, I read it to my husband, and I share your stories with friends. I love the laughter. I love the way you make my mind hungry for more knowledge."

—Debora K.

"Your books are such a CLASSY collection of information. I have become one of your bigger fans. You folks are GREAT!"

—John D.

"I love your material. I now have three of your books. Guests coming to my place can't wait to use the facilities because of your books. In fact, I'm thinking that I might change the color scheme of my bathroom so it doesn't clash with your books."

—Darren McK.

"Just wanted to tell you I live to read your next book...love you guys! Thanks!"

—Missy H.

"I just wanted to let you know that I think the *Bathroom Readers* are fantastic! My husband got me two for my birthday. And then, being the terrific guy that he is and knowing how much I loved this kind of book, he continued to buy them for me until I owned every one. It's almost as though these were books written especially for me."

—Dafna H.

"Thank you for making something that makes me want to read. I have a short attention span, but the *Bathroom Readers* keep me reading. I'm on my third book! They're the only books I've been able to read start to finish. I just want to say thank you, and please, don't stop making books."

—Michelle F.

Uncle John's

Ahh-Inspiring Bathroom Reader

By the
Bathroom Readers'
Institute

Bathroom Readers' Press
Ashland, Oregon

UNCLE JOHN'S AHH-INSPIRING
BATHROOM READER®

For information, write
The Bathroom Readers' Institute,
P.O. Box 1117, Ashland, OR 97520
www.bathroomreader.com
541-488-4642

Cover design by Michael Brunsfeld,
San Rafael, CA (*Brunsfeldo@comcast.net*)
BRI "technician" on back cover: Larry Kelp

Uncle John's
Ahh-Inspiring Bathroom Reader®
by The Bathroom Readers' Institute

ISBN: 1-57145-873-5

Library of Congress Catalog Card Number:
2002114026

Printed in the United States of America

Fifth Printing
14 13 12 11 10 9 8 7 6

* * * * *

"Once you can accept the universe as matter
expanding into nothing that is something,
wearing stripes with plaid comes easy."

—*Albert Einstein*

"Parliamentary Manners" by Scott Feschuk, Paul Mather, and Peter McBain as "Ask Miss Parliamentary Manners" in the *National Post*: This Week In Review, April 27, 2002. © National Post. Reprinted with permission.

"How to Toilet Train Your Cat" by Karawynn Long, found on her website *www.karawynn.net/mishacat/toilet*.

"Buried Treasure in the U.S." from THE PEOPLE'S ALMANAC © 1975 by David Wallechinsky and Irving Wallace. Reprinted with the kind permission of the authors.

Here are a few books the BRI's Throne Room would be empty without:

Lies Across America, by James W. Loewen, and author of the best-selling *Lies My Teacher Told Me*. Copyright © 1999.

An Underground Education, by Richard Zacks. Copyright © 1997 by Richard Zacks.

Joke Stew: 1,349 More Hilarious Servings from Today's Hottest Comedians, edited by Judy Brown. Copyright © 2000.

It's a Conspiracy! by the National Insecurity Council, Copyright 1992 by Michael Litchfield; published by EarthWorks Press.

What's the Number for 911? by Leland Gregory III Copyright © 2000. Andrews & McMeel Publishing.

A special thanks to some regular readers for submitting good stuff:

Max L. Israel
Sera Kirk
Gavin Sheehan
Joel & Wendy McNeil
Dean Bliss
Mike Schuster
Adam Brucker
Jonathan Gewirtz
Charles Surine
Roger Shaheen
David Whitman
Dee & Kellar Smith
Chris O'Rourke
Joe Gayeski
Janet K. Behning
Patte Rosebank
Aaron Allermann
Glen & Janese Granholm

THANK YOU!

The Bathroom Readers' Institute sincerely thanks the people whose advice and assistance made this book possible.

Gordon Javna
John Dollison
Jennifer & Zipper
Jeff Altemus
Jay Newman
Julia Papps
Thom Little
Sharilyn Hovind
Michael Brunsfeld
Janet Spencer
Lori Larson
Sam Javna
Jim McCluskey
Maggie Javna
Jeff Cheek
Jesse Clark
Sharon Freed
Jess Brallier
Bryan Henry
Gideon Javna
Angela Kern
Allen Orso
Georgine Lidell
Dylan Drake
Bernadette Baillie
Paul Stanley
Jenny Baldwin
Barb Porsche
Paula Leith
John Javna
Mike Nicita
Claudia Bauer
Hazel Daniels
Teri Morin
William Coleman
Pat Perrin
Mustard Press
Scarab Media
Porter the Wonder Dog
Sydney Stanley
Marley & Catie Pratt
Thomas Crapper

* * *

KBRX Radio, for their part of this insanity: Scott Poese and Nicole Kennedy, Dog House Morning Show

"My life has no purpose, no direction, no meaning, and yet I'm happy. I can't figure it out. What am I doing right?"

Charles M. Schulz

Hiya Sophie! Hiya Jessie!

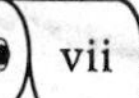

CONTENTS

Because the BRI understands your reading needs, we've divided the contents by length as well as subject.

Short—a quick read
Medium—2 to 3 pages
Long—for those extended visits, when something a little more involved is required
***Extended**—for those leg-numbing experiences

INTRODUCTION

Here we go again. Can it be a year since we've put out a *Bathroom Reader*? Wait a minute, let me look at the calender. Yes, it's time for a new edition. Every year we think we'll never be able to do another book, and every year we do.

This is our 15th year and, if I do say so myself, we've outdone ourselves. Is that immodest of me? Perhaps, but I can't help it—I think this is a great book. I've asked everyone here at the Bathroom Readers' Institute and they agree: it is immodest of me.

If this is your first *Bathroom Reader*, welcome to our family. If you're one of our loyal readers, it's good to have you back. You're the reason we keep writing these books. Of course, we love researching and writing—it gives us an excuse to keep learning about, say, shrunken heads (page 291)—but knowing you're out there, loving what we do, is the real payoff for us. How do we know you're out there? We get enthusiastic letters of support every day. Thanks... keep 'em coming and let us know what you'd like to see us write about.

Speaking of that, this year we've included a bunch of articles our readers have been asking for: the Origin of Video Games, the History of Professional Wrestling, and stories of the Stanley Cup to mention a few. And here are some more great ones you'll find in the book: Number Two's Wild Ride (that's from John D), *Saturday Night Live* (that's by Jay), The Opossum (Little Thom), Death of a Princess (from Jim) and the San Francisco Earthquake (by Janet).

Some notes:

• First of all, this book wouldn't be possible without the gargantuan efforts of the BRI team (thank you Jennifer, thank you Jeff, thank you Jay, Julia, John, and Thom—great job, everybody).

• There are a few articles which may look familiar to BRI stalwarts. We've revisited a couple of topics from previous *Bathroom Readers*; expanding on what we wrote about eleven or twelve (or thirteen) years ago. We are not repeating ourselves. We are not repeating ourselves.

• Joyous news! We just had a baby...book. It's *Uncle John's Bathroom Reader For Kids Only* (shameless plug). Over the years we've gotten so many letters from young readers that we decided to do a book just for them.

• A special thanks to Terry Budden. We put out the word that we were looking for articles by any BRI members who were "experts." Beyond our expectations, Terry sent us a great article he wrote about the town of Gander, Newfoundland. Are you an expert on something? Let us know at *www.bathroomreader.com* (second shameless plug).

Well, that's all for now. The book's done (we always write the introduction last), it will soon be off to the printer and we're all ready for hibernation (translation: we're taking the weekend off). See you next year.

And as always, remember,

Go with the Flow!

Uncle John and the BRI Staff

P. S. Did we mention our website: *www.bathroomreader.com?*

YOU'RE MY INSPIRATION

It's always fascinating to find out where the architects of pop culture get their ideas from. These may surprise you.

VULCAN HAND SALUTE. Leonard Nimoy invented this for Mr. Spock during the filming of a *Star Trek* episode. The gesture was borrowed from the Jewish High Holiday services. The Kohanim (priests) bless the congregation by extending "the palms of both hands...with thumbs outstretched and the middle and ring fingers parted." Nimoy used the same gesture for Spock, only with one hand.

SNOOPY. Based on the black-and-white dog that Peanuts creator Charles Schulz owned when he was 13 years old. The real dog's name was Spike, which Schulz used as the name of Snoopy's brother.

SAVING PRIVATE RYAN. Steven Spielberg's WWII drama was inspired by a real-life story: A few weeks after D-Day, Sergeant Fritz Niland learned that his three older brothers had been killed in action. Army policy states that no family should suffer the loss of more than two sons, so, over Niland's protests, he was sent home.

ANIMAL (the Muppets' drummer). Apparently Jim Henson was a rock 'n' roll fan. He based the out-of-control drummer on another out-of-control drummer: The Who's Keith Moon.

COSMO KRAMER. While Larry David and Jerry Seinfeld were laying the groundwork for *Seinfeld*, David's eccentric neighbor, Kenny Kramer, would often pop in and bug them. Just like his TV counterpart, Kramer had no real job but dabbled in schemes and inventions (he patented glow-in-the-dark jewelry). "Unlike the TV Kramer," says Kenny, "my hairbrained schemes work."

DR. EVIL. Mike Myers's inspiration for Austin Powers's archenemy comes from the James Bond villain, Blofeld, in *You Only Live Twice*. But Dr. Evil's famous mannerism comes from a 1979 photograph of Rolling Stones guitarist Keith Richards. It shows the rocker "in the exact pinky-biting pose favored by Dr. Evil."

Monday is the only day of the week that has an anagram: dynamo.

COURT TRANSQUIPS

The verdict is in! Court transcripts make some of the best bathroom reading there is. These were actually said, word for word, in a court of law.

Judge: I know you, don't I?
Defendant: Uh, yes.
Judge: Alright, how do I know you?
Defendant: Judge, do I have to tell you?
Judge: Of course, you might be obstructing justice not to tell me.
Defendant: Okay. I was your bookie.

Lawyer: How do you feel about defense attorneys?
Juror: I think they should all be drowned at birth.
Lawyer: Well, then, you are obviously biased for the prosecution.
Juror: That's not true. I think prosecutors should be drowned at birth, too.

Judge: Please identify yourself for the record.
Defendant: Colonel Ebenezer Jackson.
Judge: What does the "Colonel" stand for?
Defendant: Well, it's kinda like the "Honorable" in front of your name—not a damn thing.

Judge: You are charged with habitual drunkenness. Have you anything to say in your defense?
Defendant: Habitual thirstiness?

Plaintiff's Lawyer: What doctor treated you for the injuries you sustained while at work?
Plaintiff: Dr. J.
Plaintiff's Lawyer: And what kind of physician is Dr. J?
Plaintiff: Well, I'm not sure, but I remember that you said he was a good plaintiff's doctor.

Q: Do you have any children or anything of that kind?

Q: Do you have any suggestions as to what prevented this from being a murder trial instead of an attempted-murder trial?
A: The victim lived.

Q: You don't know what it was, and you didn't know what it looked like, but can you describe it?

Defendant: If I called you a son of a bitch, what would you do?
Judge: I'd hold you in contempt and assess an additional five days in jail.
Defendant: What if I thought you were a son of a bitch?
Judge: I can't do anything about that. There's no law against thinking.
Defendant: In that case, I think you're a son of a bitch.

It takes 4,000 grains of sugar to fill a teaspoon.

HUMAN HAILSTONES

Hailstones are formed when ice crystals in a thunderhead are tossed around, gathering successive coats of ice. But people can get caught in thunderheads, too.

THE PILOT

In 1959 Lt. Col. William Rankin bailed out of his single-engine plane when the engine failed at 47,000 feet above Virginia. A storm was in progress, and he fell right through the middle of it. It would normally take a man 13 minutes to fall 47,000 feet, but Rankin got caught in the updrafts and remained aloft for 45 minutes. He tumbled about in –70° temperatures, covered with ice and sleet, his body bruised by hailstones. Fortunately, his parachute opened at 10,000 feet and he landed intact in a tree in North Carolina, 65 miles from where he'd bailed out. He made a complete recovery.

THE GLIDERS

In 1930 a German glider society held an exhibition. Five glider pilots flew into a towering thunderhead hoping to set new altitude records by using the updrafts. But the updrafts were more than they had counted on—the gliders were torn to pieces by the violent winds. The pilots bailed out but were carried to the upper regions of the cloud, where they were coated by ice. All but one froze to death before finally falling to the ground.

THE PARACHUTIST

In 1975 Mike Mount jumped from a plane 4,500 feet over Maryland, expecting a two-minute fall to Earth. Although thunderstorms were building, Mount had over 400 jumps under his belt and thought he could steer himself through the clouds. He couldn't. He was sucked into the storm and pulled up to 10,000 feet. The storm swept him up and dropped him again and again. He debated whether to cut himself free of his main chute and freefall through the storm, relying on his reserve chute to save him. But he wasn't sure he'd be able to see the ground approaching. Finally the storm released its grip and he landed, cold but unharmed, nine miles from his intended drop zone. His wild ride had lasted 30 minutes.

Mars attacks: In 1911 a meteor from Mars fell to Earth in Nakhla, Egypt, killing a dog.

PENNY WISE

Some people collect coins; Uncle John collects trivia about coins.

Abraham Lincoln was the first president to be depicted on a U.S. coin, a penny issued in 1909. The penny is the only U.S. coin where the person faces right instead of left.

Why was the Lincoln penny issued beginning in 1909? To commemorate the 100th anniversary of Abraham Lincoln's birth.

When the Citizens Bank of Tenino, Washington, closed on December 5, 1931, the town was without ready cash to do business, so denominations of 25 cents, 50 cents, and $1 were printed on three-ply Sitka spruce wood, the first wooden money issued as legal tender in the U.S.

Spanish doubloons were legal tender in the United States until 1857.

Until 1965, pennies were legal tender only up to 25 cents. A creditor couldn't be forced to accept more than 25 pennies in payment of a debt. Silver coins were legal tender for amounts not exceeding $10 in any one payment.

The 1921 Alabama Centennial half-dollar was the first U.S. coin designed by a woman, Laura Gardin Fraser.

During World War II, the United States minted pennies made of steel to conserve copper for making artillery shells.

Booker T. Washington was the first African American to be depicted on a U.S. coin, a half-dollar issued in 1946.

Codfish were depicted on many of the early coins of the infant United States from 1776 to 1778.

The first U.S. cent, which was the size of today's 50-cent piece, was coined in 1793. In 1856 the Mint produced the first penny of today's size.

In 1932 Congress issued a commemorative coin—the Washington quarter—to celebrate the 200th birthday of George Washington. The quarter was intended to be used for only one year, but it was so popular that it was continued as a regular-issue coin from 1934 on.

OOPS!

Everyone enjoys reading about someone else's blunders. So go ahead and feel superior for a few minutes.

CUT IT OUT!

"Lyn Thomas was working on a home-improvement project when he cut through a gas main, requiring the entire street to be evacuated. Moments after the gas engineers left, he went back to work...and promptly broke a water main, flooding his and his neighbor's properties."

—U.K. Mirror

GETS RID OF PLAQUE

"A plaque intended to honor deep-voiced actor James Earl Jones at Lauderhill, Florida's 2002 celebration of Martin Luther King Day, caused city officials incredible embarrassment. Somehow the plaque's maker inscribed this extremely incorrect message:

'Thank you James Earl Ray for keeping the dream alive.'

"Ray was the man convicted of assassinating King in Memphis, Tennessee, in 1968."

—ABCNews.com

WHAT A TANGLED WEB WE WEAVE

"A married couple in Beijing, China, ended up brawling after realizing they had unwittingly courted each other over the Internet. After a month of secret online flirting, the man arranged to meet up with his mystery girlfriend, only to discover it was actually his wife. He had known only her user name, I Want You.

"They each agreed to carry a certain newspaper to identify themselves, but were shocked when they came face to face and started fighting in the street. Passersby eventually alerted security guards, who had to separate the two."

—Ananova.com

TRAVELIN' LIGHT

"In 1986 an Orion Airways chartered jetliner took off from Birmingham, England, carrying 100 passengers to the Greek island of Crete. A few minutes into the flight the captain announced the

Fat City: Each employee at Ben & Jerry's headquarters gets three pints of free ice cream a day.

plane had to return to the Birmingham Airport. Technical difficulties? No, they forgot the luggage."

—Kickers: All the News That Didn't Fit

DON'T ASK, DON'T TELL

"It was the law in the ancient Greek city of Amyclae to hold one's tongue. The Amyclaeans had often panicked when they heard rumors that the powerful Spartan army was coming, so to put an end to defeatism, a law was passed forbidding rumors. Violators were to be executed.

"When the Spartans actually did appear, no one had the courage to report it, and the city was overcome without a fight."

—Amazing Lost History

A TAXING EXPERIENCE

"Eager to spread the word of the Bush administration's $1.3 trillion tax cut in 2001, the IRS sent more than half a million notices to taxpayers informing them they were going to receive the maximum possible tax cut refund check...when in fact they weren't.

"Officials placed the blame on a computer program. 'What we're doing now,' the IRS announced when the goof was discovered, 'is working to get a corrected notice out to the taxpayers—all 523,000 of them.'"

—The Denver Post

GOIN' BATTY

"A man trying to warn sleeping relatives about a fire in their garage at 4:00 in the morning was mistaken for a burglar and beaten with an aluminum baseball bat. Police said Joe Leavitt of Florence, Alabama, who was visiting his parents, suffered bruises to the back and a gash to the head that required stitches."

—MSNBC

CAN'T PULL THE WOOL OVER THEIR EYES

"According to British researchers, five years of studying sheep brains to determine if mad cow disease may have jumped species must now be thrown out because someone mislabeled the brains. They were studying cow brains the whole time."

—"The Edge," ***The Oregonian***

Smallest, shallowest ocean on Earth: The Arctic Ocean.

"HERE SPEECHING AMERICAN"

Let's face it: English can be pretty tough to grasp, especially if it's not your first language. Uncle John gives the authors of these signs and labels an "A" for affort.

In an Austrian ski lodge:
Not to perambulate the corridors in the house of repose in the boots of ascension.

In a Japanese hotel room:
Please to Bathe inside the tub.

From a chopstick wrapper in a Chinese restaurant:
Can you eat with chopsticks
Doctor told us / Be intell /
eat by using chopsticks /
Lots of people use chopsticks /
So try eat your chopsticks /
Right Now!

Air conditioner directions in a Japanese hotel room:
Cooles and Heates: If you want just condition of warm in your room, please control yourself.

Outside a Russian monastery:
You are welcome to visit the cemetery where famous Russian and Soviet composers, artists, and writers are buried daily except Thursday.

In a Finland hostel:
If you cannot reach a fire exit, close the door and expose yourself at the window.

In a Copenhagen airport:
We take your bags and send them in all directions.

From a Majorcan (Spain) shop entrance:
Here speeching American.

Warning label on Chinese lint-cleaning roller:
1. Do not use this roller to the floorings that made of wood and plastic.
2. Do not use this roller to clean the stuffs that dangerous to your hands such as glass and chinaware.
3. Do not use the roller to people's head, it is dangerous that hair could be sticked up to cause unexpected suffering.

In a Nairobi restaurant:
Customers who find our waitresses rude ought to see the manager.

But can it shoot a basket? A bison can jump as high as six feet off the ground.

FAMILIAR PHRASES

We're back with one of our regular features. Here are the origins of some common phrases.

TO TRIP THE LIGHT FANTASTIC

Meaning: To dance

Origin: "Coined by English author John Milton, best known for his 1667 masterpiece, *Paradise Lost.* Milton's poem 'L'Allegro'—which means the cheerful or merry one—was written in 1631. He writes: '*come, and trip it as ye go / On the light fantastic toe.*'" (From *Inventing English*, by Dale Corey)

TO FEEL GROGGY

Meaning: To feel dazed

Origin: "This phrase originally referred to drunkenness, and got its name from the ration of rum, known as 'grog,' which was issued to sailors in the Royal Navy until 1971." (From *Everyday Phrases*, by Neil Ewart)

IN LIKE FLYNN

Meaning: Assured success

Origin: "This is often assumed to refer to Errol Flynn's notorious sexual exploits. The earliest example of the phrase, however, in a glossary of air force terms from WWII, claims that the allusion is to the ease with which Flynn accomplished his swashbuckling cinematic feats." (From *Jesse's Word of the Day*, by Jesse Sheidlower)

TO BE WELL-HEELED

Meaning: To have plenty of money or be well-to-do

Origin: "It might be assumed that *well-heeled* originally alluded to the condition of a rich person's shoes. But that is not the case. In the 18th century, it was a fighting cock that was 'well-heeled,' that is, fitted with an artificial spur before facing an opponent in the pit. From that, men began to 'heel' themselves, to carry a gun, before entering a trouble zone. Perhaps because most troubles can be alleviated by money, the expression took on its present financial aspect." (From *Heavens to Betsy!*, by Charles Earle Funk)

Odds that a grain of rice grown in the U.S. will end up being brewed into beer: 1 in 10.

PROMOTIONS THAT BACKFIRED

When a company wants to drum up new business, they sometimes sponsor special promotions... but things don't always work out as planned. Here are two promos that these companies wish they could take back.

Promotion: Disco Demolition Night

What Happened: In 1979, Chicago DJ Steve Dahl came up with this idea to get fans to a Chicago White Sox doubleheader, and the team's promotional director, Mike Veeck, thought it was great: any fan who brought a disco record to the stadium would get in for 98¢. Then, between games the disco records would be blown up. Veeck announced it for the July 12 games against Detroit and told the security crew to be ready for about 35,000 fans.

The Backfire: *Sixty thousand* fans showed up... ready for destruction. They were drinking, burning effigies of John Travolta, and throwing disco records at opposing players throughout the first game. When Dahl dynamited over 1,000 disco records after the first game, the crowd went crazy. Thousands of fans mobbed the diamond. They ripped up the pitcher's mound, tore down fences, and started a bonfire in center field, causing thousands of dollars in damage. Riot police were finally called in and they got the crowd off the field, but it was too late. The White Sox had to forfeit the second game—only the fourth time that's happened in Major League history.

What happened to Mike Veeck? He was forced to resign. He developed a drinking problem and didn't work in baseball again for 10 years. "I went down the sewer," he said.

Promotion: "Monday Night Winning Lineup" scratch-off game

What Happened: Chicago-based food giant Beatrice Inc. came up with this campaign in 1985. The cards were given away at grocery stores around the country and players had to scratch off tiny footballs on the cards to pick the correct number of touchdowns in eight NFL games. Prizes ranged from food coupons and TV sets to the Grand Prize: a trip to the Super Bowl or the cash equivalent—$5,500.

Linonophobia **is a fear of string.**

Frank Maggio of Atlanta got 50 of the cards off a store display rack and played them. And he noticed a pattern. Turns out there were only 320 different cards. He kept getting more cards until he had a complete set. That meant he could scratch off the top row of numbers on a new card, match it up to a master, and know what the rest of the numbers would be. "It was like picking off sitting ducks," he said.

He and a friend, Jim Curl, started grabbing all the cards they could get their hands on, in stores, from sales representatives, and even in the mail directly from the company. They started scratching.

The Backfire: Three weeks later, Maggio and Curl turned in their tickets—worth several million dollars. Beatrice immediately canceled the contest and refused to pay, even though the men had offered to show them their mistake and take a measly $1 million for their trouble.

The two men went home...and *really* started scratching. "That weekend cost Beatrice about $10 million," said Maggio. In 1988 the legal battle was finally over, and Beatrice paid out $2 million in a class-action settlement to 2,400 other winners and settled separately with Maggio and Curl for an undisclosed sum (estimated to be about $12 million). Maggio's friends reported that the 25-year-old salesman left town and retired.

* * *

CONTROVERSY AND *SATURDAY NIGHT LIVE*

• *Saturday Night Live* always airs live...almost. Twice the show was broadcast on a seven-second delay. NBC demanded it so that censors would have a chance to bleep out swearing. Who was too risky for live TV? Richard Pryor (December 13, 1975) and Andrew Dice Clay (May 12, 1990). Nora Dunn boycotted Clay's show; so did scheduled music guest Sinead O'Connor.

• Two years later, O'Connor stirred up controversy when she ripped up a picture of Pope John Paul II after her second song. NBC received 4,484 complaints. But the most severe complaint came from the Vatican, which used its clout to force NBC to edit out the ripping in reruns. O'Connor has since been ordained as a minister.

Democrats are more likely than Republicans to own a cat.

FAMOUS FOR 15 MINUTES

Here's proof that Andy Warhol was right when he said that "in the future, everyone will be famous for 15 minutes."

THE STAR: Dennis Tito, a millionaire businessman

THE HEADLINE: *Money Talks; Man Become's World's First Space Tourist*

WHAT HAPPENED: Tito, a former NASA aerospace engineer, had always wanted to be an astronaut, but engineer was about as far as he got...until he switched careers. He became a financial consultant, made millions of dollars, and then decided to buy his way into space. He found a willing seller: the cash-strapped Russian Space Agency agreed to blast him into space for $20 million, which covered nearly the entire cost of the launch.

NASA and its counterparts in Europe, Canada, and Japan all opposed Tito's trip, but Tito started his training in Russia anyway. Everything went smoothly until about a week before the launch, when he and his crew went to the Johnson Space Center in Houston for a week of preflight training and NASA refused to admit him to the facility. When the Russian astronauts announced that they wouldn't train either, NASA blinked—and let them in.

In April 2001, Tito rocketed into orbit aboard a Russian spacecraft. He spent six days aboard the International Space Station and then returned to Earth. "They might not know it," Tito told reporters after the trip, "but this is the best thing that's happened to NASA."

THE AFTERMATH: Tito must have been right, because in February 2002, NASA adopted a set of guidelines for selecting future "guests" to the Space Station. Since then, a South African Internet tycoon named Mark Shuttleworth became space tourist #2, and 'N Sync star Lance Bass nearly became #3, but his trip was canceled when sponsors couldn't come up with the cash.

THE STAR: Kate Shermak, a fifth-grader at Jamestown Elementary School in Jamestown, Michigan

If you live an average lifespan, you'll spend a total of about six months on the toilet.

THE HEADLINE: *Ask and Ye Shall Receive...Forever, for Free*

WHAT HAPPENED: In 2002 Kate's fifth-grade teacher John Pyper gave the class an unusual assignment, designed to teach kids that letter-writing can be fun: he told them to write to a local business and make an "outrageous request." Kate wrote to the Arby's franchise in nearby Hudsonville. "My outrageous request is to get a lifetime supply of curly fries for free," she wrote. "They're my favorite fries. If you can't meet my outrageous request, I understand."

To Kate's surprise, Arby's said yes, and presented her with a certificate good for a lifetime supply of free curly fries.

THE AFTERMATH: The *Grand Rapids Press* printed the story a few days later; it was picked up by the Associated Press and soon appeared in newspapers all over the world. Not everyone in Kate's class was as lucky with their requests—one student wrote to his future sixth-grade teacher asking to be excused from a year's worth of homework. (Request denied.)

THE STAR: An unknown *Star Wars* fan

THE HEADLINE: *Phantom Phan Phixes Philm*

WHAT HAPPENED: In 1999 the fan, whose identity has never been revealed, went to see *Star Wars Episode 1: The Phantom Menace*. Like a lot of people, he was disappointed by what he saw; unlike anyone else, he decided to do something about it. When the movie came out on VHS, he used his computer to re-edit it, as he (or she) put it, "into what I believe is a much stronger film by relieving the viewer of as much story redundancy, pointless Anakin action and dialog, and Jar Jar Binks as possible." He called his new, 20-minute-shorter version of the film *The Phantom Edit*.

The Phantom Editor never tried to sell his version of the film, but he did give it to friends...and they gave copies to their friends...and soon thousands of copies of the re-edit were circulating all over the Internet, making it arguably the most successful bootleg in Hollywood history. Many who saw it thought *The Phantom Edit* better than the original.

THE AFTERMATH: The popularity of the first re-edit prompted scores of wannabes to do their own versions with names like *Episode 1.2* and *The Phantom Re-Edit*. The phenomon began to get covered by the mainstream press; newspapers as prestigious as the *Chicago*

So that's why they call him King of the Jungle: Lions can mate more than 50 times a day.

Tribune even began printing movie reviews of the bootleg versions.

Lucasfilm had initially chalked the re-edits up to fans having fun, but as the craze continued to grow, the studio threatened legal action against bootleggers. Ultimately the Phantom Editor—or someone claiming to be him (or her)—e-mailed an apology to Lucas via a website called *Zap2it.com*, calling his film "a well-intentioned editing demonstration that escalated out of my control." If you look hard enough, you can probably still find the film online.

THE STAR: Randee Craig Johnson

THE HEADLINE: *Can-do: Candidate for Sheriff Brings Unique Qualifications to the Race*

WHAT HAPPENED: When Crawford County Sheriff Dave Lovely took early retirement in February 2002, the panel of three county officials invited applications from the public to fill the position of interim sheriff until the next election. One person who wrote in to apply was Randee Craig Johnson, 41, who cited his military experience and his "familiarity with the law" as things that made him a good candidate for the job.

What did Johnson mean, exactly, by his "familiarity with the law"? Johnson wrote his letter from a cell inside the Crawford County Jail, where he'd been held since July 2001 while awaiting trial for murder. In his letter, Johnson predicted that he would be acquitted and asked the panel to look past his current circumstances when they made their choice. "I believe everyone deserves a chance to prove themselves," he wrote.

The Traverse City *Record-Eagle* ran a story on Johnson's candidacy; it was picked up by the national wire services. The contest for Crawford County Sheriff wasn't actually a real election, it was just three panel members appointing a temporary sheriff; but even so, when Johnson entered the race, newspapers all over the country ran the story, making it the most widely covered sheriff's race in the United States.

THE AFTERMATH: Johnson lost his bid for sheriff—the panel promoted Undersheriff Kirk Wakefield without even considering Johnson's application. But he did prove himself in the end: On May 24, 2002, a jury unanimously acquitted him of murder and after 307 days in jail he walked out a free man.

SUV drivers are twice as likely to talk on a cellphone as drivers of other kinds of cars.

HOLY PUNCTUATION

Isn't it funny how the funniest things in life are usually not meant to be funny? These church bulletins from BRI stalwart Jim deGraff are a great example.

Due to the rector's illness, Monday's healing service will be discontinued until further notice.

The eighth graders will be presenting Shakespeare's *Hamlet* on Friday. The congregation is invited to attend this tragedy.

The audience is asked to remain seated until the end of the recession.

Low Self-Esteem Support Group will meet Thursday at 7:00 p.m. Please use the back door.

Remember in prayer the many who are sick of our church and community.

A songfest was hell at the Methodist church Tuesday.

Don't let worry kill you. Let the church help.

Thursday night potluck supper. Prayer and medication to follow.

Pastor is on vacation. Massages can be given to church secretary.

Ushers will eat latecomers.

The Rev. Adams spoke briefly, much to the delight of his audience.

The Senior Choir invites any member of the congregation who enjoys sinning to join the choir.

Today—Christian Youth Fellowship House Sexuality Course, 1 p.m.–8 p.m. Please use the rear parking lot for this activity.

Smile at someone who is hard to love. Say "hell" to someone who doesn't care much about you.

The Outreach Committee has enlisted 25 visitors to make calls on people who are not afflicted with any church.

Scouts are saving aluminum cans, bottles, and other items to be recycled. Proceeds will be used to cripple children.

Weight Watchers will meet at 7 p.m. Please use large double door at the side entrance.

Will the last person to leave please make sure that the perpetual light is extinguished.

Makes sense: The horsefly can pierce horse hide with its mouth.

OVER MY DEAD CHICKEN!

Are you an activist? How far would you be willing to go for a cause you believed in? Here are some folks who went pretty far.

PROTESTOR: Larry Eaton of Wilsonville, Oregon
BURNING ISSUE: Six months after Eaton finished building his $300,000 dream house, the state announced it was going to build a minimum security prison across the street. The 40-year-old Eaton and several of his neighbors demanded that the zoning be changed from residential to commercial, so they could sell their houses for a reasonable price, but state officials refused.
WHAT HE DID: In October 2001, after four years of attending city council meetings and begging for help, Eaton finally had had enough. He got a backhoe, dug some huge holes in his front yard and started planting school buses, nose down. He said they represented the family values the state buried when they put the prison in. He also said he'd plant a new one every month until the zoning was changed. "I promise you," he said, "these buses won't move until I do."
OUTCOME: He was up to five front-yard buses at last count. But even though it made national news, the state still won't change the zoning. "It looks like Easter Island," said one reporter.

PROTESTOR: Chuay Kotchasit of Thamuang, Thailand
BURNING ISSUE: In the early 1990s, Kotchasit invested his life savings of 580,000 bahts—about $13,000—in a mutual fund at the Government Savings Bank. The 65-year-old had hoped to use the interest from his nest egg for his retirement. But by 2001, the fund had lost two-thirds of its value. Kotchasit blamed the bank.
WHAT HE DID: On August 14, 2001, Kotchasit walked into the local branch of his bank with a bag, tore it open, and drenched himself with human excrement. "It is more bearable than the stink of mismanagement," he said. He told reporters that he had spent five days planning the protest.
OUTCOME: Account closed.

Shakespeare's daughter was illiterate.

PROTESTORS: Six hundred women in Escravos, Nigeria
BURNING ISSUE: The exploitative practices of oil giant ChevronTexaco, whose multibillion-dollar refinery operations took place next to their impoverished villages.
WHAT THEY DID: In July 2002, the women—unarmed—stormed Nigeria's main oil export terminal and threatened to strip naked. They took 1,000 workers hostage and completely halted all traffic in and out of the terminal and said that if any of the workers tried to leave the plant, they would take off their clothes—a powerful shaming gesture in Nigeria. Furthermore, they vowed to stay until negotiations with oil officials began.
OUTCOME: Talks began immediately, and after 10 days the women agreed to end the siege. They won a written contract from the company to hire local workers, build schools and hospitals, and provide electricity and water to their villages.
AFTERSHOCK: The success of the Escravos protest spurred copycat protests at five more refineries over the next month. Those protests also ended with deals from ChevronTexaco to improve the areas they did business in.

PROTESTORS: Chicken supporters in Sonoma, California
BURNING ISSUE: In early 2002, city officials in Sonoma started "removing" flocks of wild chickens that had lived freely and roamed the city for decades. Officials claimed the chickens were a danger to children, were a health hazard, and generally stunk up the town. The protestors argued that the birds were part of the town's old-country charm and that the officials and real-estate developers were "ruining it in the name of progress."
WHAT THEY DID: "Chicken drops." As soon as officials began removing the birds, other birds would mysteriously appear in the middle of the night—at the library, in the plaza, and at the Chicken Carwash, where a flock of more than 100 had once lived. Officials would take them away, but more would appear to take their place.
OUTCOME: The conflict continues. Officials keep taking the chickens away, and protestors keep dropping off new ones. Says one chicken-hating resident, "It's a comedy and it seems funny—until it's happening to you."

Is it a pine? Is it an apple? It's neither—the pineapple is actually a very big berry.

UNDERWORLD LINGO

Every profession has its own jargon—even the criminal world. These terms were compiled by someone else. We stole them fair and square... and we're not giving them back, and no copper's gonna make us!

Walk the plank. Appear in a police lineup.

Barber a joint. Rob a bedroom while the occupant is asleep.

Chop a hoosier. Stop someone from betting because they've been continuously winning.

Dingoes. Vagrants who refuse to work even though they claim to be looking for a job.

California blankets. Newspapers used to sleep on or under.

Wise money. Money to be wagered on a sure thing.

Ride the lightning. Be electrocuted.

Rolling orphan. Stolen vehicle with no license plates.

Put [someone] in the garden. Swindle someone out of their fair share of money or property.

Swallow the sours. Hide counterfeit money from the police.

Frozen blood. Rubies.

Square the beef. Get off with a lighter sentence than expected.

Toadskin. Paper money—either good or counterfeit.

Vinegar boy. Someone who passes worthless checks.

Trojan. A professional gambler.

White soup. Stolen silver melted down so it won't be discovered.

Grease one's duke. Put money into someone's hand.

Irish favorites. Emeralds.

Fairy grapes. Pearls.

High pillow. The top man in an organization.

Nest with a hen on. Promising prospect for a robbery.

Trigging the jigger. Placing a piece of paper (the trig) in the keyhole of a door to a house that is suspected to be uninhabited. If the trig is still there the next day, a gang can rob the house later that night.

The muscles that power a dragonfly's wings make up 23% of its bodyweight.

FICTIONARY

The Washington Post *runs an annual contest asking readers to come up with alternate meanings for various words. Here are some of the best (plus a few by the BRI).*

Carcinoma (n.), a valley in California, notable for its heavy smog.

Abdicate (v.), to give up all hope of ever having a flat stomach.

Esplanade (v.), to attempt an explanation while drunk.

Unroll (n.), a breadstick.

Mortar (n.), what tobacco companies add to cigarettes.

Flabbergasted (adj.), appalled over how much weight you've gained.

Balderdash (n.), a rapidly receding hairline.

Innuendo (n.), an Italian suppository.

Semantics (n.), pranks conducted by young men studying for the priesthood.

Lymph (v.), to walk with a lisp.

Gargoyle (n.), an olive-flavored mouthwash.

Instigator (n.), do-it-yourself reptile kit. Just add water.

Laughingstock (n.), an amused herd of cattle.

Coffee (n.), one who is coughed upon.

Hexagon (n.), how a mathematician removes a curse.

Reincarnation (n.), the belief that you'll come back as a flower.

Paradox (n.), two physicians.

Prefix (n.), the act of completely breaking a partially broken object before calling a professional.

Atheism (n.), a non-prophet organization.

Rectitude (n.), the dignified demeanor assumed by a proctologist immediately before he examines you.

Flatulence (n.), emergency vehicle that transports the victims of steamroller accidents.

Eyedropper (n.), a clumsy optometrist.

Zebra (n.), ze garment which covers ze bosom.

Think (Boston) tea is Massachusetts's state beverage? Try again—it's cranberry juice.

THE COST OF WAR (MOVIES)

Here's a behind-the-scenes look at the role the Pentagon plays in shaping how Hollywood depicts the military.

PROFITEERS

If you're going to make a war movie, chances are you're going to need army tanks, fighter planes, ships, and maybe even submarines to film some of your scenes.

There are two ways to get them: One is to pay top dollar to rent them on the open market from private owners or the militaries of foreign countries like Israel and the Philippines. That can add tens of millions of dollars to the budget. The other is to "borrow" them from the U.S. military, which makes such items available to filmmakers at a much lower cost.

Critics charge that Pentagon cooperation with the film industry is a waste of taxpayer money, but the all-volunteer U.S. military sees it differently: Supporting a movie like *Top Gun*, for example, doesn't cost all that much, and the resulting film is a two-hour-long Armed Forces infomercial starring Tom Cruise.

NO FREE LUNCH

The catch is that the military will only support films that cast the Armed Forces in a positive light. If a movie producer submits an unflattering script, the Pentagon will withhold its support until the script is changed. If the producer refuses to make the recommended changes, the Pentagon withholds its support, and the cost of making the film goes through the roof.

The original script for *Top Gun*, for example, called for Tom Cruise's character to fall in love with an enlisted woman played by Kelly McGillis. Fraternization between officers and enlisted personnel is against Navy rules, so the Navy "suggested" that producer Jerry Bruckheimer rework the McGillis character. "We changed her to an outside contractor," Bruckheimer told *Brill's Content* magazine. The resulting movie was such an effective recruiting tool that the Navy set up booths in theater lobbies, to sign up enthusiastic recruits after they saw it.

THE PENTAGON SEAL OF APPROVAL

Here's a look at a few films that have been through the Pentagon's screening process:

***Independence Day* (1996),** starring Will Smith and Jeff Goldblum

Story Line: Evil aliens try to destroy the world.

Status: Cooperation denied. "The military appears impotent and/or inept," one Pentagon official complained in a memo. "All advances in stopping aliens are the result of civilians."

***G.I. Jane* (1997),** starring Demi Moore

Story Line: A female Navy recruit tries out for the Navy SEALs.

Status: Cooperation denied. The title was bad, for one thing, because "G.I." is an Army term and there are no G.I.s in the Navy. The military also objected to a bathroom scene in which a male SEAL who shares a foxhole with Moore has difficulty urinating in front of her. As one naval commander put it, "the urination scene in the foxhole carries no benefit to the U.S. Navy."

***Goldeneye* (1995),** starring Pierce Brosnan as James Bond

Story Line: Russian mobsters and military men are out to rule the world using the GoldenEye—a device that can cut off electricity in London to control world financial markets.

Status: Cooperation approved. The military did, however, object to one character in early drafts of the script, a U.S. Navy admiral who betrays America by revealing state secrets. "We said, 'Make him another Navy,'" the Pentagon's Hollywood liaison, Philip Strub says. "They made him a French admiral. The Navy cooperated."

***Forrest Gump* (1994),** starring Tom Hanks

Story Line: The life story of a developmentally-disabled man named Forrest Gump, who spends part of the movie fighting in Vietnam.

Status: Cooperation denied. The Army felt the film created a "generalized impression that the Army of the 1960s was staffed by the guileless, or soldiers of minimal intelligence," as one memo put it, arguing that such a depiction is "neither accurate nor beneficial to the Army." Separately, the Navy objected to the scene where Gump shows President Lyndon Johnson the battle scar on his buttock, complaining that "the 'mooning' of a president by a uniformed soldier is not acceptable cinematic license."

***Windtalkers* (2002),** starring Nicolas Cage and Christian Slater
Story Line: Based on true events, the film is about Navajo Indians who served as "code-talkers" during World War II. Their Navajo-based code so confused the Japanese military that they were never able to crack it. The top-secret code-talkers were so valuable that each was protected by a bodyguard who also had instructions to kill him rather than let him be captured by the Japanese.
Status: Cooperation approved...but only after the producers agreed to tone down the "kill order." The characters *imply* that there's an order to kill, but they never get to say it because the military "would not let them say the words 'order' or 'kill.'"

***Courage Under Fire* (1997),** starring Denzel Washington and Meg Ryan
Story Line: A military investigator (Washington) tries to solve the mystery of how a helicopter pilot (Ryan) died in combat.
Status: Cooperation denied. "There were no good soldiers except Denzel and [Meg]," says the Pentagon's Strub. "The general was corrupt. The staff officer was a weenie."

***Apocalypse Now* (1979),** starring Marlon Brando and Martin Sheen
Story Line: An Army officer (Sheen) is sent to Vietnam to "terminate" a colonel who has gone insane (Brando).
Status: Cooperation denied. *Apocalypse Now* ran into the same problem with semantics that *Windtalkers* did: the military balked at supporting a film that portrays it ordering one officer to kill another. Director Francis Ford Coppola refused to change the word "terminate" to "arrest" or "detain," so the Pentagon withdrew their support. Coppola ended up having to rent helicopters from the Philippine Air Force. That cost a fortune and helped put the film months behind schedule...because the helicopters kept getting called away to battle Communist insurgents.

40% of U.S. Army personnel are members of an ethnic minority.

HEADLINES

These are 100% honest-to-goodness headlines. Can you figure out what they were trying to say?

Factory Orders Dip

SUN OR RAIN EXPECTED TODAY, DARK TONIGHT

PSYCHICS PREDICT WORLD DIDN'T END YESTERDAY

CAPITAL PUNISHMENT BILL CALLED "DEATH ORIENTED"

CHICAGO CHECKING ON ELDERLY IN HEAT

TIPS TO AVOID ALLIGATORS: DON'T SWIM IN WATERS INHABITED BY LARGE ALLIGATORS

Here's How You Can Lick Doberman's Leg Sores

Coroner Reports on Woman's Death While Riding Horse

CHEF THROWS HIS HEART INTO HELPING FEED NEEDY

CINCINNATI DRY CLEANER SENTENCED IN SUIT

High-Speed Train Could Reach Valley in Five Years

FISH LURK IN STREAMS

KEY WITNESS TAKES FIFTH IN LIQUOR PROBE

JAPANESE SCIENTISTS GROW FROG EYES AND EARS

SUICIDE BOMBER STRIKES AGAIN

DONUT HOLE, NUDE DANCING ON COUNCIL TABLE

POLICE NAB STUDENT WITH PAIR OF PLIERS

MARIJUANA ISSUE SENT TO JOINT COMMITTEE

Girl Kicked by Horse Upgraded to Stable

KILLER SENTENCED TO DIE FOR SECOND TIME IN TEN YEARS

COURT RULES BOXER SHORTS ARE INDEED UNDERWEAR

Nuns Forgive Break-in, Assault Suspect

ELIMINATION OF TREES COULD SOLVE CITY'S LEAF-BURNING PROBLEM

No wonder they're skinny: lobsters can crawl as far as a mile a day looking for food.

UNCLE JOHN'S STALL OF FAME

We're always amazed by the creative way people get involved with bathrooms, toilets, toilet paper, etc. That's why we've created Uncle John's "Stall of Fame."

Honoree: Henry Pifer, a truck driver from Arkansas
Notable Achievement: Standing up for the rights of workers who are sitting down...you know where
True Story: In June of 1999 Pifer was hit by a coworker's truck while he was at work. His injuries were serious enough that he had to take time off from his job, so he applied to the state Workers' Compensation Commission for benefits...and was turned down. Reason: At the time of the accident, Pifer was returning from a bathroom break. "Doing your business" at your place of business doesn't count as work, the commission concluded, because it is not an "employment service." Your boss isn't paying you to poop.

Rather than take the decision sitting down, Pifer fought it all the way to the Arkansas Supreme Court...and won. In March 2002 the court ruled that Pifer's bathroom break "was a necessary function and directly or indirectly advanced the interests of his employer."

Little Rock attorney Philip Wilson called the ruling "a landmark decision, because it's the first time the Supreme Court has defined employment services with respect to going to the bathroom."

Honoree: The Toto Company of Japan, the world's largest manufacturer of toilets and plumbing fixtures
Notable Achievement: Creating the "Miracle Magic Pavilion"
True Story: In 2002 Toto wanted to make a big impression at Japan's Kitakyusyu Expo trade show, so they spent a lot of money making a promotional movie touting the company's plumbing fixtures. Rather than just project it onto an ordinary boring movie screen, the company commissioned the "Miracle Magic Pavilion," also known as the "Toilet Theater." It's just what it sounds like it is: a toilet so big that it can be used as a movie theater. Viewers

Parrots never, ever, get appendicitis. (They don't have an appendix.)

enter through a door built into the side of the huge toilet bowl, then sit on genuine life-sized toilets to watch the film.

Have you ever been at a movie and had to use the bathroom really bad, but you didn't want to leave your seat for fear of missing an important scene? Even in the Toilet Theater, you'd still be out of luck—none of the toilet-seat theater seats are actually hooked up to plumbing. More bad news: Toto has no plans to screen feature films in its enormous toilet, either. You get to watch Toto infomercials. That's it.

Honoree: Max Reger, a turn-of-the-century German composer
Notable Achievement: Being best remembered for something he composed...in the bathroom
True Story: Have you ever heard of Max Reger? Probably not; his name isn't even that familiar to music buffs. In fact, Reger is remembered less for his music than for his response to a scathing review of his work written by a critic named Rudolph Louis in 1906.

"Dear sir," Reger wrote in reply, "I am sitting in the smallest room of my house. I have your review before me. In a moment it will be behind me."

Honoree: The Rowanlea Grove Entertainment Co. of Canada
Notable Achievement: Putting Osama Bin Laden in his place
True Story: It wasn't long after 9/11 that the folks at Rowanlea decided to sit down and be counted: they downloaded a picture of Osama Bin Laden from the Internet and printed it on a roll of toilet paper; now anybody that wants to pay him back with a little "face time" can do it. Rowanlea also prints Osama's face on tissue paper, garbage bags, air-cushion insoles for your smelliest pair of shoes, and even sponges for use on those really disgusting cleaning jobs. Bonus: printing Osama's face on toilet paper without his permission violates his "right to publicity."

Osama "Ex-Terrorist-Commando X-Wipe" rolls aren't cheap—they sell for $19.95 for one or $49.95 for a pack of four, plus shipping and handling. The inkjet ink runs and may irritate sensitive skin, which is why Rowanlea recommends an alternative to wiping: "placing a sheet in the toilet bowl before doing your business. Then bombs away!"

Construction of the Great Wall of China was financed—in part—by lotteries.

SPECIAL TIPS FOR HIRING WOMEN

We've come a long way, baby. And it should be obvious once you read this article, which originally appeared under the title "Eleven Tips on Getting More Efficiency Out of Women Employees" in the July 1943 edition of Mass Transportation *magazine.*

There's no longer any question whether companies should hire women for jobs formerly held by men. The military draft and the manpower shortage have settled that point. The important things now are to select the most efficient women available and to know how to use them to the best advantage. Here are 11 helpful tips on the subject from Western Properties:

1. If you can get them, pick young married women. They have these advantages: they usually have more of a sense of responsibility than their unmarried sisters; they're less likely to be flirtatious; as a rule, they need the work or they wouldn't be doing it—maybe a sick husband or one who's in the army; they still have the pep and interest to work hard and to deal with the public efficiently.

2. When you have to use older women, try to get ones who have worked outside the home at some time in their lives. Most companies have found that older women who have never contacted the public have a hard time adapting themselves and are inclined to be cantankerous and fussy. It's always well to impress upon older women the importance of friendliness and courtesy.

3. While there are exceptions to this rule, general experience indicates that "husky" girls—those who are just a little on the heavy side—are likely to be more even-tempered and efficient than their underweight sisters.

4. Retain a physician to give each woman you hire a special physical examination—one covering female conditions. This step not only protects against the possibilities of lawsuit but also reveals whether the employee-to-be has any female weaknesses which would make her mentally or physically unfit for the job. Companies that follow this practice report a surprising number of women turned down for nervous disorders.

5. In breaking in women who haven't previously worked outside the home, stress the importance of time—the fact that a minute or two lost here and there makes serious inroads on schedules. Until this point is gotten across, service is likely to be slow.

6. Give the female employee a definite schedule of duties so that she'll keep busy without bothering the management for instructions every few minutes. Numerous companies say that women make excellent workers when they have their jobs cut out for them but that they lack initiative in finding work themselves.

7. Whenever possible, let the employee change from one job to another at some time during the day. Women are inclined to be nervous and they're happier with change.

8. Give every girl an adequate number of rest periods during the day. Companies that are already using large numbers of women stress the fact that you have to make some allowances for femi nine psychology. A girl is more efficient if she can keep her hair tidied, apply fresh lipstick, and wash her hands several times a day.

9. Be tactful in issuing instructions or in making criticisms. Women are sensitive; they can't shrug off harsh words the way that men do. Never ridicule a woman—it cuts her efficiency.

10. Be considerate about using strong language around women. Even though a girl's husband or father may swear vociferously, she'll grow to dislike a place of business where she hears too much of this.

11. Get enough size variety in uniforms so that each girl can have a proper fit. This point can't be stressed too strongly as a means of keeping women happy.

* * *

"The first problem for all of us, men and women, is not to learn, but to unlearn."

—Gloria Steinem

Price of a box of Girl Scout Cookies when they debuted in 1936: 25¢.

GREAT SCOTT!

Workplace wisdom from Scott Adams, creator of "Dilbert," America's favorite anticorporate comic strip.

"I've discovered what I call the Bill Gates effect. That is, the more successful you are, the uglier you get."

"Informed decision making comes from a long tradition of guessing and then blaming others for inadequate results. This is the principle behind lotteries, dating, and religion."

"Reporters are faced with the daily choice of painstakingly researching stories or writing whatever people tell them. Both approaches pay the same."

"The only risk of failure is promotion."

"Nothing defines humans better than their willingness to do irrational things in the pursuit of phenomenally unlikely payoffs."

"It's hard to argue with the government. Remember, they run the Bureau of Alcohol, Tobacco and Firearms, so they must know a thing or two about satisfying women."

"There are two ways to predict the future. You can use horoscopes, tea leaves, tarot cards, a crystal ball, and so on, collectively known as the 'nutty methods.' Or you can put well-researched facts into sophisticated computer models, more commonly referred to as 'a complete waste of time.' I find it a lot easier to simply make stuff up."

"Always avoid meetings with time-wasting morons."

"In the future, the most important career skill will be a lack of ethics."

"A Mission Statement is defined as 'a long, awkward sentence that demonstrates management's inability to think clearly.' All good companies have one."

"By definition, risk-takers often fail. So do morons. In practice, it's difficult to sort them out."

"The Dilbert Principle: People are idiots."

Dividing something into squares is known as *graticulation*.

OLD HISTORY, NEW THEORY

We tend to believe what science tells us about history—until science tells us something else. Here is a new finding that may change the history books…for now.

The Event: The sinking of the *Titanic*. The luxury liner sank on its maiden voyage in 1912, killing more than 1,500 passengers and crew members.

What the History Books Say: Just before midnight on April 14, 1912, the *Titanic* struck an iceberg in the North Atlantic. The impact gouged a hole in the hull so large that the "unsinkable" ship went down in just two hours and 40 minutes. What remains in question is exactly how the hull was breached…and why.

One popular theory is that the steel used to make the hull was defective, and that when chilled by the icy cold waters of the North Atlantic, it became so brittle that the steel plates fractured on impact when the ship hit the iceberg.

The theory fails on two points. The steel used by the Harland and Wolff shipyards was "battleship quality," strong enough to be used in warships, not just ocean liners. And at the time of impact, the water in the *Titanic*'s ballast tanks was unfrozen, indicating that the North Atlantic wasn't nearly cold enough that night to turn steel brittle, even if it were defective. The theory also fails to explain a strange sound that passengers heard during the impact. One witness described it sounding "as though we went over about a thousand marbles."

New Theory: The discovery of the wreck of the *Titanic* in 1985 has helped to shed light on the mystery. Submersibles recovered some of the iron rivets that were used to secure the steel plates together, and one of the rivets ended up in the hands of Dr. Tim Foecke, a metallurgist with the National Institute of Standards and Technology. Foecke cut the rivet in half…and found a flaw: pieces of "slag," or glass added to the wrought iron to give it strength, were not evenly distributed in the iron as they should have been. Instead, they were concentrated in clumps, which

Bittersweet: Ancient Romans paid their taxes with honey.

weakens the iron instead of strengthening it.

A properly formed rivet would stretch but remain intact during a collision with an iceberg, but if it were defective the head of the rivet could pop off, leaving a hole in the steel plate about an inch in diameter. Pop enough rivets in a line along the hull—something that might sound "as though we went over about a thousand marbles"—and the plates would separate, letting in enough seawater to sink a ship. And even if the steel plates remained in place, there would be enough one-inch holes in the hull to take on water and send the *Titanic* to her watery grave.

Still, one defective rivet does not sink a ship. So when Foecke learned the submersible was making another trip down to the *Titanic*, he asked them to bring him back some more to study. The submersible brought back 48 rivets. Nineteen of them were defective.

* * *

K...FOR KILLER

In 1917 the British Admiralty decided to build a fleet of "K-boats"—325-foot-long steam-powered submarines. Bad idea:

- K2 caught fire on its maiden dive.
- K3 sank for no apparent reason (with the Prince of Wales aboard) and then mysteriously surfaced again. Later it was rammed by K6 and sank for good.
- K4 ran aground.
- K5 sank and all on board were killed.
- K6 got stuck on the sea bottom.
- K7 rammed K17 and went to the junk heap.
- K14 started leaking before ever leaving the dock, and was later rammed by K22 and sank.
- K17 went out of control and sank.
- K22 was rammed by an escorting cruiser.
- In 1918 (after the deaths of some 250 British sailors) the K project was abandoned.

HE SLUD INTO THIRD

These were actually uttered on the air by sports announcers.

"He dribbles a lot and the opposition don't like it—you can see it all over their faces."

—Ron Atkinson,
soccer announcer

"This is really a lovely horse, I once rode her mother."

—Ted Walsh,
horse racing announcer

"And here's Moses Kiptanui, the 19-year-old Kenyan, who turned 20 a few weeks ago."

—David Coleman,
track and field announcer

"We now have exactly the same situation as we had at the start of the race, only exactly the opposite."

—Murray Walker,
motor sports announcer

"It's a partial sellout."

—Chip Caray,
baseball announcer

"The Phillies beat the Cubs today in a doubleheader. That puts another keg in the Cubs' coffin."

—Jerry Coleman,
baseball announcer

"Anytime Detroit scores more than 100 points and holds the other team below 100 points, they almost always win."

—Doug Collins,
basketball analyst

"There are no opportune times for a penalty, and this is not one of those times."

—Jack Youngblood,
soccer announcer

"Coming on to pitch is Mike Moore, who is six-foot-one and 212 years old."

—Herb Score,
baseball announcer

"That was a complicated play, folks. So let's have a replay for all of you scoring in bed."

—Bob Kelly,
hockey announcer

"He slud into third."

—Dizzy Dean,
baseball announcer

"We'll be back with the recrap after this message."

—Ralph Kiner,
baseball announcer

First animated characters on TV commercials: the Ajax pixies. They sold cleanser.

WHEN THE BIG ONE HIT

The Great San Francisco Earthquake was one of the costliest—in both lives and money—natural disasters to hit the United States in the 20th century. Here's the story.

A TUESDAY LIKE NO OTHER

Most of San Francisco's 450,000 people were asleep at 5:13 a.m. on Tuesday, April 18, 1906. Firefighters lay exhausted in their beds after fighting a fire at the California Cannery Company the night before. *The Daily News* was about to go to press with an article noting that San Franciscans had collected $10,000 for the victims of the recent earthquake in Formosa. It mentioned that committees had been meeting in town to discuss how to handle such a disaster should it ever happen in San Francisco.

Then it happened. The jolt from the earthquake was felt from Los Angeles to Coos Bay, Oregon, a distance of 730 miles. San Francisco stood at the epicenter. It's not known how high on the Richter scale the quake was—some estimates say more than 8.5—but when the earth shook, electric lines came down, trolley tracks twisted, water pipes shattered, bridges collapsed, and buildings crumpled. In some areas, the ground moved 20 feet. It was over in 48 seconds.

All services—including communication, transportation, and medical—were either completely gone or heavily damaged. The city lay in ruins, and the casualties mounted. The situation was bad...and it was about to get worse.

IGNITION

Smaller earthquakes had hit the town in 1857, 1865, 1868, and 1890. As the city was reconstructed over the years, people built their homes out of wood, knowing it withstood shaking better than brick. But there was a problem with wood: it burned. So anywhere a gas line was ruptured, a stove was upset, or a lantern was overturned, there was enough ready fuel to start a serious fire...and that's exactly what happened.

People reported more than 50 fires within the first half hour following the quake, but because the city's alarm system was out, San Francisco's 585 firefighters had no way of pinpointing the locations. And even if they could, there was little they could do because most of the water mains were broken. Worse yet, Fire Chief Dennis Sullivan lay dying of injuries suffered in the quake. The fires quickly began to consume San Francisco.

HERE COMES FUNSTON

Brigadier General Frederick Funston, stationed at the Presidio, an army outpost on the northern edge of San Francisco, was flung from his bed by the quake. He immediately sprang into action. Funston knew that army troops were needed to help with the disaster, but he also knew that federal law prevented soldiers from entering the city without first being invited by local authorities. So he headed to City Hall to find Mayor Eugene Schmitz. What he found instead was the building in ruins, fires in the distance, and no sign of the mayor. He decided that troops were needed—whether or not the proper channels were followed. He sent messengers to the Presidio and to Fort Mason, which was also at the north end of the city, and less than two hours after the quake the first of 500 soldiers were on their way into the stricken city. Later they would be joined by sailors, marines, and the National Guard.

Funston organized survivors, ordering some people to gather and distribute all the food that they could find. Others were sent to find wagons and go to neighboring towns for food and supplies. More were sent in search of any bakeries still standing with orders to help get them back in business. And still others were ordered to begin collecting and burying the dead. At 10:15 a.m., Funston sent a telegram to Washington, D.C., asking Secretary of War William Howard Taft for emergency assistance and tents for 20,000 people. It wasn't long before he revised the request to 100,000. Even that wouldn't be enough.

MAYOR'S ORDERS

Mayor Schmitz finally arrived at City Hall at 7 a.m., as bodies were being pulled from the rubble. He immediately moved into the Hall of Justice and later moved his headquarters four more times as the fires grew and spread. His first order of business was to send out messengers—one to find a telegraph office that was still operating, one to Oakland to ask for fire engines, hoses, and dynamite, and one to the governor requesting that food and water be sent with all possible haste.

There's about as many nerve cells in your brain as there are stars in our galaxy.

Schmitz also ordered troops to shoot looters on sight, a rule that was so strictly enforced, it was claimed that people were shot while searching through the rubble of their own homes. Others claimed the troops did most of the looting.

NOWHERE TO RUN

Fires continued to pop up, grow, and join with other blazes to become huge walls of flame. By 9:00 a.m., a fire was moving across the city, devouring entire blocks at a time. In some areas, the flames advanced as fast as a human can run. By noon, 11 blocks had burned and Market Street had turned into a flaming tunnel.

Meanwhile, the streets became clogged with refugees, soldiers, firefighters, and police. Sightseers coming from outlaying areas to view the damage soon found themselves trapped by the crowds and confusion. And before long they were all trapped by the flames. The entire city of San Francisco and many of its citizens were in danger of being reduced to ashes.

Turn to page 251 to find out how the city was saved.

* * *

PROCLAMATION
BY THE MAYOR

The Federal Troops, the members of the Regular Police Force and all Special Police Officers have been authorized by me to KILL any and all persons found engaged in Looting or in the Commission of Any Other Crime.

I have directed all the Gas and Electric Lighting Co.'s not to turn on Gas and Electricity until I order them to do so. You may therefore expect the city to remain in darkness for an indefinite time.

I request all citizens to remain at home from darkness until daylight every night until order is restored.

I WARN all Citizens of the danger of fire from Damaged or Destroyed Chimneys, Broken or Leaking Gas Pipes or Fixtures, or any like cause.

E. E. SCHMITZ, Mayor

Dated April 18, 1906

Call me Rock: The odds that a stage or screen actor has changed their name is about 75%.

CANNED DELICACY

We found a bunch of disgusting foods and put them in Uncle John's Bathroom Reader For Kids Only. *Here are the leftovers.*

BRAINS

Armour Star, the company that makes Armour hot dogs, also makes canned pork brains. The front of the label has a photo of pork brains prepared in milk gravy, and on the side of the can, Armour suggests a "delicious" recipe for eggs 'n' brains. However, once you discover that one can of brains contains 3500 mg of cholesterol—1,170% of the recommended daily value—you might want to skip the eggs (just a thought).

GAME

Tired of tuna fish? Try some Cajun Style Alligator. The Native Game Company offers a variety of meats that you won't find on the shelves of your local grocery store (available only through mail order). Pick up a can of Smoked Rattlesnake, Elk, or Buffalo *Au Jus*, for a wild all-natural taste. Some other meat to order: emu, turtle, and kangaroo.

TONGUE

Australia's Bronte Industries has been marketing lamb's tongues for more than three decades. The blue and gold can familiar to most Aussies reads "Bronte Tongues in Jelly." Oddly, Bronte only advertises them in movie theaters.

INSECTS

People have been snacking on fresh bugs for centuries. But now, thanks to modern food technology, Sakon Nakhon Agricultural Research and Training Centre offers canned grasshoppers, locusts, water beetles, mole crickets, plain crickets, red ant eggs, and silk-worm pupae. The company explains, "Four of the products are made as crunchy snacks that go so well with a cold beer, while the ant eggs are perfect served on hot toast." They're a good source of protein, too!

QUEEN OF THE JAIL

From our Dustbin of History files: Here's a true story of danger, seduction, betrayal, and a deadly escape.

THE SETTING

Allegheny County Jail, Pittsburgh, Pennsylvania, 1901

THE CAST

Katherine Soffel	Ed Biddle	Jack Biddle	Peter Soffel
The warden's beautiful wife	Famous outlaw	Ed's accomplice and younger brother	The prison warden

PROLOGUE

Jack and Ed were "the Biddle Boys," leaders of a gang of small-time outlaws who relied more on brains than brawn to carry out their nefarious crimes. Sometimes they used chloroform to render their potential victims unconscious; sometimes they used beautiful women as distractions. They carried guns, too... just in case.

On April 12, 1901, the gang was robbing a house next to a small grocery store in Mt. Washington, Pennsylvania. A female accomplice kept the grocer occupied while the boys searched the adjoining house, looking for a pile of cash. The distraction didn't work, though—the grocer heard a noise and went to investigate. A struggle ensued, shots were fired, and the grocer ended up dead on his living-room floor. The Biddle brothers fled the scene and holed up in a safehouse, but the police soon caught up with them. After a violent shootout, the outlaws were arrested, but not before a policeman was killed. The trial was quick and the sentence severe: the Biddle Boys were to be hanged for their crimes on February 25, 1902.

SECRET LOVE AFFAIR

Peter and Katherine Soffel were in the midst of a divorce when the Biddles arrived at the Allegheny County Jail. Katherine, who had previously spent time in an asylum, showed no interest in her husband. Instead, she spent most of her time visiting the prisoners, offering them spiritual advice and bringing them Bibles. For the

President Lyndon Johnson had an aunt named Frank. (Her parents wanted a son.)

inmates, Katherine Soffel was a welcome sight. They called her "Queen of the Jail."

She first went to see the Biddles out of curiosity; their exploits throughout the Midwest had made them somewhat notorious. Ed's charm and good looks soon won her over, though. She became infatuated and visited him more and more often, at least 25 times over the next few months, sneaking him food and books. The warden knew his wife had taken an interest in the outlaw but must not have realized just how keen an interest. He allowed her to keep visiting.

After a few months, Ed and Jack convinced Katherine that they were innocent and asked her to help them escape so they could live honest lives as coal miners in Canada. She agreed.

DARING ESCAPE

As luck would have it, Ed's cell could be seen from Katherine's bedroom window. The two designed a secret alphabet code with which Katherine could point to various body parts, representing different letters, and spell out messages about the warden's movements. This allowed the Biddles to devise a plan. Then they had Katherine—at great risk to herself—smuggle in two saws and a revolver.

On Wednesday night, January 29, 1902, the boys cut through their cell bars. They apprehended three guards and locked them in a cell. As they were leaving the prison, they were met by a waiting Katherine, which was *not* a part of the plan. She was supposed to lay low and meet them in Canada a month later. But Katherine, mad with love, took a page out of the Biddles' book and chloroformed her husband, then snuck away in the night. She didn't want to be away from Ed Biddle.

The warden awoke to a nasty headache and an empty house. When he was told the Biddle Boys had escaped, he knew Katherine was involved and immediately put out an all-points-bulletin on the three of them.

ON THE RUN

Meanwhile, Ed agreed to let Katherine come along, much to the dismay of Jack, who thought she'd slow them down. But Ed was the boss. They stole a horse and a sleigh from a nearby farm and made it to Cooperstown, 38 miles north of Pittsburgh. They

There are enough calories in a Big Mac to run a vacuum cleaner for 98 minutes.

planned to have a quiet breakfast there and slip away unnoticed, but news of the breakout had beat them to the town. The Pennsylvania winter was harsh, and the three fugitives didn't have any warm clothes. They were easily identified and the police were now hot on their trail. They stopped for lunch in Mount Chestnut, 54 miles from Pittsburgh, and Ed and Katherine consummated their relationship. Time, however, was running out.

FINAL SHOWDOWN

With their horse and sleigh, the Biddle Boys and Katherine Soffel left Mount Chestnut on the snowy afternoon of January 31, 1902. They had only traveled a few miles when a posse met them head-on at the crest of a hill. Ed stopped the sleigh, handed the reins to Katherine, and he and Jack jumped off, each with gun in hand. The sherriff told them to surrender. Ed told them to go to hell and opened fire. The lawmen responded with a hail of bullets.

When the shootout was over, Ed was shot twice, Jack 15 times, and Katherine—who had grabbed a gun and joined in the fray—was shot once by Ed after pleading for him to take her life. She didn't want to live without him.

The three were taken to nearby Butler Hospital. Katherine's wound was treatable; Ed and Jack were not so lucky. As they lay on their deathbeds, they told police varying accounts of what had happened. Ed claimed he'd never loved Katherine, that he just used her to help him escape. Katherine claimed that Ed was just saying that to protect her. Love letters he wrote her while still in prison backed her up, but only Ed knew for sure. He and Jack both died on the night of February 1, 1902.

POSTMORTEM

The Biddle Boys' bodies were put on display at the Allegheny County Jail for two hours. More than 4,000 people came to see the famous bandits. Katherine served 20 months in prison and lived out the rest of her life in shame. She died a brokenhearted woman on August 30, 1909.

* * *

"We wouldn't have been captured if we hadn't stuck to the woman."

—Jack Biddle

Q: How many toothpicks can you make from one cord of wood? A: 75 million.

IT'S A WEIRD, WEIRD WORLD

Proof that truth really is stranger than fiction.

WORD RAGE

"A man who becomes upset when he hears certain words was sentenced to six years in prison for shooting his girlfriend because he thought she was about to say 'New Jersey.' Thomas Mitchell, 54, was convicted earlier this month of aggravated assault for shooting Barbara Jenkins in March 1999. Jenkins survived the attack. His relatives testified that Mitchell gets angry, curses and bangs on walls when he hears certain words or phrases, including 'New Jersey,' 'Snickers,' 'Mars,' and 'Wisconsin.'"

—Associated Press

CUT IT OUT

"An Oregon man who was shot in the leg removed the bullet himself with an X-acto knife, and then sold it back to the shooter for $200 to hinder the prosecution's case against him."

—The Bend *Bulletin*

A STONE'S THROW AWAY

"More than 600 people were injured in this year's Stone-Throwing Festival in central India. The ritual, in which residents of two villages form groups on either side of the river Jaam and hurl stones at each other, is held every year. Last year, only 250 were injured."

—Reuters

INDECENT PROPOSAL

"Who said romance is dead? Twenty-five-year-old Paul Armstrong proposed to his girlfriend by having 'Connie, Will You Marry Me?' tattooed on his butt, which she then discovered while giving him a massage. 'How could I say no after that?' said Connie, a schoolteacher. A week later, he discovered on her rear end the tattoo, 'Yes!' And they were married."

—London Daily Telegraph

What did they use before that? The first chalkboard was used in a school in 1714.

Q&A: ASK THE EXPERTS

Everyone's got a question or two they'd like answered—basic stuff, like "Why is the sky blue?" Here are a few of those questions, with answers from some of the nation's top trivia experts.

THEY'RE NO CHICKENS

Q: *Do ostriches bury their heads in the sand?*

A: "No, they do not. This ancient belief may have come about because baby ostriches often fall on the ground and stretch out their long necks when they are frightened. This largest of all birds cannot fly and therefore does need protection, but burying its head is not the answer. The ostrich's protection from danger lies in its very powerful legs and its ability to run at speeds of about 40 miles an hour." (From *The Question and Answer Book of Nature*, by John R. Saunders)

HOT STUFF

Q: *What makes food sizzle?*

A: "There is water inside food. When you put it in a hot pan, the water comes out in tiny drops. As soon as they hit the hot pan, the drops dance around, exploding into little puffs of steam. Dancing and exploding, they make little waves in the air that travel to your ears as a sizzling sound." (From *Why Does Popcorn Pop?*, by Catherine Ripley)

THAT'S SWELL

Q: *Why do your feet swell up in an airplane?*

A: "It is a common myth that feet swell up when you ride in an airplane because of changes in atmospheric pressure due to high elevation. Feet swell up on planes, especially during long flights, for the same reason they swell up on the ground—inactivity.

"And it does not matter if you leave your shoes on or off; they will swell either way. If left on, they will provide external support, but will inhibit circulation a bit more and probably feel tighter

More Americans claim German ancestry (46.5%) than any other. Irish ancestry is #2 at 33%.

during the latter part of the flight. If taken off, comfort may be increased, but the shoes are likely to be more difficult to put on once the flight is over.

"Podiatrists normally recommend 'airplane aerobics' to help circulation—including help for swelling feet." (From *The Odd Body: Mysteries of Our Weird and Wonderful Bodies Explained*, by Dr. Stephen Juan)

STORM'S A-BREWIN'

Q: *Why do clouds darken to a very deep gray just before it's about to rain or prior to a heavy thunderstorm?*

A: "Clouds normally appear white when the light which strikes them is scattered by the small ice or water particles from which they are composed. However, as the size of these ice and water particles increases—as it does just before clouds begin to deposit rain—this scattering of light is increasingly replaced by absorption. As a result, much less light reaches the observer on the ground below and the clouds look darker." (From *The Last Word 2*, edited by Mick O'Hare)

MY HEART GOES BOOM!

Q: *If nitroglycerin is an explosive, why don't people who take nitroglycerin for heart conditions explode?*

A: "We all know that nitroglycerin is a highly explosive compound. It's a volatile chemical cocktail combining carbon, hydrogen, nitrogen, and oxygen. 'Nitro' taken in pill form helps heart patients by acting directly on the wall of the blood vessels. It dilates the vessels, which both increases the blood supply to the heart and reduces the work of the heart by reducing blood pressure.

"But according to Dr. Thomas Robertson, chief of the cardiac diseases branch of the U.S. National Institutes of Health, the amount of 'nitro' in heart medications is too small to cause any possible danger of a patient exploding—even if the patient overdosed a little and jumped up and down." (From *The Odd Body: Mysteries of Our Weird and Wonderful Bodies Explained*, by Dr. Stephen Juan)

* * *

Youth is a malady of which one becomes cured a little every day.

—Italian proverb

Q: How did *cranberries* get their name?...

FREE PORK WITH HOUSE

Have you ever been stuck in the bathroom with nothing to read? (Our greatest fear.) Try flipping through the classifieds to look for ones like these.

FREE

Beautiful 6-month-old kitten, playful, friendly, very affectionate **OR...** Handsome 32-year-old husband—personable, funny, good job, but hates cats. Says he goes or cat goes. Come see both and decide which you'd like.

Free! 1 can of pork & beans with purchase of 3-Bedroom, 2-bath home

German Shepherd 85 lbs. Neutered. Speaks German.

FOR SALE

1-man, 7-woman hot tub, $850

Amana Washer Owned by clean bachelor who seldom washed.

Cows, Calves never bred... also 1 gay bull for sale.

Tickle Me Elmo, still in box, comes with its own 1988 Mustang, 5l, Auto, Excellent Condition $6800

Georgia Peaches California Grown—89¢ lb.

Fully cooked boneless smoked man—$2.09 lb.

Kellogg's Pot Tarts: $1.99 Box

Exercise equipment: Queen Size Mattress & Box Springs—$175

Used tombstone, perfect for someone named Homer Hendelbergenheinzel. One only.

For Sale: Lee Majors (6 Million Dollar Man)—$50

Turkey for sale: Partially eaten, eight days old, drumsticks still intact. $23 obo

MISCELLANEOUS

Have Viagra. Need woman, any woman between 18 & 80.

Shakespeare's Pizza—Free Chopsticks

Hummels—Largest selection. "If it's in stock, we have it!"

Wanted: Somebody to go back in time with me. This is not a joke. You'll get paid after we get back. Must bring your own weapons. Safety not guaranteed. I have only done this once before.

Hairobért: If we can't make you look good...You ugly!

Tired of cleaning yourself? Let me do it.

...A: From *crane berry*—they grow on a stalk that looks like a crane's neck.

LUCKY FINDS

Ever found something really valuable? It's one of the best feelings in the world. Here's an installment of a regular Bathroom Reader *feature.*

HONEST STAN

The Find: $20,000

Where It Was Found: In a drawer

The Story: On January 29, 2002, home inspector Stan Edmunds was checking out a house in Hinsdale, New Hampshire, for a prospective buyer. To get to the attic, he had to go through a closet, and an odd wooden shelf support kept catching his eye. The third time through, he pulled on it—and out slid a hidden drawer. Inside it: $20,000 in $100 bills.

Edmunds could have put it in his pocket and walked away, but he didn't—he called the real-estate agent. The agent contacted the heirs of the homeowner, who divided the money up. And one of them sent Edmunds a check for his honesty...for $50. He said he would be donating it to charity.

CHICAGO HOPE

The Find: Superbowl Championship ring

Where It Was Found: In a couch

The Story: In 1996 retired Hall of Fame running back Walter Payton was coaching a high school basketball team outside of Chicago. As an exercise in trust, he gave one of the boys, Nick Abruzzo, his 1986 Superbowl ring—complete with his name and 41 diamonds—to hold for a few days. Nick and his friends passed it around in awe...and then lost it.

Five years later, college student Phil Hong bought an old couch for his dorm room from his friend Joe Abruzzo—Nick's younger brother. One day, while looking in the couch for a lost dog toy, he found the ring. The longtime Chicago fan knew what it was immediately. "Growing up, Walter Payton was my idol," he said. Unfortunately, Payton died of cancer in 1999, but Hong returned the ring to his widow, Connie Payton. "This ring was what he worked for his whole life," he said. "It needs to be back in the family."

In Greenland there's a place called Thank God Harbor.

HANGING IN PLAIN SIGHT

The Find: Masterpiece painting

Where It Was Found: Hanging on a wall

The Story: In July 2001, an elderly couple in Cheltenham, England, decided to sell an old painting that had been hanging on a wall in their house for decades. They figured it was worth a few thousand dollars. They wrapped it in a blanket and took it to Christie's auction house. "They arrived in their van and I came outside to look at what they had," said appraiser Alexander Pope. "It was a classic valuation moment." It turned out to be a masterpiece by 17th-century French artist Nicolas Poussin. Sale price at auction: $600,000.

GIVE ME A RING SOMETIME

The Find: Diamond ring

Where It Was Found: In a bar in Vancouver, British Columbia

The Story: In 1998 a man selling costume jewelry approached 21-year-old Tanya Tokevich while she was sitting in a Vancouver bar. She ended up buying a ring for $20. "It didn't look like much," she said. "It was dull, but I just thought it was nice." She decided to have it appraised to find out whether she'd gotten a good deal. She had. It wasn't costume jewelry—it was an antique engagement ring with a 2.05-carat diamond worth $11,000.

THE CASE OF THE MISSING LIST

The Find: Famous list

Where It Was Found: In a suitcase in Germany

The Story: When a Stuttgart couple found an old suitcase in their parent's loft after they died in 1999, they didn't think much of it—until they saw the name on the handle: O. Schindler. Inside were hundreds of documents—including a list of the names of the Jewish slave-laborers and their fake jobs that factory owner Oskar Schindler gave to the Nazis during WWII. The bold move saved 1,200 Jews from extermination and inspired the movie *Schindler's List.* Apparently, friends of Schindler's had used the loft as a storage space decades earlier and then forgot about it. The couple gave the suitcase and all the documents to a newspaper, but asked for no money in return. It now resides in Yad Vashem Holocaust Museum, in Jerusalem.

Makes sense: *Radish* comes from the Latin *radix,* meaning "root."

CLIFF'S NOTES

Some questionable wisdom from one of our heroes, Cliff Clavin, the know-it-all mailman from the 1980s TV sitcom Cheers.

On suntans:

"It's a little-known fact that the tan became popular in what is now known as the Bronze Age."

On Freud:

"A Freudian slip is when you say one thing when you're really thinking about a mother."

On intelligence:

"The human brain can only operate as fast as the slowest brain cells. Excessive intake of alcohol, as we know, kills brain cells. But naturally it attacks the slowest and weakest brain cells first. In this way, regular consumption of beer eliminates the weaker brain cells, making the brain a faster and more efficient machine. That's why you always feel smarter after a few beers."

On Music:

"I wonder if you know that the harp is a predecessor of the modern day guitar. Early minstrels were much larger people. In fact, they had hands the size of small dogs."

On pigs:

"It's a little-known fact that the smartest animal is a pig. Scientists say if pigs had thumbs and a language, they could be trained to do simple manual labor. They give you 20 to 30 years of loyal service and then at their retirement dinner you can eat them."

On women:

"Ah, just like all women. If they're not turnin' down your proposal of marriage, they're accusing you of suspicious behavior in the lingerie changing room."

On politics:

"If you were to go back in history and take every president, you'll find that the numerical value of each letter in their name was equally divisible into the year in which they were elected. By my calculations, our next president has to be named Yellnick McWawa."

On dating:

"There's no rule against postal workers dating women. It just works out that way."

Largest living thing on Earth: an underground mushroom in Oregon, 3.5 miles across.

WEDDING SUPERSTITIONS

If you're planning a wedding, there's a lot to remember. And if you're superstitious, you may have even more to juggle.

THE BIG DAY

Good Luck: Pick a date when the moon is waxing (increasing in size) and an hour when the tide is rising. Also be sure to time the wedding ceremony so that it ends in the second half of the hour, when the minute hand is rising on the face of the clock. Don't stop there: Everything associated with the wedding should be moving up, up, up! Anything that rises or grows promises rising fortunes for you and your spouse.

Bad Luck: *Don't* schedule the wedding for early in the morning. That will bring bad luck—and it's not just a superstition: in the old days the groom, and sometimes even the bride, needed ample time to clean themselves up after morning farm chores, lest they risk showing up at church smelling of animals and manure. (Nowadays it gives the groom a chance to recover from his bachelor party or whatever antics went on the night before.)

THE DRESS

Good Luck: White has been a lucky color for formal weddings in the West for more than a century; for informal ceremonies, any color will do...except for black or red.

Bad Luck: Black symbolizes death—only widows can wear it—and red, the color of the devil, is unlucky too. If a woman wears a red wedding dress, 1) she and her husband will fight before their first anniversary or 2) her husband "will soon die."

THE VEIL

Good Luck: The woman who puts the veil on the bride should be happily married. If possible, the bride should wear the veil her grandmother wore, to ensure "that she will always have wealth."

Bad Luck: No one other than members of the bride's family

Origin of the term *bridal shower*: English brides used to buy "bride ale" for wedding guests.

should see her veil before the ceremony, and once she is fully dressed, she shouldn't look in the mirror again until after the ceremony is over. She should leave one small article of dress, perhaps a ribbon or a pin, undone so that she can add it at the last minute without having to look in a mirror.

JEWELRY

Good Luck: Wearing earrings will bring the bride good luck.

Bad Luck: Don't wear pearls—not in the earrings or the necklace, on the dress, or anyplace else. Pearls symbolize tears. "For every pearl a bride wears, her husband will give her a reason to cry."

OMENS

Good Luck: The animals you see on the way to church are full of omens. Lambs, doves, wolves, spiders, and toads are all good luck. If birds fly directly over your car, that's also good luck—it means you're going to have a lot of kids. (Okay, maybe that's *bad* luck...)

Bad Luck: If a pig crosses your path on your way to the wedding, that's bad luck. If a bat flies into the church, that's bad luck too.

DON'T BE SHY—GO AHEAD AND CRY

Good Luck: Tears are such good luck that if the bride can't cry on her own, she should create tears "by virtue of mustard and onions" if necessary. Tears symbolically wash the bride's old problems away, giving her a fresh start.

Bad Luck: *Not* crying is *very* bad luck. This is a throwback to the days when people believed that witches can only shed three tears, and these only from her left eye. By crying, a bride demonstrated to the assembled guests that she was not a witch, thereby avoiding being burned at the stake (also bad luck).

MISCELLANY

Good Luck: When she enters and leaves the church, the bride should step across the threshold with her right foot first.

Bad Luck: The bride shouldn't have anything to do with making either her wedding cake or her wedding dress. Don't eat anything while you're getting dressed, either—that's bad luck too.

Hands off: On average, kids aged 2 to 5 put their hands in their mouths 10 times an hour.

STRANGE LAWSUITS

These days, it seems that people will sue each other over practically anything. Here are some real-life examples of unusual legal battles.

THE PLAINTIFF: Wawa, a food store chain
THE DEFENDANTS: Tamilee Haaf and George Haaf, Jr., owners of the HAHA market
THE LAWSUIT: In late 1996, Wawa, which controls 500 convenience store outlets in eastern Pennsylvania, filed a suit claiming that HAHA is too similar in sound and could confuse people into believing that HAHA is affiliated with Wawa. The Haafs claim they have a right to use the name since it is simply an abbreviation of their last name.
THE VERDICT: It may sound funny, but HAHA lost. The judge ruled that "HAHA" sounds so close to "Wawa" that it dilutes Wawa's trademark. HAHA boo-hoo, Wawa yee-ha.

THE PLAINTIFF: Associate Humane Societies
THE DEFENDANT: Frank Balun
THE LAWSUIT: Balun went into his Hillside, New Jersey, garden in July 1993 to check on his tomato vines and discovered that some of the plants had been eaten by rats. So he set a squirrel trap, hoping to catch one. He did. Then he called the Humane Society to pick it up. But before they could respond, the rat tried to escape and Balun hit it on the head with a broom handle, killing it. The Humane Society in Newark then filed charges against Balun for "needlessly abusing a rodent." Complaining that Balun should have dealt with it more humanely, the Humane Society said, "It may only be a rat, but it's a living creature, and there is no reason to abuse a living creature."
THE VERDICT: A municipal judge dismissed the charges, citing a statute that allows people to kill vermin that attack their "crops."

THE PLAINTIFF: State of Colorado
THE DEFENDANT: Eugene Baylis

Makes sense: ***Sahara*** **comes from the Arabic word** ***sahra*** **meaning "desert."**

THE LAWSUIT: Forty-two-year-old Baylis walked into a biker bar in Colorado Springs, armed with an AK-47 rifle, four hand grenades, and a pistol. Seeing the heavily armed man, several of the bar's regular patrons advanced on him—allegedly to keep him from doing any harm. But Baylis got scared and opened fire, killing two people and injuring five.

In court, Baylis argued that he'd gone to the bar to look for a man who'd shot him with a pellet gun earlier in the day. He claimed he merely wanted to hold his attacker until the police arrived, but when he was accosted by the men in the bar, he felt he had no choice but to shoot them...in "self-defense."

THE VERDICT: Incredibly, a jury found Baylis not guilty on all counts. One of the jurors said the prosecution never proved Baylis had had any real intentions of killing anyone when he entered the bar and "didn't disprove that Baylis acted in self-defense."

THE PLAINTIFF: Peter Maxwell

THE DEFENDANT: Peter Maxwell

THE LAWSUIT: Maxwell owned a urethane-manufacturing company in Chino, California. He was also on the payroll as a worker, taking a salary of $10,000 a year. One day while he was operating a mixing machine, his sweater got caught on an exposed bolt. He was pulled into the device and severely injured. Maxwell, the employee, hired an attorney and sued Maxwell, the owner, for negligence. Maxwell, the owner, hired another lawyer to defend the company against the lawsuit.

THE VERDICT: Both Maxwells decided they could settle their dispute out of court and negotiated that Maxwell, the owner, should pay Maxwell, the employee, $122,500 for his injuries.

AFTERMATH: When the IRS caught wind of the deal, they demanded that Maxwell, the employee, pay $64,185 of the settlement in income tax. They also wanted Maxwell, the owner, to cough up $58,500 because he tried to write off the payment as a business expense. Maxwell was outraged—and so was Maxwell. Maxwell, the owner, side by side with Maxwell, the employee, appealed the IRS's judgment to the U.S. Tax Court. In 1990 Judge Robert Ruwe ruled that Maxwell, the employee, could have the settlement income tax-free and that Maxwell, the owner, could deduct the entire amount as a business expense.

During 33 seasons on the air, Mr. Rogers's trolley traveled more than 100 miles on its track.

UNCLE JOHN'S "CREATIVE TEACHING" AWARDS

Another round of the BRI's Creative Teaching Awards, because we're just so proud of teachers who continue to make education an exciting and creative experience.

SUBJECT: Animal care
WINNER: Leslie Davis, of Savannah, Georgia
APPROACH: In May 2002, Davis assembled her elementary school students and took them to a nearby park—where they stole a duck from the pond. Then they went back to the school, where they planned to release the duck as a prank.
REACTION: The 23-year-old teacher was charged with public drunkenness, obstruction, and contributing to the delinquency of minors.

SUBJECT: Fashion
WINNER: Vice Principal Rita Wilson, Rancho Bernardo High School, Poway, California
APPROACH: During the 2002 April Dance, Ms. Wilson wanted to make sure that female students were following the dress code. So, as they were entering the building, she lifted up the girls' skirts to see if they were wearing thong underwear, which was prohibited. According to a source, she even did so in front of male students.
REACTION: The Poway Unified School District investigated and concluded that the vice principal "used poor judgment"...then demoted her to a classroom teaching job.

SUBJECT: Civics
WINNER: School administrators at Hamilton High School, in Chandler, Arizona
APPROACH: As part of a law-enforcement training class, four students took part in a "gun drill," storming school hallways with fake guns, shouting "Don't make me do it!" But apparently someone had failed to warn the faculty about the drill.

First African American to win the Nobel Peace Prize: Ralph Bunche, in 1950.

REACTION: Panicked students and teachers locked down the classrooms until they were sure they were safe. The instructor who planned the drill—Police Officer Andy McIlveen—was asked not to return to the school district. Said Assistant Principal Dave Constance, "This is not an appropriate way to teach school safety."

SUBJECT: Humanities
WINNER: Ronald Cummings, of Santa Ana, California
APPROACH: For some reason, Cummings drove a group of students—a 14-year-old boy and two 18-year-olds—to a gang fight and then gave them a cigarette lighter that looked exactly like a pistol.
REACTION: Immediately put on leave from the school, he was charged by police with contributing to the delinquency of minors, making terrorist threats, and using a fake firearm in a threatening manner. He faces eight years in prison.

SUBJECT: History
WINNER: School officials in West Palm Beach, Florida
APPROACH: To make sure students would fulfill state requirements in history, the officials developed a 100-question test—and then required that students answer only 23 of them correctly to pass.
REACTION: Not much. Some teachers complained, but the school board defended the low grade scale...and the test went on anyway. Bottom line: The students can get three-quarters of the answers wrong and still pass.

SUBJECT: Ethics
WINNER: Third-grade teacher Betty Bettis and gym teacher Thomas L. Sims, of Kansas City, Missouri
APPROACH: When a lunch money collection in Bettis's class came up $5 short, the teacher strip searched the students. She took the girls into a restroom, had them strip to their underwear, and then had them check each others' panties. Sims took the boys into a gym and had them strip and then shake their underwear.
REACTION: Outraged parents made the story international news. One student even went on a talk show to describe the incident. By the way, they found the missing money in a rest room...but not as a result of the strip search.

The traditional gift for a 44th wedding anniversary is...groceries.

THE WORLD'S FIRST VIDEO GAME

Ever heard of William Higinbotham? He's the guy who invented the world's first video game. But he never made a cent off his invention and hardly anyone has heard of him. Uncle John thinks it's time he got the credit he deserves.

HOWDY, NEIGHBOR

How would you feel if a nuclear reactor came online just down the street from your house? Would knowing that it was just a "small" research reactor, dedicated to finding "peaceful uses" for atomic energy, make you feel any better? That's what happened in 1950 at the Brookhaven National Laboratory in Long Island, New York.

Despite all of its public assurances, local residents were visibly concerned about the potential dangers of the new plant. One way the facility tried to ease public fears was by hosting an annual "Visitor's Day," so that members of the community could look around and see for themselves what kinds of projects the scientists were working on. There were cardboard displays with blinking lights to look at, geiger counters and electronic circuits to fiddle with, and dozens of black-and-white photos that explained the different research projects underway at the lab.

In other words, Visitor's Day was pretty boring.

SOMETHING TO DO

In 1958 a Brookhaven physicist named William Higinbotham decided to do something about it. Years earlier, Higinbotham had designed the timing device used to detonate the first atomic bomb; now he set his mind to coming up with something interesting for Visitor's Day. "I knew from past visitor's days that people were not much interested in static exhibits," he remembered. "So that year, I came up with an idea for a hands-on display."

FOLLOW THE BOUNCING BALL

Looking around the labs, Higinbotham found an electronic testing device called an oscilloscope, which has a cathode ray tube display similar to a TV picture tube. He also found an old analog computer (modern computers are digital, not analog) that he could hook up to the oscilloscope in such a way that a "ball" of light would bounce randomly around the screen.

"We found," Higinbotham remembered, "that we could make a game which would have a ball bouncing back and forth, sort of like a tennis game viewed from the side." The game he came up with looked kind of like this:

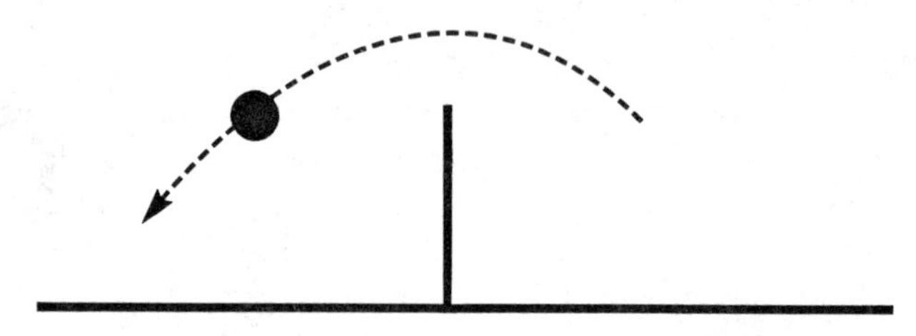

Two people played against one another using control boxes that had a "serve" button that hit the ball over the net, and a control knob that adjusted how high the ball was hit. And just as in real tennis, if you hit the ball into the net, it bounced back at you.

BEST OF SHOW

It took Higinbotham two hours to draw up the schematic diagram for "Tennis for Two," as he called it, and two weeks of tinkering to get it to work. When Visitor's Day came around and Higinbotham put it on a table with a bunch of other electrical equipment, it only took the visitors about five minutes to find it. Soon hundreds of people were crowding around it, some standing in line for more than an hour for a chance to play the game for a minute or two. They didn't learn much about the peaceful applications of nuclear energy that Visitor's Day in 1958. But they sure had fun playing that game.

Higinbotham didn't have an inkling as to the significance of what he'd done. "It never occurred to me that I was doing anything very exciting," he remembered. "The long line of people I thought wasn't because this was so great, but because all the rest of the things were so dull."

Seeing is believing: Frogs use their eyeballs to push food down their throat.

GAME OVER

So what happened to Higinbotham's video tennis game? He improved it for Visitor's Day 1959, letting people play Tennis for Two in Earth gravity, or low gravity like on the moon, or very high gravity like that found on Jupiter.

Then, when Visitor's Day was over, he took the video game apart and put the pieces away. He never brought them out again, never built another video game, and never patented his idea.

Willy Higinbotham would probably be completely forgotten today were it not for a lawsuit. When video games began taking off in the early 1970s, Magnavox and some other early manufacturers began fighting in court over which one of *them* had invented the games. A patent lawyer for one of Magnavox's competitors eventually learned of Higinbotham's story and brought the Great Man into court to prove that he, not Magnavox, was the true father of the video game.

OUCH!

In 2001 Americans spent more on video game systems and software—$9.4 billion—than they did going to the movies—$8.35 billion. What did Higinbotham, who died in 1994, have to show for it? Nothing. He never made a penny off his invention. Not that he could have—he worked for a government laboratory when he invented the game, so even if he had patented the idea, the U.S. government would have owned the patent.

"My kids complained about this," he joked, "And I keep saying, 'Kids, no matter what, I wouldn't have made any money.'"

For more about the history of video games, follow the bouncing ball to page 180 for "Let's Play Spacewar!"

* * *

SEA-ING THINGS

Dolphins sometimes play chase in long lines, like people doing a snake dance or snap-the-whip. Sailors, seeing this long line of something moving in the water, have sometimes reported seeing huge sea serpents.

It's easy to spot someone with *hexadectylism:* six fingers on one hand or six toes on one foot.

"I SPY"...AT THE MOVIES

You probably remember the kids' game "I spy, with my little eye..." Moviemakers have been playing it for years. Want to play? Here are some in-jokes and gags you can look for the next time you see these films.

SPIDER-MAN (2002)

I Spy... Lucy Lawless, star of *Xena: Warrior Princess*

Where to Find Her: She appears as the red-haired punker who makes the astute observation: "A man with eight arms? Sounds like a good time to me!" (*Spider-man* director Sam Raimi worked as a producer on *Xena*.)

AMERICAN PIE (1999)

I Spy... Blink 182

Where to Find Them: During the Internet scene, the popular band can be seen watching the Webcast. Their song "Mutt" is playing in the background.

HOW THE GRINCH STOLE CHRISTMAS (2000)

I Spy... Director Ron Howard's favorite hat

Where to Find It: On the Grinch's head—when he is "directing" his dog Max to become a reindeer. Legend has it that Jim Carrey stole the hat and ad-libbed an imitation of Howard. Howard thought the bit was funny and left it in the movie, hat and all.

ERIN BROCKOVICH (2000)

I Spy... The real Erin Brockovich

Where to Find Her: When the fake Erin (Julia Roberts) is in a restaurant with her kids, their waitress is the real Erin. Her name tag reads "Julia."

SPIES LIKE US (1985)

I Spy... Blues legend B.B. King

Where to Find Him: He's one of the CIA agents at the drive-in theater/missile silo. In the credits, he's listed as "Ace Tomato Agent."

FERRIS BUELLER'S DAY OFF (1986)

I Spy... References to several of director John Hughes's movies

Where to Find Them: On the license plates of various cars. VCTN (*National Lampoon's Vacation*), TBC (*The Breakfast Club*), MMOM (*Mr. Mom*), and 4FBDO (*Ferris Bueller's Day Off*).

MONSTERS, INC. (2001)

I Spy... Pixar's phone number

Where to Find It: At the end of the simulation that begins the film, a monster reaches for a knob on the control panel. Just below it and to the left is a series of 10 numbers. Dial them and you'll reach Pixar, the studio that made the movie.

THE MATRIX (1999)

I Spy... Andy and Larry Wachowski, the film's directors

Where to Find Them: They're the two window washers outside the office where Neo is being chastised for arriving late to work.

THE SHAWSHANK REDEMPTION (1994)

I Spy... A photograph of Morgan Freeman's son

Where to Find It: The parole papers that repeatedly receive a rejected stamp show a picture of Red (Morgan Freeman) when he was a young man. Morgan's son Alfonzo was used for the shot.

GEORGE LUCAS MOVIES

I Spy... THX-1138

Where to Find It: *THX-1138* was the name of Lucas's first feature film, and he has paid homage to it throughout his career. A license plate in *American Graffiti* reads "1T1H3X8." Luke Skywalker rescued Princess Leia from Cell Block 1138 in *Star Wars*. In *Raiders of the Lost Ark*, a loudspeaker in the submarine dock states, "*Ein, Ein, Drei, Acht*" ("One, one, three, eight" in German). A battle droid in *The Phantom Menace* has the designation—you guessed it—1138. (Note: We don't know if there are any references to it in *Howard the Duck*—we couldn't make it through a complete viewing.)

* * *

One falsehood spoils a thousand truths.
Ashanti wisdom

THE TIGER, THE BRAHMAN, AND THE JACKAL

This classic story of deception and trickery comes from a book of Indian fairy tales published in 1892. For those not familiar with Indian culture, a Brahman is a Hindu of the highest caste: the priest caste.

ONCE upon a time, a tiger was caught in a trap. He tried in vain to get out through the bars, and rolled and bit with rage and grief when he failed.

By chance a poor Brahman came by.

"Let me out of this cage, oh pious one," cried the tiger.

"Nay, my friend," replied the Brahman mildly, "you would probably eat me if I did."

"Not at all," swore the tiger with many oaths. "On the contrary, I should be forever grateful, and serve you as a slave!"

Now when the tiger sobbed and sighed and wept and swore, the pious Brahman's heart softened, and at last he consented to open the door of the cage. Out popped the tiger, and, seizing the poor man, cried, "What a fool you are! What is to prevent my eating you now, for after being cooped up so long I am just terribly hungry!"

In vain the Brahman pled for his life; the most he could gain was a promise by the tiger to abide by the decision of the first three things he chose to question as to the justice of the tiger's action.

So the Brahman first asked a pipal tree what it thought of the matter, but the pipal tree replied coldly, "What have you to complain about? Don't I give shade and shelter to everyone who passes by, and don't they in return tear down my branches to feed their cattle? Don't whimper—be a man!"

Then the Brahman, sad at heart, went farther afield until he saw a buffalo turning a well wheel; but he fared no better from it, for it answered, "You are a fool to expect gratitude.

Look at me. While I gave milk they fed me on cotton seed and oil cake, but now that I am dry they yoke me here, and give me refuse as fodder!"

The Brahman, sadder still, asked the road to give him its opinion.

"My dear sir," said the road, "how foolish you are to expect anything else. Here am I, useful to everybody, yet all, rich and poor, great and small, trample on me as they go past, giving me nothing but the ashes of their pipes and the husks of their grain!"

On this the Brahman turned back sorrowfully, and on the way he met a jackal, who called out, "Why, what's the matter, Mr. Brahman? You look as miserable as a fish out of water!"

The Brahman told him all that had occurred. "How very confusing!" said the jackal, when the recital was ended; "would you mind telling me over again, for everything has got so mixed up?"

The Brahman told it all over again, but the jackal shook his head in a distracted sort of way, and still could not understand.

"It's very odd," said he, sadly, "but it all seems to go in at one ear and out at the other! I will go to the place where it all happened, and then perhaps I shall be able to give a judgment."

So they returned to the cage, by which the tiger was waiting for the Brahman, and sharpening his teeth and claws.

"You've been away a long time!" growled the savage beast, "but now let us begin our dinner."

"Our *dinner*!" thought the wretched Brahman, as his knees knocked together with fright. "*What a remarkably delicate way of putting it*!"

"Give me five minutes, my lord!" he pleaded, "in order that I may explain matters to the jackal here, who is somewhat slow in his wits."

The tiger consented, and the Brahman began the whole story over again, not missing a single detail, and spinning as long a yarn as possible.

"Oh, my poor brain! Oh, my poor brain!" cried the jackal, wringing its paws. "Let me see! How did it all begin? You were in the cage, and the tiger came walking by—"

"Pooh!" interrupted the tiger, "What a fool you are! *I* was in the cage."

"Of course!" cried the jackal, pretending to tremble with

During Prohibition, half of all federal prison inmates were in jail for violating liquor laws.

fright. "Yes, I was in the cage—no I wasn't—dear, dear, where are my wits? Let me see—the tiger was in the Brahman, and the cage came walking by—no, that's not it, either! Well, don't mind me, but begin your dinner, for I shall never understand!"

"Yes, you shall!" returned the tiger, in a rage at the jackal's stupidity; "I'll *make* you understand! Look here—I am the tiger..."

"Yes, my lord!"

"And that is the Brahman..."

"Yes, my lord!"

"And that is the cage..."

"Yes, my lord!"

"And I was in the cage—do you understand?"

"Yes—no—please, my lord..."

"Well?" cried the tiger impatiently.

"Please, my lord I—how did you get in?"

"How I—why in the usual way, of course!"

"Oh, dear me!—my head is beginning to whirl again! Please don't be angry, my lord, but what is the usual way?"

At this the tiger lost patience and, jumping into the cage, cried, "This way! Now do you understand how it was?"

"Perfectly!" grinned the jackal, as he dexterously shut the door, "and if you will permit me to say so, I think matters will remain as they were."

* * *

RANDOM FACTS

• In 1992, 29,000 rubber ducks and other bath toys fell into the middle of the Pacific Ocean during a shipping accident. Eleven months later, the toys started washing up along the North American seaboard. Scientists used the duckies to help them study ocean currents.

• What's the botanical difference between green peppers, yellow peppers, and red peppers? There is none—the only difference is their age. They start out green, then turn yellow, then red, then purple, then brown. And as they mature, they get progressively sweeter (until they spoil).

• After Congress reduced the postage rate from 5¢ to 3¢ in 1851, a 3¢ piece was minted to make it easier to buy stamps.

How did *bonfires* get their name? From "bone fires," or funeral pyres.

THE FINAL DAYS OF KING CHARLES II

Next time you feel yourself coming down with a cold, thank your lucky stars for 21st-century medicine.

MONDAY

On the morning of February 2, 1685, King Charles II of England was preparing to shave when he suddenly cried out in pain, fell to the floor, and started having fits. Six royal physicians rushed in and administered emergency "aid."

- They let (drained) 16 ounces of blood.
- Then they applied heated cups to the skin, which formed large round blisters, in order to "stimulate the system."
- They let 8 more ounces of blood.
- They induced vomiting to purify his stomach, gave an enema to purify his bowels, and made him swallow a purgative to clean out his intestines.
- Then they force-fed him syrup of blackthorn and rock salt.
- They shaved his hair and put blistering plasters on his scalp. The king regained consciousness. The treatment seemed to be working, so they kept at it.
- They gave him another enema.
- Then they applied hellebore root to the nostrils, more blistering plasters to the skin, and powdered cowslip flowers to the stomach.
- Special plasters made from pigeon droppings were attached to his feet. After 12 hours of care, they put the ailing king to bed.

TUESDAY

- Charles awoke and seemed much improved. The attending physicians congratulated themselves and continued the treatment.
- They let 10 more ounces of blood.
- They gave him a potion of black cherry, peony, lavender, crushed pearls, and sugar. Charles slept for the rest of the day and throughout the night.

Woof: Dogs have 42 permanent teeth, 10 more than humans do.

WEDNESDAY

- He awoke, had another fit, and was bled again.
- They gave him senna pods in spring water, and white wine with nutmeg.
- They force-fed him a drink made from "40 drops of extract of human skull" of a man who had met a violent death.
- They made him eat a gallstone from an East Indian goat.
- Then they proudly announced that King Charles was definitely on the road to recovery.

THURSDAY

- The king was near death.
- He was blistered again, re-bled, repurged, and given another enema.
- He was given Jesuits' powder—a controversial malaria remedy—laced with opium and wine. His doctors were mystified by the king's weakening condition.

FRIDAY

- Showing no improvement, the king was bled almost bloodless.
- They scoured the palace grounds and created a last-ditch antidote containing "extracts of all the herbs and animals of the kingdom."

SATURDAY

The king was dead.

Postmortem: It was rumored at the time that King Charles II had been poisoned, but no proof was ever found. Modern doctors offer three theories as to cause of death:

1. He *was* poisoned—but not by an enemy—by himself. He often played with chemicals in an unventilated palace laboratory, where he contracted acute mercury poisoning.

2. He suffered from kidney failure.

3. He had a brain hemorrhage.

Would the king have survived without treatment? Probably not. But at least his death wouldn't have been so excruciating.

OPENING LINES

The Oscars and the Grammys are all right. But we at the BRI have always been fascinated by things that are so bad they're good. Here's the story behind one of our favorite awards, the Bulwer-Lytton.

"IT WAS A DARK AND STORMY NIGHT..." The line has been plagiarized and satirized by a multitude of writers. Sometime in the 1970s, a graduate student named Scott Rice set out to find its origin and discovered it was the opening line of the 1830 novel *Paul Clifford* by English author Edward George Bulwer-Lytton:

> It was a dark and stormy night; the rain fell in torrents—except at occasional intervals, when it was checked by a violent gust of wind which swept up the streets (for it is in London that our scene lies), rattling along the housetops, and fiercely agitating the scanty flame of the lamps that struggled against the darkness.

Years later, while working as an English professor at San Jose State University, Rice served as a judge in numerous writing contests. Impressed by the high quantity of bad writing he saw, in 1982 Rice decided to run his own contest. His unusual literary challenge: compose the opening sentence to the worst of all possible novels. This "whimsical competition" soon turned into a formal contest, which Rice named for the master of longwindedness: the Bulwer-Lytton Fiction Contest.

Today the contest attracts thousands of entries from all over the world. The rules are simple: the entry can only be a single sentence. It may be of any length, but all entries must be original and previously unpublished. Here are some of the winners from the past 20 years.

• **As the fading light of a dying day** filtered through the window blinds, Roger stood over his victim with a smoking .45, surprised at the serenity that filled him after pumping six slugs into the bloodless tyrant that mocked him day after day, and then he shuffled out of the office with one last look back at the shattered computer terminal lying there like a silicon armadillo left to rot on the information superhighway.

—Larry Brill, Austin, Texas (1994 winner)

President George W. Bush's 2001 tax cut added 14,368 pages to the U.S. Tax Code.

• **She wasn't really my type,** a hard-looking but untalented reporter from the local cat box liner, but the first second that the third-rate representative of the fourth estate cracked open a new fifth of old Scotch, my sixth sense said seventh heaven was as close as an eighth note from Beethoven's Ninth Symphony, so, nervous as a tenth grader drowning in eleventh-hour cramming for a physics exam, I swept her into my longing arms, and, humming "The Twelfth of Never," I got lucky on Friday the thirteenth.
—William W. Ocheltree, Port Townsend, Washington (1993 winner)

• **The bone-chilling scream split** the warm summer night in two, the first half being before the scream when it was fairly balmy and calm and pleasant for those who hadn't heard the scream at all, but not calm or balmy or even very nice for those who did hear the scream, discounting the little period of time during the actual scream itself when your ears might have been hearing it but your brain wasn't reacting yet to let you know.
—Patricia E. Presutti, Lewiston, New York (1986 winner)

• **The countdown had stalled** at T minus 69 seconds when Desiree, the first female ape to go up in space, winked at me slyly and pouted her thick, rubbery lips unmistakably—the first of many such advances during what would prove to be the longest, and most memorable, space voyage of my career.
—Martha Simpson, Glastonbury, Connecticut (1985 winner)

• **As the newest Lady Turnpot** descended into the kitchen wrapped only in her celery-green dressing gown, her creamy bosom rising and falling like a temperamental soufflé, her tart mouth pursed in distaste, the sous-chef whispered to the scullery boy, "I don't know what to make of her."
—Laurel Fortuner, Montendre, France (1992 winner)

• **The moment he laid eyes** on the lifeless body of the nude socialite sprawled across the bathroom floor, Detective Leary knew she had committed suicide by grasping the cap on the tamper-proof bottle, pushing down and twisting while she kept her thumb firmly pressed against the spot the arrow pointed to, until she hit the exact spot where the tab clicks into place, allowing her to remove the cap and swallow the entire contents of the bottle, thus ending her life.
—Artie Kalemeris, Fairfax, Virginia (1997 winner)

Shortcut: Danny DeVito once studied to be a hairdresser.

AMAZING ANIMALS: THE OPOSSUM

When we saw the opossum on a list of wildlife that thrives in cities, it made us curious about how it manages to survive in such a hostile environment. Turns out that this tough little critter is quite an amazing animal.

OLD-TIMER

Of all the mammals on Earth, opossums are among the oldest. Fossil records show it going back more than 100 million years. Remarkably, the gray-and-white, pink-nosed, rat-tailed opposums we see in our backyards today are almost identical to the ones that walked around with the dinosaurs. They have survived that long with very few evolutionary changes.

The opossum is a *marsupial*, a primitive type of mammal distinguished by its unique reproductive system. It gives birth to embryos that develop into viable "pups" in an external pouch—like a kangaroo. There used to be thousands of species of marsupials in North America, but over tens of millions of years they migrated south, into what is now South America.

Continental drift prevented them from returning until fairly recently (less than eight million years ago) and by that time another type of mammal had evolved: *placental* mammals, which develop their young *inside* their bodies. Placental mammals dominated. Of all the South American marsupial species that could have survived in North America, only one did: the opossum.

SURVIVOR

The evolutionary cards are stacked against the opossum.

It's not fast: it has a top speed of 1.7 mph.

It's not large: adults range from 6 to 12 pounds.

It's not exceedingly smart: it has almost the smallest brain-to-body ratio of any land mammal.

It's not aggresive, nor well-suited for fighting to defend itself. So why is the primitive opossum the only marsupial that made it in

How long have mammals been on Earth? 200 million years. Homo sapiens? 150,000 years.

North America? Here are some features that helped opossums beat the odds:

• They'll eat anything. They can survive on worms, snails, insects, snakes, toads, birds, fruits, vegetables, or garbage. (They'll also eat cat food and dog food.)

• Opossums are unusually resistant to diseases, including rabies. They're also very resistant to snake venom—a dose of rattlesnake venom that would kill a horse barely affects an opossum.

• They have a prehensile (grasping) tail that they can use to gather branches and grass for nesting, climb trees, and escape predators.

• Opossums are the only animals besides primates that have an opposable thumb. It's on their hind feet, and they use it to grasp with, like humans do.

• Male opossums have another unique appendage: a forked penis. Females have a two-channel vagina, so everything has to line up correctly for successful mating. This means that the opossum can't crossbreed with other species, which is another reason it has changed so little over the eons.

PLAYING 'POSSUM

Another unique trait that plays a big part in the opossum's survival is its ability to "play dead." Is it playing? Not exactly.

When an opossum is threatened by an enemy, it doesn't have a lot to work with. It doesn't want to fight and avoids it at all costs. It hisses and growls, baring its mouthful of teeth—it has 50, the most of any land mammal. It will even emit a foul odor, vomit, or defecate to repel the enemy. Sometimes these strategies work.

But if the predator is really hungry and still a threat, the opossum has one more weapon. It passes out. It's not an act, it's an involuntary reaction to overwhelming danger. It goes into a coma or shocklike state: the heart rate drops drastically, the body temperature goes down, the tongue hangs out, and it drools. It is, for all appearances, dead. Why is that good? Most predators won't eat dead animals. They'll usually sniff around, then leave it alone.

After a while, as short as a minute or as long as six hours, the opossum will "wake up" and waddle on its way to survive another day, another week, and who knows, maybe another 100 million years.

In 2000 Italian pastry chefs built an edible Ferrari out of 40,000 cream pies.

LIVE FROM NEW YORK, IT'S SATURDAY NIGHT!

In our Third Bathroom Reader, *we covered the origin of* Saturday Night Live. *Why write about it again? Because it's one of the most influential TV shows of all time. Over the years, it has had its ups and downs, but it remains essentially the same show Lorne Michaels devised back in 1975.*

A CONSERVATIVE MEDIUM

In the late 1960s, America's youth spoke out against the war in Vietnam, against racism, and against a government they saw as a growing threat to the freedom of speech. How did the big three TV networks react to this dissent? They mostly ignored it.

Take the popular variety show *Laugh-In*, which was marketed to younger people. It featured a head writer who also happened to be a Nixon speechwriter. The result: More fluff than substance. And *The Smothers Brothers Comedy Hour* coasted along fine until Tommy Smothers began speaking out openly against the war. CBS swooped in and quickly canceled the show in 1969. By the end of the decade, the message was clear: "The revolution will not be televised."

UNDERGROUND COMEDY

In the early 1970s, the revolution took an unexpected turn: it showed up in underground comedy. *MAD* magazine and *National Lampoon* spread the anti-establishment message on their pages; comedy troupes such as Second City in Chicago and Toronto and The Groundlings in Los Angeles performed cutting-edge satire with no rules, no limits, and no censorship—all things that TV network executives stayed well away from. To them, comedy was Johnny Carson and Dick Cavett for adults, and *The Brady Bunch* and *Gilligan's Island* for kids.

There was, however, one word that the network brass has always pricked up its ears for: ratings. And NBC's late-night Saturday ratings were so low in 1975 that they were giving away advertising spots in the time slot as a free bonus to attract primetime advertis-

Most-groped dummy at Madame Tussaud's Wax Museum: Elle MacPherson.

ing deals. They blamed the low ratings on the time of night rather than on what they were broadcasting: *Tonight Show* reruns. But everyone was growing tired of having Johnny on six, and sometimes seven, nights a week. NBC was ready to replace the reruns with something else. They were considering a weekly variety show hosted by impressionist Rich Little and singer Linda Rondstadt.

They gave the task of creating the new show to a young executive named Dick Ebersol, who didn't even bother pursuing Little; he wanted to do something new and fresh that younger viewers could identify with. A fellow executive told him, "Dick, there's only one guy you should talk to."

LORNE MICHAELS

By the time he was 30 years old, Canadian Lorne Michaels (born Lorne Lipowitz) had graduated with an English degree from the University of Toronto, sold cars in England, starred as one-half of a comedy team on Canadian television, been a writer for *Laugh-In* (all of his jokes about Nixon were rejected), produced a TV special for Lily Tomlin, and submitted an idea for a late-night variety show to NBC—twice.

But the timing for his show wasn't right until 1975, when Ebersol sought him out. At their first meeting, Michaels told Ebersol: "I want to do a show for the generation that grew up on television." His concept was already mapped out: an anything-goes comedy show featuring edgy satire, commercial parodies, fake news, rock music, and a celebrity host. It had to be live—a practice network television had abandoned in the 1970s—otherwise it wouldn't have the spontaneity it needed. Ebersol agreed and pitched the idea to the network, selling it as a "youth" show and pointing to the dismal ratings NBC was getting in the 18 to 34-year-old market. To Ebersol's and Michaels's amazement, the network was convinced... mostly.

HEEERE'S JOHNNY

By the 1970s, Johnny Carson had as much clout as anybody at NBC. The *Tonight Show* had done so much for the network that what Johnny wanted, Johnny got. And one thing Johnny *didn't* want was competition. Worried that a new comedy show would compete with his "King of Late Night" status, Carson summoned Michaels and Ebersol.

But one of Michaels's strengths was his diplomatic skill—he calmly reassured the "Great One" that his show would be very different than Carson's: no interviews, a bunch of unknowns, a completely different format aimed at a completely different audience. Carson was duly impressed with the two young men and gave them—and the network—his approval. He would come to regret that decision.

PUTTING IT TOGETHER

Michaels signed a deal with NBC, fittingly, on April 1, 1975. He and Ebersol were given Studio 8H on the 17th floor of New York's Rockefeller Center. Michaels wanted to call the new show *Saturday Night Live*, but ABC was putting together a show by the same name—hosted by Howard Cosell and featuring the "Primetime Players." So they called it *NBC's Saturday Night*, then just *Saturday Night*. (The show wasn't called *Saturday Night Live* until the March 26, 1977, episode.)

Michaels began a search for "enlightened amateurs"—comedians who, according to Doug Hill and Jeff Weingrad in their book *Saturday Night*, spouted "drug references, casual profanity, a permissive attitude toward sex, a deep disdain for show business convention, and bitter distrust for corporate power." Michaels wanted to combine that rawness with the style of his all-time favorite comedians: Monty Python's Flying Circus.

Michaels approached one of the hottest comedians of the mid-1970s, Albert Brooks, with the idea of hiring him as the permanent celebrity host. Brooks declined, saying that he wanted to focus on a movie career. He did, however, offer an alternative idea. "You don't want a permanent host anyway," he told Michaels. "Every show does that. Why don't you get a different host every week?" So they did. But they still needed a cast.

STAR SEARCH

That summer, word of the new show quickly spread through the show biz world. Ads for auditions went into trade papers all over the country. In New York, comedy clubs put their best acts on when the *Saturday Night* people arrived. But Michaels wanted more than stand-up comedians, he wanted socially conscious performers who could act, improvise, do impressions, sing, and dance. He scoured the ranks of *National Lampoon*, comedy troupes, even serious reper-

Mark your calendars: Nov. 12 is "National Pizza with the Works Except Anchovies Day."

tory theaters. Michaels could only pay his performers $750 per episode, but he was offering something most couldn't refuse: exposure on national television. One more rule: none of *Saturday Night*'s talent would be over 30 years old.

THE NOT READY FOR PRIMETIME PLAYERS

First hired was Gilda Radner, whom Michaels had performed improv with in the 1960s. In 1975 Radner was with Second City in Chicago, along with Dan Aykroyd, Bill Murray, and John Belushi. Michaels was reluctant about Belushi—who was known as much for being uncontrollable as he was for being a brilliant comedian. But Belushi did so well as a samurai pool hustler in his audition that he was hired over Murray, who had already signed a tentative deal with ABC's *Saturday Night Live*.

From the improvisational group The Proposition he found Jane Curtin, who fit the bill as the "white bread" woman, and from The Groundlings in Los Angeles, Laraine Newman. She was chosen partly for her audition performance and partly for her red hair, which would offset Curtin's sandy blonde and Radner's brunette locks. To round out the appearance of the cast, Michaels wanted a black man. He'd originally hired Garrett Morris as a writer. But even though Morris had no comedic experience, Michaels was impressed with his acting ability in the 1972 film *Cooley High*, so Morris was made a cast member instead. Now that the cast was set, they needed a name. Michaels mocked ABC's Saturday-night show by calling NBC's performers the "Not Ready For Primetime Players."

In addition to performers, Michaels also sought out talented young writers, including the team of Al Franken and Tom Davis, a cynical *Lampoon* writer named Michael O'Donoghue (who was responsible for a lot of *SNL*'s darker material), and a former *Smothers Brothers Comedy Hour* writer named Chevy Chase. Chase wanted to act, but there was no more money in the budget for cast members, so Michaels signed him as head writer (which actually paid more money than the players were getting). Michaels and Chase immediately became buddies, and Chase got preferential treatment, including the "Weekend Update" job, much to the dismay of the cast. It was a sign of things to come.

The cast and crew were set. Now all Michaels and Ebersol had to do was make a show. ***Turn to page 199 for Part II of the story.***

Official state dance of Utah: square dance.

CELEBRITY FAVORITES

Famous people—for some reason we can't get enough of them. Knowing a celebrity's favorite color won't make your life any better, but it's fun to know anyway.

COLORS

Cary Grant: Red

Christina Aguilera: Turquoise

Angelina Jolie: Black

Walter Cronkite: Blue

Justin Timberlake: Baby blue

FOODS

Barbra Streisand: Coffee ice cream

Cameron Diaz: French fries

Red Hot Chili Peppers: Bananas

Sarah Michelle Gellar: Pasta

Jennifer Love Hewitt: McDonald's cheeseburgers

MOVIES

Lynn Redgrave: *Jules et Jim*

Scott Adams: *Star Wars*

Ben Stein: *Gone with the Wind*

Sandra Bullock: *The Wizard of Oz*

HOBBIES

Leonardo DiCaprio: Writing poetry

Tanya Tucker: Cutting-horse contests

Henry Fonda: Model airplanes

Winona Ryder: Reading

Brad Pitt: Interior design

BANDS

Ani DiFranco: The Beatles

Drew Barrymore: The Beatles

Roseanne Cash: The Beatles

Bob Weir: The Beatles

Moby: Donna Summer

RELIGIONS

Harrison Ford: Buddhism

Mel Gibson: Catholocism

Natalie Portman: Judaism

Tom Crusie: Scientology

Christopher Reeve: Atheism

BOOKS

Woody Harrelson: *A People's History of the United States* by Howard Zinn

Larry King: *Catcher in the Rye* by J. D. Salinger

Bryant Gumbel: *The Autobiography of Malcolm X*

Gloria Steinem: *Little Women* by Louisa May Alcott

Uncle John: *Affliction* by Russell Banks

Jeff Foxworthy: *You Might Be a Redneck if...* by Jeff Foxworthy

JOBS THEY'D LIKE TO HAVE

James Brown: Big League Pitcher

Roseanne: Teacher

Matthew Broderick: Construction worker

Tom Hanks: Cartoonist

Melanie Griffith: Brain Surgeon

World's most admired bachelor, according to one survey: Jesus.

DON'T!

Thinking of skipping this page?
Take our advice: don't.

"Don't get mad. Don't get even. Just get elected…then get even."
—James Carville

"Don't marry a man to reform him—that's what reform schools are for."
—Mae West

"Don't ever send a man window shopping. He'll come back carrying a window."
—*A Wife's Little Instruction Book*

"Don't take life too seriously. You'll never get out alive."
—Tex Avery

"Don't worry if you're a kleptomaniac, you can always take something for it."
—Robert Benchley

"Don't worry about people stealing an idea. If it's original, you'll have to ram it down their throats."
—Howard Aiken

"Don't meet trouble halfway. It's quite capable of making the entire journey."
—Stanislaw Jerzy Lec

"Don't carry a grudge. While you're carrying the grudge, the other guy's out dancing."
—Buddy Hackett

"Don't steal. The government hates competition."
—Anonymous

"Don't blame God. He's only human."
—Leo Rosten

"Don't dig for water under the outhouse."
—Cowboy proverb

"Don't judge each day by the harvest you reap but by the seeds that you plant."
—Robert Louis Stevenson

"Don't just do something, stand there."
—Dean Acheson

"Don't compromise yourself. You're all you've got."
—Janis Joplin

"Don't worry about the world coming to an end today. It's already tomorrow in Australia."
—Charles Schulz

31% of men say they look at other women when they're with their…

WEIRD CANADA

Canada: land of beautiful mountains, clear lakes, bustling cities... and some really weird news reports. Here are some of the oddest entries from the BRI newsfile.

SNOW DAY

In January 2002, a 30-year-old Ontario man named Nona Thusky was charged with public drunkenness and violation of probation. He was kept in custody awaiting sentencing on a previous conviction for assaulting a police officer when, two weeks later, he was suddenly released. Why? Because it snowed.

Mr. Thusky is a member of the Algonquin tribe from the Barriere Lake reservation, and he's the only community member who knows how to operate the snowplow. After a severe February snowstorm, judge Jean-Francois Gosselin decreed that "community service"—i.e., clearing snow from the streets—made more sense than jail time.

I THOUGHT THEY WERE A HOCKEY TEAM

Toronto Mayor Mel Lastman found himself in a storm of criticism in January 2002. He had staged a photo session shaking hands with and receiving a T-shirt from a member of the Hell's Angels. Members of the notorious motorcycle gang had been involved in a vicious six-year drug war with rival gangs in Quebec in which more than 150 people were killed. Police organizations, city officials, and citizens blasted the mayor for the move, calling it grossly insensitive. Mayor Lastman threw the T-shirt away and apologized, saying he didn't know that the Hell's Angels... dealt drugs. Afterwards, the gang demanded an apology from the mayor—for throwing away the present they gave him.

BEYOND THE CALL OF DOOTY

In 1943, 17-year-old Hugh Trainor enlisted in the army and passed a preliminary test in his hometown on Prince Edward Island. He then traveled by ferry to an army barracks in Halifax, Nova Scotia. Once there, he failed his medical test and never officially became a member of the armed forces. But Trainor claimed that his time on the ferry—about a 10-mile ride—qualified as "war service," because German submarines had previously attacked ships in Canadian waters. In 2002 the Federal Court of Canada ruled that 75-year-old Trainor was entitled to veteran's benefits for his service and awarded him $1,000 a month for the rest of his life.

THE PLOP THICKENS

The state provincial fair in Calgary, Alberta, offered a new thrill to attendees in 2002: Cow Patty Bingo. They divided a field up into squares, painted numbers on them, and let people bet on the numbers. Then they let the cows into the field. The person whose square got the first "lucky patty" won a prize. Organizers denied claims that the cows had been given laxatives to speed the game up.

*   *   *

HOOT OFF THE PRESS

WANTED

"Salespeople needed. If you are now employed but wish to improve your position, or in a dead-end job, call now for opportunity in cemetary sales."

—*Toronto Star*

"Career opportunity for a firefighter position: 'We offer a smoke-free work environment.'"

—*Calgary Herald*

ANNOUNCEMENTS

"All residents will now be collected on Thursday."

—Ontario waste-systems company notice

"At a meeting of the cemetary commission, the burial rates were increased slightly to reflect the higher cost of living."

—Nova Scotia church bulletin

CLASSIFIEDS

"Visitors are needed for a man having trouble with blindness and a German-speaking woman."

—*The Ottawa Citizen*

"Lots of stuff! All ex-hubby's remains."

—*South Delta Today*, B.C.

"Wedding gown worn once by mistake. Size 9–10. Asking $20."

—*Oshawa Times*

NEWS FLASH

"A third grain-elevator fire in east-central Alberta has investigators wondering if there's a cereal arsonist at work."

—*Calgary Herald*

Canada has more doughnut shops per capita than any other country.

INTERNATIONAL ELVIS

Decades after his death, Elvis is more popular than ever. He sells more records, generates more revenue, and has more fans worldwide than he did when he was alive. If you need proof, look to these Elvis impersonators.

LATINO ELVIS (Robert Lopez, a.k.a. "El Vez," Mexico)
Claim to Fame: First Mexican Elvis to think he was the *second* Mexican Elvis
Taking Care of Business: Lopez, who is famous all over Mexico and has appeared on MTV and *The Tonight Show*, grew up absolutely convinced that Elvis Presley was Mexican. "When I was a kid in the '60s, I had uncles with continental slacks and pompadours in that Elvis style," he says. "I thought Elvis looked like my uncles."

Lopez got a rude awakening when he realized that the King wasn't in Mexico even when he was *supposed* to be: "The first movie I ever saw him in was *Fun in Acapulco*. I found out later that it wasn't even filmed in Mexico, but on a sound stage." No matter—El Vez is still dedicated to emulating the King. "I don't think that you can do this unless you love and admire Elvis," he says. "This isn't just some fat-man-on-pills parody."

REFUSNIK ELVIS (Vassil Angelov, Bulgaria)
Claim to Fame: Put his life on the line by impersonating the King
Taking Care of Business: When he was a young man in the 1960s, Angelov had to hide his admiration of Elvis because sideburns and rock music were illegal in communist Bulgaria. But the communist era ended in 1990 and today Angelov runs Bulgaria's only Elvis fan club and openly tours the country imitating his idol. Someday he hopes to travel the world. "I want to look for people and places," he says, "where I can show off my God-given talent."

TOKYO ELVIS (Mori Yasumasa, Japan)
Claim to Fame: Became the first non-American to win an Elvis impersonator contest in Memphis, Tennessee, the Elvis capital of the world

It's worth it: After a three-week vacation, your IQ can drop by as much as 20%.

Taking Care of Business: Yasumasa didn't even hear his first Elvis song until he was 18, but quickly made up for lost time. It wasn't long before he had perfected an Elvis imitation and was performing on U.S. Army bases all over Japan. In 1992 he made the trip of a lifetime when he traveled to Memphis, entered the International Elvis Impersonator Contest... and won. The victory has only deepened his appreciation of the King. "Although he didn't compose or write his songs and leave any deep messages, I believe that he himself is the message," Yasumasa says. "He was using his own body and soul to convey the message of freedom to the world. This to me is really incredible."

KIWI ELVIS (Brian Childs, New Zealand)

Claim to Fame: He's living the life of Elvis... in reverse

Taking Care of Business: Elvis was a singer who collected police badges and always wanted to be in law enforcement—and Brian Childs was a New Zealand police constable who always wanted to be the King. He started out impersonating Elvis in his spare time, but his chief didn't like it and in January 2002, told him he'd have to quit his hobby. Constable Childs quit his job instead. Today he is the reigning champion Elvis Presley impersonator in neighboring Australia and is considering suing the force for wrongful dismissal.

FILIPINO ELVIS (Rene Escharcha, a.k.a. "Renelvis", Philippines)

Claim to Fame: He takes care of business—by telephone

Taking Care of Business: It's not easy to stand out from the crowd when you're an Elvis impersonator—even if you're a Filipino Elvis living in North Carolina. One of the ways Escharcha makes his mark is by whipping out his long-distance phone card in the middle of a performance and calling his cousin in the Philippines (also an Elvis impersonator) so that they can belt out Elvis tunes together, a cappella, over a speakerphone. Escharcha also keeps the King's legacy fresh by writing his own songs. In "Elvis on Terrorism," Escharcha sings, "I wonder if Elvis were here today, what would he do? I can assure you, he would do something."

Why is he so dedicated to being the King? "If you want to be somebody, you have to work at it," Renelvis explains.

43% of single American men say they didn't go on a date in 2001.

FAMILIAR PHRASES

Here are more origins of some common phrases.

BASKET CASE

Meaning: An overly anxious or stressed person who can't function normally (yup, that's Uncle John)

Origin: "First appeared as a slang term in WWI meaning 'a quadruple amputee.' Soldiers who had lost all their limbs actually were carried in baskets, because if they were carried on stretchers, they'd be too likely to fall out." (From *Jesse's Word of the Day*, by Jesse Sheidlower)

HANG IN THERE

Meaning: To refuse to give up; to stick with it

Origin: "This hails from the world of boxing, where managers exhort exhausted fighters to clinch their opponents, or hang on to the ropes, to finish a round or a bout. In recent years the expression has come to be used as common parting words to someone in trouble since everyone in this life is usually up against the ropes in one way or another." (From *Grand Slams, Hat Tricks, and Alley-oops*, by Robert Hendrickson)

TO SHOW YOUR TRUE COLORS

Meaning: To be yourself

Origin: "*To sail under false colors* was to disguise a pirate ship by flying the flag of a friendly nation. Camouflaged in this way, pirates could usually sail fairly close to the ship he wanted to attack without raising an alarm. When the moment was right, he'd *show his true colors* by raising his own flag." (From *Scuttlebutt…& Other Expressions of Nautical Origin*, by Teri Degler)

TO HAVE SOMEONE OVER A BARREL

Meaning: To have the upper hand

Origin: "In the days before mouth-to-mouth resuscitation, lifeguards placed drowning victims over a barrel, which was rolled back and forth while the lifeguard tried to revive them. The person 'over the barrel' is in the other person's power or at his

The call of the koala bear sounds like a handsaw cutting wood.

mercy." (From *The Facts on File Encyclopedia of Word and Phrase Origins*, by Robert Hendrickson)

ROLLING OVER IN ONE'S GRAVE

Meaning: The action of a dead person, as if appalled by something that has happened or been proposed

Origin: "The first-known reference to this phrase is in Mark Twain's 1894 novel, *The Tragedy of Pudd'nhead Wilson*. Twain says: 'You has disgraced yo' birth. What would yo' pa think o' you? It's enough to make him turn in his grave.'" (From *The Phrase That Launched 1,000 Ships*, by Nigel Rees)

SKID ROW

Meaning: A run-down part of town

Origin: "Seattle swells with pride in the well-documented knowledge that *skid row* had its origins there. In the mid-19th century a logging road along which logs were skidded led from the forest to Yesler's Mill. The *Skid Road* became a road populated by lumberjacks, sailors, prostitutes, and panhandlers. It soon became known as *Skid Row*, but today is always spelled with small letters." (From *Cassell Everyday Phrases*, by Neil Ewart)

TO THROW IN THE TOWEL

Meaning: To give up

Origin: "From the 17th-century expression, *throw in the sponge*, which was the practice of throwing up the sponge used to cleanse a boxer's face at a prize-fight, a signal that the fighter had had enough—that the sponge is no longer required. In today's pugilistic encounters one is more likely to hear that the manager of one contestant throws in a towel, rather than a sponge, but the original occasion for the expression still stands." (From *Heavens to Betsy!*, by Charles Earle Funk)

* * *

"Some mornings it just doesn't seem worth it to gnaw through the leather straps."

—***Emo Phillips***

Monkeys given paints and paper on which to draw will scream in anger when an unfinished...

WEIRD SENTENCES

These sentences may have made sense at the time they were handed down...but we doubt it.

• Leah Marie Fairbanks of Duluth, Minnesota, pleaded guilty to first-degree assault charges and was sentenced to 14 months probation...plus she had to read seven classic novels and the Declaration of Independence and then write reports on each one.

• Anna Mae Leach of Castle Shannon, Pennsylvania, was jailed for a week for not returning three videotapes. (The charges turned out to be false.)

• Gloria Cisternas of Santiago, Chile, was sentenced to seven days in jail for failing to pay a $63 (U.S.) fine. She had been fined for failing to keep her lawn green.

• *USA Today* reported that Utah's Tom Green had been convicted for polygamy and criminal nonsupport. Sentence: "0–5 years in prison."

• Tony and Angelica Flores spent a night in jail after failing to appear for their court date. Criminal charges had been filed against them in Peoria, Arizona, for keeping their Christmas lights up too long.

• In Louisville, Kentucky, Luther Crawford, father of 12 kids by 11 different women, was $33,000 behind on child support payments. He avoided going to prison by accepting the judge's offer that he refrain from sex until he has paid up.

• A wealthy Finnish man was fined $103,000—for a speeding ticket. In Finland, traffic fines are levied in proportion to the driver's income.

• Four Swedish teenagers were convicted of high treason for their plot against King Carl Gustaf. Their plot: to throw a strawberry cream pie at him.

...work is taken from them. But they don't object to having a finished painting taken.

POLITALKS

Politicians aren't getting much respect these days—but then, it sounds like they don't deserve much, either.

"Wherever I have gone in this country, I have found Americans."

—Alf Landon (R-KS)

"We shall reach greater and greater platitudes of achievement."

—Richard J. Daley (D), ***mayor of Chicago***

"I hope I stand for anti-bigotry, anti-Semitism, anti-racism."

—George H. W. Bush

"This is the worst disaster in California since I was elected."

—Gov. Pat Brown (D-CA), ***discussing a flood***

"Mr. Nixon was the thirty-seventh president of the United States. He had been preceded by thirty-six others."

—Gerald Ford

"If God had wanted us to use the metric system, Jesus would have had ten apostles."

—Jesse Helms (R-NC)

"This legislation has far-reaching ramifistations."

—Gib Lewis (D-TX)

"I didn't intend for this to take on a political tone. I'm just here for the drugs."

—Nancy Reagan, ***asked a political question during a "Just Say No" rally***

"I am not a chauvinist, obviously....I believe in women's rights for every woman but my own."

—Harold Washington (D), ***mayor of Chicago, 1984–87***

"Those who survived the San Francisco earthquake said, 'Thank God, I'm still alive.' But, of course, those who died—their lives will never be the same again."

—Barbara Boxer (D-CA)

"The state of California has no business subsidizing intellectual curiosity."

—Gov. Ronald Reagan, (R-CA), ***responding to student protests on college campuses***

"Politics would be a helluva good business if it weren't for the goddamned people."

—Richard Nixon

THE KING OF COTTON

When you hear the name Eli Whitney, you probably think of his invention, the cotton gin. But you may not realize how profoundly it (and his other inventions) changed the world. Here's the history they never taught you in school.

LOOKING FOR WORK

In 1792 a 27-year-old Massachusetts Yankee named Eli Whitney graduated from Yale University and landed a tutoring job in South Carolina. He was glad to get it—he needed the money to pay off his school debts. But when he arrived there he discovered that the job paid half of what he'd been promised, which meant he'd never be able to save any money. He turned the job down.

Suddenly he was jobless, penniless, and stranded in the South, hundreds of miles from home. But he'd made the trip from New York with a friend named Phineas Miller, who was escorting *his* employer, a widow named Mrs. Greene, back to Georgia. When Greene invited Whitney to spend a week at her plantation outside of Savannah, he gladly accepted. He had no place else to go.

Whitney repaid Mrs. Greene's generosity by designing an embroidery frame for her. Greene was impressed by the cleverness of the design, and it got her thinking. If Whitney was this clever, maybe he could solve a problem that plagued her and other planters—how to "gin," or remove the seeds from, cotton...without doing it by hand.

Upland cotton, the only kind that grew in the interior regions of the South, had seeds that were "covered with a kind of green coat resembling velvet," as Whitney put it. These fuzzy seeds stuck to the cotton fibers like Velcro. Removing them by hand required so much labor—one person could clean only about a pound of cotton per day—that upland cotton was essentially worthless.

MASS PRODUCTION

If a way could be found to remove the seeds more easily, upland cotton had the potential to become a very valuable export crop. Why? The Industrial Revolution had transformed the English tex-

The word *ecology* comes from the Greek word for "household."

tile industry (which turned the cotton into thread and the thread into cloth) into a monster and caused demand for cotton to soar.

As late as the 1730s, spinners and weavers made cloth just as they had for centuries: slowly and by hand. One person, sitting at a spinning wheel, could spin raw cotton into only one string of yarn at a time. It took 14 days to make a pound of yarn, which one or two weavers could then weave into a single piece of cloth.

In the mid-1700s, English inventions with colorful names like the flying shuttle (1733), the spinning jenny (1764), the water frame (1769), and the mule (1779), changed all that; so did the introduction of steam power in 1785. Now a single unskilled laborer—even a child or someone formerly thought too old to work—could tend machines that made hundreds and eventually thousands of strands of yarn at once, or that wove it into yards and yards of cloth, faster than the eye could see.

THE BIG BANG

Because of these inventions, the English textile industry's appetite for cotton became enormous and grew exponentially from year to year. In 1765 spinners and weavers in England had turned half a million pounds of cotton into cloth; by 1790 the new machines were consuming 28 million pounds of cotton per year, nearly all of it imported from other countries. As demand for raw cotton soared, it got harder and harder to find enough of it to feed all of the new machines.

How much of the imported raw cotton came from the American South? Almost none. As late as 1791, the year before Whitney arrived in Georgia, exports for the entire South totaled a few hundred bags at most. But not for long.

NO PROBLEM

So how long did it take Whitney to solve the problem that had vexed Southern planters for years? Ten days. It took several months to perfect the design, but after just 10 days, this Yankee, who'd landed at Greene's plantation purely by chance, managed to invent this revolutionary machine.

The design was so simple that it was a wonder nobody else had thought of it before. It consisted of a wooden roller with wire "teeth" that grabbed the cotton fibers and pulled them through a

Q: How did the names Jessica and Sylvia become popular? A: Shakespeare used them in his plays.

slotted iron screen. The slots in the screen were wide enough to let the teeth and the cotton fibers through, but they were too narrow for the seeds, which separated out and fell into a box.

A rapidly rotating brush then removed the cotton fibers from the teeth and flung them into a bin. This allowed the user to feed raw cotton into the machine indefinitely, without having to stop every few minutes to clean the teeth.

Using Whitney's cotton gin, in one day a laborer could clean as much as 10 pounds of upland cotton, which before would have taken 10 days to clean by hand. If a larger gin powered by water or a horse was used, a laborer could clean as much cotton in one day as would have taken more than *seven weeks* to clean by hand.

BRAVE NEW WORLD

Over the next several decades, Whitney's cotton gin transformed the South. Tens of thousands and eventually millions of acres of wilderness were cleared to make way for enormous cotton plantations. By 1810 U.S. exports of cotton to England had grown from almost nothing to 38 million pounds, making the South the largest supplier of cotton to that country.

And that was only the beginning. By the start of the Civil War, the Southern "cotton belt," as it came to be known, was exporting *920 million* pounds of cotton to England each year, more than 90% of its cotton imports. Cotton had become, as one historian described it, "the largest single source of America's growing wealth." Cotton was king.

THE CLOTHES ON YOUR BACK

But Whitney's invention had more far-reaching effects than increasing U.S. exports. The industrialization of cotton production vastly increased the supply of cotton cloth. That changed cotton from one of the most expensive fabrics on Earth to one of the cheapest—and in the process, it clothed the world.

Between 1785, the year that steam power was introduced to the textile industry, and the early 1860s, the price of cotton cloth fell by more than 99%. That's the equivalent of a price of Tommy Hilfiger jeans falling from $5,000 to $50.

In the past almost no one had been able to afford cotton, (how many $5,000 pairs of jeans could you afford?), and things like

Odds that someone caught shoplifting is a teenager: 50%.

leather and wool made poor substitutes. (Don't believe it? Treat yourself to a pair of wool underpants and you'll see what we mean.) "Most of humanity," historian Paul Johnson writes in *A History of the American People*, "were unsuitably clothed in garments which were difficult to wash and therefore filthy."

Cheap, abundant cotton cloth changed that, too. "There is no instance in world history where the price of a product in potentially universal demand came down so fast," Johnson writes. "As a result, hundreds of millions of people, all over the world, were able to dress comfortably and cleanly at last."

CHAINS OF COTTON

There is yet another aspect to Eli Whitney's cotton gin—an ugly, inhuman side, that cast a shadow over all of the good it did. Many Americans think of Whitney's invention as an emancipator, a machine that freed the slaves from having to do the hand ginning of cotton. On the contrary, the rise of cotton cultivation in the South actually helped to entrench the institution of slavery, condemning millions of black Americans to its horrors just when many opponents of slavery thought it might finally be dying out.

Between 1775 and 1800 the price of slaves had fallen from about $100 per slave to $50, and abolitionists predicted that if the institution were left alone, it would die on its own. Or at the very least, as slavery weakened, it would become easier to abolish.

But the invention of the cotton gin changed everything. As the amount of acreage brought under cultivation in the South soared, so did the demand for slaves to work the plantations. Between 1800 and 1850, the price of a slave rose from $50 to as much as $1,000. Slavery, formerly thought to be in decline, quickly became integral to the new Southern economy.

As such, the leaders of the Southern states became increasingly militant in their determination to defend it and even expand it beyond the South. For a new generation of Southern leaders, the institution of slavery—because of the prosperity that came with it—was something to be defended, even to the death.

The cotton gin had made it happen...and made the Civil War inevitable.

Part II of the story of Eli Whitney starts on page 239.

Dolphins can hear underwater sounds from as far as 15 miles away.

IS THIS BRAIN LOADED?

Before they allow some people to buy guns, maybe police should skip the background check and give the applicants an IQ test. Here's why.

• A Washington man became frustrated trying to untangle Christmas lights in his driveway and became even more frustrated when his daughter came home and drove over them. So he went inside, got his .45-caliber pistol, took it into his backyard, and fired several shots into the ground, after which he was arrested.

• A man at Dallas–Fort Worth Airport damaged a window and caused panic among passengers when he accidentally fired his hunting rifle at a security checkpoint. The gun went off while he was demonstrating to guards that it wasn't loaded.

• A 32-year-old man was treated for a gunshot wound in his thigh in a Kentucky hospital. He had accidentally shot himself, he explained, while practicing his quick draw...with a snowman.

• Daniel Carson Lewis was charged with criminal mischief, driving while intoxicated, weapons misconduct, and assault after shooting a hole in the Alaskan Pipeline north of Fairbanks. Result: 280,000 gallons of crude oil were spilled over two acres of tundra before crews could stop the leak, the worst in about 20 years. Cleanup costs were estimated at $7 million. He did it, said his brother, "just to see if he could." He faces up to 10 years in prison.

• Chaddrick Dickson, 25, was treated for wounds received while trying to get the gunpowder out of a .22-caliber bullet by holding it with pliers and smashing it on the floor. The bullet exploded, hitting him in the leg. Dickson needed the gunpowder, he said, to put in his dog's food "to make him meaner."

• To get the attention of officers in a passing police car after getting a flat tire, a man in Pretoria, South Africa, shot his gun at it. The officers didn't help him with the flat, but they did charge him with attempted murder.

Most popular seafood in America: tuna. The average American eats 3.6 pounds a year.

INVASION OF THE FRANKENFISH

We don't want to scare you, but some strange creatures have been showing up on our doorsteps lately. They weren't invited... and they won't go away.

INVADING SPECIES: Golden Apple Snail

BACKGROUND: A native of South America, the golden apple snail became a popular addition to aquariums around the world because it is considered "pretty." In the early 1980s, some private snail farms found a new use for the easy-to-raise, protein-rich snails. They were shipped to snail farmers in Taiwan and the Philippines in the hopes of starting escargot industries.

LOCK THE DOORS, HERE THEY COME: Unfortunately, the escargot business never took off and prices plummeted, so farmers simply dumped the snails. Bad idea. Golden apple snails are voracious eaters, munching continuously for up to 24 hours a day, and their preferred food is rice seedlings. And what's the primary source of food and employment in Asia? Rice.

Laying as many as 500 eggs a week, the renegade snails quickly multiplied. By the mid-1990s they had destroyed an estimated two million acres of rice fields in the Philippines alone, and had spread to nearly every Asian nation, causing billions of dollars in damage.

And they're not done yet. The snails were discovered in U.S. waters in the 1990s, probably escapees or throwaways from aquariums. Several states have made owning a golden apple snail a crime.

INVADING SPECIES: Zebra Mussel

BACKGROUND: Originally from the Caspian Sea in Russia, by the 1800s, this freshwater mollusk had spread into other waterways in western Europe. In 1988 the zebra mussel showed up on this side of the Atlantic. How? Transatlantic ships probably brought the mussels over in their ballast tanks and unknowingly dumped them into North American ports.

LOCK THE DOORS, HERE THEY COME: Female zebra

mussels produce as many as a million eggs per year, with a very high survival rate. Once they appear, they take over, depleting rivers and lakes of oxygen and killing off native clams, snails, and fish. Not only that, they get into water pipes that feed to power plants and public waterworks, causing massive clogs. It's estimated that they cause $5 billion of damage every year. By 2002 they had spread to the Mississippi, Arkansas, Illinois, Ohio, and Tennessee Rivers...and they're still on the move.

MORE BAD NEWS: The zebra mussel brought a friend. The small (10-inch) but superaggressive round goby fish tagged along in the ballast tanks and has found a new home in the Great Lakes. Its long breeding period and ability to feed in complete darkness give it a competitive edge over native fish species...which it eats. The fact that it eats baby mussels too—though not enough to control them—means that the goby has an unlimited food source and will likely follow the zebra mussel, wreaking havoc throughout the Mississippi River system and beyond.

INVADING SPECIES: Northern Snakehead Fish

BACKGROUND: This Chinese fish is considered a delicacy in Asia. You can find them in some Asian markets in the United States. In June 2002, a man was fishing a pond in Crofton, Maryland, when he caught a fish he didn't recognize. Biologists later identified the 26-inch specimen as a snakehead. How'd it get there? An unnamed man admitted to dumping his two pet snakeheads after he got tired of feeding them. A subsequent search of the pond turned up more than 100 babies.

LOCK THE DOORS, HERE THEY COME: The snakehead, dubbed "Frankenfish" by the press, can get up to three feet long and an adult can eat prey as large as itself...including birds and small mammals. Worse: With no natural predators, it can devour everything in sight. Then, if conditions are just right, it can use its long fins as legs to *crawl across land to find a new pond or river*. It can actually survive on land for up to four days.

Officials are hoping that hasn't happened yet and said they'll use a pesticide to kill the snakeheads—and everything else in the pond—just so the Frankenfish doesn't spread. "It's not a dead or alive thing," biologist Bob Lunsford told the *Washington Post*, "we just want it dead."

...Western astronomers did. (And then many Westerners mistook them for planets.)

THE LAST LAUGH: EPITAPHS

Some unusual epitaphs and tombstones from the U.S. and Europe, sent in by our crew of wandering BRI tombstonologists.

In Arizona:
Ezikel Height
Here lies young
Ezikel Height
Died from jumping
Jim Smith's claim;
Didn't happen at
the mining site,
The claim he jumped,
was Jim Smith's
dame.

In England:
Mike O'Day
This is the grave of
Mike O'Day
Who died
maintaining his
right of way.
His right was clear,
his will was
strong.
But he's just as dead
as if he'd been
wrong.

In Guilford, Vermont:
Henry Clay Barney
My life's been hard
And all things show
it;
I always thought so
And now I know it.

In Georgia:
Anonymous
Due to lack of ground
in this cemetery,
Two bodies are
buried in this
one plot.
One of them was
a politician,
The other was
an honest man.

In England:
Emily White
Here lies the body
of Emily White,
She signalled left,
and then turned
right.

In Vermont:
John Barnes
Sacred to the memory
of my husband
John Barnes
Who died
January 3, 1803
His comely young
widow, aged 23,
Has many
qualifications of a
good wife,
And yearns to be
comforted.

In England:
Anonymous
It is so soon that
I am done for,
I wonder what I
was begun for.

In England:
Anonymous
Stop stranger as you
pass by
As you are now so
once was I
As I am now so will
you be
So be prepared to
follow me.

In Vermont:
Anonymous
Here lies our darling
baby boy
He never cries nor
hollers.
He lived for one and
twenty days
And cost us forty
dollars.

In Pawtucket, Rhode Island (on a boulder):
William P. Rothwell
This is on me.

Among the artifacts Columbus brought back from his second voyage: a swordfish sword.

I WANT TO RIDE MY BICYCLE!

It took dozens of tries and more than a century—not to mention a lot of scraped knees and broken bones—to develop the bicycle. Here's the story.

ROLL CALL

Humanity has had the wheel for thousands of years, but not until about 200 years ago were people able to use the wheel to get around without the aid of a horse or some other animal.

Exactly when and where the idea for the bicycle originated is unknown. Some historians claim that images of crude machines resembling bikes appeared on the walls of Egyptian tombs. Others argue that the ancient Romans had them in the city of Pompeii. There is even a drawing of a machine that resembles a modern bicycle in *Codex Atlanticus*, a collection of Leonardo da Vinci's mechanical drawings from 1493, but whether or not Da Vinci drew it is heavily disputed (many argue it was forged by the monks who were restoring the drawings in the 1970s). So for all intents and purposes, the history of the bicycle doesn't begin until very recently: the turn of the 19th century.

STOP HORSING AROUND

The first known bike was based on a toy. In 1790 in Versailles, France, the Comte Mede de Sivrac built an adult-sized version of a child's hobbyhorse. He called it the *velocifere*, Latin for "fast" and "carry." Judith Crown and Glenn Coleman describe it in their book *No Hands*:

> It must have been a delightfully silly sight: two wood wheels joined by a stub of beam, saddled and shaped to resemble a horse, with de Sivrac running wildly astride it until the thing rolled fast enough to coast a few yards. Fashionable aristocrats soon were huffing across the royal gardens on their own velociferes—some machines outfitted as horses, others as lions or serpents—lifting their legs gleefully as they spun past amused pedestrians.

As much fun as the velocifere may have been, it was equally dangerous. It lacked two important features—steering and brakes. Riders and unsuspecting pedestrians were injured so often that the craze soon fizzled out and wouldn't be tried again for almost 30 years.

YABBA DABBA DO

A German man named Baron Karl von Drais de Saverbrun wasn't fond of horses, finding them stubborn and moody, difficult to groom and saddle, and constantly leaving piles in their wake. Unfortunately, his job required that he ride one. He was the "master of forests," a land surveyor for the wealthy duke of Baden's very large estate. Von Drais needed some way to travel short distances without a horse.

In 1817, using the velocifere for inspiration, von Drais invented a new machine. It looked sort of like a modern bike but operated more like something out of the *Flintstones*: it had no pedals, so it required "foot power" to move it along. Von Drais's machine was constructed entirely out of wood, weighed about 50 pounds, and was steered by handlebars connected to the front wheel. The rider leaned forward on a belly brace—a cushioned piece of wood that rested beneath the handlebars—and pushed off with his feet. By leaning forward, the rider could coast along at speeds of up to 10 mph. Von Drais called it the *Laufsmachine*, or "walking machine," but most people referred to it as the *draisienne*.

Von Drais sold several of his machines to the French postal service. They were praised at first, but complaints of injuries soon started coming in. Although draisiennes rode well on the smooth fields that surrounded Duke of Baden's property, they were no match for the potholes, hills, and harsh weather that the postal carriers often encountered—not to mention the fact that the rider's feet were the closest thing the draisienne had to brakes. But despite its shortcomings, the draisienne got people excited about the possibilities of self-propelled machine travel.

IRONING OUT THE ERRORS

Working around the same time as von Drais, an English coach maker named Denis Johnson came up with a better solution. He created the "hobby horse," a version of the draisienne made out of wrought iron instead of wood. Like the draisienne, his machine lacked pedals, but the durable iron body was a vast improvement

More ships have been sunk by hurricanes than by warfare.

over wood and made for a much smoother ride. Johnson sold some "hobby horses" to wealthy Londoners, but creating them was so expensive, time consuming, and unprofitable that he soon stopped production.

PUT THE PEDAL TO THE METAL

Sometimes necessity is the mother of invention; at other times, boredom is. In 1839 a Scottish blacksmith named Kirkpatrick MacMillan changed transportation forever when he decided to pass the hours of a slow day away by tinkering with an old "hobby horse." He pondered the idea of attaching iron rods and foot pedals to the rear wheel. That way, he figured, riders could move the machine without having to push their feet against the ground. Rather, the rods and the pedals would crank the rear wheel and create motion, much like the locomotive, another recent invention. MacMillan built a prototype, gave it a ride, and lo and behold, it worked!

Being a natural showman, MacMillan amazed townspeople by riding his contraption at top speeds through the streets. But instead of being revered as a great invention, his new "hobby horse" was viewed as a dangerous menace. MacMillan could often be seen crashing into trees and flying over the handlebars. His escapades were put to an abrupt end when he was arrested for knocking down a small child in 1842 (the first known cyclist-related offense).

Although he never really marketed his invention and died before it caught on with the masses, many regard MacMillan as the father of the modern bicycle. A plaque is displayed at the site of his blacksmith shop which reads: "Kirkpatrick MacMillan: He builded better than he knew."

Round and round and round she goes. For Part II of the story, just follow your nose...to page 286.

SHARK ATTACK!

Ever since Uncle John saw Jaws, *he's been afraid of the ocean. This list of shark facts didn't help.*

• Sharks can detect the heartbeats of other fish.

• Mako sharks have been known to jump into the very fishing boats that are pursuing them.

• Bull sharks have been known to kill hippopotamuses in African rivers.

• Approximately 10 times more men than women are attacked by sharks.

• While in a feeding frenzy, some sharks bite their own bodies as they twist and turn.

• A 730-pound mako shark caught off Bimini in the Bahamas contained in its stomach a 120-pound swordfish—with the sword still intact.

• Lemon sharks grow a whole new set of teeth every two weeks.

• Sharks have a sixth sense. They can navigate by sensing changes in the Earth's magnetic field.

• Sharks will continue to attack even when disemboweled.

• Greenland sharks have been observed eating reindeer when they fall through ice.

• Three men who spent five days adrift in the Atlantic in 1980 had a shark to thank for their rescue. They fell asleep, but when the attacking shark nudged their raft, they woke up...in time to flag down a passing freighter.

• Some sharks can detect one part of blood in 100 million parts of water.

• Bull sharks have been known to pursue their victims onto land.

• The jaws of an eight-foot shark exert a force of 20 tons per square inch.

• The average shark can swallow anything half its size in one gulp.

• The original idea for steak knives derived from shark teeth.

• Approximately 100 shark attacks on humans occur worldwide each year.

Chicken à la King is named after King Edward VII.

"HOLY CATCHPHRASE, BATMAN!"

Every TV show wants one, but few achieve it: a catchphrase. The best ones not only propel their show into the limelight, but eventually take on a life of their own, sometimes getting into the dictionary, sometimes even electing a president.

Catchphrase: "D'oh!"
From: *The Simpsons* (1989–)
Here's the Story: Dan Castellaneta, the voice of Homer Simpson, came up with Homer's signature line himself. "It was written into the script as a 'frustrated grunt,'" he explains, "And I thought of that old Laurel and Hardy character who had a grunt like 'D'owww.' Matt Groening (*Simpsons* creator) said 'Great, but shorten it.' ...No one thought it would become a catchphrase." But it did—in a big way. The sitcom is seen by more than 60 million people in more than 60 countries. In 2001, "D'oh!" earned a spot in the *Oxford English Dictionary*.

Catchphrase: "Holy _______, Batman!"
From: *Batman* (1966–68)
Here's the Story: Uttered by Robin (Burt Ward) whenever he was dumbfounded, this silly phrase helped make the show a hit... and also led to its demise. During the first season, which aired two nights a week, *Batman* was fresh. ABC quickly realized that one of the things viewers loved was Robin's quirky line, so they milked it for all it was worth. But by the end of the second season, the plots were all recycled and the "Holy whatever, Batman!" had lost its impact. It didn't do much for Burt Ward's career either; he was never able to get past the Boy Wonder image.

In the 1995 film *Batman Forever,* Chris O'Donnell's Robin gave a nod to this famous catchphrase in the following exchange with Val Kilmer's Batman: "Holy rusted metal, Batman!" exclaims Robin. "Huh?" asks Batman. "The island," explains Robin, "it's made out of rusted metal... and holey... you know." "Oh," says Batman dryly.

Fore! *Golf* probably comes from the Dutch word *Kolf,* which means "club."

Catchphrase: "What'chu talkin' 'bout, Willis?"

From: *Diff'rent Strokes* (1978–86)

Here's the Story: Gary Coleman's snub-nosed delivery helped keep *Diff'rent Strokes* going for eight years. After the show's demise, the struggling Coleman began to use it at public appearances and in TV cameos to help keep his career afloat. But in recent years he's grown so sick of the line—and the TV business in general—that he's vowed never to say it again.

Catchphrase: "Sock it to me!"

From: *Laugh-In* (1968–73)

Here's the Story: The phrase came from pop music (Aretha Franklin's *Respect*). But the popular variety show *Rowan and Martin's Laugh-In* turned it into a mindless slapstick sketch…and repeated it week after week. Here's how it worked: An unsuspecting person (usually Judy Carne) would be tricked into saying "Sock it to me!" Then he or she was either hit by pies, drenched with water, or dropped through a trap door. Viewers loved it; they knew what was coming every time, and they still loved it. It quickly became an "in" thing to get socked.

This catchphrase was more than popular—it may have altered history: On September 16, 1968, presidential candidate Richard Nixon appeared on the show. He was set up in the standard fashion but surprised everyone by changing the command into a question: "Sock it to *ME?*" It did wonders for Nixon's staid, humorless image, and may have helped propel him into the Oval Office.

Catchphrase: "Beam me up, Scotty."

From: *Star Trek* (1966–69)

Here's the Story: Although Captain Kirk (William Shatner) never actually said this exact phrase (the closest he came was on the *Star Trek* animated series: "Beam *us* up, Scotty"), it has somehow been transported everywhere—feature films, advertisements, and even bumper stickers ("Beam me up, Scotty—there's no intelligent life down here.") Sometimes it even finds its way into the news: when 39 members of the Heaven's Gate cult committed suicide in 1997, expecting to leave their bodies and join with a spaceship, the press dubbed them the "Beam Me Up Scotty" cult.

Pound for pound, wood is stronger than steel.

THE GODMOTHERS

In 1990 the Italian police started rounding up underworld leaders all over Italy. But once the men were gone, the women took over... and proved that queenpins can be just as ruthless as kingpins.

ALL IN THE FAMILY. In June 1999, police in Sicily arrested Concetta Scalisi, the Godmother of an area known as the "Triangle of Death." She had ruled over her crime family's dealings in heroin, extortion, and violence in three towns on Mount Etna in Sicily after the death of her father. She was personally wanted for three murders.

SHE'LL NEVER CHANGE HER SPOTS. In December 2000, police arrested Erminia Giuliano, of the Camorra, Naples' version of La Cosa Nostra. "The Godmother" had inherited the job when the last of her five brothers was arrested. Police claim she had ruthlessly and casually ordered numerous executions of rivals, and was ranked one of Italy's 30 most dangerous criminals. When arrested, the 45-year-old made a special request of the police—she wanted to go to the hairdresser and be allowed to wear a leopard-skin outfit to prison.

MOB BOSS MADAM. Erminia Guiliano's rival in Naples was Maria Licciardi, who took over her family after her husband's arrest. She built the family's business by forging alliances with several other Camorra clans and by adding prostitution—regarded by old-school Mafia as an "immoral" business—to heroin trade and extortion. The alliances eventually broke down and between 1997 and 1998 she dragged her family through gang wars that killed more than 100 people. She was arrested on June 14, 2001.

BAD HAIR DAY. On May 5, 2002, there was an argument in a Naples hair salon between Clarissa Cava and Alba Graziano. The Cavas and the Grazianos had been bloody rivals for 30 years. Several days later, Graziano and her two daughters, aged 21 and 22, drove up to the car occupied by Cava, 21, her two aunts and and her sister—and machine-gunned them. Cava and her two aunts were killed. The Graziano's were later heard laughing and toasting the killings on police surveillance tapes.

Hot stuff: Hawaii is the only state that has never recorded a temperature below 0°F.

WRITING ON THE WALL

Why do writers write? These quotes from famous authors may provide some answers.

"I write for the same reason I breathe—because if I didn't, I would die."

—Isaac Asimov

"The good writing of any age has always been the product of *someone's* neurosis, and we'd have mighty dull literature if all the writers that came along were a bunch of happy chuckleheads."

—William Styron

"My first rule is, if it sounds like writing, rewrite it. Another rule is to try to leave out the parts people skip. Oh, and never start with the weather. With those rules you can go all the way."

—Elmore Leonard

"Contrary to what you might think, a career in letters is not without its drawbacks—chief among them the unpleasant fact that one is frequently called upon to sit down and write."

—Fran Lebowitz

"I'm so sick of Nancy Drew I could vomit."

—Mildred Benson, *author of 23 Nancy Drew novels*

"You don't write because you want to say something; you write because you've got something to say."

—F. Scott Fitzgerald

"The best time for planning a book is when you're doing the dishes."

—Agatha Christie

"People want to know why I do this, why I write such gross stuff. I like to tell them that I have the heart of a small boy...and I keep it in a jar on my desk."

—Stephen King

"I don't want to sound commercial, but I'm in it for the money, not the awards. This is my job; it's how I feed my family. What do I care if someone reads my books a hundred years from now? I'll be dead."

—Tom Clancy

"We write to taste life twice."

—Anais Nin

"There are three rules for writing a novel. Unfortunately, no one knows what they are."

—W. Somerset Maugham

OLD HISTORY, NEW THEORY

We tend to believe what science tells us about history... until science tells us something else. Here are some new findings that may change the history books, for now.

The Event: The Black Death, which wiped out about a third of the population of Europe in the mid-1300s

What the History Books Say: The Black Death was caused by an outbreak of bubonic plague, spread by rats.

New Theory: Dr. James Wood, professor of anthropology at Penn State University, believes historians have been too quick to attribute the Black Death to bubonic plague. Wood and his team of researchers are using computer analysis of church records and other documents to map out how the plague spread across Europe, and they say that if the epidemic really had been caused by bubonic plague, it would have spread differently than this one apparently did.

Rat-borne bubonic plague has to reach epidemic levels in the rat population before it can cause an epidemic in humans, Wood says. The Black Death seems to have spread faster among humans than it could possibly have spread among rats. And there's little evidence of a rat epidemic in the historical record. "There are no reports of dead rats in the streets in the 1300s," he says.

Also, symptoms of bubonic plague are stark and unmistakable: high fever, bad breath, body odor, coughing, and vomiting of blood, followed by swollen lymph nodes and red bruising on the skin that turns purple and then black. Yet, Wood says, 14th-century descriptions of the Black Death are vague. They're "usually too non-specific to be a reliable basis for diagnosis," he says.

In-Conclusion: So what does Dr. Wood think really caused the Black Death? Ebola? A now-extinct strain of bubonic plague that behaves differently than the more modern strains we're familiar with? Stay tuned—according to news reports, Dr. Wood is still in the early stages of his research and "is not ready to suggest an alternative disease."

GREAT STORY... JUST CHANGE THE ENDING

It might surprise you to learn that some of your favorite movies were changed from the originals to "improve" them. Did it work? Here are a few examples. You be the judge.

***A FISH CALLED WANDA* (1988)**

Original Ending: More in line with the dark and deceitful nature of the characters, Otto (Kevin Kline) gets killed by the steamroller. And Wanda (Jamie Lee Curtis) ditches Archie (John Cleese) at the airport, keeping all of the stolen jewels for herself.

But Wait: Test audiences didn't approve. Two more endings were filmed before viewers were satisfied—Otto lives, and Wanda and Archie go to South America together. The result: *A Fish Called Wanda* was a box-office smash, bringing in nearly $200 million.

***BLADE RUNNER* (1982)**

Original Ending: Director Ridley Scott's original existential ending confused test audiences, leaving many questions unanswered, most notably Deckard's (Harrison Ford) identity. Was he a replicant or not?

But Wait: Warner Bros. had invested a lot in the film and ordered Scott to "fix it." Reluctantly, he added narration by Ford and filmed a more typically violent Hollywood ending in which Deckard is indeed a replicant. Ten years later, in one of the first "director's cut" videos, Scott restored the film to his original vision. Which one is better? Both are available, so you can decide for yourself.

***THE SCARLET LETTER* (1995)**

Original Ending: Hollywood is notorious for altering novels but it outdid itself with this one. In Nathaniel Hawthorne's classic tale, Hester Prynne is judged an adulteress and sentenced to wear the letter "A" for the remainder of her days. After her secret lover confesses to the people, he dies in Hester's arms—an ending that echoed the sentiment of the times.

The Cliffs Notes edition of *The Scarlet Letter* outsells Nathaniel Hawthorne's edition by 3 to 1.

But Wait: Demi Moore's Hester is a bit more "modern"—she gets revenge on her oppressors and the reunited family lives happily ever after. Defending the new ending, Moore attested that "not many people have read the book anyway." Even fewer people saw the movie.

FATAL ATTRACTION (1987)

Original Ending: Dan (Michael Douglas) is charged with murder as we hear a voice-over of Alex's (Glenn Close) suicidal confession. Test audiences yawned their disapproval.

But Wait: Months after filming was completed, the cast was called back to film the more climactic ending in which Dan's wife (Anne Archer) murders Alex in the bathtub.

BUTCH CASSIDY AND THE SUNDANCE KID (1969)

Original Ending: Paul Newman's and Robert Redford's characters are shot by soldiers in a gruesome death scene.

But Wait: The version released to the public ends with a freeze-frame of the two stars making their final charge, thereby immortalizing them instead of killing them.

THELMA AND LOUISE (1991)

Original Ending: Similar to *Butch Cassidy and the Sundance Kid,* Geena Davis and Susan Sarandon's car falls all the way to the canyon floor, presumably smashing them to bits.

But Wait: Fearing a negative reaction to killing off the film's stars, the theatrical release shows their car sailing off the cliff, but leaves their fates up in the air, so to speak. The DVD includes the alternate ending.

THE PRINCESS DIARIES (2001)

Original Ending: The original finale had Mia (Anne Hathaway) simply agreeing to fly off to the fabled European kingdom of Genovia to become a princess.

But Wait: Director Garry Marshall's five-year-old granddaughter felt shortchanged; she wanted to see the castle. Marshall acquiesced and had Disney buy stock footage of a European castle and digitally add the flag of Genovia to it. "It cost us a penny or two," explained Marshall, "but it made my granddaughter happy."

Charge! First year Americans used credit cards more than cash: 1995.

MOTHERS OF INVENTION

There have always been women inventors... even if they've been overlooked by the history books. Here are a few you may not have heard of.

MARY ANDERSON

Invention: Windshield wipers

Background: In 1903 Anderson, an Alabaman, took a trip to New York City. One snowy afternoon she decided to tour the city by streetcar, but instead of sightseeing found herself staring at the streetcar conductor, who had to keep stopping to wipe the snow off his windshield.

On the spot, Anderson made a drawing in her sketchbook of a device consisting of a lever that "activated a swinging arm that mechanically swept off the ice and snow" from the windshield. She got her patent the following year; ten years later windshield wipers were standard equipment on automobiles.

DONNA SHIRLEY

Invention: Sojourner Mars Rover

Background: In 1991 Shirley, an aerospace engineer, was appointed manager of NASA's Mars Explorer Program. Her team was charged with developing the rover vehicle that would go to Mars aboard the unmanned Pathfinder spacecraft. The rover was to be about the size of a pickup truck, with rockets to blast it off the surface of Mars and back to the Pathfinder for its return to Earth. They'd already built a one-eighth-scale prototype; now they were using it to design the full-scale rover.

There was just one problem: sending a truck-sized rover to Mars and then returning it to Earth was too expensive. The craft only had a budget of $25 million. That may seem like a lot but, says Shirley, "for a planetary spacecraft it's incredibly cheap; $25 million would pay for a few commercials for the Super Bowl."

That's when Shirley got the idea that saved the mission. "While her male colleagues were ready to scrap the whole project,

A man once lost his car in parking garage for two years. The tab: $3,400.

Shirley suggested that perhaps size was not that important," Ethlie Vare writes in *Patently Female*. "Could not the prototype of the rover become the vehicle itself?"

It could and it did: On July 4, 1997, the Sojourner Rover landed on Mars and began exploring the surface. It's going to be there a while, too—the rockets that were supposed to send it home got cut from the budget.

LAURA SCUDDER

Invention: Potato chip bag

Background: Before a Southern California businesswoman named Laura Scudder came along in the mid-1920s, potato chips were sold in bulk in large barrels. When you bought chips at the store, the grocer scooped them out of the barrel and into an ordinary paper bag. If you got your chips from the bottom of the barrel, they were usually broken and stale.

It was Laura Scudder who hit on the idea of taking wax paper and ironing it on three sides to make a bag, then filling it with potato chips and ironing the fourth side to make an airtight pouch that would keep the chips fresh until they were eaten. Scudder's self-serve, stay-fresh bags were instrumental in turning potato chips from an occasional treat into a snack food staple.

MARTHA COSTON

Invention: Signal flare

Background: Martha Hunt was only 14 when she eloped with a Philadelphia engineer named Benjamin Coston...and only 21 when he died bankrupt in 1848, leaving her destitute with four small children. Not long after his death she found something interesting among his possessions: a prototype for a signal flare. She hoped that if it worked, she could patent it and use it to restore her family's fortunes.

But it didn't—so Martha started over from scratch, and spent nearly 10 years perfecting a system of red, white, and green "Pyrotechnic Night Signals" that would enable naval ships to communicate by color codes over great distances at night. (Remember, this was before the invention of two-way radio.) The U.S. Navy bought hundreds of sets of flares and used them extensively during the Civil War. They are credited with helping main-

Amount Tiger Woods's caddie made in 2000: $1 million.

tain the Union blockade of Confederate ports, and also with saving the lives of countless shipwreck victims after the war.

ROMMY REVSON

Invention: Scünci

Background: In 1987 Revson was divorced from Revlon cosmetics heir John Revson, and the divorce settlement was so bad that she had to find a job to support herself. Appearances count, so she had her hair bleached before she started applying for jobs. Big mistake—the chemicals damaged her hair to the point that "it was coming off in handfuls," Revson remembers. She decided the only thing to do was pull her hair back into a ponytail, but it was so brittle that she couldn't use rubber bands. She came up with something better: an elastic band covered with soft fabric.

So did Revson ever get around to applying for a job? Who knows—she decided to patent her ponytail holder instead, naming it the Scünci after her Lhasa Apso puppy. Today they're better known as "scrunchies," and at last count Revson has sold more than two billion of them.

* * *

SPEEDY JUSTICE

Defendant: John Cracken, a Texas personal injury lawyer

The Crime: Flaunting his wealth in public

Background: In 1991 Cracken represented a disabled widow in a lawsuit against her husband's employer, the Rock-Tenn Company. Rock-Tenn was a recycling company, and the man was killed in a bailing machine. Cracken sued for $25 million, but Rock-Tenn's case was so weak that there was talk that the jury might award as much as $60 million. Shortly before deliberations were to begin, however, some of the jurors happened to spot Cracken in the courthouse parking garage, driving a brand-new red Porsche 911.

The Sentence: The jury awarded Cracken's client only $5 million. Why so little? One juror explained, "There was no way I'm going to buy that lawyer another fancy car."

IT'S A RACKET

Sports are part of the fabric of our culture. They're part of our language, too. Here are the origins of a few common sports terms.

ALLEY-OOP

Meaning: In basketball, a high pass caught in midair by a teammate who tries to stuff the ball in the basket before landing

Origin: "Probably coined by American soldiers during World War I. It's from the French *allez* (go) plus *oop*, a French pronunciation of the English *up*. During the 1920's, *allez-oop* became *alley-oop*, commonly said upon lifting something. In the late 1950s, San Francisco 49er quarterback Y. A. Tittle invented a lob pass called the alley-oop that was thrown over the heads of defenders to his very tall receiver, R. C. Owens. By the 1970s, it had been adapted to describe the schoolyard basketball play it is today." (From *Grand Slam, Hat Tricks & Alley-oops*, by Robert Hendrickson)

BOGEY

Meaning: In golf, one stroke over par

Origin: "*Bogey*, 'an imaginary thing that causes fear,' gives us the *bogeyman*, who scares children, and a popular 1890 song called 'Colonel Bogey.' In England, when you were doing exceptionally well it was said that Colonel Bogey was playing with you. When someone did well on a particular hole, they thought the Colonel was lending a hand; a player doing poorly was said to be losing to Bogey. As golf became organized, par became the standard score and a bogey became one more than the duffer's aim." (From *Where in the Word?*, by David Muschell)

BONEHEAD PLAY

Meaning: A very stupid play

Origin: "The original bonehead play was made in 1908 by Fred Merkle, the New York Giants first baseman. It was the bottom of the ninth innning. There were two outs. Moose McCormick was on third and Merkle was on first. The next man up singled to center, and McCormick scored the winning run. But Merkle ran into the

Downtown: Downtown London has sunk about one inch since 1997.

dugout—he never touched second base. Johnny Evers of the Cubs got the ball and stepped on second, forcing Merkle out. The winning run was nullified and the Giants lost. The Cubs and Giants finished the season tied for first place, and the Cubs won the pennant in a play-off game. A sportswriter's reference to Merkle's blunder as a 'bonehead play' introduced the phrase into the lexicon." (From *Grand Slam, Hat Tricks & Alley-oops*, by Robert Hendrickson)

HAT TRICK

Meaning: The scoring of three consecutive goals in a game—usually hockey or soccer—by the same player

Origin: "This American phrase comes from the 19th-century tradition of awarding a new hat (or the proceeds of passing a hat) to British cricket bowlers when they bowled down three wickets with three successful balls. Although it's now mainly associated with hockey, *hat trick* has also been used for a jockey who wins three consecutive races, or a soccer player who scores three goals in one game." (From *Southpaws & Sunday Punches*, by Christine Ammer)

RACKET

Meaning: In tennis, a bat with an oval frame, strung with nylon

Origin: "Tennis balls were originally hit with the palm of the hand, called *raquette*, probably from the Arabic *rahat* meaning the same. As tennis evolved, gloves were used, then boards, then paddles, and finally the long-handled racket used today. All were called by the name *raquette*, which became the English word *racket*. The French still call tennis *le jeu de paume* (the palm game)." (From *Word Mysteries & Histories*, by the American Heritage Dictionary)

TEE

Meaning: The small peg with a concave head that is placed in the ground to support a golf ball before it is struck

Origin: "The first tees were just small handfuls of sand or dirt off which golf balls were hit. The Scottish word was first recorded in 1673 as *teaz*, but people thought this was the plural of *tee* and over the years, *tee* became the singular form. The little wooden pegs we call tees today were invented in the 1920s by William Lowell, a dentist from New Jersey." (From *Word and Phrase Origins*, by Robert Hendrickson)

Queen of fashion: When she died in 1603, Queen Elizabeth I owned 3,000 dresses.

UNCLE JOHN'S PAGE OF LISTS

Some random bits from the BRI files.

5 Most Germ-ridden Places at Work

1. Phone
2. Desktop
3. Water fountain handle
4. Microwave door handle
5. Keyboard

5 Movies That Feature a One-Armed Man

1. *Bad Day at Black Rock* (1955)
2. *The One-Armed Swordsman* (1967)
3. *The Fugitive* (1993)
4. *The Blade* (1995)
5. *Twin Peaks: Fire Walk with Me* (1992)

7 States with Lowest Life Expectancy

1. South Carolina
2. Mississippi
3. Georgia
4. Louisiana
5. Nevada
6. Alabama
7. North Carolina

4 Forest Service Tips on What to Do if You Encounter a Cougar

1. Don't "play dead"
2. Be aggressive Don't act like prey
3. Don't run
4. Blow an air horn (if one's handy)

3 Most Dangerous Foods to Eat in a Car

1. Coffee
2. Tacos
3. Chili

2 Topics at the 2002 Taiwan Toilet Seminar

1. Practical Means to Eliminate Bad Smells in Toilets
2. Citizen's Satisfaction of Public Toilets in Korea

2 Famous Number Threes

1. Dale Earnhardt
2. Babe Ruth

7 Places You Can Legally Carry a Concealed Weapon in Utah

1. A car
2. A city bus
3. A train
4. A mall
5. A bar
6. A church
7. A school

3 Things Rats Can Do

1. Wriggle through a hole the size of a quarter
2. Survive being flushed down a toilet
3. Multiply so fast a single pair could have 15,000 descendants in a year

5 Things That Have Been Sold in Vending Machines

1. Emu jerky
2. Poached eggs
3. Holy water
4. Beetles
5. Live shrimp

A humpback whale can eat 5,000 fish in a single sitting. (Who knew they could sit?)

YOU AIN'T GOT IT, KID

It's hard to imagine anyone rejecting the opportunity to hire Harrison Ford, but people make mistakes. Here are a few examples of a few unbelievable rejections.

What They Said: "With your voice, nobody is going to let you broadcast."
Who Said It: CBS producer Don Hewitt, 1958
Rejected! Barbara Walters (she signed with NBC)

What They Said: "Stiff, unappealing. You ain't got it, kid."
Who Said It: Columbia producer Jerry Tokovsky, 1965
Rejected! Harrison Ford

What They Said: "You have a chip on your tooth, your Adam's apple sticks out too far, and you talk too slow."
Who Said It: Universal Pictures executive, 1959
Rejected! Clint Eastwood

What They Said: "The girl doesn't have a special perception or feeling which will lift that book above the curiosity level."
Who Said It: Anonymous publisher, 1952
Rejected! *The Diary of Anne Frank*

What They Said: "Go learn to cook. Your book will never sell."
Who Said It: A literary agent in the early 1970s
Rejected! Danielle Steel, who got a new agent, and has since sold over 350 million books.

What They Said: "The band's okay but, if I were you, I'd get rid of the singer with the tire-tread lips."
Who Said It: BBC radio producer at a 1963 audition
Rejected! The Rolling Stones—and their lead singer, Mick Jagger

What They Said: "His ears are too big. He looks like an ape."
Who Said It: Talent scout Darryl F. Zanuck
Rejected! Clark Gable

Companion comes from the Latin word _com_, "with," and...

HAS ANYONE SEEN MY STRADIVARIUS?

Everybody knows a Stradivarius is the world's most valuable kind of violin. (Read more on page 359.) So how could anyone lose one? Here are a few amazing stories of violins that got away.

VALUABLE VIOLINS

Master violin maker Antonio Stradivari created more than 1,100 instruments during his lifetime. The several hundred that survive are so valuable and so well documented, you'd think nobody would try to steal one because it would be immediately identified as stolen property. Considering their worth, you'd also think their owners would take good care of them. Guess again.

Missing! The Gruenberg Stradivarius, made in 1731; estimated value (1990): $500,000

Background: In July 1990, violinist Erich Gruenberg arrived at Los Angeles International Airport and was met by a friend. As he was loading his luggage into the friend's trunk, he let his violin case out of his sight for just a moment. When he looked back, it was gone.

Outcome: Police put out an international bulletin alerting the music world to the theft…and in April 1991, police in Honduras arrested 30-year-old Nazario Ramos when he tried to sell the violin to a member of a local orchestra. Police speculate that he was just a petty airport thief who didn't know what he was stealing until after he got it.

The violin was secretly flown back to Los Angeles. It was met at the airport by an armored car and taken immediately to a bank vault, where an insurance company executive verified that it was the genuine article. News of the violin's return was kept secret for several days. "We weren't going to give anyone a chance to steal it again," says police spokesman Bill Martin.

…*panis*, "bread"—someone you break bread with.

Missing! The Davidoff Stradivarius, made in 1727; estimated value: $3.5 million

Background: The Davidoff Stradivarius vanished from the Manhattan apartment of its owner, 91-year-old Erika Morini (considered one of the greatest violinists of all time) as she lay dying in a hospital a few blocks away. For years the former child prodigy had kept the violin locked away in a closet rather than in a safe, because she wanted it to be within close reach. While Morini was hospitalized, someone entered her apartment, unlocked the closet, and stole the violin, leaving an inferior violin in its place. It was insured for only $800,000.

The theft was discovered when Morini's goddaughter Erica Bradford and her daughter Valerie Bradford let themselves into the apartment to prepare it for Morini's return. Morini made it back home and lived out her last few days in the apartment, but the violin never did. Friends substituted a fake so that when she asked to see if the violin was safe, they could point to it and assure her that it was.

Outcome: The Davidoff Stradivarius is still missing. Reward: $100,000. According to news reports, Valerie Bradford "keeps failing lie detector tests and doesn't quite know why." The question she keeps failing: "Do you know who took the violin?"

"I guess I get nervous," she says.

Missing! The Duke of Alcantara, made in 1732; estimated value (1994): $800,000

Background: The Duke of Alcantara was owned by the University of California. On August 2, 1967, David Margetts, a second violinist with the UCLA string quartet, borrowed the Duke from the university collection for a rehearsal in Hollywood. On his way home he bought some groceries and then stopped at a restaurant. When he got back to his car—which was *unlocked*—he realized the violin was gone. To this day, Margetts can't remember if he put the violin in the car after rehearsal—which would mean that somebody stole it—or if he simply left it on the roof of his car and drove off.

In January 1994, a violin dealer recognized the violin he was working on as an authentic Stradivarius. He looked it up in a reference book, found a photograph of the same violin, and discovered that it had been missing from UCLA for 27 years. It turned out the violin's "owner" was an amateur violinist named Teresa

Salvato, who had gotten it from her ex-husband as part of their divorce settlement. He had gotten it from his aunt, who claimed to have found it beside a freeway in 1967. "That sort of matches the violin-left-on-the-top-of-the-car version," says Carla Shapreau, an attorney for UCLA.

Outcome: At first Salvato refused to give the violin back, but she eventually agreed to relinquish all claims of ownership in exchange for $11,500. She claims she only wanted to do the right thing for the instrument. "UCLA lost it once. They're really not very careful," she explains.

Missing! The Ex-Zimbalist, made in 1735; estimated value: $1 million

Background: In 1949 an NBC Symphony Orchestra violinist named David Sarser scraped together all the money he had and borrowed a little more so that he could buy the Stradivarius being sold by Efram Zimbalist, Sr. (father of *The FBI* star Efram Zimbalist, Jr.). It cost him about $30,000.

"Buying that Strad got me a different life," Sarser remembers. "I was in the newspaper. I took it everywhere with me, and everyone was in awe." He planned on eventually selling the violin and living off the money in retirement, but his plans were dashed when the instrument was stolen from his studio in the mid-1960s.

Sarser says that at one point the FBI was close to solving the crime, but the instrument vanished a second time and was apparently sold to a buyer in Japan. The Ex-Zimbalist has since been photographed in Japan and even displayed in a department store, but Sarser hasn't been able to retrieve it or identify the new owner. "I have no desire to play any other instrument," he says. "It became part of me, and I became part of it."

Missing! The Gibson Stradivarius, made in 1713; estimated value: $1.2 million (1988)

Background: Polish virtuoso Bronislaw Huberman may be the only person ever to have the same Stradivarius stolen from him twice. In 1919 the Gibson was stolen in Vienna, then recovered a few days later when the thief tried to sell it to a dealer. In 1936 it was stolen from Huberman's dressing room while he was onstage at Carnegie Hall. He never saw it again—the violin was still missing when he

A human jaw can open 30 degrees; a snake jaw can open 130 degrees.

died in 1947. Lloyd's of London paid him $30,000 for his loss.

In 1985 an ex-con and former café violinist named Julian Altman summoned his wife, Marcelle Hall, to his deathbed and told her to take good care of his violin after he was gone. "That violin is important," he told her. He also instructed her to carefully examine the violin case. She did...and found newspaper clippings from the 1936 theft stuffed inside. She confronted her dying husband. At first he told her he had bought it from the thief for $100. Later he confessed that he'd stolen it by distracting a guard with a fine cigar, sneaking into the dressing room, and walking out with the Stradivarius under his coat. Unlike other thieves, he didn't want to sell it, he just wanted to play it. "Julian didn't get rid of it," Hall told reporters, "he played it for 50 years."

Outcome: After Altman died, Hall turned the violin over to Lloyd's of London. They must have believed Hall's claim that she didn't know anything about the theft until Altman confessed, because when they sold the Gibson Strad to a British violinist for $1.2 million, they paid her a $263,475 finder's fee.

"You know, Julian would tell people that his violin was a Stradivarius," remembers Altman's friend David Gartner. "They would just laugh at him. They thought he was kidding."

* * *

WHAT'S IN *YOUR* CANDY BAR?

In 1972 the Oregon Health Department discovered that the chunks in Hoody Chunky Style Peanut Butter were not peanuts, but rat droppings. Company executives were sentenced to 10 days in prison for health violations, and the U.S. Food and Drug Administration issued strict new guidelines on the amount of foreign matter permissible in packaged foods. They include:

1. No more than 50 insect fragments or two rodent hairs per 100 grams of peanut butter.

2. No more than 10 fruit fly eggs in 100 grams of tomato juice.

3. No more than 150 insect fragments in an eight-ounce chocolate bar.

—*Wrong Again!*

Detroit has more "registered" bowlers than any other American city.

IT'S SLINKY, IT'S SLINKY

Uncle John wants to know why Slinky is such a popular toy. Sure, it's fascinating, but let's face it—once you've "walked" it down the stairs a few times, there's not much more you can do with it. Never mind. It's a classic. We love it. It's Slinky!

1. What happened when the Slinky first hit the shelves of Macy's department store in New York City in 1949?

a) Sales were so poor that creators Richard and Betty James pretended to be customers and started buying Slinkys in the hope of drawing attention to their display

b) Slinkys were so popular that they had to be removed from the store's shelves because the crowds of people were creating a fire hazard

c) After several accidents where children became tangled in the Slinky's wire coils, they were banned from the store

d) The weight of the metal Slinkys caused the shelves to collapse, leaving one salesman dead and two customers badly injured

2. Slinkys were used to make all of the following, except which one?

a) A pecan-picker

b) Makeshift radio antennas for soldiers during the Vietnam War

c) A therapeutic tool for stroke victims

d) A device used to display toupees

3. All of the following Slinkys were really made, except which one?

a) A gold-plated Slinky

b) Felt-covered Slinky Pets with animal faces and tails

c) A novelty telephone called the Slink-a-Phone

d) A slinky board game called the Amazing Slinky Game

4. What company used the Slinky jingle in an ad campaign?

a) Isuzu Amigo

b) Hershey Kisses

c) Pepto-Bismol Chewables

d) North Face Sneakers

5. In 1999 Slinky won what honor?

a) Asked to appear on a U.S. postage stamp

b) Received an honorary Oscar for numerous film appearances

c) Awarded a Junior Nobel Prize for combining physics with play

d) Sealy created a Slinky mattress in recognition of Slinky's outstanding work with springs

6. How much wire is used to make a Slinky?

a) 30 feet

b) 55 feet

c) 80 feet

d) 112 feet

7. How did the inventor come up with the name Slinky?

a) He named it after his secretary's favorite black dress (it was actually his favorite dress, too)

b) His wife found it in the dictionary—it took her two days of searching before she found a word that described the toy

c) He was inspired by his out-of-work brother-in-law's nickname: "Slinky" Wilson

d) The toy fell in the toilet and got stuck—the plumber had to use a tool he called a Slinky to unclog it

8. Slinky has been to which of the following?

a) Outer space—aboard a NASA Space Shuttle to test the power of a Slinky in zero gravity

b) Egypt—to test its ability to "climb" down the side of the Great Pyramid at Giza

c) Arctic Circle—to test the magnetic effect of the North Pole on a Slinky

d) White House—a gift to President Eisenhower in 1953 as an example of "American ingenuity"

Answers

1.b; 2.d; 3.c; 4.a; 5.a; 6.c; 7.b; 8.a

It takes 10 pounds of milk to make 1 pound of cheese.

NEW VIETNAM

Most families vacation in Florida because of the warm weather and abundance of theme parks. You can shake hands with Mickey Mouse at Disney World, feed the dolphins at SeaWorld... and duck and cover in New Vietnam. Well, at least that was the idea.

BACKGROUND

In 1975 Reverend Carl McIntire, a New Jersey fundamentalist preacher and pro-Vietnam War activist, began construction on what was to be "New Vietnam." Spread out over 300 acres of land in Cape Canaveral, Florida, McIntire and his partner, former Green Beret Giles Pace, envisioned a theme park where people could get a glimpse of the Vietnam War.

What would the theme park look like? Here are a few of the attractions McIntire planned:

• ***Sampan* ride.** A *sampan* is an Asian sailboat. Tourists would take a sampan ride around a moat that encircled a recreated Vietnamese village with a neighboring Special Forces camp.

• **Special Forces camp.** The camp would be made up of simple concrete barracks displaying weapons "used by the Commies in Vietnam." Around the barracks would be trenches and mortar bunkers complete with sandbag walls and sham machine guns.

• **The perimeter.** The camp would be surrounded with row upon row of barbed wire, *punji* stakes, and fake Claymore mines to add to the atmosphere. "We'll have a recording, broadcasting a firefight, mortars exploding, bullets flying, Vietnamese screaming," McIntire explained, while hired GIs shoot blanks at the enemy. Visitors would be encouraged to take cover in the barracks or station themselves behind a machine gun and get in on the action.

• **A Vietnamese village.** The village would be made up of 16 thatched huts and four concrete upper-class Vietnamese homes that would double as retail shops and snack bars serving traditional Vietnamese cuisine. So after working up an appetite manning the machine guns, park visitors could stop in for a bowl of rice and noodles. The village was to be completely authentic, with irrigated

That little statue on the grill of every Rolls Royce car has a name: "Spirit of Ecstasy."

paddies, water buffalo, cows, chickens, ducks, and palm trees.

• **Vietnamese people.** Vietnamese people—real refugees from the real war—would travel through the village in traditional outfits and make New Vietnam come to life. McIntire planned this as a make-work program for Vietnamese refugees arriving in Florida at the end of the war. "Every penny will go back to the Vietnamese. The Bible says love your neighbor."

"They'll work anywhere for a paycheck," Pace commented. "And this will be work that won't be in competition with anyone else. There's nothing offensive about it."

INTO THE MORASS

The idea bombed and the park was never completed. Vietnamese refugees, having just experienced the horrors of a real war, weren't about to participate in a fake one. "My wife won't walk around that village in a costume like Mickey Mouse," refugee Cong Nguyen Binh told reporters. "We want to forget. We want to live here like you. We don't want any more war."

* * *

MISNOMERS

• The rare **red** coral of the Mediterranean is actually **blue.**

• The **gray** whale is actually **black.**

• Whale**bone** is actually made of **baleen**, a material from the whales' upper jaws.

• The Atlantic **salmon** is actually a member of the **trout** family.

• **Heart**burn is actually pyrosis, caused by the presence of gastric secretions, called reflux, in the lower **esophagus.**

• The Caspian **Sea** and the Dead **Sea** are both actually **lakes.**

• The horseshoe **crab** is more closely related to **spiders** and **scorpions** than crabs.

• The Douglas **fir** is actually a **pine** tree.

• A **steel**-jacketed bullet is actually made of **brass.**

• Rip**tides** are actually **currents.**

HAPPY HOLIDAYS

Here's some holiday trivia you may not have come across before.

LABOR DAY

In 1893 amid growing labor unrest, President Grover Cleveland sent 12,000 federal troops to stop a strike at the Pullman train car company in Chicago. The strike was broken, but two men were killed and many more were beaten. For Cleveland and the Democrats, the move backfired—the pro-business brutality only served to bolster the growing union movement.

To win back constituents, Congress passed legislation the following year making the first Monday in September a national holiday honoring labor. It was a presidential election year, so President Cleveland promptly signed the bill into law, hoping it would appease American workers. It didn't. Cleveland was defeated…but Labor Day was established for good.

GROUNDHOG DAY

February 2, the midpoint between winter solstice and spring equinox, has been celebrated for eons. The Celts called it *Imbolc* ("in the belly"—for sheep pregnant with lambs); Romans had *Lupercalia*, a fertility celebration. For other cultures, too, the day was marked by rituals of "rebirth" and hope for a bountiful new growing season.

According to Irish tradition, a snake emerges from "the womb of Earth" and tests the weather to see if spring has arrived. The Germans had a similar tradition, except that they watched for badgers waking from hibernation. If the day was a sunny, shadow-casting day, more winter weather was to come. No shadow meant an early spring.

When German settlers came to Pennsylvania in the 1700s, they brought the custom with them…but there were no badgers, so they substituted another hibernating animal: the groundhog.

~~COLUMBUS~~ AMERICAN INDIAN DAY

Attempts to designate a national day honoring Native Americans have been made—unsuccessfully—for nearly a century. In 1914 Red Fox James, a Blackfoot Indian, rode 4,000 miles on horseback

The carnation's name means "fleshlike." (Their pink color reminded people of meat.)

in support of a national day of recognition for Native Americans. He ended the journey in Washington, D.C., where his proposal for the holiday was adopted by 24 state governments. The state of New York became the first to officially designate an American Indian Day, in May 1916.

While it has yet to be recognized as a national holiday, several states, South Dakota being the first, have officially changed another time-honored holiday to American Indian Day: the second Monday in October—Columbus Day.

MERRY MITHRAS

The Bible doesn't say when Jesus was born, but many historians think it was in April. So why is Christmas celebrated on December 25? One possible reason: *Mithras*. Mithras was a Persian diety known as The Conquering Sun, and his birthday was traditionally celebrated at the winter solstice in late December. Mithraism and Christianity were both becoming popular in the Mediterranean region at about the same time. But early Christians were determined to prevail, so they adopted December 25 as the date of the Nativity. By the third or fourth century A.D., the already popular day was firmly entrenched as Christmas.

* * *

THIS AIN'T NO PARTY

In April 2002, a Veterans of Foreign Wars group in Utah issued a resolution demanding that the date of Earth Day be changed. Why? April 22 is former Soviet leader Vladimir Lenin's birthdate. The group refused to celebrate on the birthday of "the godless master of manipulation, misinformation, and murder."

Not only that, members claim the day was chosen intentionally and that former Wisconsin senator Gaylord Nelson, founder of Earth Day, is a communist sympathizer. "He voted against funding the Vietnam War," said one post commander.

The 86-year-old Nelson says it was a coincidence. "Several million people were born on any day of the year. Does the VFW want to change it to another day on which, undoubtedly, some really evil person was born? Hitler? Mussolini? Genghis Khan?"

Another April 22 birthday: St. Francis of Assisi.

Q: What do you get when you add zinc to copper? A: Brass.

AMAZING COINCIDENCES

We're constantly finding stories about amazing coincidences, so in this Bathroom Reader, *Uncle John listed a few of his favorites.*

NEEDS WORK

While eating dinner at Notting Hill Gate restaurant in 1992, a London publisher had her car broken into. One of the things taken from the car was a manuscript she had been reading and found extremely promising. Apparently the thieves weren't interested in literature, though—they threw the manuscript over a fence while driving away. On Monday morning she was desperately trying to come up with a way to explain how she lost the manuscript when the author called. Before she got a chance to apologize, the author asked, "Why did you have my manuscript thrown over my front fence?"

STROKE OF LUCK

During the 1988 Olympic games in Seoul, South Korea, Karen Lord of Australia and Manuella Carosi of Italy swam in different heats of the women's 100-meter backstroke. Both finished with times of exactly one minute 4.69 seconds, tying them for 16th place. Only one swimmer could hold a lane in the consolation final, so Lord and Carosi were forced to swim again. Amazingly, after the swim-off the officials reported the times were exactly the same, one minute 5.05 seconds. Officials decided that the two had to swim yet one more time. At the end of the unprecedented third consecutive race Carosi was declared the winner. Her time: one minute 4.62 seconds. Lord's time: one minute 4.75 seconds—13 hundredths of a second behind.

LONG SHOT

In 1893 Henry Ziegland of Texas jilted his fiancé, and she killed herself over it. Her brother swore revenge. He took his gun and went after Ziegland, shot him in the face and then turned the gun on himself. But the bullet only grazed Ziegland and then got

The city of Edinburgh, Scotland, is built on top of an extinct volcano.

lodged in a tree. Twenty years later, Ziegland was removing the tree that had the bullet buried in it, using dynamite to make the job easier. The explosion blasted the bullet out of the tree... striking Ziegland in the head and killing him.

BANK ON IT

In 1977 Vincent Johnson and Frazier Black broke into the Austin, Texas, home of Mr. and Mrs. David Conner and stole two TVs and a checkbook. A few hours later, the two men showed up at a local bank with a check made out to themselves for $200. When they asked the teller to cash it for them, she asked them to wait a minute, and then called security. Why? The bank teller was Mrs. David Conner.

OTHERWISE ENGAGED

Brenda Rawson became engaged to Christopher Firth in 1961. He gave her a diamond ring, but she lost it while they were on vacation in Lancashire, England. In 1979 she was talking to her husband's cousin, John. For some reason the conversation turned to metal detectors and John mentioned that 18 years earlier, one of his kids had discovered a diamond ring near Lancashire. It was her ring.

SPARE ME

In 1971 Mrs. Willard Lovell of Berkeley, California, accidentally locked herself out of the house. She had spent 10 minutes trying to find a way in again when the postman arrived with a letter for her from her brother, who'd been staying with her a few weeks earlier. The letter contained a spare key to the house, which he had borrowed and forgotten to return.

* * *

EAT YOUR WORDS

- *Zucchini* comes from an Italian word meaning "sweetest."
- The Sanskrit word *naranga*, meaning "fragrant," gives us our *orange*.
- *Tangerines* were named after the city of Tangier, Morocco, which was well known for the fruit.

CELEBRITY LAWSUITS

These days, it seems that people will sue each other over practically anything. Here are a few real-life examples of unusual legal battles involving celebrities.

THE PLAINTIFF: Singer/composer Tom Waits
THE DEFENDANT: Frito-Lay
THE LAWSUIT: In 1988 Frito-Lay ran radio commercials featuring a singer with a raspy, gravelly voice that sounded amazingly like Waits. He had already been approached to do commercials by the same ad agency...and refused. So they used an impersonator. Waits sued for "voice misappropriation," claiming the idea that he would use his music to sell Doritos sullied his reputation with his fans.
THE VERDICT: Waits won. In 1992 he collected $2.4 million, the first-ever punitive award involving a celebrity soundalike.

THE PLAINTIFF: John Hartman, former Doobie Brother
THE DEFENDANT: Petaluma, California, Police Department
THE LAWSUIT: He left the band to join the force, then left the force to rejoin the band. When he wanted to get back on the force in 1994, the former drummer was turned down. So he sued for discrimination, claiming that he should be classified as disabled because he'd done so many drugs in the early 1970s.
THE VERDICT: He lost. The judge ruled that Hartman hadn't done enough drugs to qualify as disabled.

THE PLAINTIFFS: James and Laurie Ryan
THE DEFENDANTS: MTV, Las Vegas's Hard Rock Hotel, and actor Ashton Kutcher
THE LAWSUIT: Mr. and Mrs. Ryan walked into their room at the Hard Rock Hotel and discovered a mutilated corpse in the bathroom. Horrified, they tried to flee, but two "security guards" and a "paramedic" forced them back into the room. After some time, Kutcher came in and told them the whole thing was a joke, a prank staged for the MTV series *Harassment*. The Ryans didn't think it was funny and sued for $10 million in damages.
THE VERDICT: Pending.

Why is the first vertebra of your neck called the *atlas*? Because it holds up your head.

THE PLAINTIFF: Hollywood producer Steve Bing
THE DEFENDANT: Movie-studio mogul Kirk Kerkorian
THE LAWSUIT: Kerkorian's ex-wife, Lisa Bonder, sued for $320,000 *a month* in child support for their four-year-old daughter. Billionaire Kerkorian claimed he couldn't possibly be the father—he was sterile. He also said he had proof that the real father was Bonder's ex-boyfriend, multimillionaire Bing. How did he know? His private detectives had collected DNA evidence—they went through Bing's garbage and found some used dental floss. Probability that Bing's the dad: 99.993%. Bing sued for invasion of privacy, asking a staggering $1 billion in damages.
THE VERDICT: They settled quietly and the suit was dropped.

THE PLAINTIFF: Florence Henderson
THE DEFENDANT: Serial Killer Inc.
THE LAWSUIT: Henderson, the actress who played Carol Brady on the TV show *The Brady Bunch*, sued clothing maker Serial Killer Inc. in 1999 when they put out a T-shirt that showed her picture with the caption "Porn Queen." The suit called the caption "highly offensive... and false."
THE VERDICT: Serial Killer pulled all the offending merchandise out of stores the day after the suit was filed. No word on the outcome of the suit.

THE PLAINTIFFS: Anna Kournikova, Judith Soltesz-Benetton
THE DEFENDANT: *Penthouse* magazine
THE LAWSUIT: *Penthouse* published photos it claimed were of the famous Russian tennis player bathing topless. Kournikova denied it was her and threatened to sue. But the magazine's editors said they had studied the photos in "painstaking detail" and refused to back down. It seemed *Penthouse* might win until Soltesz-Benetton (of the Benetton clothing family) came forward and said *she* was the woman in the photos... and then filed a $10 million lawsuit.
THE VERDICT: *Penthouse* settled with Soltesz-Benetton out of court. But that's not the end: Kournikova's suing, too. Will that put the struggling magazine out of business for good? Verdict pending.

Remember him? *Time* magazine's Man of the Decade for the 1980s was Mikhail Gorbachev.

SMELLS LIKE...MURDER

Premature death seems almost like an occupational hazard among rock stars. But that doesn't make fans—or conspiracy theorists—any less suspicious, particularly in the case of suicide. And this one seems more suspicious than most.

The Deceased: Kurt Cobain, leader of Seattle grunge band Nirvana. Gained notoriety with the 1991 angst-filled anthem "Smells Like Teen Spirit."

How He Died: On April 8, 1994, an electrician spotted Cobain's dead body lying on the floor of a greenhouse room above the detached garage at the musician's Seattle residence. Police determined that Cobain had injected himself with heroin, then stuck a shotgun into his mouth and pulled the trigger. Near the body they found a "suicide note." According to media reports, Cobain's wallet, open to his driver's license, was next to the body, ostensibly to make identification easier after the blast to the head.

To the police (and most of the media), it looked like a clear case of another rock star destroyed by his demons. But did the police overlook evidence that might point to a different conclusion?

SUSPICIOUS FACTS

• At the time Cobain was shot, he had three times the lethal dose of heroin in his blood. According to experts, even an addict like Cobain would be comatose with that level of the drug in his body, incapable of positioning a gun and pulling the trigger. Cobain had two fresh needle marks, one on each arm. Did he inject himself twice? If he was intent on committing suicide, why didn't he just let the overdose do its work? Or were the second injection and the shotgun blast the work of someone else?

• There were no legible fingerprints on the shotgun that killed Cobain. (The gun wasn't even tested for fingerprints until nearly a month after his death.) Fingerprints can be wiped off a gun, but is that what happened here? If so, who wiped the gun clean, and why?

• Only part of the "suicide note" found by Cobain's body sounds like he planned to kill himself—the last four lines—and some experts

So *that's* why we bail water: The handle of a bucket or a kettle is called the *bail*.

question whether those lines are in his handwriting.

Most of the note is an anguished apology to his fans for his lack of enthusiasm and seems more about his resignation from the music industry than suicide. (Shortly before his death he decided not to headline the Lollapalooza tour.) Only the last four lines are addressed to his wife and daughter. Was suicide an afterthought, or did he actually have no intention of killing himself?

• The driver's license by the body wasn't left there by Cobain—the first police officer on the scene found Cobain's wallet nearby and displayed the license by the body for photographs.

• Someone attempted to use Cobain's credit card until just hours before the body was discovered, even though, according to the coroner's report, Cobain had died four days earlier. Cobain himself had last used the card to buy a plane ticket from Los Angeles to Seattle on April 1. The card was not found in his wallet.

WHAT REALLY HAPPENED?

If suicide seems unlikely, accidental death looks next to impossible. How could Cobain, a hardened addict, so seriously misjudge his heroin dose? After such a dose, could he have accidentally positioned the shotgun on his chest and pulled the trigger? And if suicide and accident are ruled out, that leaves only...murder. But who would have wanted to kill Cobain and make it appear a suicide?

THE LOVE CONNECTION

Cobain's wife, rock star Courtney Love, was in the L.A. area at the time Cobain's body was discovered. But according to Tom Grant, an L.A. private investigator, Love may have been involved in a conspiracy to kill her husband, possibly with the aid of Michael Dewitt, the male nanny who lived at the Cobain residence. Possible motives according to Grant:

✔ Cobain may have told Love he was leaving her; if the pair divorced, Love would get half of Cobain's estate. With a suicide she would get it all.

✔ Cobain's record sales would increase after a suicide, giving Love even more money.

✔ Her own career would benefit. (Love's band, Hole, headlined the Lollapalooza tour in place of Cobain and Nirvana.)

Gossip: Why did young Courtney Love do time in juvenile hall? For shoplifting a Kiss T-shirt.

IS THIS LOVE?

Grant has a unique perspective—Love hired him to find Cobain after Cobain escaped from a drug rehab center just a few days before he died. Grant continued his investigation after the body was found and was disturbed by the inconsistencies and contradictions in Love's behavior:

✔ Love phoned in a missing persons report on April 4, the day Cobain died, according to the coroner's report. Claiming she was Cobain's mother, Love told Seattle police he had bought a shotgun and was suicidal. But a receipt found on Cobain's body showed that his best friend Dylan Carlson bought the gun for him almost a week earlier, *before* Cobain entered rehab. According to Carlson, Cobain wanted the gun for protection, not suicide. By phoning in the report, was Love trying to plant the idea that Cobain was suicidal?

✔ Love directed Grant to look for Cobain in a number of Seattle hotels and to check out his drug dealers. Even though Dewitt, the nanny, had told Love he'd talked with Cobain at their residence on April 2, Love did not tell Grant he'd been seen there. Was Love trying to keep Grant from finding Cobain too soon?

✔ When Grant visited the Cobain residence with Carlson the day before Cobain's body was found, there was evidence that Dewitt had been there recently. (Neither Grant nor Carlson looked in the greenhouse.) Later that day Dewitt told friends he was leaving for Los Angeles. Grant says he had the feeling Dewitt was avoiding him.

✔ The electrician who found Cobain's body was hired by Love to check the security system at the residence and, according to Rosemary Carroll, Love's entertainment lawyer, she specifically told him to check the greenhouse. Was she setting him up to find the body?

FADE AWAY

In the note found beside Kurt Cobain's body, his last words, before the disputed last four lines, were "...it's better to burn out than to fade away." Did he think shooting himself was the only way out of his apathetic malaise, or did he simply plan to leave the music scene near the peak of his popularity to avoid becoming just another mass-marketed rock star, ultimately drifting into irrelevance? The police investigation is closed...so we'll probably never know.

DUMB CROOKS

Here's proof that crime doesn't pay.

PSSST!

"In Albuquerque, New Mexico, Timothy E. Beach, 23, was arrested for allegedly robbing a Taco Bell restaurant that he used to manage. According to police, Beach could not resist identifying himself to a former co-worker during the heist, and briefly lifted his ski mask to say, 'It's me, Tim.'"

—Universal Press Syndicate

NAKED NIMROD

"Barry Darrell Freeman, 29, was convicted of attempted rape last year near Philadelphia. According to testimony, the victim asked Freeman to take off his own clothes and then taunted him until he did. With his clothes off, the woman saw that he wasn't carrying a weapon and ran away, eventually outrunning him to safety. During the chase, according to the victim, she heard Freeman muttering something about not being able to trust a woman."

—*News of the Weird*

WHAT'S HIS IQ?

"When a Des Moines, Iowa, convenience store clerk tried to tell police about a man who had just robbed his store, he got some unexpected help. 'He's about 5'10",' Harpal Singh told police over the phone. Then the suspect, who had inexplicably returned to the store, corrected him. 'I'm 6'2",' the man said.

'About 6'2",' Mr. Singh told the police, 'and about 38 years old.'

'I'm 34,' the man said, correcting Mr. Singh again. Moments later, a sheriff's deputy arrived and arrested Steven Hebron, 34, who was charged with robbery."

—*Pittsburgh Post-Gazette*

NAUGHTY NANNY

"Twenty-five-year-old nanny Ildiko Varga, on the run and wanted for trashing an employer's home and mistreating a toddler in a New York City suburb, was finally caught when she stopped a

Only one state—California—is allowed by federal law to set its own air pollution regulations.

police officer on the street to show him the article the *New York Post* had written about the crime and to ask him if he thought she had a good case for a slander lawsuit."

—Newsday

TAKE ME WITH YOU

"An Elgin, Illinois, man, wanted on an outstanding warrant, went down to his local police department to take part in the Ride Along program, which allows citizens to accompany police officers during patrols and see, among other things, criminals getting arrested, which he was."

—"The Edge," *The Oregonian*

CHECK IT OUT

"Gary Harvey has been jailed for trying to pay his back taxes with a phoney $1 million-dollar check...and then demanding a refund. Judge Ann Aiken gave Harvey ten months behind bars."

—USA Today

PLUMB STUPID

"Advertising doesn't always pay. Robert Peter Nelson III, a Washington County plumber, was arrested early Sunday and charged with robbery. Police said that Nelson had held up a Shop'n'Go at 2:30 am and a Uni-Mart at about 4:30 am. As he was driving away from a third store just minutes later, the clerk got a look at the van. Emblazoned on the side was a phone number and the name 'Nelson Plumbing and Heating.' Said Police Superintendent James Morton, 'He made it pretty easy to solve.'"

—Pittsburgh Tribune Review

OLD DOG, NEW TRICKS

"Thieves in Essex, England, tried to snort a bag of powder they found in Dee Blythe's living room—not realizing it was the ashes of her dead dog. As they made off with her TV, her VCR, and her stereo, they must have thought they'd hit the jackpot when they saw the powder marked 'Charlie'—street slang for cocaine—in a vase on the mantlepiece. 'It was horrible knowing they were in my house,' said Ms. Blythe, 'but the idea of them trying to get high on a dead dog's ashes certainly made me feel a bit better.'"

—The Sun

No wonder they're f-a-a-a-t: Pound for pound, sheep out-eat cows by seven to one.

DEATH...IT'S A LIVING

In Uncle John's Giant Bathroom Reader, *we told the story of how Elvis Presley's estate, which nearly went bankrupt after he died, went on to make more money than the King ever did when he was alive. It turns out that Elvis isn't the only one who got rich too late...*

PICTURE PERFECT

Not long after Mark Roesler graduated from law school in 1981, he was hired by the publisher of the *Saturday Evening Post* to protect the artwork of the late Norman Rockwell, who had painted more than 300 covers for the magazine.

Roesler's work with the Rockwell estate caught the attention of the Elvis Presley estate, which had been slowly sliding toward bankruptcy since the King's death in August 1977. The Presley estate hired Roesler, and he was instrumental in putting it on a sound financial footing.

Working with the Rockwell and Presley estates made Roesler realize how great the potential demand for his services was. He started a company, now known as CMG Worldwide, to manage and protect the legal rights of dead celebrities. Today CMG represents more than 200 of the world's most famous dead people, including Mark Twain, Buddy Holly, Amelia Earhart, James Dean, Princess Diana, George S. Patton, Jr., Ty Cobb, Malcolm X, and three of the original Little Rascals.

(FINANCIAL) LIFE AFTER DEATH

Lawyers like Roesler have revolutionized the field of "intellectual property." In the old days, the assumption was that when a famous person died, their right to control their image—their "right of publicity," as it's called—died with them and that anyone could use their image and likeness in any way they pleased. But Roesler and others have successfully argued that the "right of publicity" is an asset just like any other, and when a celebrity dies, ownership and control of that asset should pass on to the heirs. Several states have since passed laws that explicitly guarantee just that.

DEAD TO RIGHTS

In the process of defining and protecting the rights of the famous dead, the lawyers have helped the value of these estates to soar. And their success hasn't gone unnoticed: *Forbes* magazine, long famous for its list of the 400 richest Americans, now also publishes an annual list of "Richest Deceased Celebrities." More than 25 years after his death, Elvis is still the King: his estate earned an estimated $37 million between June 2001 and June 2002, easily beating *Peanuts* creator Charles Schulz, who came in second at $28 million. Here's a look at how the fortunes of five other famous dead people are faring:

1. JAMES DEAN

Dean had made only three movies when he crashed his Porsche on California's Highway 46 in 1955 and died. He was just 24. But since then his face has become a classic Hollywood icon, and the licensing of his image in advertising, movie posters, coffee mugs, T-shirts, and other products earned his estate more than $30 million between 1984 and 1998 alone. The estate continues to pull in about $3 million a year—far more than Dean himself made during his brief career.

Perhaps the most morbid licensing arrangement came in 2002, when Porsche dealers in New Zealand marketed—with the Dean family's permission—a limited-edition Boxster sportscar, a bizarre attempt to use the fact that Dean was killed in one of the company's products...in order to sell more of the company's products.

2. BABE RUTH

For many years Ruth's daughter Julia Ruth Stevens had no means of controlling who got to use her famous father's image or how they used it. "Most people didn't bother to ask me for permission to use daddy's name, and there wasn't a lot I could do about it," she says. The only people who paid money were those who felt guilty using it for free; because of this Stevens might get a token $100 "royalty" check every couple of years. Not anymore—since signing with CMG Worldwide she has collected more than $100,000 a year. "It's funny that in daddy's best year, he made only $80,000, and now I'm receiving more than that," she says.

...made liquor so strong it could knock someone out.

3. TUPAC SHAKUR

The prolific gangsta rapper was only 25 when he was killed in a drive-by shooting in Las Vegas in 1996. He left behind more than 200 unreleased tracks, and after his death his mother, Afeni Shakur, sued his record label to win control of the recordings. By 2002 she had released five new albums, and more are in the works. (Shakur released only four albums while he was alive.) Tupac's estate has earned an estimated $40 million since 1998—more than he made when he was alive—and currently pulls in about $7 million a year.

4. JIMI HENDRIX

When 27-year-old Hendrix died of a drug overdose, he left no will, so his entire estate—including hundreds of hours of unreleased recordings—was inherited by his father, James "Al" Hendrix. Al handed over management of the estate to attorney Leo Branton, who methodically combed through the recordings looking for material that could be released in new albums. Today there are more than 400 Hendrix releases, including dozens of bootlegs. When Branton tried to sell the rights to Hendrix's music to MCA for a reported $50–75 million in 1993, Al Hendrix sued to stop him, arguing that the music was worth closer $90 million. Hendrix won, and the rights are still in the family. The estate earned $8 million in 2001–2002, landing Jimi in ninth place on the *Forbes* list.

5. DALE EARNHARDT, SR.

Earnhardt was already America's most popular race-car driver when he was alive, but when he died in February 2001 after crashing his car at the Daytona 500, he became an almost-mythical figure to racing fans. They snapped up more than $20 million worth of Dale Earnhardt merchandise in the year following his death.

Sales of Dale Earnhardt books, T-shirts, model race cars, Monopoly games, cell-phone faceplates, commemorative Coke cans, and other merchandise dropped off a bit in 2002, but the family draws inspiration from the fact that 25 years on, the Elvis Presley estate is still selling more than $37 million worth of stuff each year. "If Dale Earnhardt gets the same reaction," says estate spokesman J. R. Rhodes, "everyone involved will be ecstatic."

Alien Nation: In 2002 alone, UFO sightings in Canada increased by 42%.

VIDEO TREASURES

Here's our latest installment of great movies you may have never seen. Take this with you the next time you go to the video store with no idea what to rent.

SAY ANYTHING (1989) *Comedy*
Review: "Satisfying teenage comedy-drama about a self-assured loner (John Cusack) who goes after the class brain (Ione Sky), and finds her surprisingly human. Amusing, endearing, and refreshingly original; written by first-time director Cameron Crowe." (*Leonard Maltin's 2001 Movie & Video Guide*)

RAISE THE RED LANTERN (1991) *Foreign/Drama*
Review: "Director Zhang Yimou spins an intimate, intense tale of an oppressed woman's descent into madness. Set entirely within the claustrophobic compound where a Chinese nobleman lives with his four wives, the film is always engrossing, enlivened by the director's stunning use of color." (Stephen Farber, "Movieline")

SIX DEGREES OF SEPARATION (1993) *Drama*
Review: "A young man (Will Smith) arrives on the doorstep of a sophisticated New York couple (Stockard Channing and Donald Sutherland) claiming to be a friend of their children... and the son of Sidney Poitier. Witty, complex, always engaging study of identity and more." (*Halliwell's Film and Video Guide 2001*)

THINGS CHANGE (1988) *Comedy*
Review: "Director David Mamet and co-writer Shel Silverstein have fashioned a marvelously subtle and witty comedy about an inept, low-level gangster (Joe Mantegna). He goes against orders to take an old shoe-shine 'boy' (Don Ameche) on one last fling before the latter goes to prison for a crime he didn't commit." (*Video Movie Guide 2001*)

SILENT RUNNING (1971) *Science Fiction*
Review: "The future: Plants do not exist on Earth anymore. Greenhouses in orbit contain the last samples of Earth's dying forests. But one day the government decides that the program has

Poll result: 50% of Americans believe humans lived at the same time as dinosaurs.

to be stopped. Directed by Douglas Trumbull, master of special effects who worked on *2001: A Space Odyssey*. A cult movie for SF fans." (Scifi.com)

THE KILLER (1989) *Foreign/Action*

Review: "John Woo's best film features Chow Yun-Fat as an honorable assassin trying to get out of the business. Impeccable pacing and incredible action choreography create an operatic intensity that leaves you feeling giddy. Available both dubbed and in Cantonese with English subtitles." (*Video Movie Guide 2001*)

THE TAKING OF PELHAM ONE TWO THREE (1974) *Suspense*

Review: "Ruthless Robert Shaw and three cohorts hijack NYC subway train, hold passengers for one million in cash—to be delivered *in one hour!* Outstanding thriller, laced with cynical comedy, bursts with heart-stopping excitement, terrific performances, and first-rate editing." (*Leonard Maltin's 2001 Movie & Video Guide*)

MONSOON WEDDING (2001) *Drama*

Review: "Rarely do films come along that are as intelligent and moving as *Monsoon Wedding*. Director Mira Nair's kaleidoscopic portrait of an Indian family preparing for their daughter's marriage succeeds in creating a vivid panoply of characters and telling a variety of stories." (Reel.com)

SLAP SHOT (1977) *Comedy*

Review: "A profane satire of the world of professional hockey. Over-the-hill player-coach Paul Newman gathers an oddball mixture of has-beens and young players and initiates them, using violence on the ice to make his team win. Charming in its own bone-crunching way." (*VideoHound's Golden Movie Retriever 2001*)

TWENTY BUCKS (1993) *Drama*

Review: "Whimsical film follows a $20 bill from its 'birth' in a cash machine to its 'death' as it is returned to the bank, tattered and torn, for shredding. The bill is passed from owner to owner, sometimes simply and briefly, sometimes altering fate." (*VideoHound's Golden Movie Retriever 2001*)

Tomatoes have more flavor at room temperature than they do when chilled.

AN A-PEEL-ING HISTORY

According to one legend, the fruit that Eve found irresistible in the Garden of Eden was not an apple, but a banana. Is it true? Who knows? But for thousands of years, the banana has been a source of pleasure...and sometimes trouble.

HOW THEY SPREAD

• Bananas are believed to have originated in the rainforests of Southeast Asia, where a wide variety of species still grow.

• Arab traders brought the banana to the Middle East and Africa in the seventh century. But these weren't the large fruit we know today—they were just a few inches in length. In fact, some historians believe "banana" comes from *banan*, the Arabic word meaning "finger."

• By the late 1400s, bananas were a staple food along the western coast of Africa where Portuguese sailors collected plants and brought them to the Canary Islands, between Africa and Spain.

• In 1516 Tomás de Berlanga, a Spanish priest, brought banana stalks to the New World, to the island of Hispañiola (now Haiti and the Dominican Republic). And he took plants with him to the mainland when he was made bishop of Panama in 1534.

• Another priest, Vasco de Quiroga, brought banana plants from Hispañiola to Mexico in the mid-16th century. From there, bananas spread and flourished throughout the Caribbean basin, leading many to believe—erroneously—that they were native to the region.

COMING TO AMERICA

Despite the banana's popularity in the tropics, it remained virtually unknown in the United States until the late 1800s. It was formally introduced to the American public at the 1876 Centennial Exposition in Philadelphia, which included a 40-acre display of tropical plants. A local grocer sold individual bananas, wrapped neatly in tinfoil, for 10¢—an hour's wage at the time. The fruit would remain an expensive luxury for years.

But bananas never would have become a popular snack food if

On-the-job injury: Pool shark Minnesota Fats was once hospitalized for "cue-tip-chalk lung."

it hadn't been for a few enterprising entrepreneurs. Cape Cod sea captain Lorenzo Baker was the first merchant to successfully capitalize on the banana when he discovered the curious fruit in Jamaica and brought a load of them to New Jersey in 1870. He sold 160 bunches for a substantial profit and soon began shipping them back to the East Coast on a regular basis. In 1885 he and Boston businessman Andrew Preston formed the Boston Fruit Company.

GETTING ON TRACK

At about the same time, an ambitious 19-year-old from Brooklyn discovered bananas too. In 1871 Minor Keith and two of his brothers went to Costa Rica to work for their uncle, who had won a government contract to build a railroad line from the capital, San José, to the port city of Limón. It was a treacherous project over miles of dense mountainous jungle and ultimately claimed the lives of some 5,000 workers, including Keith's brothers and uncle.

In spite of the hardship, however, Keith persisted. And as the railroad construction proceeded, he planted banana plants on any and all nearby land. Why? The quick-growing fruit was a cheap way to feed the workers.

The railroad was completed in 1890, but Keith was in financial trouble. The Costa Rican government refused to pay him, and there weren't enough passengers to support the line. What could he do? Forced to find another source of revenue, Keith decided to experiment with the bananas he'd planted: his railroad could cheaply transport them to Limón, where they could be shipped to markets in the United States. The experiment was so successful that the banana business quickly overshadowed his meager passenger service.

MERGER

Despite a decade of success, in 1899 Keith once again found himself in trouble. His financial partner went bankrupt, leaving him without enough money to run the railroad. So, as a way to preserve his business, he went to Boston and arranged with Lorenzo Baker and Andrew Preston to merge their two companies. (The company they formed, the United Fruit Company, still exists as part of United Brands.)

By the end of the century, advances in refrigerated steamship

Slow down! One hundred cups of coffee consumed in 4 hours can cause a heart attack.

and rail transportation made it possible to ship bananas to all parts of North America. As improved production led to lower prices, the United Fruit Company was poised for a banana boom. Now affordable, the banana quickly became a popular snack, and production shifted into high gear. But there was a dark side to the business that the American public knew little about.

BANANA REPUBLICS

Behind the scenes, the banana business played a huge part in the economy and politics of Central America. The United Fruit Company, as well as other banana companies such as Standard Fruit (today part of Dole), made sweetheart deals with Central American dictators, buying or leasing vast tracts of land at bargain prices and paying little, if any, taxes.

While bananas created wealth in Central America, it mostly enriched government officials—without benefitting the common people. In 1910 American author O. Henry coined the term *banana republic*, and by the 1930s, it was commonly used to describe the corrupt Central American countries controlled largely by banana companies.

GUNBOAT DIPLOMACY

U.S. foreign policy stood firmly behind the banana companies too. Under President William Howard Taft (1909–1913), the goal of diplomacy was to support (or create) stable governments favorable to U.S. interests. And later, when "dollar diplomacy" failed, the U.S. government resorted to "gunboat diplomacy." American troops were sent in to ensure the pro-U.S. outcome of elections in Honduras, Nicaragua, and other Latin American countries.

In the 1950s, for example, Jacobo Arbenz, a progressive Guatemalan president, proposed reclaiming lands owned by the United Fruit Company and other large landowners and distributing them to landless peasants. It never happened—in 1954, citing the threat of communism, the United States backed a military coup that ousted Arbenz and ended the immediate threat of land reform.

But times were changing for the banana companies. Worker strikes led to labor reforms. The monopoly of United Fruit Company was broken by an antitrust suit in 1958 that forced it to sell parts of the company to competitors and Guatemalan entrepreneurs.

Today, imperialist politics have taken a backseat to more modern business practices. But bananas are still big business, and remain America's most popular fruit.

BANANARAMA

- Americans eat an average of 75 bananas a year per person.
- The banana split was invented in 1904 by Dr. David Strickler, a drugstore pharmacist in Latrobe, Pennsylvania.
- Technically the banana is a berry.
- Ever wonder why bananas have no seeds? Because of natural mutations, the kind we eat don't have any. The dark dots in the center are all that's left. (They reproduce by underground stems, or rhizomes.)
- There are several hundred varieties of bananas worldwide, but the one that most of us slice on our cereal is the Cavendish. The Cavendish is favored by commercial producers for its size, flavor, and, most importantly, resistance to diseases.
- A banana has about 110 calories and is high in fiber, potassium, and vitamin C.
- The banana has never been a Fruit-of-the-Month selection.
- The song "Yes, We Have No Bananas" was an enormous hit in 1923—selling at the rate of 25,000 copies of sheet music per day. The popularity of the song spurred a new craze: dancing the Charleston on banana peel–covered floors.
- A few forgotten banana products: banana wine, banana flour (cheaper than wheat flour), banana ketchup, banana pickles, banana vinegar, and Melzo, a powdered-banana drink mix.
- To let the public know that bananas should be allowed to ripen at room temperature, not in the refrigerator, in 1944 United Fruit commissioned a song and a character: Chiquita Banana. The song was so popular it was once played on the radio 376 times in one day. And Chiquita herself was named "the girl we'd most like to share our foxhole with" by American servicemen.

*　　*　　*

"Great men never feel great. Small men never feel small."

—Chinese proverb

FLUNKING THE PEPSI CHALLENGE

Lots of companies have ad campaigns that flop, but Pepsi seems to have more than its share. Here are a few classic bombs.

KEEP ON TRUCKIN'

For its "Pepsi 400" contest in the summer of 2001, Pepsi offered to send the holders of five winning tickets on an all-expenses-paid trip to Florida's Daytona 400 auto race. One of the five would get to drive home in the grand prize, a brand-new Dodge truck; the other four would each get $375 worth of free gas. There was just one problem: contest organizers accidentally printed 55 winning tickets instead of five. Rather than risk alienating the winners—not to mention millions of Pepsi drinkers—Pepsi sent all 55 winners to Daytona, gave away five trucks instead of one, and spent $20,625 on free gas instead of $1,825. Estimated cost of the error: about $400,000.

OVER-STUFFED

In April 1996, Pepsi canceled its "Pepsi Stuff" merchandise giveaway campaign months ahead of schedule. Reason: Too many winners. The company underestimated how many people would redeem the points by 50%, forcing it to spend $60 million more than expected on free merchandise. "We're outpacing our goals on awareness," a company spokesperson explained.

JET LAG

Another disaster from the "Pepsi Stuff" campaign: 21-year-old John Leonard tried to redeem seven million award points for the Harrier fighter jet he saw offered in a Pepsi Stuff TV ad. The rules stipulated that contestants could buy points for 10¢ apiece, so that's what he did. Leonard (who studied flawed promotions in business school) raised $700,000 to buy the required points and then sent the money to Pepsi, along with a letter demanding they hand over the $50 million jet. When Pepsi refused, claiming the offer was made "in jest," Leonard filed suit in federal court. Three years later, a judge ruled that "no objective person could reason-

Heavy! Water weighs more per unit of volume than wine does.

ably have concluded that the commercial actually offered consumers a Harrier jet." Pepsi lucked out...case dismissed.

THE KING OF (SODA) POP

Even Pepsi's biggest successes can become colossal flops. In 1983 they signed the largest individual sponsorship deal in history with pop singer Michael Jackson. It was a multi-year deal and Pepsi made millions from it...only to find itself linked to one of the most lurid scandals of the 1990s when Jackson abruptly cancelled his Pepsi-sponsored "Dangerous" tour in 1993. Jackson's reasons for quitting: (1) stress generated by allegations that he had sexually molested a young boy, and (2) addiction to painkillers he took "to control pain from burns suffered while filming a Pepsi ad."

THE NAME GAME

In 1983 another Pepsi contest ran into budget trouble when the company offered $5 per letter to any customer who could spell their own last name using letters printed on Pepsi bottle caps and flip tops. Pepsi hoped to control the number of cash prizes by releasing only a limited number of vowels...but it failed to take into account people like Richard "no vowels" Vlk, who turned in 1,393 three-letter sets and pocketed $20,985 for his efforts. Vlk, a diabetic who does not drink Pepsi, collected the letters by taking out classified ads offering to split the winnings with anyone who sent him a matching set. "I don't even remember making one whole set myself," he says. "I didn't buy any Pepsi." (The company got even by mailing him his winnings in $15 increments, one check for each winning set.)

THEY CAN SEE CLEARLY NOW

In 1992 Pepsi introduced Crystal Pepsi, an attempt to cash in on the booming popularity of see-through soft drinks like Clearly Canadian. Sales were less than half of what Pepsi projected, even after the company reformulated the product. Marketing experts point to two critical flaws that they say doomed Crystal Pepsi from the start: (1) customers balked at paying extra for a product that, because it was clear, was perceived to have fewer ingredients than regular Pepsi, and (2) after more than a century of conditioning, consumers *want* colas to be dark brown in color. "Clear colas are about as appetizing as brown water," an industry analyst explains.

A single mushroom can produce as many as 40 million spores in a single hour.

TRUST ME...

Call it doublespeak, call it spin, call it "a different version of the facts." The truth is—it's still a lie.

TRUST ME... "I wouldn't call it an accident. I'd call it a malfunction."

SAID BY: Dr. Edward Teller, "father of the hydrogen bomb," referring to Three Mile Island, 1979

THE FACT: It was a real accident—250,000 gallons of radioactive waste leaked out.

TRUST ME... "Our one desire is that... the people of Southeast Asia be left in peace to work out their own destinies in their way."

SAID BY: President Lyndon B. Johnson, 1964

THE FACT: Maybe he meant "left in pieces"—the war in Vietnam was well underway and escalating.

TRUST ME... "I have no more territorial ambitions in Europe."

SAID BY: Adolf Hitler, 1938

THE FACT: Within two years of saying this, Germany invaded Czechoslovakia, Denmark, Norway, Holland, Belgium, and France.

TRUST ME... "I would have never owned those ugly-ass shoes."

SAID BY: O. J. Simpson, in a 1996 civil lawsuit, denying he owned a pair of Bruno Magli "Lorenzos"

THE FACT: A month later, 30 photographs were discovered that showed Simpson wearing the shoes at a 1993 Buffalo Bills game.

TRUST ME... "The army is the Indian's best friend."

SAID BY: General George Armstrong Custer, 1870

THE FACT: He then wiped out most of the Sioux nation before being killed at Little Big Horn.

TRUST ME... "As long as I own the Cleveland Browns, they will remain in Cleveland."

SAID BY: Brown's owner Art Modell, 1993

THE FACT: He moved the franchise to Baltimore in 1996.

97 out of 100 Americans who buy engagement rings this year will buy one with a diamond.

SHAKES' TAKES

Some hilarious lines from the late comedian Ronnie Shakes.

"A lot of people wonder how you know if you're really in love. Just ask yourself this one question: 'Would I mind being destroyed financially by this person?'"

"They say that hell is hot, but is it humid? Because I can take the heat; it's the humidity I can't stand."

"After twelve years of therapy my psychiatrist said something that brought tears to my eyes. He said, 'No hablo ingles.'"

"I was going to buy a copy of *The Power of Positive Thinking*, and then I thought: What the hell good would that do?"

"My doctor gave me two weeks to live. I hope they're in August."

"I like life. It's something to do."

"We live in a mobile home. Hey, there are advantages to living in a mobile home. One time, it caught on fire. We met the fire department half way."

"I spend money with reckless abandon. Last month I blew five thousand dollars at a reincarnation seminar. I got to thinking, 'what the hell, you only live once.'"

"I was an ugly baby. On my birth certificate there was a listing for 'Probable Cause.'"

"One question on hospital admittance forms really gets me. 'Sex: Male or Female?' Do I want to be in a hospital where they can't tell the difference?"

"As a teenager I just wanted to fit in, just be one of the boys. It was tough. I went to an all-black school. I went so far as to have them print my negative in the yearbook. I think it was the black teeth that gave me away."

"I wouldn't mind being the last man on Earth—just to see if all of those girls were telling me the truth."

"I fear that one day I'll meet God, He'll sneeze, and I won't know what to say."

Lead melts at a temperature of 620°F; tin at 446°F. Mix them...

FADS

Here's a look at the origins of some of the most popular obsessions from days gone by.

THE SMURFS

Created by Belgian storybook illustrator Pierre "Peyo" Culliford in 1957, the Smurfs developed followings in Germany, Italy, Spain, and Scandanavia (where the blue creatures were known as Schlumpfe, Puffo, Pitufo, and Smolf, respectively), but they remained more or less unknown in the rest of the world.

Then in 1978, British Petroleum launched an advertising campaign featuring the creatures, which it renamed the Smurfs for the English audience. The ads sparked a Smurf craze in England, prompting an American importer to bring them to America... where they caught the eye of the daughter of the president of NBC. Her enthusiasm prompted dad to order up a Saturday morning Smurf cartoon show for the network. The show became an enormous hit, turning NBC into a Saturday morning juggernaut and launching a Smurf craze in the United States. By 1982 the Smurfs were the biggest-selling toy merchandising line in the country, outselling even *E.T.* and *Star Wars*.

"BABY ON BOARD" SIGNS

In 1984 an executive recruiter named Michael Lerner decided to start his own consumer products business. The only problem: he couldn't think of any products to sell. Lucky for him, an old college friend told him about a couple who'd just come back from a vacation in Germany, where they'd seen small signs suction-cupped to automobile windows warning motorists to drive carefully because a baby was on board. The couple wanted to start selling the signs in the United States.

Lerner offered them a deal: If they would agree to let *him* market the signs, he would give them a royalty. Deal! Lerner founded a company called Safety 1st; by the end of 1985 he was selling 500,000 of the little diamond-shaped yellow signs a month. The couple made more than $100,000 for doing absolutely nothing.

Soon imitators stole his idea and swamped the market with

humorous signs like "Beam Me Up Scotty" and "Ex-Husband in Trunk." Lerner couldn't sue—he didn't have a patent, but that wasn't a problem: He just used his Baby On Board profits to branch out into other child-safety products. He eventually took Safety 1st public, and in April 2000 it sold to a Canadian company for $195 million.

PAINT BY NUMBERS

In 1952, a Detroit paint-company owner named Max Klein got together with an artist named Dan Robbins and formed Craft Master, a company that sold the world's first paint-by-numbers kits. The kits consisted of numbered jars of paint and a rolled-up canvas (later cardboard) stamped with the outline of a painting; each section of the painting had a number that corresponded to a particular color of paint. Price, including paints and brush: $1.79

So who did Klein and Robbins get the idea from? Leonardo da Vinci. "I recalled reading about da Vinci, and when he got large and complicated commissions, he would give numbered patterns to his apprentices to block in areas for him that he'd go back and finish himself," Robbins explains. "It took two years to get off the ground; then they took off like a rocket." By 1954 more paint-by-numbers paintings were hanging in American homes than were original works of art.

At the peak of the fad, Craft Master was producing 50,000 kits a day. Their slogan was "Every man a Rembrandt." Among the Rembrandts: Nelson Rockefeller, Ethel Merman, Andy Warhol, J. Edgar Hoover...and even President Dwight D. Eisenhower.

SLOT CARS

The world's first toy slot cars were introduced by the Aurora Plastics Company in 1960. Aurora's cars came with special slotted tracks that kept the cars on the road, thanks to a small projection under the car's nose that inserted into the slot. Cost: $3.00 to $8.00 per car, or $20–40 for an entire racing set, which made them affordable for just about everyone. The cars went up to 600 mph in scale, and since the "drivers" were in continuous control of their vehicles' speeds, the cars were more challenging—and more fun—to operate than toy cars had ever been.

Because of all of this, the cars became hugely popular. Entrepreneurs built huge multilevel slot-car racing centers that competed with pinball arcades for America's pocket change, and home enthusiasts spent $1,500 or more building their own elaborate speedways at home. In all, Americans spent $100 million on slot cars and tracks in 1963—more than they spent on model railroads—and by 1965 more than 3.5 million Americans were racing slot cars on a regular basis. For a time it seemed that slot cars might even become more popular than bowling, but the fad didn't last long—sales dropped off sharply in 1967 and never recovered.

INSTANT TANS

Dihydroxyacetone is a drug that's used as an antidote for cyanide poisoning. It has a side effect: It stains human skin brown on contact. A sun worshipper named John Andre noticed this in the late 1950s and decided to mix the medicine with alcohol and fragrances and sell it as a self-tanning aftershave called Man-Tan. Andre sold $3 million worth of the stuff in 1960, giving both aftershave and suntan lotion companies quite a scare. They needn't have worried: paint-on tans were just a flash in the pan, and sales "virtually disappeared" the following year. (Update: Man-tan is still gone, but thanks to the established link between sunlight and skin cancer, paint-on tans are more popular than ever.)

SHMOOS

In 1948 cartoonist Al Capp added a new character to his L'il Abner comic strip: the *shmoo*, a strange creature, described as "a cross between Casper the Ghost and a misshapen dinosaur." In Capp's comic-strip world, the shmoos were as much a part of the food supply as they were a part of the story line: they laid eggs, produced butter, and gave milk in glass bottles. If you broiled them, they turned into steak; if you boiled them, they turned into chicken.

And if you made a toy out of them, manufacturers learned in the late 1940s, they sold by the millions. Companies made fortunes selling shmoo ashtrays, clocks, piggy banks, pencil sharpeners, clothing, candy, and even shmoo meat products. By 1950 more than $25 million worth of shmoo items had been sold, yet for some reason, Capp decided to write the characters out of the story line. He created a "shmooicide squad" that gunned down every single shmoo in the strip, and the fad died out soon after that.

The skin of a tiger shark is 10 times as strong as ox hide.

A FAMOUS PHONY

Most people have fantasized about being someone else, but few of us have actually done it. Here's an amazing story of a man who pretended to be someone he wasn't... and pulled it off.

BACKGROUND: Ferdinand Waldo Demara, Jr. was one of the most prolific imposters in history. Born in Lawrence, Massachusetts, in 1921, the high school dropout had successfully passed himself off as a doctor of philosophy, a zoologist, a Trappist monk, a prison counselor, a biologist doing cancer research, a sheriff, a soldier, and a sailor by the time he was in his 30s.

MOMENT OF "TRUTH": His greatest ruse came during the Korean War when he used the identity of Dr. Joseph Cyr, and enlisted in the Royal Canadian Navy in 1951. He served aboard a destroyer off the Korean coast. Under intense battle conditions, Demara *was* the ship's surgeon: he pulled teeth, removed tonsils, administered anaesthesia, and even amputated limbs. But most incredibly, after studying the procedure in a book, he successfully removed a bullet from a wounded soldier that was less than an inch from his heart. Onlookers let out a cheer as he completed the impeccable operation and saved the man's life. In all his time as a doctor in Korea, he never lost a single patient.

UNMASKED: His success turned out to be his undoing—photographs of the heroic doctor made it into Canadian newspapers. The real Dr. Cyr's mother saw them and alerted authorites. Amazingly, no charges were filed; Demara had saved too many lives. A naval board of inquiry released him—with back pay. Demara was later arrested for posing as a teacher in the United States and served a six-month sentence. When asked why he did it, noting that he didn't get rich from his escapades, he answered, "Rascality, pure rascality."

IMMORTALITY ACHIEVED: In 1961 Hollywood made a movie based on the Demara story, *The Great Imposter*, starring Tony Curtis and Karl Malden. Director Robert Mulligan was a finalist for the Director's Guild Award for the film. And Demara himself got a minor part in another movie: In 1960 he appeared in the melodrama *The Hypnotic Eye*. He played... the doctor.

Number of documented deaths-by-piranha in human history: Not even one.

THE MAN IN THE MASK

Classical "Greco-Roman" wrestling can trace its roots all the way back to the ancient Greeks and Romans. But what about "professional" wrestling—the kind where costumed buffoons hit each other with folding chairs? How old is that? Older than you might think.

WORLD-CLASS WRESTLING

In 1915 some fight promoters organized an international wrestling tournament at the Opera House in New York. A rising American star named Ed "Strangler" Lewis headlined a roster of other top grapplers from Russia, Germany, Italy, Greece, and other countries. These were some of the biggest matches to be fought in New York City that year.

There was just one problem: almost nobody went to see them.

HO-HUM

Wrestling, at least as it was fought back then, could be pretty boring for the average person to watch. As soon as the bell rang or the whistle was blown, the two wrestlers grabbed onto each other and then might circle round...and round...and round for hours on end, until one wrestler finally gained an advantage and defeated his opponent. Some bouts dragged on for nine hours or more.

Wrestling could also be hard to understand, which made it even more boring. In baseball, an outfielder either caught a fly ball or they didn't. In football, the person with the ball either got tackled or they didn't. Wrestling was different—when two grapplers circled for hours, who could tell at any point in the match who was winning? Did anyone even care?

Even by wrestling standards, 1915 was a particularly boring year because the world's youngest and best wrestlers were all off fighting in World War I. Those that were left were often past their prime and not very entertaining. Not surprisingly, the organizers of the tournament at the Opera House were having trouble filling seats. For the first day or two it looked like they were going to lose a lot of money.

For the first day or two.

38% of American companies say they monitor their employees' e-mails.

MYSTERY MAN

Things were about to change, thanks to one spectator. He was huge, but he didn't stand out just because of his size—he stood out because he was wearing a black mask that covered his entire head. There was no explanation for what the man was doing there or why he was wearing the mask. He just sat there watching the matches each day, and when they ended he left as silently as he came.

Then, a few days into the tournament, the masked man and a companion suddenly stood up and loudly accused the promotors of banning the masked man from the tournament. He was the best wrestler of all and the promoters knew it, they claimed. That was why he was being kept out of the tournament, and they demanded that he be let back in. Security guards quickly hustled the pair out of the building, but they came back each day and repeated their demands, generating newspaper headlines in the process. By the end of the week, much of New York City was demanding that the masked man be allowed into the tournament.

OH, ALL RIGHT

Finally, on Saturday, the promotors gave in to the pressure and agreed to let him compete. Just days earlier, some of the world's most famous wrestlers had battled one another in a nearly empty Opera House. No one cared. Now throngs of New Yorkers ponied up the price of admission to watch the mysterious masked man fight, even though—or more likely *because*—they had no idea who he was or whether he even knew how to fight.

Sure enough, the Masked Marvel delivered—although not quite as much as he promised, because he lost one match and only wrestled "Strangler" Lewis to a draw. But he whipped everyone else he wrestled, bringing the packed tournament to a thrilling end. Considering the amount of exitement that led up to those final bouts, it's a good bet that the people who saw the masked man fight remembered the experience for the rest of their lives.

MYSTERY REVEALED

The following year, the Masked Marvel was officially *un*masked after losing a match with a wrestler named Joe Stecher. He turned out to be…Mort Henderson, a railroad detective from Altoona,

When kids were asked to name "the most important person in the world"…

Pennsylvania, who made his living throwing hobos off trains when he wasn't in the ring. Henderson had wrestled for years under his own name, but he lost many of his matches and had gone nowhere in the sport. Even when he *wasn't* wearing a mask, nobody knew who he was.

So how did Henderson do so well at the Opera House? The whole thing was a setup—the promoters planted him in the audience hoping that he would generate publicity and sell tickets. The other wrestlers were in on the scam, too; that was how he won so many fights.

Many New Yorkers realized that they'd been had, but nobody seemed to mind. The Masked Marvel was *fun*.

FROM SPECTACLE...TO SPORT...TO SPECTACLE

Wrestling had long been full of colorful characters. After all, legitimate professional wrestling traced its roots back to the days when carnival strongmen traveled the country offering cash prizes to any locals who could pin them to the mat.

By 1915 wrestling had matured into a legitimate sport, a test of strength and skill, not quite as exciting as boxing but still a sport that took itself seriously. Mort Henderson could not have realized it at the time, but on the day he donned his mask the first time in 1915, he changed professional wrestling forever. It was "at this point," Keith Greenberg writes in *Pro Wrestling: From Carnivals to Cable TV*, "promoters began copying techniques from vaudeville to keep spectators interested."

PUTTING ON A SHOW

A lot of the credit for changing pro wrestling into what it is today goes to a former vaudeville promoter named Joseph "Toots" Mondt. Mondt saw wrestlers as little different from theatrical performers, and their matches as just another act to be managed so that profits were maximized.

Rather than let a match run on for hours, he set time limits, which allowed him to book more fights back to back. His traveling troupe of wrestlers fought the same fights—with the same rigged outcomes—in every town they visited. Since the wrestlers didn't have to focus on winning, they were free to thrill audiences with moves like flying drop kicks, airplane spins, and leaps across

...God came in 19th place, just after *Harry Potter* author J. K. Rowling.

the ring feet first to kick opponents in the chest.

Landing fake body blows like these—ones that appeared devastating without actually causing serious physical harm—was elevated to a fine art. "When a grappler threw a punch, he tried to connect using a forearm instead of a fist, softening the blow," Greenberg writes. "A man diving on a foe from the ropes actually grazed the man with a knee or elbow, rather than landing on him directly and causing injury."

ONE-RING CIRCUS

The next big wave of innovation came during the Great Depression of the 1930s, when dwindling ticket sales forced promoters to resort to even greater gimmickry to draw crowds. Wrestlers assumed false ethnic identities so that blue-collar immigrants could root for someone of their own ethnic group, and also to capitalize on whatever geopolitical goings-on might make for an interesting villian. Evil German counts and Japanese generals were popular during World War II; in peacetime, crazy hillbillies and snooty English lords filled the bill, grappling with the noble Indian chiefs and scrappy Irish brawlers that the audiences loved.

Wrestlers fought tag-team matches. They battled it out in cages. They wrestled while chained together. They fought in rings filled with mud (of course) as well as ice cream, berries, molasses, and other gooey substances. Women wrestled. Midgets wrestled. Giants wrestled. Morbidly obese people wrestled, and so did people with disfiguring diseases. Maurice Tillet, the French Angel, suffered from a glandular disease called *acromegaly* that gave him enlarged, distorted facial features. He was such a successful villain that he spawned a host of imitators, including the Swedish Angel, the Golden Angel, the Polish Angel, and the Czech Angel, a number of whom suffered from the same disease.

OLD SCHOOL

What happened to the "genuine" professional wrestlers, the guys who refused to showboat and took their sport seriously? They continued to wrestle one another in honest matches for legitimate championship titles. In 1920, for example, Ed "Strangler" Lewis won a world championship match against Joe Stecher in a three-hour-long bout; he held the title off and on for the next 13 years.

90% of all insects live in the soil for at least part of their lives.

After that the title turned over several times before it passed to a wrestler named Lou Thesz, who would win and lose it several times into the 1950s.

Not that anyone cared. Thesz wasn't above a little showmanship—his specialty holds were the Kangaroo and the Airplane Spin—but "there was little interest in the championship among the public," Graeme Kent writes in *A Pictorial History of Wrestling*. "This was mainly because Thesz scorned gimmicks, relying on his wrestling ability to carry him through."

STAY TUNED...

Yet it was a gimmick at the end of World War II that would provide the biggest boost to professional wrestling. The emerging medium of TV—and a wrestling innovator called Gorgeous George—helped bring wrestling into American living rooms.

The Masked Marvel was responsible for turning wrestling from a sport into a spectacle, but Gorgeous George deserves the credit for bringing professional wrestling into full bloom. That story is on page 340.

*   *   *

IT'S A WEIRD, WEIRD WORLD

"Alain Robert, the French 'spider-man' famous for climbing the Eiffel Tower and Empire State Building, walked away from China's 88-story Jinmao Tower—too risky. In February 2001, Han Qizhi, a 31-year-old shoe salesman, just happened to be passing the popular landmark and was 'struck by a rash impulse.' When security guards weren't looking, Han, who had never climbed before, launched himself upon the skyscraper and began to climb. 'He walked around Jinmao a couple of times, told his colleague he was going up, dropped his jacket, and started climbing,' said a police spokesman. Han, bare-handed and dressed in ordinary street clothes, was grabbed by policemen just short of the summit."

—Reuters

What are a *carapace* and a *plastron*? The top and bottom parts of a turtle shell.

KNOW YOUR OLOGIES

You may have heard of psychology, biology, and ecology, but chances are you've never heard of any of these "ologies."

Rhinology: The study of noses

Nosology: The study of the classification of diseases

Hippology: The study of horses

Dactylology: Communication using fingers (sign language)

Ichthyology: The study of fish

Myrmecology: The study of ants

Potamology: The study of rivers

Anemology: The study of wind

Sinology: The study of Chinese culture

Mycology: The study of fungi

Glottochronology: The study of when two languages diverge from one common source

Neology: The study of new words

Oenology: The study of wines

Conchology: The study of shells

Otology: The study of ears

Oneirology: The study of dreams

Semiology: The study of signs and signaling

Cetology: The study of whales and dolphins

Vexillology: The study of flags

Deontology: The study of moral responsibilities

Axiology: The study of principles, ethics, and values

Phantomology: The study of supernatural beings

Histology: The study of tissues

Trichology: The study of hair

Malacology: The study of mollusks

Dendrochronology: The study of trees' ages by counting their rings

Morphology: The study of the structure of organisms

Oology: The study of eggs

Eschatology: The study of final events as spoken of in the Bible

Don't let the name fool you: Mississippi Bay is off the coast of Yokohama, Japan.

HOW THE PEOPLE GOT BEER

How long have young men used beer to buck up their courage around young women? Longer than you think. Here's the story that the Bura people of northern Nigeria used to explain where beer comes from.

Long, long ago there was no such thing as beer. The people were happy. God had put people in the world, but he had not told them that there was such a thing as beer. God did not want them to know about beer.

There was once a man who wanted to take a girl from a village far away to be his wife. He would go to talk with the girl, but her people would not give him a chance. He did not know what to say to them, for he was very bashful. Every day he would go, but they would not let him have her for his wife. He was getting very tired of going and not getting her.

One day he started to visit the girl's folks. Halfway between his village and their village, he met a devil. The devil said, "I see you go on this road very often, but I never see you bring anything back. I just wonder why you go. Do you want something over this way?" The man said, "Yes, I want to take a wife in a village over this way, but they will not give her to me. I do not know what to say to them for I am too bashful." The devil said, "If I give you my advice, will you take it?" "Yes," said the man excitedly, "I will. Tell me, please."

The devil said, "When you go home, thresh some corn and separate the male grains from the female grains. Put the male grains in water and leave them until they sprout. Grind the female grains into flour and pour this flour into a jar of water. When the male grains have been in the water a few days, take them out and let the sprouts grow a little more. Then put them in the sun to dry. Next, put a pot on the fire, and with the flour which has been soaking in the jar, make mush. When the mush is made, put it out to cool. When the mush is cold, put it back into the jar of water. Grind the sprouted grains of corn which have been drying, and put that flour into the same jar with the mush. Mix up the mush and corn flour and the water. When you have mixed them well, cover the jar and let it stand for a day. It will get sweet, and on the second day it will foam. Get a strainer and strain it. After you have strained it, drink some of it. After you have drunk all you can, go and get your wife. You will see then what this thing will do for you. The name of it is beer."

The man said, "Thank you, thank you very much, my father. You have given me very good advice." And each went his way.

The young man went home and threshed corn, and divided the male grains from the female grains. He did everything that the devil told him to do. He made beer, strained it, and drank all that he could. The beer made him drunk and he did not know what he was doing. His understanding became warped. He started off to see the girl's people. They said, "Welcome," and he went into the compound and saluted them.

He began at once to ask for her, but he did not talk like a bashful man any more. He talked fast and loud. Her people were amazed. They said, "Always before, this young man was bashful, but today, he is not like he always was. What is the matter?"

The man said, "No, no more chitchat. If you do not give me my wife today, you give me back my cotton which I have given in payment for her. I will not have small talk any longer. I have always been bashful, but now I am tired of it and I will not have it any longer. Our negotiations will finish today. If I take her, all right; if I do not take her, all right, and that is that."

Her people were amazed by what he said to them. They decided together that they had better give him his wife. They allowed him to take his wife home with him that day. The man said, "I tell you beer is something wonderful."

This is how the Bura people began to make beer. One man began first, and even until today, men still make it. Beer is of the devil, and there is no argument, for he told them how to make that which was his own.

* * *

"I read about the evils of drinking, so I gave up reading."

—**Henny Youngman**

HOMER VS. HOMER

On the left we have the wisdom of Homer, Greek poet and philosopher, who lived 3,000 years ago. And on the right we have the other Homer.

Homer the Greek	*Homer the Simpson*
"It is the bold man who every time does his best."	"I don't know, Marge. Trying is the first step toward failure."
"The charity that is a trifle to us can be precious to others."	"You gave both dogs away? You know how I feel about giving!"
"The fates have given mankind a patient soul."	"Give me some peace of mind or I'll mop the floor with you!"
"Nothing in the world is so incontinent as a man's accursed appetite."	"Ahh, beer...I would kill everyone in this room for a drop of sweet beer."
"I detest he who hides one thing in his heart and means another."	"But, Marge, it takes two people to lie: one to lie, and one to listen."
"The man who acts the least, disrupts the most."	"It is better to watch things than to do them."
"A sympathetic friend can be quite as dear as a brother."	"Television—teacher, mother, secret lover!"
"A multitude of rulers is not a good thing. Let there be one ruler, one king."	"I'd blow smoke in the president's stupid monkey face and all he'd do is grooooove on it!"
"Never, never was a wicked man wise."	"I am so smart! S-M-R-T, I mean S-M-A-R-T."
"How mortals take the gods to task! Yet their afflictions come from us."	"I'm not normally a religious man, but if you're up there, save me, Superman!"

Bad luck? The Confederate flag had 13 stars...but there were only 11 Confederate states.

NUMBER TWO'S WILD RIDE

Uncle John feels a responsibility to "eliminate bathroom ignorance." So for this edition of the Bathroom Reader *we're going to answer the basic question: What happens after you flush? (It's more complicated than you think.)*

READY, SET, GO!

For you, the trip has ended. You've "done your business," (hopefully you've also had a few minutes of quality reading time), you've flushed the toilet, and you've moved onto the next thing.

But for your "business," a.k.a. organic solid waste, a.k.a. "Number Two," the trip is just beginning. Here's a general idea of what happens next.

CONNECTIONS

If you live in a rural area, your house is probably hooked up to a septic tank. We'll get to that later.

Before the 20th century, "sanitary systems" typically dumped raw sewage directly into rivers, streams, and oceans. Today, if you live in an urban area or a suburb, chances are your toilet and all of the water fixtures in your house—the sinks, showers, bathtubs, dishwasher, washing machine, etc.—are all hooked into a sewer system that feeds into a wastewater treatment plant. So the journey begins when Number Two mixes with all of the rest of the wastewater leaving your house. Then it enters the *sewer main* that runs down the center of your street (usually about six feet beneath the road surface), and mixes with the wastewater coming from the your neighbors' homes.

From there the sewer main probably joins with other sewer mains to form an even bigger sewer main. Depending on how far you are from the wastewater treatment plant, the sewer mains may repeatedly join together to form ever larger pipes. By the time you start getting close to the plant, the pipe could be large enough in diameter to drive a truck through it.

In 1876 an English cricket player hit the ball 37 miles. (It landed on a moving railroad car.)

PRIMARY TREATMENT

By now Number Two has a lot of company, especially if any storm drains feed into your community's system. Anything that can be swept into the the storm drains—old shoes, tree branches, cardboard boxes, dead animals, rusty shopping carts—is now heading through the giant pipes toward the treatment plant.

This floating garbage would destroy the equipment in the plant, so the first step is to remove it from the wastewater. This is accomplished by letting the water flow through a series of screens and vertical bars that trap the really large objects but let everything else—including Number Two—float through. The big stuff is then removed and disposed of, often in landfills.

THE NITTY GRITTY

Now the trip starts to get a little rough:

• The wastewater flows into a grinder called a *communitor*. The communitor is like a huge garbage disposal: It takes everything that's still in the water, Number Two included, and grinds it down into a sort of liquified mulch that's easier to treat chemically and easier to remove. Number Two has now "become one," so to speak, with all the other solid matter still in the wastewater.

• Next this slurry flows into a *grit chamber*, where inorganic materials—stuff that can't rot, like sand, gravel, and silt—settle to the bottom of the chamber. Later, they're disposed of in a landfill.

• The wastewater then flows from the grit chamber into a closed *sedimentation tank*, where it is allowed to sit for a while so that the organic matter still in the water has a chance to settle to the bottom of the tank, where it can be removed.

• Have you ever dropped a raisin into a glass of 7-Up and watched the bubbles carry it to the top of the glass? So have the folks that design treatment plants. Some plants use a *flotation tank* instead of a sedimentation tank: They force pressurized air into the wastewater, then pump this mixture into an open tank, where the bubbles can rise to the surface. As they float up, the bubbles carry a lot of the organic matter to the surface with them (including what's left of poor Number Two), making it easier to skim from the surface and remove.

By the time the wastewater has been processed through the

What is piperine? The stuff in black pepper that makes you sneeze.

sedimentation tank or the flotation tank, as much as 75–80% of solid matter has been removed.

THE SLUDGE REPORT

So what happens to all of the organic solid matter (i.e., Number Two and all his friends) that has just been removed from the sedimentation tank? It gets turned into fertilizer.

- It goes into a *thickener*, where it's—you guessed it—thickened.
- Then it's fed into a closed anaerobic tank called a *digester*, where it's—right again—digested. Enzymes break down the solid matter into a *soluble* (dissolvable) form. Then acid-producing bacteria ferment it, breaking it down even further, into simple organic acids. Bacteria then turns these organic acids into methane and carbon dioxide gasses. The entire process of decomposition can take anywhere from 10 to 30 days, during which time it will reduce the mass of the organic matter by 45–60%.
- What's left of the digested sludge is pumped out onto sand beds, where it's allowed to dry. Some of the liquid in the sludge percolates down into the sand; the rest evaporates into the air. The dried organic material that's left can then be used as a soil conditioner or a fertilizer. (Moral of the story: wash your vegetables before you eat them.)

SECONDARY TREATMENT

That takes care of the organic matter—the part of the process known as *primary treatment*. Number Two's trip is now at an end. But what about the liquid in the sedimentation and flotation tanks? Taking care of that is known as *secondary treatment*:

- Some treatment plants pump the water through a *trickling filter*, where the water flows over a bed of porous material that's coated with a slimy film of microorganisms. The microorganisms break the organic matter down into carbon dioxide and water.
- Another process utilizes *activated sludge*—living sludge that is made up millions upon millions of bacteria cells. The wastewater is pumped into a tank containing the sludge, and the bacteria absorb any remaining organic matter.
- Finally, the wastewater is processed in something called a *secondary clarifier*, which removes the bacteria before they are discharged back into the environment.

Is your Adam's apple larger than normal? That means you're "cock-throppled."

• Some water treatment facilities don't use trickling filters or activated sludge, they just pump the water into a lagoon or a *stabilization pond*, where the water is allowed to sit while naturally occurring bacteria and other microorganisms do the same job on their own, only a little slower.

ADVANCED TREATMENT

Most wastewater that has received both primary and secondary treatment is considered safe enough to go back into the environment. But some water does require further treatment, especially if it is going to be reused by humans.

• Processes with such names as *reverse osmosis* and *electrodialysis* can remove "dissolved" solids—solids that can pass easily through other kinds of filters. Then the water is filtered and treated chemically to remove phosphorous, ammonia, nitrogen, and phosphates.

• If the water is going to be made safe for drinking, it is also treated with chlorine or disinfected by ozone.

That's it! The water is clean. (Uncle John wouldn't want to drink it, but that doesn't mean it isn't clean.)

DOWN-HOME FLUSHING

Not everyone is hooked up to a water treatment facility. If you live out in the country, you may be hooked up to a septic tank, which performs the same wastewater treatment functions, only more simply and naturally:

• The water from your toilets, bathtubs, showers, and sinks feed into a simple tank, usually made of concrete, cinder blocks, or metal.

• Solid matter settles to the bottom and the liquid remains on top.

• The liquid overflows into a system of underground trenches, often filled with rocks or gravel, where it can safely dissipate into the surrounding soil and biodegrade naturally.

• The solids settle at the bottom of the tank and break down organically. You can help the process along by adding special yeast and other treatments to the septic tank; if this isn't enough, it may have to be pumped out.

* * *

"Power corrupts. Absolute power is kind of neat."

—John Lehman, US secretary of the Navy

Fastest way to wake up a penguin, according to French scientists: Touch their feet.

BRI BRAINTEASERS

BRI stalwart David Zapp collected these puzzles...and dared us to solve them. Naturally, Uncle John immediately took them to our "research lab" and pronounced them bona fide bathroom reading. Now, we "pass" them on to you. *(Answers are on page 516.)*

1. A murderer is condemned to death. He has to choose between three rooms. The first is full of raging fires, the second is full of assassins with loaded guns, and the third is full of lions that haven't eaten in three years.

Which room is safest?

2. Can you name three consecutive days without using the words Monday, Tuesday, Wednesday, Thursday, Friday, Saturday, or Sunday?

3. A man is found dead in the Arctic with a pack on his back.

What happened?

4. A man pushes a car up to a hotel and tells the owner he's bankrupt.

What's going on?

5. You have two plastic jugs filled with water. How can you put all the water into a barrel, without using the jugs or any dividers, and still tell which water came from which jug?

6. This is an unusual paragraph. I'm curious how quickly you can find out what is so unusual about it? It looks so plain you would think nothing was wrong with it. In fact, nothing is wrong with it. It is unusual, though. Study it, think about it...but you still may not find anything odd.

7. A carrot, two lumps of coal, and a pipe lie together in the middle of a field.

What happened?

8. A woman shoots her husband. Then she holds him under water for over five minutes. Finally, she hangs him. But five minutes later, they both go out and enjoy a wonderful dinner together.

How can this be?

9. What's black when you buy it, red when you use it, and gray when you throw it away?

10. A man is born in 1972 and dies in 1952 at age 25.

What's the deal?

Longest name in the Bible: Mahershalalhashbaz (Isaiah 8:1).

LEMME EXPLAIN...

Free advice from Uncle John: When you're caught red-handed, it's better just to fess up and take your lumps. Here are a few people who would have done well to follow his advice.

SCOOBY-DOOFUS

In August 1996 in Tampa, Florida, police arrested Robert Meier and charged him with credit fraud for marrying his comatose girlfriend only hours before she died...so he could rack up more than $20,000 in charges on her credit cards. Meier's excuse: It was his girlfriend's dog's fault. According to a police spokesperson, "He said the dog told him she would want him to have a better life, so it would be OK to use her credit cards."

WHO'S KIDDING WHO?

In February 1997, Cathleen Byers, former manager of the Oregon Urban Rural Credit Union, was arrested for embezzlement. Was she guilty? Byers admitted stealing $630,000 over six years but claimed that she wasn't *really* guilty because she suffers from multiple personality disorder. One of her other personalities—Ava, Joy, Elizabeth, Tillie, Claudia, C. J., Katy, Roman, Cookie, Mariah, Frogger, Chrissy, or Colleen—must have done it without her knowledge. An expert testified that whichever alter-personality took the money didn't know right from wrong and that Byers wasn't even aware of what her alter-self was up to. The judge didn't buy it, arguing that Byers "should have been clued in by the new house and the luxury cars."

DRIVEN TO DRINK

After only one month on the job, Calgary, Alberta, school bus driver Marvin Franks was arrested for driving his bus while under the influence of alcohol. Police pulled Franks's bus over and administered a breath test after a terrified student called 911 using her cell phone. The bus driver was found to have a blood-alcohol level three times the legal limit. In an interview with the *Calgary Sun,* Franks admitted to having two beers before starting his route, on top of being hungover from drinking the night before. But he blamed his drinking on job stress, which he

The only four countries on Earth with one-syllable names: Chad, France, Greece, and Spain.

blamed on the kids he drives to school. "If you had these kids on your bus, you'd drink too," he explained.

LOUNGE LIZARD

In March 2002, 47-year-old Susan Wallace, a former British Airways flight attendant, was convicted of animal cruelty after she threw Igwig, her three-foot-long iguana, at a doorman and then later at a policeman following an altercation in a pub. Wallace maintains that she is innocent because Igwig acted of his own volition. "He probably jumped in defense of me. He's done that before," she said. (Igwig is now banned from the pub.)

STRAIGHT SHOOTER

In May 2001, David Duyst of Grand Rapids, Michigan, was convicted of murdering his wife and was then sentenced to life without parole. Yet to this day, Duyst insists that he's not guilty, despite a mountain of forensic evidence against him. So how'd she die? According to Duyst, she committed suicide by shooting herself... *twice*, in the *back* of her head.

SIDE ORDER OF COMPASSION, PLEASE

In October 2001, professional boxer Waxxem Fikes, 35, served five days in an Akron, Ohio, jail after assaulting a waiter at Swenson's restaurant. According to testimony, Fikes was "aggressively complaining" that the onions on his double cheeseburger were unsatisfactory. "I told him that I expect the onions to be crisp, tender and succulent, and bursting with flavor," Fikes testified. "They were not. My hands are lethal weapons or whatever, I know that. But he had no compassion for what I was talking about."

BODY OF EVIDENCE

In March 2001, a woman in Munich, Germany, saw a neighbor carrying a dead body into his apartment. She called the police. When the suspect answered the door in a "surprised and disturbed state," officers thought for sure that they had a murderer on their hands. Not quite. As the embarrassed man explained, the "dead body" was actually a life-sized silicon doll that he'd just bought at an adult bookstore.

Q: What's the French word for walkie-talkie? A: *Talkie-walkie.*

UNDERWEAR IN THE NEWS

A cosmic question: when is underwear newsworthy?
The answer: it's newsworthy when it's...

HEAD-WARMING UNDERWEAR

In March 2002, Reuters reported that maternity wards in Sweden were using underpants as caps for newborns. Why? Because when they use real baby caps, people steal them. "We got tired of buying new caps all the time," said one nurse; so they started using adult hospital-issue underwear instead. She said if you roll up the underpants nicely on the baby's tiny head, it doesn't look that bad.

MODERN ART UNDERWEAR

In April 2001, San Francisco conceptual artist Nicolino unveiled his latest sculpture: a 1,000-pound "Bra Ball" made up of bras donated by 20,000 women, including supermodel Naomi Campbell. That wasn't Nicolino's first brassiere-inspired work. He once tried to fly a 40,000-bra tapestry over the White House using 10 breast-shaped helium balloons to support it.

PRISONERS' UNDERWEAR

Officials in Linn County, Oregon, have banned underwear for jail inmates, saying it's too expensive to wash and replace. It's also dangerous: an inmate recently tried to hang himself with the elastic on his briefs, said a sheriff. When a prisoner protested the new policy, claiming that it's his "constitutional right" to wear underpants, Sheriff Dave Burright noted, "I don't remember Thomas Jefferson putting anything about underwear in the Constitution."

"SHOW-ME" UNDERWEAR

Every July, people from all over the world travel to Berlin, Germany, to celebrate "freedom and sensuality" at the city's annual "Love Parade." In 2002 city officials came up with an odd promotion for the event: they decided to sell pairs of thong underwear as tickets to the subway. Available in black or white, the unisex garments cost 12 euros (about $8) and were good for travel all day. To get on the train, all riders had to do was show their thongs. Ticket inpsectors said that people wouldn't have to remove the underwear to get on the train...but they would need to be "flashed."

DUTY-FREE UNDERWEAR

Customs officers in the Czech Republic stopped a car at the border and promptly arrested the driver for smuggling. To avoid paying import duties, the man had hidden contraband inside every door and seat of the car and even behind the dashboard. The contraband: 1,400 pairs of ladies' panties.

EDIBLE COSMIC UNDERWEAR

In 1999 Russian scientists reported that they were working to solve a problem as old as the space program: what to do with the dirty underwear? Storage space is precious on the ever-longer trips, and engineers have increasing difficulty finding room for used undies. Cosmonauts complain when they're ordered to wear their underwear too long, so the scientists came up with a solution: develop a bacteria that can eat underwear. They hope to have it perfected by 2017. Bonus: The bacteria will also release methane gas, which could then be used as fuel.

HAVOC-WREAKING UNDERWEAR

In June 2001, after two sewer breakdowns that caused massive "solid-waste" flooding, officials in Kannapolis, North Carolina, issued this plea to residents: Stop flushing your underwear down the toilet. According to Jeff Rogers, operations manager with the Sewer Department, workers pulled wadded rags from the lift station pump...and they looked a lot like underwear. "People flush all kinds of different things that they shouldn't be flushing," he said. "We definitely don't want them flushing any underpants."

SANCTIFIED UNDERWEAR

Two women have opened a store in Raleigh, North Carolina, hoping to create a new market: lingerie for religious women. The Seek Ye First Lingerie shop appeals to women who want to be "alluring, but not sleazy," said the two Baptist owners. Apparently customers like the idea of it's-no-sin underwear—the owners report brisk sales at the "thong rack."

Population of the American colonies in 1610: 350.

MY BODY LIES OVER THE OCEAN

When someone passes away and their remains are buried or cremated, it's said that they are being "laid to rest." Unfortunately, that's not always the case. For some people, the journey is just beginning.

DOROTHY PARKER

Claim to Fame: Writer, critic, and member of New York's famous Algonquin Round Table in the 1920s and 1930s

Final Resting Place: Her ashes were interred in 1988, after spending more than 15 years in a filing cabinet.

Details: Parker died in June 1967. She left instructions that her body be cremated, but didn't specify what she wanted done after that. When nobody showed up to claim the ashes, the funeral home stored them (for a few years), then mailed them to her lawyers. The lawyers put the box containing her ashes on top of a filing cabinet, apparently waiting for Parker's friend and executor, Lillian Hellman, to collect them. Hellman never did, so when she died in 1984, the law firm began meeting with Parker's surviving friends to figure out what to do.

Parker had left her entire estate to Martin Luther King, Jr. (whom she had never met), and when he was assassinated, everything went to the NAACP. When both the Algonquin Hotel (her legendary hangout) and the *New Yorker* magazine (her publisher) turned down Parker's ashes, the NAACP volunteered to create a memorial garden for her at their headquarters in Baltimore. Finally, in 1988, Parker's ashes were placed in an urn next to a marker inscribed with Parker's self-penned epitaph: "Excuse My Dust."

THOMAS PAINE

Claim to Fame: Founding Father and author of "Common Sense," a political pamphlet that helped spark the American Revolution

Final Resting Place: Unknown

Details: Paine didn't mince his words; he offended just about everyone he knew in the United States, England, and France.

There are over 15,000 miles of neon lights in the signs along the Las Vegas strip.

When he died in 1809 at the age of 72, he had few friends left among the Founding Fathers. He was buried on his farm in New Rochelle, New York; only six people attended his funeral.

Ten years later, an English admirer named William Cobbett decided to return Paine to England, where he could be given a proper funeral and burial. Rather than getting permission from Paine's relatives or the new owners of his farm, Cobbett just dug the body up and snuck it to England in a shipping crate. But since he didn't have money for a funeral or a decent grave, Cobbett had to stage a series of "bone rallies" across England, raising money by charging for a peek at Paine's corpse.

No luck—the public wasn't interested. When Cobbett couldn't even interest people in buying locks of the dead man's hair, he finally gave up and stored the bones under his bed.

When Cobbett died penniless in 1835, the bones were seized as part of his estate and scheduled to be auctioned off to pay his creditors. Even that plan failed—the auctioneer balked at the idea of selling human remains to satisfy a debt. Paine's skeleton was turned over to Cobbett's son, and what he did with it remains a mystery.

THE HEART OF LOUIS XIV

Claim to Fame: King of France from 1643 to 1715

Final Resting Place: An English dinner plate

Details: During the French Revolution, as the country collapsed into anarchy, Louis XIV's tomb was raided and his embalmed heart was stolen. It was eventually purchased by an English nobleman named Lord Harcourt. Harcourt sold it to the Reverend William Buckland, dean of Westminster Cathedral; when Buckland died in 1856, the heart was passed on to his son Francis.

Francis Buckland was a peculiar man with some peculiar theories. He believed that the way to assure national security was to make England completely food self-sufficient and that the best way to do that was to raise—and eat—exotic animals. How exotic? Over time Buckland graduated from eating ostrich and buffalo to more unusual fare, including moles, flies, slugs, and porpoise heads. He eventually decided that even the king of France himself was fair game as a protein source, so one night he cooked up the royal heart and ate it. "Never before," he told his astonished dinner guests, "have I eaten the heart of a king."

Bad omen? If you add up all the numbers of the roulette wheel (1 to 36), the sum is 666.

AMAZING LUCK

Sometimes we're blessed with it, sometimes we're cursed with it—dumb luck. Here are some examples of people who lucked out...for better or worse.

DOMO ARIGATO

Jason Powell worked on a grass farm in Corvallis, Oregon. In early 2002, he lost his wallet somewhere in the fields and figured it was gone for good. But it wasn't. Apparently it was picked up by a combine, then baled up with the straw and exported to Japan. Six months later, Powell received the wallet in the mail—returned to him by the Japanese farmer who found it—with his driver's license, credit cards, and $6 still inside.

GOOD THING THEY DIDN'T CLEAN UP

While visiting their sons in Nebraska, Larry and Leita Hatch stopped at a local Burger King. Larry bought a soft drink and when he peeled off the "Cash Is King" game sticker, he became the only $1 million winner in the entire country. (Wait, it gets better.) He stopped at a grocery store to make a copy of the ticket, but when he got to his son's house, he found he'd lost the original. So he went back to the grocery store—three hours later—and calmly picked up the ticket where it was lying...on the floor in the checkout line.

GOOD THING THEY DIDN'T CLEAN UP, PART II

Even if you have a winning lottery ticket, you have to turn it in before the deadline in order to claim your prize. In 1994 Duane and Nancy Black of Bullhead City, Arizona, read about an unclaimed lottery ticket. Value: $1.8 million. So just for the heck of it they decided to look through their stash of old tickets—and they found the winner. They immediately got on a plane to Phoenix and claimed their prize...two hours before the six-month ticket expired.

HEEEERE, LITTLE FISHY

In October 1999, 56-year-old Bev Marshall-Smith was surf-fishing off New Zealand's North Island when a large fish chased her lure into the shallows. Thrilled, she grabbed a piece of driftwood and charged into the water to get it. She must not have been able to see what she'd caught because when the fish refused to go quietly, she started clubbing it. "Every time he wrestled, I hit him," she said. Ultimately, she beat it to death...but the wrestling match could have ended differently. When she went in to collect her prize, she discovered she'd been wrestling with a six-foot blue shark.

THE LUCKIEST-UNLUCKIEST AWARD

On April 3, 1996, Mohamed Samir Ferrat, an Algerian business associate of U.S. Commerce Secretary Ron Brown, was scheduled to fly with Brown from Bosnia to Croatia. In a bizarre twist of fate, Ferrat backed out of the trip at the last minute. Brown's plane crashed, killing all 35 passengers. Ferrat probably felt like a lucky man, but only three months later, on July 17, he boarded TWA flight 800, which exploded over Long Island Sound, killing all 230 passengers and crewmembers...including Ferrat.

PICK *ME* A WINNER

Every year the Dearborn Heights Police Supervisors Association holds a raffle in Taylor, Michigan, and because it's a fundraiser for the police, they're careful to be sure everything is aboveboard. The prize for the 2001 raffle was a $20,000 Harley-Davidson Road King Classic; the winning ticket was to be picked by the 2000 winner, an autoworker named Tom Grochoki. There were 7,800 tickets in the barrel. Grochoki picked one, handed it to Lt. Karl Kapelczak, and went back to the crowd to hear the winner's name announced. The winner: Tom Grochoki.

THE UNLUCKIEST-LUCKIEST AWARD

It was bad luck when a 20-year-old Greek man accidentally shot himself in the head with his speargun while fishing off the island of Crete. A lifeguard found him floating in the water six hours later, the spear entering his jaw, going through his brain, and protruding from the top of his skull. But it was incredibly good luck when surgeons discovered that the spear had passed through one of the spaces in the brain that are nonfunctional—if it was just millimeters to the left or right he would have suffered serious brain injury or died. They removed it in a three-hour operation that left the man with no brain damage and no health problems.

To pass U.S. Army basic training, men have to do 40 push-ups...

CAUGHT IN THE ACT

Things aren't always as they seem, and savvy marketers can turn lying into an art form. But sometimes they get caught.

THE PRODUCT: Heinz Ketchup

YOU ASSUME: When you buy a bottle of ketchup that says "20 oz." on it, you get 20 ounces of ketchup.

WOULD THEY LIE TO US? Bill Baker of Redding, California, bought a 20-ounce bottle of ketchup for his wife's meatloaf. The recipe called for 20 ounces exactly, but when they poured it in the measuring cup, it was an ounce and a half short.

EXPOSED: Bill got ticked off. "If it says 20 ounces, it should be 20 ounces," he said. He called the state's Division of Measurement, setting off a five-year statewide investigation of H. J. Heinz Co. What did they find? Heinz's bottled products, from the 20-ounce to the 64-ounce size, were regularly 0.5% to 2% short. That may not seem like much, but officials estimated that Californians had been cheated out of 10 million ounces—78,124 gallons—of the red stuff. That's $650,000 worth of ketchup. Heinz was ordered to pay $180,000 in civil penalties, and agreed to overfill their bottles for one year—by about 10 million ounces.

THE PRODUCT: Used cars

YOU ASSUME: When you buy a used car from big-name automaker's dealership, you're getting a safe, reliable car.

WOULD THEY LIE TO US? Auto manufacturers buy back about 100,000 cars every year because of defects. Under federal "lemon laws," if they can't fix a car's problem, they have to buy it back. Where does it go from there? For years automakers claimed they would never resell a defective car; it would either be destroyed or studied by their engineers.

EXPOSED: In March 2001, in a lawsuit over a "laundered lemon" sold to a North Carolina couple, DaimlerChrysler was forced to reveal some incriminating facts: Between 1993 and 2000, the auto giant had paid $1.3 billion to buy back more than 50,000 vehicles—and resold nearly all of them, recouping two-thirds of the buyback cost. They had been sold to Chrysler dealers who then resold them to the public. And, most damaging to the company, many of the legally required disclosure forms were unsigned, meaning buyers were told nothing about the cars' histories.

In July 2001, Chrysler settled with the couple for an undisclosed amount, but the company was still facing a class-action suit inspired by the case. In December 2001, another couple in California won a similar case against Ford Motor Co., who, the jury ruled, had knowingly resold them a lemon. Amount the jury ordered Ford to pay: $10 million.

THE PRODUCT: Movie reviews

YOU ASSUME: The movie reviews you read in newspapers and magazines are from authentic, unbiased movie critics.

WOULD THEY LIE TO US? In 2001 several advertisements for Sony-made films featured quotes from reviews by "David Manning" of "*The Ridgefield Press*," a small paper in Connecticut. Manning always seemed to give Sony's movies high praise. His take on *A Knight's Tale* star Heath Ledger: "This year's hottest new star!"

EXPOSED: After *Newsweek* reporter John Horn questioned the authenticity of the ads in June 2001, and the state of Connecticut investigated, Sony admitted they'd written the reviews themselves. David Manning didn't exist, and the real *Ridgefield Press* knew nothing about it. The investigation also revealed that people appearing in Sony's TV commercials—who seemed to be genuine moviegoers—were actually Sony employees. "These deceptive ads deserve two thumbs down," said state Attorney General Richard Blumenthal. In February 2002, Sony was fined $325,000 and agreed to stop the practice. After the case, Universal Pictures, 20th Century Fox, and Artisan Entertainment all admitted that they, too, had used employees and actors posing as moviegoers in their TV ads.

OVEREXPOSED: Shortly after the fake reviewer was revealed, two men in California filed a class-action lawsuit against Sony for "deliberately deceiving consumers." By July, 10 more had been filed against all of Hollywood's major movie studios over deceptive advertising practices. The verdict? Coming soon to a courthouse near you.

Face facts: In a standard deck of cards, the king of hearts is the only king with no moustache.

WARNING LABELS

Some things in life should go without saying, but there's always the occasional moron who needs to be told not to use a blowtorch while sleeping.

On a Duraflame fireplace log: "Caution—Risk of Fire."

On a compact disc player: "Do not use the Ultradisc 2000 as a projectile in a catapult."

On a propane blowtorch: "Never use while sleeping."

On a box of rat poison: "Warning: Has been found to cause cancer in laboratory mice."

On an air conditioner: "Avoid dropping air conditioners out of windows."

On a vacuum cleaner: "Do not use to pick up anything that is currently burning."

On a Batman costume: "Warning: Cape does not enable user to fly."

On a bottle of hair coloring: "Do not use as an ice cream topping."

On a curling iron: "Warning: This product can burn eyes."

On a cardboard sunshield for a car: "Do not drive with sunshield in place."

On a toner cartridge: "Do not eat toner."

On a toilet bowl cleaning brush: "Do not use orally."

On a pair of shin guards: "Shin pads cannot protect any part of the body they do not cover."

On a portable stroller: "Caution: Remove infant before folding for storage."

On a plastic, 13-inch wheelbarrow wheel: "Not intended for highway use."

On a laser pointer: "Do not look into laser with remaining eye."

In a microwave oven manual: "Do not use for drying pets."

In the instructions for a digital thermometer: "Do not use orally after using rectally."

First state to require license plates on cars: New York, in 1901.

LET'S PLAY SPACEWAR!

Three years after a government physicist named William Higinbotham created the first video game, Tennis for Two (see page 65), some students at MIT invented a game called Spacewar! Here's their story.

NOT EXACTLY A LAPTOP

If you ever get a chance to see a picture of the Electronic Numerical Integrator and Computer (ENIAC for short), you probably won't recognize it for what it is. Completed in 1945, the ENIAC is considered to be the first practical digital computer ever made.

ENIAC was *the* supercomputer of its day. It was as big as a three-bedroom house and weighed more than 60,000 pounds. It contained more than 18,000 vacuum tubes, each one the size of a lightbulb. And because the tubes burned out so frequently (2,000 a month on average), ENIAC was out of order about a third of the time.

Even when it was working, ENIAC couldn't do very much: Its operators programmed it manually, spending hours or even days flipping switches and rewiring circuits. And ENIAC couldn't store these "programs," so each time the operators finished one computational task (calculating the path of an artillery shell, for example) and wanted to start another (nuclear weapons research), they had to flip the switches and rewire the whole computer all over again. ENIAC didn't have a keyboard or video screen, and it was more than 10,000 times slower than a modern personal computer.

COLLEGE SCREENING

Computers evolved slowly. Computers with video monitors, for example, were extremely rare through the 1960s. Only three universities in the entire United States—Stanford, the University of Utah, and MIT—had one.

So if it took 15 years for computer technology to progress to the point where exactly three American universities could own computers with video screens, how long do you think it took students at these universities to program the first video games into these supercomputers? A couple of months, at most.

SOMETHING TO SEE

MIT's legendary Whirlwind computer, for example, had a demonstration program called Bouncing Ball. Technically, it wasn't a video game because the viewer didn't do anything. You could only watch as a ball appeared at the top of the screen, then fell to the bottom and bounced around the screen, with a *thwok!* sound coming from the computer's speaker at each bounce. Eventually the ball lost its momentum and settled on the floor, finally rolling off to one side and out of the picture, at which point another ball would drop from the top of the screen.

But Bouncing Ball and the computer "games" that followed weren't supposed to be taken seriously. They were just things the early programmers dreamed up to amuse themselves and to demonstrate the number-crunching power of the Whirlwind computer. The best games were designed to tax the abilities of the computers to the limit. But other than that, they were "hacks," as they were called even then—programs with no constructive purpose whatsoever. The people who made them called themselves "hackers."

Mouse in the Maze was one of the earliest hacks. Designed for a supercomputer called the TX-O, it consisted of a mouse (the animal), a maze, and a piece of cheese. Using a special light pen, the player drew a maze right on the screen and then placed the cheese in the maze. Then the mouse searched through the maze and ate the cheese, leaving crumbs wherever it ate. An "improved" version had the mouse searching for martinis and after drinking the first one, staggering around the maze looking for the rest. There were other games—Tic-Tac-Toe, and a pattern-generating program called HAX—but nothing that would hold the interest of players for more than a few minutes.

COMPUTER TRAINING

Then in the fall of 1961, the Digital Equipment Corporation donated a state-of-the-art computer called the Programmable Data Processor (PDP-1) to MIT. The PDP-1 was smaller than the TX-O, much faster, and a lot easier to use.

Even before it arrived at MIT, the PDP-1 had captured the imagination of the university's Tech Model Railroad Club (TMRC). Club members had already spent several years "requisitioning" com-

South-pollywog: According to *Sesame Street,* Kermit the Frog is left-handed.

puter equipment from around campus and using it to automate their huge model railroad. They'd also spent a lot of time learning how to program the TX-O, so when the PDP-1 finally arrived on campus, they were already the best computer programmers around. And they were ready to hack.

The PDP-1 came with no software at all; almost everything had to be programmed from scratch. MIT students were doing much of the programming for little or no pay, so the professors who controlled access to the computer agreed to give them plenty of hack time in return. And what did they do with the hack time? They invented games.

LOST IN SPACE

Many TMRC members were science-fiction buffs; so it didn't take them long to decide what kind of game they wanted to create for the PDP-1: a space game—one that would push the computer's processing power to its limits. "The basic rules developed quickly," MIT alumnus J. M. Graetz remembers. "There would be at least two spaceships, each controlled by a set of console switches.... The ships would have a supply of rocket fuel and some sort of a weapon—a ray or a beam, or possibly a missile."

SPACEWAR!

TMRC member Steve "Slug" Russell wrote the first version of the game, taking about six months and 200 hours of computer time to do it. The game he came up with consisted of two spaceships, one wedge shaped, the other long and thin, which flew around the screen and battled one another by shooting "torpedoes"—dots of light—at each other. Each ship was controlled by a different set of four toggle switches on the PDP-1 console. One toggle switch made the ship rotate clockwise; a second made it rotate counterclockwise; a third switch provided thrust; and a fourth fired the torpedoes. (Ever play Asteroids? The controls were pretty much the same.)

Both ships were controlled by human players. There was no way to play the computer as your opponent, because once everything else had been programmed into it, "there wasn't enough computing power available to do a decent opponent," Russell remembered. He named his game Spacewar!

The "average" American CEO's pay has increased more than 600% since 1990.

A THOUSAND POINTS OF LIGHT

As soon as Russell got the game up and running, other TMRC members began making improvements:

• At first the game had no stars in the background, but the blank screen made it difficult to tell whether slow-moving ships were drifting closer to each other or farther apart. So Russell added a series of random dots...but they didn't last long. Using an astronomical reference book, another club member, Pete Samson, programmed in an accurate map of the night sky, including the relative brightness of each star.

• Another TMRC member named Dan Edwards inserted a sun—complete with accurate gravitational field—into the center of the screen. Now instead of sitting still in empty space, the ships were constantly being pulled toward the sun, and if they crashed into it they were destroyed. That helped to make the game more interesting, because it inserted an element that was beyond the players' control. It also made strategy more important, because skilled players could figure out ways to use gravity to their advantage.

• Graetz added a feature called "hyperspace." If a player got into trouble and was about to get killed, flipping the hyperspace toggle caused the ship to disappear for a few seconds and then reappear somewhere else on the screen, hopefully someplace less dangerous and not close to the sun. Graetz also inserted an element of risk—if a player hit hyperspace one too many times, their ship would be destroyed.

TOO MUCH OF A GOOD THING

The improvements made the game more interesting...which created a new set of problems. Spacewar! addicts played for hours on end, frantically flipping the toggle switches on the $120,000 computer until their elbows hurt. Needless to say, the computer wasn't designed with that kind of use (or abuse) in mind.

Rather than risk breaking the $120,000 computer, a couple of TMRC members scrounged wire, switches, and other parts from the model railroad and made another innovation—individual game controllers that they connected to the PDP-1 with lengths of electrical wire. Now the players could stand back from the computer and play as furiously as they wanted to, without damaging the computer or getting sore elbows.

Walt Disney World generates about 56 tons of trash every day.

BIRDS OF A FEATHER

So what do Steve Russell and the developers of Spacewar! have in common with Willy Higinbotham, creator of Tennis for Two? Two things—they never patented their invention; and they never made any money from it. Digital Equipment ended up giving Spacewar! away as a diagnostic program and it became popular with computer engineers and programmers all over the country... including a University of Utah student named Nolan Bushnell, who later founded Atari.

It turns out there was a way to make money off of Spacewar!... it just involved waiting for the price of computer technology to come down. In the mid-1970s, well after the video arcade craze was underway, an MIT graduate student named Larry Rosenthal decided to build an arcade version of Spacewar! as his master's thesis project. The game he created—sold as Space War and then as Space Wars—happened to hit the arcades in 1977, the same year that *Star Wars* hit the big screen.

Space War(s) had nothing to do with *Star Wars*, of course, but nobody cared. It quickly became the most popular arcade game ever... until a game called Space Invaders came along in 1978.

MEETING OF THE MINDS

As for Steve Russell, he not only never made a penny off the game he was largely responsible for creating, he never even graduated from MIT. He relocated to Seattle and got a job with a computer time-share company. One of his responsibilities was hiring local high school kids to come into the office and see if they could get the computers to crash. Lots of kids tried, but, according to Russell, only one kid had enough computer savvy to make the computers crash every time, no matter how hard Russell and his colleagues tried to thwart him.

The kid's name was Bill Gates. He never graduated from college, either.

The next phase of the history of video games will take us to the video arcade, so turn to page 314 and let's play Pong.

No matter how hard they try, scientists can't train houseflies to do tricks.

LOST INVENTIONS

True or false: Ever since some caveman got the bright idea of making tools, it's been a steady advance of ideas and innovation, from the wheel to the automobile and beyond. False. History is much messier than that. Many inventions have been made, lost, and reinvented later. Here are a few examples.

THE ELECTRIC BATTERY

The National Museum of Iraq has a collection of clay jars made by the Parthians, who once ruled the Middle East. One jar, however, dating from about 200 B.C., is not your ordinary container.

It's just over five inches high by three inches across. The opening was once sealed with asphalt, with a narrow iron rod sticking through it. Inside the jar was a copper sheet rolled into a tube and closed at the bottom with a copper disc. The iron rod hung down in the center of the tube.

The odd jar didn't attract much attention until around 1960, when researchers discovered that if the jar was filled with an acidic liquid (vinegar or fermented grape juice), it generated a small current, between 1.5 and 2 volts. Their conclusion: the jar was an electric battery. In the acidic liquid, electrons flowed from the copper tube to the iron rod—much like the batteries invented by Italian physicist Alessandro Volta around 1800.

But what would anyone in ancient Baghdad use a battery for? The most likely explanation is that they linked a series of batteries that were used to electroplate gold onto silver. Electroplating is a way of covering the surface of one metal with another metal, creating the false appeareance of a solid gold object. It involves passing an electric current through a solution, forcing positively charged metal particles onto a negatively charged surface. Experiments have shown that electroplating can indeed be done with modern batteries just like that ancient jar.

THE COMPUTER

In 1900 sponge divers found the wreck of an ancient ship 140 feet under water, near the Greek island of Antikythera. Many of the

Odds that a battery was bought during the Christmas season: 40%.

items retrieved from it were taken to the National Archaeological Museum in Athens, among them lumps of corroded bronze that looked like parts of a statue. But an archaeologist noticed some words inscribed on the metal and then found gears—and then realized it wasn't a statue, it was a machine.

Originally held together by a wooden box that fell apart when taken out of the water, the mechanism had dials on the outside and a complicated arrangement of wheels and differential gears inside. The inscription dated it between 100 B.C. and 30 A.D. and indicated that the contraption had something to do with astronomy.

A 1959 *Scientific American* article compared the object to "a well-made 18th-century clock." The "Antikythera mechanism," it said, was a model of the solar system which, like a modern computer, "used mechanical parts to save tedious calculation." Turned by hand, or perhaps by water power, the machine would calculate and display the position of the sun, moon, planets, and stars.

The find meant that historians had to rethink their whole concept of the ancient Greek world—and their concept of when computing machines were first invented.

THE SEISMOGRAPH

Domemico Salsano, an Italian clockmaker, is usually credited with inventing the seismograph in 1783. His "geo-sismometro" used an inked brush attached to a pendulum. The brush recorded earth-shaking vibrations on an ivory slab. It was sensitive enough to register quakes from 200 miles away.

But 1,500 years before that, a Chinese philosopher named Chang Hêng had already invented a device for detecting distant earthquakes. It was shaped like a big wine jar, about six feet across. On the outside were eight dragon heads with an open-mouthed toad beneath each one. Each dragon held a ball in its mouth. When a distant earthquake occurred, the dragon pointing in the direction of the quake dropped the ball into the mouth of the toad.

Nobody is sure exactly what mechanism was inside the jar, but modern seismologists assume that a pendulum was connected to the dragons. And, according to ancient records, the dragon jar worked.

Water freezes before a cockroach's blood will.

SPACE BATHROOM ALPHA

We're always interested in how astronauts "take care of business" in the weightlessness of space. Now that the International Space Station is up and running, we figured that it's time to revisit the subject.

BRAVE NEW WORLD

As we told you on page 25, millionaire American businessman Dennis Tito made history in April 2001 when he bought his way onto the International Space Station, also known as Space Station Alpha, by paying the Russian Space Agency a cool $20 million for the privilege of becoming the world's first space tourist.

Since then, NASA has agreed to allow more such trips. So in case you're planning to take a Space Station vacation, you might like to know what to expect if you get up there and have to... use the facilities.

The toilet on Space Station Alpha has a toilet seat and a bowl, but that's where any similarity to Earth toilets ends. Since there's no gravity in the space station, they can't use water to flush the toilet—there's no way to keep it in the bowl. The toilet flushes with "air currents." What does that mean? That's NASA's polite way of saying that you're pooping into a toilet bowl hooked up to a vacuum cleaner.

LOOKING OUT FOR NUMBER ONE

As for peeing, there's a special vacuum hose in the bathroom designed for that purpose. Everyone has to use the same hose, but each astronaut is issued their own custom-fitted "personal urine funnel" (yes, the male funnels are shaped differently from the female funnels). These special attachments help to prevent leakage into the Space Station's atmosphere and also helps to minimize the "yuck" factor associated with everyone having to pee into the same hose.

What happens next? Unlike the Space Shuttle, where the urine is collected into a storage tank and periodically vented into outer space, Space Station Alpha doesn't have that luxury. The Space Shuttle makes short trips and returns to Earth on a regular basis, so

The city of Chicago tows 55,000 junked cars to wrecking yards per year.

its water tanks are refilled before each new mission. But Space Station Alpha (hopefully) is never coming back down, and the astronauts who live and work there will be in space for weeks or even months on end. Sending up fresh supplies of water every couple of months would cost a fortune, so NASA developed a different strategy: the station is designed to recycle every single drop of water possible, including sweat, including the moisture the astronauts exhale when they breathe, *and* their urine.

WASTE NOT, WANT NOT

The Space Station toilet pumps the astro-urine into a machine called a Urine Processor, or UP (pronounced "you pee") for short. It works kind of like the spin cycle on a washing machine: the urine enters a cylindrical drum that rotates more than 300 times a minute; this causes the liquid to spread out in a thin layer across the surface of the drum. Most of the air has already been sucked out of the drum, creating a low-pressure environment that allows the water in the urine to boil off into steam at close to room temperature. The steam is then condensed back into liquid form. Everything else in the pee—minerals and salts—is collected in a filter, and the filters are changed at least once a month.

RIGHT BACK AT YOU

After the UP is finished, the "water" is pumped into a "Potable Water Processor," where it is mixed with all the other reclaimed water in the Space Station: shower water, water used when the astronauts wash their hands or brush their teeth, and moisture that's removed from the air by dehumidifiers. This waste water is pumped through a filter that removes any particles or debris. Then it's pumped through several other filters to remove any chemicals, and finally it's oxidized, or treated with oxygen, to remove any remaining chemicals and kill off any living organisms.

End result: Purified, drinkable water that is actually much cleaner than the water that comes out of your faucet at home. Really. It has almost no taste, because the water doesn't contain any dissolved minerals like tap water does on Earth. There's no smell, either. "That's easy to get rid of," says Alan Mortimer, head of Space Life Sciences at the Canadian Space Agency. "The things that smell are easy to take out."

Wasps kill more people in the U.S. every year than snakes, spiders, and scorpions combined.

HOUSTON, WE HAVE A PROBLEM

In all, the system is able to recycle about 95% of the space station's water. But what about the "solids"? The poop that's collected in Space Bathroom Alpha can't be recycled. Instead, it will be stored in sealed "toilet canisters" until one of the unmanned Russian *Progress* supply ships docks at the Space Station. After the fresh supplies are unloaded, the *Progress* is filled with the poop cans (and other garbage) and then jettisoned away from the station. Gravity pulls it back into the Earth's atmosphere, where it burns up on reentry.

These flaming fireballs of space poop are a huge improvement over the original Space Shuttle toilets. Those toilets had a 14-day holding capacity and could not be emptied during a mission. As soon as they filled up, the astronauts had to either return to Earth...or improvise. And even back on Earth, the toilets were not easily emptied. They had to be removed from the shuttle and flown to Houston to be cleaned by highly trained technicians.

WASHING UP

The International Space Station also has a shower, something the shuttle astronauts had to do without. (They had to make do with sponge baths and shampoo, originally designed for hospital patients, that didn't need to be rinsed out.)

Taking a shower in space is similar to taking one on Earth, except that in the absence of gravity, the water doesn't fall to the floor. It just floats around inside the shower stall, which is sealed to prevent the water from escaping into the rest of the Space Station. One advantage: Since the water floats around instead of going down the drain, you don't need as much to take your shower as you would on Earth. You only use about a gallon of water, and instead of moving in and out from under the showerhead, you just grab the floating globs of water and rub them on yourself. When you're finished, there's a vacuum hose attached to one wall that you use to suck up all the drops before leaving the shower.

*   *   *

According to surveys, 57% of Americans shower daily, 17% sing in the shower, 4% shower with the lights off, and 3% clean their pets by showering with them.

(About what?) According to doctors, babies dream in the womb.

THE WORLD'S WORST...

We were going to do a page of "bests"—but worsts are funnier. So put on a happy face and read about the worst...

...TRAFFIC CONGESTION A 2002 study found that traffic moved through central London at an average speed of 2.9 mph—slower than walking.

...VIEW The Grand Banks of Newfoundland, Canada, are blanketed by heavy fog for an average of one out of every three days—often for weeks at a time.

...CROSSWORD PUZZLE ANSWER In 1971, the *London Times* included this word in one of its daily puzzles: *honorificabilitudinitatibus*.

...REJECTION When King Harald Grenske of Norway proposed marriage to Queen Sigrid Storrada of Denmark in 996, she had him executed.

...MOVIE According to a nationwide poll conducted by the Hastings Bad Cinema Society, the worst movie of the 20th century was John Travolta's *Battlefield Earth*.

...VOTING "ERROR" In the 1928 Nigerian presidential election, Charles King beat Thomas Faulkner by 600,000 votes. One problem: Nigeria only had 15,000 registered voters.

...CONSTRUCTION PROJECT Workers spent 90 years building the Church of Corcuetos in Spain. The day after it was finally completed in 1625, it collapsed.

...TOURISTS According to a survey by the online travel service *expedia.com*, "Britons are the rudest, meanest, and worst-behaved holidaymakers in the world."

...HANDS IN FOOTBALL Quarterback Warren Moon fumbled the ball 161 times during his 17-year career.

...CAR Click and Clack, the *Car Talk* guys, polled listeners to find the lousiest make of car ever produced. The winner...er, we mean, loser: the Yugo.

A stone weighs slightly less at the equator than it does at the North Pole.

JUST JOSHING

Josh Billings was the pen name of humorist Henry Wheeler Shaw, born in 1818 in Massachusetts. In 1860 Shaw started writing homespun philosophies using rural dialect. In his day, Josh Billings was better known than his contemporary Mark Twain. Here are a few bits of Billings's "wizdum" in their original dialect. (By the way, the term "joshing" comes from…Josh Billings.)

"Thare iz nothing that yu and I make so menny blunders about, and the world so few, az the aktual amount ov our importance."

"Yung man, set down, and keep still—yu will hav plenty ov chances yet to make a phool ov yureself before yu die."

"He who reads and don't reflekt, iz like the one who eats and don't exercise."

"We read that Esaw sold out hiz birth rite for soup, and menny wonder at hiz extravegance, but Esaw diskovered arly, what menny a man haz diskovered since, that it iz hard work tew live on a pedigree."

"Whi iz it that we despize the man who puts himself in our power, and are quite az apt to respekt him just in proporshun az he iz out of our reach."

"Wize men go thru this world az boys go tew bed in the dark, whistling tew shorten the distance."

"Genius after all ain't ennything more than elegant kommon sense."

"Too mutch branes iz a hindrance to a bizzness man."

Q: "How fast duz sound travel?"

A: "This depends a good deal upon the natur ov the noize yu are talking about. The sound ov a dinner horn, for instance, travels a half a mile in a seckoned, while an invitashun tew git up in the morning I hav known to be 3 quarters ov an hour giong up two pair ov stairs, and then not hav strength enuff left tew be heard."

"About the best that enny ov us kan do iz tew konceal our phailings."

"It takes a smart man to conceal from others what he don't kno."

"The man who never makes enny blunders seldum makes enny good hits."

Poll result: It takes the average American 2.6 days to feel relaxed on a vacation.

LOVE AT FIRST SIGHT?

Uncle John actually fell in love at first sight. So smooth and shiny. Those perfect proportions. That beautiful white...porcelain. You thought we were talking about Mrs. Uncle John? Oh, yeah. Her too.

HERE'S LOOKING AT YOU

You're looking around a crowded room, and your eyes meet the eyes of another. Pow! A shock runs through your whole body! Are you in love? Maybe. Read on to find out. That jolt isn't imaginary. Scientists say that part of your brain actually perks up when you exchange looks with a person you consider attractive.

And just how did they discover that? British researchers used a special helmet to scan the brains of 16 volunteers (8 men and 8 women). Wearing an fMRI (functional magnetic resonance imaging) helmet, each volunteer looked at 160 photos of 40 complete strangers.

In some photos, the strangers were looking directly at the camera—which made them appear to be looking directly at the volunteer. In others, the stranger's eyes were turned away.

As the photos went flashing by—one every 3.5 seconds—the helmets recorded which part of the volunteer's brain was active. After the brain scan was finished, the volunteers went back to the pictures and rated each one for attractiveness. The results of the experiment were published in 2001 in *Nature* magazine.

REAL SPARKS

Every time a volunteer saw an attractive person looking right at them, the volunteer's ventral striatum lit up—that part of the brain is linked to the anticipation of a reward. But when the stranger in the photo was looking away, the magic didn't happen; there was much less brain activity, no matter how attractive the person in the photo. The researchers attributed that to disappointment—the volunteer had failed to make eye contact with an attractive face.

The brain response happened fast—in just nanoseconds.

Researchers think this means that it's automatic, that we're all wired for that kind of reaction.

EYES OF THE BEHOLDER

Does this mean that everybody responds to certain kinds of looks? The leading researcher, Dr. Knut Kampe of the Institute of Cognitive Neuroscience in London, commented that we all might naturally respond to people who look strong and healthy. That could be connected with survival. But Kampe said that each of the volunteers defined attractiveness in different ways, and conventional beauty wasn't the only important thing. Some looked for cheerfulness, others for a face that seemed to show empathy. Some even looked for motherliness.

IS IT LOVE?

So does it mean that love at first sight is real? Can we expect to instantly recognize our perfect mate? Probably not. Consider the following:

- Seeing a certain someone can get your brain buzzing—but so can seeing food when you're hungry. The ventral striatum that responded to the photos is the same area that lights up in hungry lab animals who think they're about to get fed. Gamblers and drug addicts have the same kind of reaction to the objects of their desire. That part of your brain gets excited when it expects *any* kind of reward.
- The brain's quick response helps explain why we make snap judgments about people we meet. But first impressions can be wrong.
- The same brain area lit up for any attractive face—no matter whether it was the opposite sex or the same sex as the volunteer. Researchers think that's because attractiveness often gets associated with social status. So maybe your brain assumes that hanging out with attractive people could improve your position. (In the case of monkeys, bonding with an animal higher up in the pecking order brings increased social status.)

So if you're expecting a future with someone based on the jolt you got when your eyes met—slow down. You'll have to engage some other part of your brain to find out whether the two of you actually get along.

The name "Ann" is used as a middle name 10 times more often than as a first name.

Q&A: ASK THE EXPERTS

More random questions, with answers from the nation's top trivia experts.

TOUCHY SUBJECT

Q: *Will you spread poison ivy if you touch the blisters?*

A: "Good news: you can't spread poison ivy by touching (or even breaking) the blisters. The belief that poison ivy spreads through the bloodstream is equally false.

"Why do blisters appear on different parts of the body days after the first signs? It probably wasn't just your skin that came in contact with the plant—it was also your clothing, gardening tools, etc. If it isn't washed off, the oil or resin from the plant can last almost indefinitely. If you're unaware you've encountered poison ivy (it takes two to four days for the first red spots to show), the resin could have been spread.

"Is there anything you can do to stop the spread? Yes. If you know you've just walked through a patch of poison ivy, wash the resin off immediately with soap and water. This also holds true for poison oak and poison sumac." (From *Old Wives' Tales*, by Sue Castle)

I YAM WHAT I YAM

Q: *I always thought yams and sweet potatoes were the same thing. However, when I asked for the yams at a recent family gathering, I was informed by one of my snotty cousins that no yams were on the menu.*

A: "Sorry, but your cousin is right. Contrary to what some grocery store produce guys may think, yams and sweet potatoes are unrelated vegetables, though in both cases you're eating the root of a tropical vine. Sweet potatoes, *Ipomoea batatas* (*batata* is the original Taino name, whence 'potato'), are an American plant of the morning glory family, whereas yams are of the genus *Dioscorea*. Yams, which are rarely seen in the United States and Canada but are a staple in tropical regions, can grow up to seven feet in length. The name is thought to derive from the West African word *nyami*, 'to eat.'" (From *The Straight Dope*, by Cecil Adams)

Cheap date: Sea urchins reproduce via a process called *fissiparity*—they split themselves in two.

ROLL THE DICE

Tired of reading palms? Sick of tea leaves? Ouija bored? Uncle John predicted that you would be. If you have a pair of dice lying around, here's another way to tell your fortune.

ASTRAGALOMANCY

Have you ever played Yahtzee or rolled dice in a bar? In Victorian England, people known as "dicers" told fortunes by tossing dice from a small cup held in their left hands. Telling fortunes with two dice is known as *astragalomancy*. (Using three dice is *cleromancy*.)

Give it a try! Tossing a pair of dice around is good for a few minutes of fun even if you aren't a true believer.

HOW TO DO IT

- Draw a circle about 12 inches in diameter on a piece of paper.
- Decide on a question that you want answered and ask it either silently or aloud as you shake the dice in your hand or in a cup. Then throw the dice into the circle, either one at a time or both at the same time.
- Add up the numbers on both dice to get the answer to your question. Sometimes the answer is precise, sometimes it's vague. (What did you expect? This *is* fortune telling, after all.)

ANSWERS

2—The answer is no.

3—If you act cautiously in the coming days, you can expect a pleasant surprise.

4—You will have good luck when you expect it least.

5—Your question will be answered in a surprising way.

6—Some form of divine intervention will provide you with an answer.

7—You will win.

8—You already know the answer to your question (so stop playing with dice and find something better to do).

9—If the answer is yes, it's only because of a twist of fate.

10—Count on success!

11—Stay calm, be prepared, know that fate is on your side.

12—Regardless of what happens, you will feel content about it.

Most widely used herb in the world: parsley.

CIRCULAR LOGIC

How many of your dice fell within the circle? That's part of your fortune, too:

- One die outside the circle means that you're likely to get the answer you want *eventually* but only "after your own thoughts set your wishes into motion."
- Two dice outside the circle: You'll get the answer you want, sooner than you think.

YES AND NO

Now here's where using dice to tell your fortune can get confusing:

- Let's say you ask the question, "Will I make a million dollars?" You want the answer to be "yes," but your roll adds up to two, so the answer is "no."
- But both dice land outside the circle, which means you'll get the answer you want—"*yes*" (instead of the "no" you just rolled), and you'll get that "yes" sooner than you think. But wait a minute—you just rolled a "yes" *and* a "no." What's that supposed to mean? Does it mean maybe? Do you roll the dice again?
- Uncle John solved the problem by asking the question, "Does fortune telling with dice really work?"

He rolled a two. You're on your own.

* * *

MORE WAYS TO TELL A FORTUNE

Ailuromancy: Observe how a cat jumps.

Sycomancy: Write a question on a leaf, leave the leaf in the sun. "If the leaf shrivels quickly, the answer is no." Otherwise the answer is yes.

Keriomancy: Study the flickering flame of a candle.

Aleuromancy: Read messages in baked balls of dough.

Oomancy: Crack an egg into a glass of water and study the shapes the egg white forms in the water.

Scrying: Study "crystals, mirrors, bowls of water, ink, blood, flames, or other shiny objects."

Ceromancy: Drop some melted wax into water and study the shapes that are formed.

D.C. FOLLIES

Some people say the best comedy is on TV.
We say it's in Washington, D.C.

DON'T QUIT YOUR DAY JOB

"Concerned that 'the pickup owners of this nation might get screwed in all this gas-guzzler talk about SUVs and vans,' **Zell Miller (D-Ga.)** introduced an amendment to keep pickup fuel economy requirements at 20.7 mpg. He also co-wrote, sang, and recorded 'The Talking Pickup Truck Blues.'

"A sample of the lyrics: 'Sure, an SUV is classy travel, / But it ain't much good for haulin' gravel, / Or hay or seed or bovine feces. / So please, don't make my pickup truck an endangered species.'"

—***Fox News***

SHAMELESS EXPLOITATION

"A controversy started September 11 when **Brian Kerns (R-Ind.)** gave the *Indianapolis Star* a harrowing account of watching a hijacked plane slam into the Pentagon during his commute on George Washington Memorial Parkway. 'I'm in shock,' he said. 'I still can't believe it. I drove into the office and told my staff to go home.'

"The *Indianapolis Star* reported, however, that the plane in question never flew over that parkway. And an American Legion official said he remembers being in Kerns's office with the congressman when networks reported the Pentagon attack. Kerns's response when pressed on whether he was mistaken about what he saw: 'Who knows?'"

—Associated Press

TOOT-TOOT

"Patrick Kennedy (D-R.I.) was accused of causing $28,000 in damage to a rented yacht on a Y2K booze cruise. He later appeared at a political roast dressed in a sailor suit and capped off the evening by singing 'Patrick the Sailor Man.' At the same roast, the admitted former cokehead joked about Senator Lincoln Chafee (R-R.I.), another admitted former cokehead: 'Now when I hear

Bess Truman is the only First Lady to have a hurricane named after her.

someone talking about a Rhode Island politician whose father was a senator and who got to Washington on his family name, used cocaine, and wasn't very smart, I know there is only a 50-50 chance it's me.'"

—*Mother Jones*

TAKE YOUR CHILD TO WORK DAY?

"Answering questions about whether his recent election was helped by nepotism (after receiving $1 million from the Republican Party's coffers), **Bill Shuster (R-Pa.)**, son of Pennsylvania representative Bud Shuster, insisted 'This is about Bill Shuster...and Bill Shuster standing on his own two feet.' Maybe. We wonder if Solicitor of the Labor Department Eugene Scalia, son of Antonin; Health and Human Services Inspector General Janet Rehnquist, daughter of William; FCC chair Michael Powell, son of Colin; and President George W. Bush feel the same way."

—*Roll Call*

ROCKET MAN

"In September 1996, **Mickey Kalinay (D)** was defeated in the Democratic primary for the U.S. Senate in Wyoming...despite his tantalizing proposal to make the space program more efficient by constructing a 22,000-mile-high tower so that space stations can be accessed by electromagnetic rail cars."

—*News of the Weird*

SOME THINGS NEVER CHANGE

"The last time **former Vice-President Dan Quayle (R)** lived in Washington, his words were parsed almost as closely as the current president's. He still lets off the occasional zinger; during an appearance on MSNBC's *Hardball*, as he tried to 'set aside the Middle East peace situation' from the war on terrorism, he asked: 'How many Palestinians were on those airplanes on September 9? None.'"

—*Salon.com*

WHAT!?!

"In 1988, **Tom DeLay (R-Tx.)** explained to reporters his lack of service in the Vietnam War, despite being eligible and healthy. 'So many minority youths had volunteered,' he claimed, 'that there was literally no room for patriotic folks like myself.'"

—online columnist, Ted Barlow

Bad news/good news: Friday the 13th comes at least once...

SNL PART II: ON THE AIR

Lorne Michaels had all of the ingredients for Saturday Night, *now he had to figure out how to mix them together.* *(Part I is on page 79.)*

BARELY CONTROLLED CHAOS

The scheduled air date for the first episode of *NBC's Saturday Night* was October 11, 1975. Just about everyone—from the executives to the crew—didn't see the show lasting an entire season... except for Lorne Michaels. He reassured his worried cast and writers on the 17th floor that their grandchildren would be watching reruns of the first episode in history class. But no one was convinced. And the chaos of the final week leading up to the premiere didn't help matters.

By the time Saturday rolled around, Michaels had no lighting director (he had fired two already); the antiquated sound system had broken down; and instead of the brick wall they were promised for a backdrop, they had a ton of uncut bricks piled in the middle of the floor.

While Michaels was busy ordering script changes and settling various arguments, Ebersol brought news that the network had ordered the show's celebrity host, George Carlin, to wear a suit and tie—the embodiment of everything *Saturday Night* was against. (Carlin compromised by wearing a sport coat with a T-shirt underneath.)

THE FIRST SKETCH

A lot of thought went into the best way to begin the show. Michaels wanted people to know from the get-go that they were seeing something different. His solution: Begin with a "cold opening." When the clock struck 11:30 p.m., viewers were pulled immediately into a sketch featuring Michael O'Donoghue and John Belushi as, respectively, professor and student.

O'Donoghue: "Let us begin. Repeat after me. I would like..."

Belushi (*in a thick foreign accent*)**:** "I would like..."

O'Donoghue: "...to feed your fingertips..."

Belushi: "...to feed your feengerteeps..."

O'Donoghue: "...to the wolverines."

Belushi: "...to thee wolvereeenes."

This goes on for a few minutes until O'Donoghue clutches his heart and keels over. Belushi sits there, shrugs, then grabs his heart and keels over. The puzzled audience is left hanging for a moment, and then **Chevy Chase** *enters wearing a stage manager's headset. He looks at the two figures lying on the floor, then breaks out into a big grin and says to the camera:* "Live from New York, it's Saturday Night!"

The show didn't go off without a hitch, but despite a few miscues, they had pulled it off—within the allotted budget—a feat that impressed the skeptical NBC brass.

SHOCKING COMEDY

The ratings for the first few episodes were considerably better than those for *Tonight Show* reruns (although still not enough to pull in major advertising dollars), while the initial reviews were a bit mixed. But a big boost came from the highly touted TV critic Tom Shales:

> NBC's *Saturday Night* can boast the freshest satire on commercial TV, but it is more than that, it is probably the first network series produced by and for the television generation....It is a live, lively, raucously disdainful view of a world that television has largely shaped. Or misshaped.

Younger viewers agreed. Here was a show that actually *made fun* of television. Dick Ebersol referred to it as "the post-Watergate victory party for the Woodstock generation."

As much as kids loved the show, grown-ups hated it. Johnny Carson echoed a lot of aging comedians' views when he described the Not Ready For Primetime Players as a bunch of amateurs who couldn't "ad-lib a fart at a bean-eating contest." It was a completely different brand of comedy than they were used to. Comedians like Bob Hope and Milton Berle made their audience comfortable, then made them laugh. By mocking the establishment, *Saturday Night* made some viewers uncomfortable. Just to make fun of politicians in general wasn't enough, this new show singled out specific politicians, particlularly presidents, and ridiculed them. All of a sudden, the revolution was being televised.

"I'M CHEVY CHASE AND YOU'RE NOT"

The first season belonged to Chase. Because he anchored "Weekend

The Bayer Aspirin Company trademarked the brand name Heroin in 1898.

Update," he got to say his name every week, and he was the only one who did. The show opened without naming any of the cast, so Chase's tagline, along with his clumsy portrayal of President Ford, thrust him into the spotlight. He alone was nominated for an Emmy Award and then was named "heir apparent to Johnny Carson" by *New York* magazine. The other cast members were jealous—especially Belushi—creating an intense air of discord backstage.

But it didn't matter. Chase left shortly into the second season to pursue a woman (he married her) and a movie career in Hollywood. He later called his departure one of the biggest mistakes of his career. Michaels, on the other hand, realized that the show had an amazing potential to make stars, so he added the cast members' names and pictures to the opening credits. Meanwhile, ABC's *Saturday Night Live* was canceled, so Bill Murray was available to replace Chase in 1976.

SECOND SEASON SUCCESS

The ensuing season saw the cast, writers, and crew start to really come together. Recurring characters like the Coneheads and the Bees (which Belushi always hated) were quickly becoming household names. Catchphrases like "Jane, you ignorant slut" and "No Coke, Pepsi!" were becoming part of the national lexicon.

In the first season, Lorne Michaels had to search long and hard for willing hosts and musical guests; in the second season, they were calling him. When stand-up comedian Steve Martin first watched the show in a hotel room, he was blown away. "They did it," he said to himself. "They did the show everyone should have been doing." And then he made it his goal to be a part of it, which he did in the second season. He has since gone on to host *SNL* more times than anyone else.

HIGH TIMES

Another part of the show's success: drugs. "From the beginning," say Hill and Weingrad, "grass was a staple of the show, used regularly and openly." Cocaine was also used, although by fewer people and behind closed doors. One of *SNL*'s early masterpieces, a sketch called "The Final Days" that chronicles Nixon's downfall, was written by writers Al Franken and Tom Davis while they were on LSD. Drugs found their way into the sketches, too, something

Percentage of (dead) people who were cremated in 1975: 7%. In 2000: 26%.

that some cast members, most notably Chase—who once demonstrated the proper way to "shoot up"—would later regret. But it was just this kind of humor that made *Saturday Night* so popular with the youth culture.

THE BLUES BROTHERS RULE

By 1977 Belushi and Aykroyd were the show's big stars, and they often flexed their muscles by threatening to quit if they didn't get their way. Meanwhile the women—Radner, Newman, and Curtin—were feeling alienated by the drugged-out and sexist behavior of the men. Michaels was running himself ragged trying (unsuccessfully) to keep everyone happy, while Ebersol was under constant pressure from the network to curb the controversial subject matter.

In 1978 Chase hit it big with his movie *Foul Play*. Aykroyd and Belushi knew that movie careers were waiting for them as well and left after the fourth season to make *The Blues Brothers*. Instead of replacing them, Michaels hired only one new cast member, comedian Harry Shearer (who, years later, would add his vocal talents to *The Simpsons*).

FEATURED PLAYERS

In his quest to find the next big star, Michaels devised a billing called "featured player." Because they didn't have full cast-member status, he didn't have to pay them as much. He tried out band member Paul Shaffer (of David Letterman fame), writers Al Franken, Tom Davis, and Don Novello (Father Guido Sarducci), as well as Brian Doyle-Murray (brother of Bill), and Peter Aykroyd (brother of Dan). The result: A disastrous 1979 season.

Bill Murray and Gilda Radner, who dated on and off during *SNL*'s previous years, now couldn't stand each other. In fact, Murray couldn't stand anything about the show—the writers, the cast, his parts—and spent most of his time launching tirades. Laraine Newman and Garrett Morris were both battling depression, drug addictions, and the realization that Hollywood didn't want them. Lorne Michaels was also exhausted, and when contract negotiations broke down for a sixth season, he quit.

Things looked bad for* Saturday Night Live. *Could it get worse? Turn to page 309 for Part III of the story.

SMARTY PANTS

Random comic quips from some of today's best comedians.

"My grandmother was a very tough woman. She buried three husbands. Two of them were just napping."

—Rita Rudner

"I celebrated last Thanksgiving in an old-fashioned way. I invited everyone in my neighborhood to my house, we had an enormous feast, and then I killed them and took their land."

—Jon Stewart

"I had a friend who was a clown. When he died, all his friends went to the funeral in one car."

—Steven Wright

"I'm paranoid. On my stationary bike I have a rear-view mirror."

—Richard Lewis

"The guy who invented the hokey-pokey just died. It was a weird funeral. First, they put his left leg in..."

—Irv Gilman

"Two guys walk into a bar. You'd think one of them would have seen it."

—Daniel Lybra

"I used to work at the unemployment office. I hated that job because when they fired me, I still had to show up at work the next day."

—Wally Wong

"When I was a kid, I couldn't wait for the first snowfall. I would run to the door and yell, 'Let me in! Let me in!'"

—Emo Philips

"Doesn't Prince Charles look like somebody kissed a frog, and it hasn't changed all the way?"

—Wendy Liebman

"Dogs hate it when you blow in their face. I'll tell you who really hates that, my grandmother. Which is odd, because when we're driving she loves to hang her head out the window."

—Ellen DeGeneres

"During the summer I like to go to the beach and make sand castles out of cement... and wait for kids to run by and try to kick them over."

—James Leemer

Q: Who is Africa's largest private-sector employer? A: Coca-Cola.

WHAT'S ON EBAY?

It's a game of virtual cat and mouse: smart alecks put crazy items up for auction on eBay and eBay pulls them off the site. Here are a few of our favorites. (The winning bids are at the end.)

ITEM: A date
DESCRIPTION: "With our co-worker Brady!!! He drives a Miata!!!"
OPENING BID: 50¢

ITEM: Frog purse, made from a real frog
DESCRIPTION: "Be the first person on your block to own a coin purse made out of most of a frog. Rest assured, you'll never be asked for spare change again."
OPENING BID: $1

ITEM: A picture of my butt
DESCRIPTION: "I'm a sexy guy from Florida, you know you want this, you pay shipping if out of USA."
OPENING BID: 75¢

ITEM: The right to legally represent a plaintiff in a lawsuit over a piece of "tainted" string cheese
DESCRIPTION: "A strand of hair is completely embedded in the cheese cylinder."
OPENING BID: $500

ITEM: One pound real Arkansas Civil War dirt
DESCRIPTION: "100% guaranteed to be from the Civil War era. Comes with certificate of authenticity if desired."
OPENING BID: $1

ITEM: "Stuff I found in my couch about an hour ago"
DESCRIPTION: Includes one pack of Big Red gum, one machine-threaded screw, 80¢ in change, two rubber bands—"one needs a little restoration."
OPENING BID: 80¢

ITEM: The sun
DESCRIPTION: "Own your very own ball of incredibly hot gas! Payment in cash only. Buyer collects."
OPENING BID: $10 million

ITEM: Pocket lint
DESCRIPTION: "Trust me, you don't want this."
OPENING BID: $12

ITEM: "Put a tattoo on my forehead for one year"
DESCRIPTION: "You must be asking why I would allow someone to tattoo my forehead. My wife and I would like to pay off our car and other bills, plus have enough money left over so I could attend school."
OPENING BID: $33,200

ITEM: Bridal wedding gown
DESCRIPTION: "Very soiled and spotted."
OPENING BID: 99¢

ITEM: "Semi-new" teriyaki vegetables and rice snack
DESCRIPTION: "M'mm. After I finished preparing the snack I realized I wasn't so hungry anymore."
OPENING BID: 25¢

ITEM: WWII novelty Hitler pincushion
DESCRIPTION: "Stick the pins in his butt. A great collectible!"
OPENING BID: $1

ITEM: Francis D. Cornworth's virginity
DESCRIPTION: "I figured with the latest eBay craze, I'd see exactly how much I could get for my virginity. I live in Miami, FL. If you live in Florida, I could probably meet you halfway up to Orlando. Otherwise you'll have to arrange to meet me."
OPENING BID: $10

ITEM: "My conscience"
DESCRIPTION: "I'm selling it, 'cause I don't want or need it."
OPENING BID: $5

...Melbourne to Sydney, covering 1,264 miles in 28 days.

ITEM: Melissa's booger—fresh from the pickin'!
DESCRIPTION: "Comes straight from the nostril to your home in less than two days. Free shipping."
OPENING BID: 1¢

ITEM: Muhammad Ali's broken-jaw X-ray
DESCRIPTION: "Used to determine the extent of his injuries following his bout with Ken Norton."
OPENING BID: $9.99

ITEM: Set of 50 "antique" prosthetic eyeballs
DESCRIPTION: "Lifelike detail; the veins in the eyes are stunning!"
OPENING BID: $50

ITEM: The raft Elian Gonzalez's family used to flee Cuba
DESCRIPTION: "A genuine piece of American history...sure to be a big moneymaker!"
OPENING BID: $20

ITEM: Cadaver bag
DESCRIPTION: "This bag is new, never used. I would have to be a sick freak to sell these used."
OPENING BID: $15

WINNING BIDS

Brady: $6.19
Frog purse: $5.50
Butt picture: $1
String cheese: No takers
Dirt: $2.75
Couch stuff: $3.06
The sun: No takers
Pocket lint: $10 million
Tattoo: No takers
Wedding dress: $15.50
Teriyaki snack: No takers
Hitler doll: No takers
Virginity: $10 million
Conscience: No takers
Booger: 1¢
Ali's X-ray: $255.01
Bag of eyeballs: $613
Elian's raft: $280 (minimum not met)
Cadaver bag: $15

TWIST ME A DIZZY

Does dealing with death and destruction on a daily basis make men loose with language? Apparently, yes. Here are a few colorful examples of wartime slang.

EGG BEATER
Helicopter. (Korean War)

GIVE A DIRTY ORB
To give a dirty look. (World War II)

CEILING WORK
High-altitude planes protecting airmen at lower levels. (World War I)

BOOM-BOOM GIRL
Prostitute. (Vietnam War)

HOT SKINNY
Rumors about important things. (Vietnam War)

LATRINE TELEGRAM
A rumored report. (World War II)

PLUTONIUM WINE
Moonshine brewed on a nuclear submarine. (Cold War)

BRAIN BUCKET
A helmet. (Korean War)

BONE JAR
Meaning "hello," a corruption of the French *bonjour*. (World War I)

MESSY BUCKET
"Thank you." From the French *merci beaucoup*, "many thanks." (World War I)

AGONY WAGON
Ambulance. (WWII)

DEEP KIMCHI
In serious trouble. *Kimchi* is a Korean cabbage dish. (Korean War)

DINKY DAU
Crazy. From the Vietnamese *dien cai dau*, "ridiculous." (Vietnam War)

BEHAVIOR REPORT
A love letter reply. (World War II)

SMOKE A THERMOMETER
To have your temperature taken. (World War I)

BOTTLED SUNSHINE
Beer. (World War II)

BOUGHT GUTS
Courage inspired by too much bottled sunshine. (World War II)

TWIST A DIZZY
To roll a cigarette. (World War II)

COMPLETELY CHEESED
Extremely bored. (World War II)

APPLESAUCE ENEMA
Mild and gentle criticism of a subordinate so he feels less "chewed out." (Vietnam War)

BIG PICKLE
The atomic bomb. (Korean War)

Most-requested care package item by U.S. troops in Saudi Arabia: toilet paper.

THE ANT AND THE PIGEON

A fable is a story with a moral. Here's one that comes from Africa.

One day an ant found a grain of corn and decided to take it home. He held it very tight and hurried as fast as he could, so that nothing would take the grain of corn from him.

There was a pond on the way home. The ant had forgotten about the pond, and he fell into it, corn and all. The corn slipped from his mouth and went to the bottom of the pond. The ant managed to stay on top of the water and struggled to find a place to get out. He began to fear that his strength would be exhausted before he could get out and that he would drown.

Suddenly a pigeon came down to the pond to drink, and when she saw the ant putting up a desperate struggle, she decided she would help the little fellow. She took a long, dry piece of grass and dropped it so that it fell near the ant. He climbed onto the grass and soon got out. The ant took a long breath and then he thanked the pigeon for saving him.

There was a boy near the pond with a bow and arrow. He was creeping up nearer and nearer to the pigeon. The ant saw what was happening and ran as fast as he could. Climbing up the boy's leg, he gave him a hard bite. The boy dropped his bow and arrow and cried out. The pigeon saw the boy and flew away to safety.

Each had saved the other. When the pigeon saved the ant, she didn't know that the ant would save her life in such a short time. If the pigeon had left the ant in the water, the boy with the bow and arrow would have killed her. Each was happier because of what they did for each other.

The Bura people say, "Every person is another's butter." Just as a big person can do something for a small one, so too can a small person do something for a big one.

According to one survey, 46% of Americans say their car is the most important...

DID THE PUNISHMENT FIT THE CRIME?

They don't give judges awards for creativity—but maybe they should. Do these guys deserve a prize? You be the judge.

THE DEFENDANT: Edward Bello, 60, a vending machine repairman and small-time crook

THE CRIME: Conspiracy to use stolen credit cards, with which he racked up more than $26,000 in charges

THE PUNISHMENT: Federal District Court Judge Alvin K. Hellerstein sentenced Bello to 10 months of home detention... *with no TV*. The tube-free environment would "create a condition of silent introspection that I consider necessary to induce the defendant to change his behavior." Despite a 30-year history of committing petty crimes, Bello has never spent a day in prison and says he's grateful to the judge for sparing him from the slammer one more time. But he's appealing the no-TV sentence anyway, claiming that it's a form of censorship and violates his First Amendment rights. "Let's face it," he says, "a television is sort of like your umbilical cord to life."

THE DEFENDANT: Albert Brown, a repeat drug offender in San Francisco, California

THE CRIME: Selling drugs to an undercover cop

A NOVEL APPROACH: Rather than decide the sentence himself, Judge James Warren of San Francisco handed Brown one of his judicial robes and told him to put it on. "This is your life," he told Brown. "You are your own judge. Sentence yourself."

THE PUNISHMENT: Brown, in tears, gave himself six months in jail. Then, according to news reports, he tacked on a "string of self-imposed conditions such as cleaning himself up for his kids, and steering clear of the neighborhood where he got busted."

"The Probation Department recommended six months and a good lecturing," Judge Warren told reporters. "But I figured, I'm

...thing in their lives. 6% say their children are most important.

not that good at lecturing. He, on the other hand, was very good at lecturing himself. And maybe this time it will stick. I had the transcript typed up and sent over to him. Just in case he forgets."

THE DEFENDANT: Alan Law, 19, of Derwent, Ohio

THE CRIME: Disturbing the peace by driving through town with his truck windows rolled down and the stereo blasting

THE PUNISHMENT: Municipal Court Judge John Nicholson gave Law a choice: pay a $100 fine or sit and listen to polka music for four hours. Law chose facing the music. A few days later, he reported to the police station and was locked in an interview room, where he listened to the "Blue Skirt Waltz," "Who Stole the Kishka," "Too Fat Polka," and other hits by Cleveland polka artist Frankie Yankovic. Law managed to sit through it and has since abandoned his plans to buy an even louder stereo for his truck.

THE DEFENDANT: A youth in the Wake County, North Carolina, Juvenile Court (names of juvenile offenders are sealed)

THE CRIME: Burglary and theft

THE PUNISHMENT: Judge Don Overby sent the miscreant home to get his most-prized possession. The kid returned with a remote-controlled car, which he handed over to the court. The judge then took a hammer and smashed it to smithereens. Judge Overby has done this with other first time offenders as well. He says he got the idea after someone broke into his house and stole his CD player, his VCR, and $300 in cash. "I remember wishing these folks could feel the same sense of loss as I did," he says.

* * *

A BRAINTEASER

Question: You are competing in a race and overtake the runner in second place. Which position are you in now?

Answer: If you answered that you're now in first place, you're wrong. You overtook the second runner and took their place, therefore you're in second.

THE REST OF THE UNITED STATES

America is more than just 50 states. You may be interested to learn that the United States owns some interesting real estate.

STATES OF THE UNION

All told, the United States owns a dozen "territories" and two "commonwealths." The definitions of both terms are a little vague but they have a few things in common: All of them are under the jurisdiction of the United States, which means the U.S. government controls their trade, foreign relations, immigration, citizenship, currency, maritime laws, declarations of war, legal procedures, treaties, radio and television regulations, and other such areas. Residents have fundamental rights under the U.S. Constitution, and U.S. citizens don't need a passport to go to there.

Residents of the commonwealths (Puerto Rico and the Northern Mariana Islands) and the inhabited territories (Guam, the U.S. Virgin Islands, and American Samoa) have a bit more in common:

- They have elected local governments, similar to those of states, but commonwealths are semi-autonomous, with a constitution and more control of their internal affairs than territories.
- They don't vote in federal elections.
- They elect non-voting delegates to Congress.
- They don't pay federal income tax (no taxation without representation).
- They do pay Social Security taxes.
- They are eligible for welfare and other federal aid programs.
- They are served by the U.S. Postal Service and have their own zip codes.
- Residents of Puerto Rico, the Northern Mariana Islands, Guam, and the U.S. Virgin Islands are U.S. citizens. Residents of American Samoa are considered U.S. nationals, not citizens.
- English is the official language (although some have a second or even third official language as well).

Twenty-four U.S. states do not allow first cousins to marry each other.

• The official currency is the U.S. dollar.

With that simplified explanation in mind, here is a list of America's island outposts.

COMMONWEALTHS

Puerto Rico

Location: Between the Caribbean Sea and the North Atlantic Ocean, east of the Dominican Republic

Size: 3,500 square miles

Population: Four million

Background: Columbus "found" this island in 1493, on his second voyage to the New World, and claimed it for Spain. He named it San Juan Bautista. When Ponce de Leon conquered it in 1509, it was inhabited by the Taino, descendents of Amazonian Indians who had migrated into the Caribbean. Most of the Taino were decimated by European diseases and mistreatment; the rest were enslaved and forced to work on sugar plantations. A recent genetic study showed that a surprising number of Puerto Ricans carry Taino blood, suggesting that many natives were assimilated.

Spain gave Puerto Rico to the United States in 1898 following its defeat in the Spanish-American War. (In the same deal, the U.S. got Guam, bought the Philippines, and won independence for Cuba.) The island became a territory of the United States in 1917. Seeking more autonomy, Puerto Ricans voted in 1951 to become a commonwealth.

Northern Mariana Islands

Location: North Pacific Ocean, between Hawaii and the Philippines

Size: 180 square miles

Population: 75,000

Background: The Northern Marianas are 14 islands in a 500-mile chain. Only the three southernmost islands of Saipan, Tinian, and Rota are developed. (There's a Wal-Mart, a McDonald's, and a Pizza Hut on Saipan.)

The native Chamorros, probably descendants of migrants from Malaysia, first encountered Europeans in 1521 when explorer Ferdinand Magellan stopped by on his round-the-world voyage. Spanish missionaries and merchants showed up in the 1600s and dominated the Chamorros for the next three centuries.

In the early 20th century, control of the islands went from Spain to Germany and then to Japan. The Americans took the islands from the Japanese in one of the bloodiest battles of World War II. It remained a U.S. territory until 1975, when the people of the Northern Marianas voted to become a commonwealth.

Today the Chamorros are about 30% of the population. About half the population—Filipinos mostly—are nonresident aliens connected to the huge garment-making industry. And the Japanese are back—as tourists spending nearly half a billion dollars a year.

INHABITED U.S. TERRITORIES

Guam

Location: North Pacific Ocean, between Hawaii and the Philippines

Size: 212 square miles

Population: 158,000

Background: Guam is the 15th island in the chain that includes the Northern Marianas.

Guam was also discovered by Magellan in 1521 and formally annexed by Spain in 1565. It was ceded to the United States by Spain in 1898, at the end of the Spanish-American War. The Japanese occupied it in 1941; the U.S. retook it three years later. A U.S. military installation dominates the island, with more than 23,000 military personnel and dependents. About half the population are Chamorros; 35% of the population are under the age of 15. Guam is currently seeking commonwealth status.

U.S. Virgin Islands

Location: Caribbean Sea and the North Atlantic Ocean, east of Puerto Rico

Size: 136 square miles

Population: 122,000

Background: This island paradise comprises three islands—St. Thomas, St. John, and St. Croix—as well as numerous smaller islets.

Columbus came across the larger archipelago in 1493 on his second voyage to the New World and named it the Virgin Islands, in honor of the 11,000 virgin followers of St. Ursula. During the 17th century, the islands were divided into two territorial units,

First food product permitted by law to have artificial coloring: Butter. (It's really white.)

one British and the other Danish. The British possessions were called the Virgin Islands; the Danish part was called the Danish West Indies.

The largest slave auctions in the world took place on St. Thomas. Sugarcane, produced by slave labor, drove the islands' economy in the 18th and early 19th centuries. And it was a shopper's paradise, as the Danes allowed Blackbeard and other pirates to openly sell their stolen treasures on the streets of St. Thomas.

Because of its strategic importance for control of the Caribbean basin and protection of the Panama Canal, the United States purchased the Danish portion in 1917 for $25 million in gold and renamed it the U.S. Virgin Islands. For clarity, the U.K. appended "British" to its territory (BVI for short).

Today tourism accounts for 70% of the islands' economy and employment, with two million visitors a year.

American Samoa

Location: South Pacific Ocean, between Hawaii and New Zealand

Size: 76 square miles

Population: 67,000

Background: Settled around 1000 B.C. by Polynesians. The first European to visit the islands of Samoa was Dutch sea captain Jacob Roggeveen, in 1722. The islands became a strategic stopover for whalers and South Sea spice traders.

Germany and the United States divided the islands between themselves in 1899. Germany was driven out by New Zealand during World War I. Western Samoa gained independence in 1962.

The U.S. part, American Samoa, is composed of five islands and two coral atolls, including the deep-water harbor of Pago Pago.

Although the Samoans embraced Christianity when the first missionaries showed up in the 1830s, in many ways they have maintained their traditions better than other Pacific islanders. Nearly all land is owned communally, and there is a social hierarchy that stresses one's responsibility to the extended family. However, Samoans have become heavily dependent on U.S. aid and imports. They spend about 40% of their income on imported food.

But wait, there's more. Check out page 459 for all of the uninhabited U.S. territories (just in case you ever want to get away from it all).

Strawberries got their name because the plant "strews" its runners across the ground.

"BOOK 'EM, DANNO"

Here are a few more of our all-time favorite TV catchphrases.

Catchphrase: "Ayyyyy."
From: *Happy Days* (1974–84)
Here's the Story: Arthur "The Fonz" Fonzarelli (Henry Winkler) was not originally intended to be the "cool" character; Potsie was. The Fonz was added as a "bad influence" to give the show more of an edge. But Winkler's hip-yet-sensitive portrayal, along with his trademark leather jacket, thumbs up, and "Ayyyyy" had such screen presence that ABC started working him into more and more storylines, making sure he got at least one "Ayyyyy" in each episode. By 1977 Winkler's billing had gone from closing credits to fifth, and finally to second. When Ron Howard left the show in 1980, Winkler was given top billing. ABC almost retitled the show *Fonzie's Happy Days*.
Blast From The Past: Check out the scene in *Pulp Fiction* where the hit-man Jules (Samuel L. Jackson) is trying to calm down the diner robbers he's terrorizing: "Let's all be good little Fonzies. And what was Fonzie like?" he asks. One of them sheepishly answers, "Coo-ol." "Correctamundo!" says Jackson.

Catchphrase: "Two thumbs up."
From: *Sneak Previews* (1975–80), renamed *At the Movies* (1980–)
Here's the Story: "Thumbs up" has been a symbol of approval since Roman times. But "*two* thumbs up" means a whole lot more to the movie industry. Gene Siskel and Roger Ebert, film critics for rival Chicago newspapers, worked together for 24 years before Siskel's death in 1999. Their opposite tastes in movies assured moviegoers that if both of these guys liked the movie, chances are you would too. Filmmakers also took note of the growing popularity of the phrase; they watched the show each week, hoping their latest project would get two thumbs up. If so, it was plastered all over movie ads. Why? Because "two thumbs up" means big box office. If not... well, have you ever seen a movie advertised that got "one thumb up"?

Of the 850 different species of bats in the world, only three drink blood.

Catchphrase: "De plane! De plane!"
From: *Fantasy Island* (1978–84)
Here's the Story: At the beginning of each episode, the vertically challenged Tattoo (Herve Villechaize) shouted this phrase to alert his boss, Mr. Roarke (Ricardo Montalban), that "de plane" was coming. The phrase did so much for *Fantasy Island* that in 1983 Villechaize asked for the same salary as Montalban. Instead, he was fired. Ratings dropped off dramatically and the show was cancelled after the following season. In 1992 Villechaize turned up in a Dunkin' Donuts commercial asking for "De plain! De plain!" donuts.

Catchphrase: "Resistance is futile."
From: *Star Trek: The Next Generation* (1987–94)
Here's the Story: This line actually made its television debut on the British TV serial *Dr. Who*. Its more recent use by the Borg, aliens out to assimilate humans, made it a household phrase. It has even become a response to the growing power of corporations and governments. A political cartoon in the late 1990s showed a Borged-out Bill Gates declaring, "We are Microsoft. We will add your biological and technological distinctiveness to our own. You will be assimilated. Resistance is futile." And now a new bumper sticker is showing up that says, "Resistance is *not* futile."

Catchphrase: "Book 'em, Danno!"
From: *Hawaii Five-O* (1968–80)
Here's the Story: Even though *Hawaii Five-O* ran for 12 years, more people today remember this catchphrase than the show itself. When he caught the bad guy, detective Steve McGarrett (Jack Lord) would smugly utter this line to his assistant Danny "Danno" Williams (James MacArthur). To say the phrase is a part of pop culture is an understatement: a 2002 Internet search found more than 1,000 entries for "Book 'em, Danno!"

* * *

"Your marriage is in trouble if your wife says, 'You're only interested in one thing,' and you can't remember what it is."

—***Milton Berle***

The automated baggage handler at Chicago's O'Hare Airport can sort 480 bags per minute.

THE LEGEND OF LINCOLN'S GHOST

Here's a trivia question you can use to win a bet: Who was the first president to claim he saw Lincoln's ghost? Answer: Lincoln himself.

BACKGROUND

Take America's "royal residence," the White House; examine tales of hauntings that have surrounded it for nearly two centuries; and add Abraham Lincoln, an odd president who believed in the occult and was murdered while in office, and you have the recipe for America's most famous ghost story.

• According to legend, shortly after Lincoln was elected to his first term in 1860, he saw a double image of himself while gazing in a mirror at his Illinois home. One was his normal reflection, the other a pale double. Mrs. Lincoln didn't see the second image but was convinced that it was a sign. The sharper image, she said, represented Lincoln completing his first term; the other was a sign that he would be reelected, but would die before completing his second term.

• As Lincoln began his first term, the nation was on the verge of the Civil War. In the midst of trying to reunify the divided country, Lincoln faced a terrible personal tragedy—his 11-year-old son, Willie, died from a fever in 1862. A grief-stricken Mrs. Lincoln conducted séances in the hopes of contacting the boy. Although the skeptical president never participated in the séances, historians say his wife's belief in the supernatural may eventually have rubbed off on him.

• Lincoln suffered restless nights filled with nightmares and premonitions of his own death. He once told his wife about a dream where he was asleep, then was woken by the sounds of someone crying. He went to the East Room and found the source of the sobs: mourners and a casket. He asked a woman, "Who died?" "The assassinated president," she told him. Lincoln walked over to the casket and saw himself inside.

Vampire slayer? King Tut had garlic bulbs buried in his tomb with him.

• Several months later, on the morning of April 14, 1865, Lincoln called an emergency meeting of the Cabinet and delivered a cryptic message: "Expect important news soon. I have had a dream," he told them, "I am on a boat, alone in the ocean. I have no oars, no rudder. I am helpless." That evening, while attending a play at Ford's Theater, Lincoln was shot from behind by John Wilkes Booth; he died the next morning at 7:22 a.m.

RESTLESS SOUL?

Parapsychologists define ghosts as "people who died with unfinished business"—and Lincoln certainly fits the bill. The Confederacy had surrendered only five days before Lincoln's assassination, but the United States was in disarray. The economy of the South had been decimated by the war; hatred and animosity were rampant. Lincoln's plans for repairing the nation were cut short by his murder. As a result, does Lincoln's ghost still roam the halls of 1600 Pennsylvania Avenue? Many subsequent residents and visitors have been convinced it does.

REPORTED SIGHTINGS

The Teddy Roosevelt White House (1901–1909)

"I think of Lincoln, shambling, homely, with his strong, sad, deeply furrowed face, all the time. I see him in the different rooms and in the halls." Skeptics maintain that this quote by President Roosevelt was taken out of context. But believers in the spirit world say that Roosevelt was speaking literally—that he actually saw Lincoln's ghost.

The Coolidge White House (1923–1929)

Calvin Coolidge's wife, Grace, claimed she saw the tall figure of Lincoln "at the window in the Oval Office, hands clasped behind his back, gazing out over the Potomac River, perhaps still seeing the bloody battlefields beyond."

The FDR White House (1933–1945)

• While sleeping in the White House, Queen Wilhelmina of the Netherlands was awakened one night by knocks at her bedroom door. When she answered it, the former president was standing before her. The queen fainted. When she came to, the ghost was gone.

Q: What is hexanol? A: The stuff that gives freshly mowed grass its smell.

• For a time, the Lincoln Bedroom was Eleanor Roosevelt's study, and the First Lady claimed she could feel the presence of the former president. "Sometimes when I worked at my desk late at night I'd get a feeling that someone was standing behind me. I'd have to turn around and look."

• A few years later in the same room, a seamstress was working on the drapes and kept hearing the sound of someone approaching the bedroom door, but no one ever came. She found a White House butler and asked him why he kept pacing back and forth. "I don't know what you're talking about," he said. "I haven't been on that floor. That was Abe."

• Winston Churchill, a frequent guest during World War II, had an "eventful" night in the Lincoln Bedroom. He was found the next morning sleeping on the floor of the room across the hall. He told no one what had happened that night and vowed never to set foot in the Lincoln Bedroom again.

The Ford White House (1974–1977)

Gerald Ford's daughter Susan was so sure she felt Lincoln's ghost in the White House that she wouldn't set foot in the Lincoln Bedroom, either.

The Reagan White House (1981–1989)

• The most prominent modern sighting comes from yet another presidential daughter, Maureen Reagan, along with her husband, Dennis Revell. One night while in the Lincoln Bedroom, they both saw "an aura, sometimes red, sometimes orange." According to Reagan, it was the ghost of Lincoln.

• Just as mysterious is the fact that the Reagan's dog Lucky would never enter the Lincoln Bedroom. She would, however, stand in the hallway and bark at something inside.

The Clinton White House (1993–2001)

"A high percentage of people who work here won't go in the Lincoln Bedroom," said President Clinton's social secretary, Capricia Marshall. According to Marshall, many White House maids and butlers swear they've seen Lincoln's ghost.

Need time off? Move to Italy. On average, Italians get 42 vacation days every year.

OOPS!

More tales of outrageous blunders to let us know that other people are screwing up even worse than we are.

POOR JUDGE OF TASTE

"British magistrate Hector Graham was about to pass sentence in his courtroom in Luton, England, when his musical tie, a gift from his wife, came to life. 'He had got to the part about how serious an offense it was when all of a sudden "Santa Claus Is Coming to Town" started up,' a court spokesman said. 'He didn't have a clue how to stop it and was extremely embarrassed, especially because after that, it went into two more Christmassy songs and finished with "We Wish You a Merry Christmas."'"

—*This Is True*

I BEG YOUR PARDON?

"A hospital patient fainted when given the news that she was to be discharged that day. She thought the nurse had said, 'We're sending you home to die.'"

—*Daily Telegraph*

MAN OF CONVICTION

"The Republican Party mistakenly invited Robert Kirkpatrick to a $2,500-a-plate fund-raising dinner with President Bush. The mistake? The invitation, complete with a letter from Vice President Dick Cheney, was sent to him at the Belmont Correctional Institution in Ohio. The letter invited him to 'join the president and Mrs. Bush for a private dinner here in Washington, D.C.' Kirkpatrick, 35, was serving three years for drug possession. 'Tell him that I'd be happy to attend,' Kirkpatrick said, 'but he's going to have to pull some strings to get me there.'"

—Associated Press

THANKS A LATTE

"Ethem Sahin was playing dominoes at the local coffeehouse in Ankara, Turkey, when a cow fell through the roof, knocking him unconscious. 'My friends told me later what happened. I couldn't believe it,' Sahin told reporters. What had happened? Apparently,

Domestic cats can run as fast as 31 mph—about 6 mph faster than humans.

the cow had wandered from the hillside where it was grazing onto the roof of the coffee house, which was built into the side of the hill. Sahin was treated for a broken leg. 'May God protect us from a worse accident,' said Sahin's wife."

—*Bizarre News*

G THAT WAS STUPID

"MSNBC has apologized for a typographical error that turned the name of an interview subject into a racial slur. The network aired an interview with Republican political consultant Niger Innis. The onscreen graphic identifying Innis, who is black, had an extra 'g' in his first name.

"Shortly after it appeared, correspondent Gregg Jarrett offered Innis a 'profuse apology.' 'It's not the first time it's happened,' replied Innis, 'but hopefully it's the last.'"

—*SFGate*

WHAT A GAS

"A German man attempted suicide by turning on the gas to his stove but then reconsidered, called police, and nearly blew himself up when he lit a cigarette to calm his nerves."

—"The Edge," *The Oregonian*

JUST ADD WATER

"Firefighters in Minot, North Dakota, were worried they might need gas masks—but it turned out they should have brought 'Nilla Wafers. Emergency responders scrambled to a report of a leaking railroad car. Initial reports said the leak was strychnine—a deadly chemical. But it turned out to be tapioca pudding mix."

—KXMC News

PLANK YOU VERY MUCH

"A woman came home to find her husband in the kitchen, shaking frantically with what looked like a wire running from his waist toward the electric kettle. Intending to jolt him away from the deadly current, she whacked him with a handy plank of wood, breaking his arm in two places. Until that moment, he had been happily listening to his Walkman."

—Associated Press

The Roman word for *secretary* meant "one who keeps a secret."

BEHIND THE HITS

Ever wonder what inspired some of your favorite songs? The answers may surprise you.

The Artist: The Beatles

The Song: "Come Together" (1969)

The Story: In 1969 Timothy Leary intended to run for governor of California against a B-movie actor named Ronald Reagan. One of Leary's battle cries was "Come together," and he asked his friend John Lennon to write a song based on it for the campaign. By the time Lennon got around to it, Leary's campaign was dead (he had to drop out when he was convicted of marijuana possession).

Lennon liked the phrase, though, and decided to build a song around it anyway. He loosely based it on the old Chuck Berry tune, "You Can't Catch Me." He even left in the line, "Here come old flat-top." Other than that, it's nothing like the Berry song, but because Lennon admitted to borrowing the line, Berry's publisher sued him. The settlement: Lennon agreed to record two Chuck Berry songs on his 1975 solo album, *Rock N Roll.* Written and recorded in a single session at the studio, "Come Together" was one of Lennon's favorites: "It's funky, it's bluesy. You can dance to it. I'll buy it!"

The Artist: Sheryl Crow

The Song: "All I Wanna Do" (1993)

The Story: After years of trying to break into the Los Angeles music scene—including singing backup on Michael Jackson's "Bad" tour—Crow finally got a record deal in 1991.

During a recording session, Crow wrote what she thought was a pretty good song…musically, anyway; she hated the words. She was stuck, so her producer ran across the street to a bookstore and bought 10 books of poetry, selected at random. He gave them to Crow, locked her in the bathroom, and told her to come out when she had something. Crow picked a poem entitled "Fun" and started singing the words, taking out some of the poet's lines and adding her own. "'All I Wanna Do' was the throwaway track of the album. It was one that wasn't going to go on the record," she recalled. Good thing it did—after A&M released it, the song won a Grammy and

Number of languages spoken in India: about 845.

propelled Crow to superstardom. Meanwhile, an English teacher in Vermont named Wyn Cooper began receiving royalty checks for a poem he'd written 10 years earlier.

The Artist: Led Zeppelin

The Song: "Whole Lotta Love" (1969)

The Story: While recording their second album, guitarist Jimmy Page came up with a bluesy riff and the rest of the band started jamming around it. Singer Robert Plant "improvised" some words, but they weren't really his. He borrowed them from a song called "You Need Love" written by blues legend Willie Dixon. And although Led Zeppelin had credited Dixon for two songs on their first album, they kept the writing credit on "Whole Lotta Love" for themselves. Why? "We decided that it was so far away in time," explained Plant. (Actually, it had only been seven years since Dixon wrote it.) "Whole Lotta Love" became the only Zeppelin song ever to reach the top 10 in the United States.

Fifteen years later, Dixon heard the song for the first time and noticed the resemblance. Dixon sued the band and settled out of court in 1987. He used the proceeds to set up the Blues Heaven Foundation to promote awareness of the blues.

The Artist: Little Richard

The Song: "Tutti Frutti" (1955)

The Story: After a long, unproductive recording session in 1955, Little Richard couldn't get the sound his producer, "Bumps" Blackwell, wanted. Exasperated, they took a lunch break and went to the local dive, the Dew Drop Inn. The place had a piano, so Richard started banging on it and wailing out some nonsense words: "Awop-Bop-a-Loo-Mop a-Good Goddam... Tutti Frutti, Good Booty!" It was the sound Blackwell was looking for.

Richard had actually written the song while he was washing dishes at a bus station in Macon, Georgia. "I couldn't talk back to the boss," he said. "So instead of saying bad words, I'd say, 'Wop-Bop-a-Loo-Bop-a-Lop-Bam-Boom,' so he wouldn't know what I was thinking." Blackwell cleaned up the lyrics ("good booty" became "aw rootie"), and they recorded it that day. The single reached #17 on the pop charts. (Believe it or not, Pat Boone covered the song and it outdid Richard's version on the hit parade.)

Old news: By the year 2050, the world's elderly will outnumber the young for the first time.

HOUDINI'S HEADLINES

Uncle John is no Houdini. When he was a little kid, he accidentally locked himself in the bathroom and couldn't get out. But it didn't matter—by the time someone answered his calls for help, he'd decided to stay.

Harry Houdini was a genius at performing death-defying feats of magic. But he was more than that—he was also a genius at getting free publicity. Everywhere he went, he staged stunts specifically designed to get newspaper headlines.

CHEEKY CHALLENGER COPS COPPERS' CUFFS!

• When Houdini first went to London, he had no bookings. He boasted about his talents to a stage manager, but the man was skeptical, and told Houdini, "I'll hire you—but only if you can get out of handcuffs at Scotland Yard." Houdini rounded up some reporters, then challenged police at Scotland Yard to cuff him.

• Wrapping Houdini's arms around a pillar, the police superintendent snapped on the cuffs, and turned to leave, saying, "We'll be back in an hour to release you."

• As they headed for the door, Houdini called out, "You better take your cuffs with you!" He had undone the handcuffs in less time than it took the cops to walk across the room.

• The reporters were impressed, and made sure Houdini got a lot of free publicity from the stunt. The result: a six-month run in London.

SNEAKY SERGEANT CAN'T STUMP HOUDINI

• From then on, challenging local police departments became one of his regular gimmicks. It always worked—even when he failed.

• In 1899 Sergeant Waldron of the Chicago police challenged Houdini to escape from his special handcuffs.

• Houdini agreed, then struggled to release himself for over an hour as the audience laughed and jeered.

• The cuffs had to be cut off—and only after the theater had emptied did Waldron admit that he had tampered with the cuffs, dropping molten lead in the lock so it would be jammed.

73% of Americans in their twenties say playing hooky from work "would improve their...

• When the trick was revealed, the local newspaper ran the story and Houdini garnered even more free publicity.

EXAMINER EXPOSÉ: HOUDINI A FRAUD!

• The *San Francisco Examiner* ran an story claiming that Houdini's secret was extra hidden keys.

• In response, Houdini announced he would pit himself against any restraint the San Francisco police could throw at him. A reporter was assigned to cover the event.

• Houdini was stripped, searched, and shackled. His hands were cuffed behind his back; his ankles were locked in irons; and 10 pairs of manacles were placed on him. He was then locked in a closet.

• Ten minutes later, he was free. The newspaper retracted their exposé and ran another story...applauding his talents.

HOUDINI JOLTS JUDGE AND JURY!

• In Germany, Houdini wanted to stage a stunt where he would jump—roped and chained—off a boat into a river. The police refused to give permission—but he did it anyway. As he pulled himself out of the river and walked up the riverbank, he was arrested.

• The only thing the cops could charge him with, though, was walking on the grass. The story made the papers all over the country.

• To get even, in 1902 the head of the Cologne police, Schutzmann Werner Graff, denounced Houdini as a fraud and a swindler.

• Houdini demanded an apology. When none was forthcoming he sued for slander. Graff told the judge and jury he could prove what he said was true just by chaining Houdini up.

• Houdini consented to be chained, then demonstrated to the judge and jury (but he refused to show Graff) exactly how he was able to release himself. He won the case, the police were fined, and Graff was ordered to apologize.

• But Graff had other plans: he appealed to a higher court. There, he produced a specially made lock that was supposed to be impossible to open. Houdini escaped in four minutes.

• This time, Graff was ordered to pay court costs and run an apology in all German newspapers. He refused again and instead took the case to Germany's highest court. Graff argued that Houdini's

...mental health and productivity." Only 50% of Americans over 65 agrees.

claim that he could escape from safes was false—yet Houdini successfully escaped from a safe right in front of the judge.

• For the third time, Graff lost his case. Thanks to the stubborn policeman, the publicity for Houdini was enormous.

HOUDINI COMMITS RANDOM ACTS OF PUBLICITY...

• Houdini became famous for escaping from straitjackets while hanging upside down from his feet over public streets. He sought out the newspapers in each town he traveled to and offered to perform the stunt while hanging from their roof. It made the front page in every town he played.

• On his first trip to Europe, Houdini hired seven bald men to sit in a row on the pavement next to a popular café. At regular intervals, the seven men would simultaneously remove their hats and nod their heads forward. Each man had one letter written on his bald head, and together they spelled "Houdini."

• In 1901 Houdini escaped from the manacles that had been worn by a sadistic murderer named Glowisky when he had been beheaded just three days earlier. It made great newspaper copy.

• A rival magician once interrupted one of Houdini's performances with loud protests that he, The Great Cirnoc, was the true handcuff king. Houdini invited him onstage to prove himself by escaping from some special cuffs. Cirnoc first insisted that Houdini demonstrate that it was possible to do (which he did, in the privacy of his cabinet, using a secret key). The Great Cirnoc then struggled to release himself from the same cuffs but couldn't. He was hooted offstage, and the papers were full of the story the next day.

...AND KINDNESS!

Popular singer Sarah Bernhardt was honored at a reception at the Met in New York. There, she was presented with a bronze bust of herself. However, no one had paid the bill for the bust. When the $350 bill was sent to her, she returned the bust to the maker. Houdini immediately stepped in and paid the bill. Within a few days, his gesture had been covered in no less than 3,756 newspapers. A reporter estimated that if Houdini had bought that much newspaper space outright, it would have cost him $56,340.

How'd he do all this stuff? Turn to page 289 to find out.

Doggone: Houdini trained his dog to escape from a pair of miniature handcuffs.

PLUMBERS BY THE HOUR

Some things never change. This piece of 19th-century humor by Charles Dudley Warner deals with a problem familiar to every 21st-century homeowner.

PLUMB BRILLIANT

There is no class of men whose society is more to be desired than that of plumbers. They are the most agreeable men I know. I suspect the secret of it is that they are agreeable by the hour.

In the driest days, my fountain became disabled. The pipe was stopped up. A couple of plumbers, with the implements of their craft, came out to view the situation. There was a good deal of difference of opinion about where the stoppage was. But I found the plumbers perfectly willing to sit down and talk about it—talk by the hour. Some of their guesses and remarks were exceedingly ingenious; and their general observations on other subjects were excellent in their way, and could hardly have been better if they had been made by the job.

WHAT, ME HURRY?

The work dragged a little—as it is apt to do by the hour. The plumbers had occasion to make me several visits. Sometimes they would find, upon arrival, that they had forgotten some indispensable tool and one would go back to the shop, a mile and a half, after it, and his companion would await his return with the most exemplary patience, and sit down and talk—always by the hour. I do not know but it is a habit to have something wanted at the shop.

They seemed to me very good workmen, and always willing to stop and talk about the job, or anything else, when I went near them. They had none of that impetuous hurry that is said to be the bane of our American civilization. To their credit be it said, that I never observed anything of it in them. They can afford to wait. Two of them will sometimes wait nearly half a day while a comrade goes for a tool.

First job of a newborn queen bee: killing the other newborn queens, so she can rule alone.

THE MOMENT IS HOURS

They are patient and philosophical. It is a great pleasure to meet such men. One only wishes there was some work he could do for *them* by the hour. There ought to be reciprocity. I think they have very nearly solved the problem of Life: it is to work for other people, never for yourself, and get your pay by the hour. You then have no anxiety, and little work.

If you do things by the job you are perpetually driven: the hours are scourges. If you work by the hour, you gently sail on the stream of Time, which is always bearing you on to the haven of Pay, whether you make any effort or not. Working by the hour tends to make one moral. A plumber working by the job, trying to unscrew a rusty, refractory nut in a cramped position, where the tongs continually slipped off, would swear; but I never heard one of them swear, or exhibit the least impatience at such a vexation, working by the hour. Nothing can move a man who is paid by the hour. How sweet the flight of time seems to his calm mind.

* * *

FROM UNCLE JOHN'S POLICE LOG

In June 2000, some kids were playing basketball at a recreational field in Moreland Township, Pennsylvania, when they heard screams for help coming from the portable toilet that serves the field. The kids ran home to mom; she called the cops. Cops found a man standing in the toilet, naked from the waist down and up to his hips in…unpleasantness. According to police, the man had dropped his keys in the toilet and became stuck when he climbed in to find them. (He says he removed his shoes, socks, and pants "so they wouldn't get dirty.")

The man spent 45 minutes trapped in the toilet; it took rescue crews another 45 minutes to free him. That doesn't include the time removing the toilet seat from the man's torso, which was wedged so tight it had to be removed by emergency room doctors. The man never found his keys, but the story did end on a positive note: police withheld his name to save him from embarrassment.

If you're an average blinker, your eyes will be blinked closed for about 30 minutes today.

NO CITY DUST HERE

We're back with another installment of anagrams...words or phrases whose letters are rearranged to form new words or phrases. Here's an extra bonus: the new phrase has more or less the same meaning as the old one.

A TELEPHONE GIRL *becomes*...**REPEATING "HELLO"**

THE COUNTRYSIDE *becomes*...**NO CITY DUST HERE**

THE PUBLIC ART GALLERIES *becomes*... **LARGE PICTURE HALLS, I BET**

THE GREAT NEW YORK RAPID TRANSIT TUNNEL *becomes*... **GIANT WORK IN STREET, PARTLY UNDERNEATH**

THE HOSPITAL AMBULANCE *becomes*... **A CAB, I HUSTLE TO HELP MAN**

HEAVY RAIN *becomes*... **HIRE A NAVY**

VACATION TIMES *becomes*...**I'M NOT AS ACTIVE**

A DOMESTICATED ANIMAL *becomes*... **DOCILE, AS A MAN TAMED IT**

CONVERSATION *becomes*... **VOICES RANT ON**

THE UNITED STATES BUREAU OF FISHERIES *becomes*...**I RAISE THE BASS TO FEED US IN THE FUTURE**

SOFTWARE *becomes*... **SWEAR OFT**

LISTEN *becomes*...**SILENT**

"THAT'S ONE SMALL STEP FOR A MAN, ONE GIANT LEAP FOR MANKIND."—NEIL A. ARMSTRONG *becomes*... **A THIN MAN RAN, MAKES A LARGE STRIDE, LEFT PLANET, PINS FLAG ON MOON! ON TO MARS!**

Christmas lite: Only 10% of U.S. households put cookies out for Santa on Christmas Eve.

PIT STOPS ON THE WORLD WIDE WEB

Uncle John's loves to bring you the best in bathroom news, so here's something he recently discovered: restroom ratings posted on the Internet. Are they legit? We don't know. Are they accurate? We don't know that, either. Are they fun? Definitely.

Finagle-A-Bagel, Boston, MA
Comments: "Large, unusually clean. Convenient location. Decent bagels, too."

Unos Pizzeria, Phoenix, AZ
Comments: "The small urinals were a ridiculous four inches from the floor. At that height, even a dwarf would have to crouch to stay on target!"

Shinjuku Subway Station Men's Room, Tokyo, Japan
Comments: "This pay toilet cost 100 yen ($1.00). Too expensive. But it smells good."

House of Blues, New Orleans, LA
Comments: "The candies were a bit stale. The after-shave was not my brand."

Castle Island, Boston, MA
Comments: "What a horrible bathroom. Dirty, smelly, perpetually 'wet' floor. I almost felt dirtier coming out than I did going in."

The Shell Station, US-219 near Lewisburg, WV
Comments: "Upon opening the door to the men's restroom, which was unlocked, a man already seated upon the toilet smiled at me as I opened the door. I quickly closed the door, never to enter again."

Tabata Subway Station Men's Room, Tokyo, Japan
Comments: "Worst toilet in Tokyo. Help! I'm nauseated."

Syracuse Carrier Dome, Syracuse, NY
Comments: "A unique bathroom. Instead of urinating into a urinal, you urinate on the wall. It then trickles down the wall into a small trough which carries the urine to God knows where."

Pazzaluna, St. Paul, MN
Comments: "The small framed photos of pasta dishes hanging above the urinals were nice."

Fifteen runners started the first-ever Boston Marathon; only 10 of them finished it.

AROUND THE HOUSE

The next time you're doing some home improvement, chances are you'll use one at least one of these three products.

TAKES THE CAKE

In 1894 Theodore Witte was applying putty around a window frame with a butter knife—and it was a messy job. Sometime later, while waiting in line at a bakery shop, he noticed a baker squeezing icing onto a cake from a tube attached to a nozzle...with complete precision. Witte went straight home and designed a "puttying tool." He patented his idea of "using a ratcheted piston to force window putty through a nozzle to effect a smooth, weatherproof seal." Witte never made much money for his invention, but to his credit, he got it right the first time; very little about the caulking gun has changed since then.

SOMETHING'S FISHY

After someone spilled raw fish oil on his metal deck, a Scottish fishing boat captain named Robert Fergusson noticed that—over time—the deck stopped rusting. So after he landed in New Orleans, Fergusson spent many years trying to formulate a fish-oil based paint that would inhibit rust and corrosion. His biggest problem wasn't getting it to work, but getting it to work without smelling fishy. Finally in 1921, after working with more fish oil than any person should ever have to, Fergusson unveiled a new paint that stopped rust, dried overnight, and left no lingering aroma: Rust-Oleum.

ROCKET SCIENCE

Norm Larsen, a chemist at the Rocket Chemical Company, had unsuccessfully tested 39 compounds that would prevent corrosion and eliminate water from electrical circuitry. He finally got it right in 1953 and labeled the compound Water Displacement Formula 40. Other workers snuck the stuff home and discovered that in addition to preventing corrosion, it also stopped squeaks and unstuck locks. So the Rocket Chemical Company marketed it for home use. The product, now called WD-40, hit store shelves in 1958. Today more than a million cans are sold every week.

Q: What do Eskimos use for toothpicks? A: Walrus whiskers.

PARLIAMENTARY MANNERS

Canadians have a well-deserved reputation for being polite. Turns out it's all an act—at least for politicians. This excerpt from the "Dear Miss Parliamentary Manners" column in the Canadian National Post *shows us that American politicians have a lot to learn.*

DEAR MISS PARLIAMENTARY MANNERS,
A recent news story contended that decorum is taking a bruising in Canadian legislatures. The article quoted a Cabinet minister as saying, "There is a certain level of civil discourse to be expected in the house even during heckling." How can you be civil and heckle at the same time?

ANSWER: Actually, it's very easy to hector with ferocity and yet remain civil and mannerly—once you've mastered the subtle nuances of the parliamentary vernacular.

Expression: "My learned colleague."
Translation: "You cheese-eating throwback."

Expression: "If the honorable member will forward his request to my department, we will provide the relevant documents."
Translation: "Talk to the hand."

Expression: "I would be happy to address the member's question."
Translation: "I yearn to bleach your skull and use it on my desk as a novelty pencil holder."

Expression: "If the member had concerns, he should have made them known at the proper time."
Translation: "Your mother didn't have any complaints last night."

Expression: "Mr. Speaker, the people of Canada deserve an answer."
Translation: "Leave my mother out of this—I swear, I'll cut you!"

Expression: "I am outraged by your craven duplicity!"
Translation: "I'm not really upset; I just wanted to get on the news. Want to have dinner tonight?"

No way: According to one expert, the most frequently used English noun is "way."

THE MIRACLE WORKER

Observations about life from Helen Keller.

"Security is mostly a superstition. It does not exist in nature....Life is either a daring adventure or nothing."

"When one door of happiness closes, another opens; but often we look so long at the closed door that we do not see the one which has been opened for us."

"Keep your face to the sunshine and you cannot see the shadow."

"Instead of comparing our lot with that of those who are more fortunate than we are, we should compare it with the lot of the great majority of our fellow men. It then appears that we are among the privileged."

"I am only one, but still I am one. I cannot do everything, but still I can do something."

"Science may have found a cure for most evils, but it has found no remedy for the worst of them all—the apathy of human beings."

"No pessimist ever discovered the secrets of the stars, or sailed to an uncharted land."

"It is wonderful how much time good people spend fighting the devil. If they would only expend the same amount of energy loving their fellow men, the devil would die in his own tracks of ennui."

"There is no king who has not had a slave among his ancestors, and no slave who has not had a king among his."

"As selfishness and complaint pervert and cloud the mind, so love clears and sharpens the vision."

"The heresy of one age becomes the orthodoxy of the next."

"Life is a succession of lessons which must be lived to be understood."

"The most pathetic person in the world is someone who has sight, but no vision."

First song ever sung in space: "Happy Birthday," to the Apollo astronauts on March 8, 1969.

RAINFOREST CRUNCH

We've heard about "saving the rainforests" for years, but why are they so important? Here are some facts about some of nature's most amazing phenomena.

RAINFORESTS ARE DIVERSE

The Facts: Rainforests—forests with an average year-round temperature of 70°F and annual rainfall of more than 60 inches—are home to 50% of life on Earth... even though they make up only 6% of the landmass.

• More types of woody plant species grow on the slopes of a single forested volcano in the Philippines than grow in the entire United States from coast to coast. Forests in the tiny country of Panama contain as many plant species as all of Europe.

• More species of fish live in the Amazon River than in the entire Atlantic Ocean. One study found more species of ants living on a single tropical stump than are found in all of the British Isles.

• Yet scientists estimate that they have discovered and identified only one-sixth of the species living in rainforests.

RAINFORESTS ARE UNIQUE ECOSYSTEMS

The Facts: The ecosystem of a rainforest is upside down compared to other forests: nutrients are stored not in the soil, but in the canopy of plants above it.

• In forests with temperate climates, the deciduous trees all drop their leaves at roughly the same time, triggered by the change of seasons. Dead leaves gradually decompose and turn into rich soil.

• That doesn't happen in the rainforest—there is no change of season; tropical trees drop their leaves gradually over the entire year.

• The constant heat and moisture of the climate spur the continuous growth of bacteria, insects, and fungi, which feed on the dead leaves—causing the forest floor to act as a huge living stomach.

• Result: Decomposition (which can take one to seven years in a temperate forest) takes only six weeks in a rainforest. Downside: The rich loamy soil that accumulates in temperate forests never gets a chance to build up on a rainforest's floor.

Most destructive disease in human history, according to health experts: malaria.

RAINFORESTS ARE FRAGILE

The Facts: The forest canopy protects the ground. Some areas of the Amazon receive up to 400 inches of rain annually. But without leaves and branches to shield the ground from pounding rain, water would run off immediately, taking any topsoil with it.

• Millions of years of daily rainfall combined with constant heat have drained nutrients from rainforests' subsoil, leaving it high in toxic aluminum and iron oxides. This makes it unable to support much plant life.

• If exposed to the sun, the ground would become unproductive, hard-packed, and cement-like. The small amounts of nutrients left in the soil would be quickly leached away.

• The balance is fragile. It's estimated that the Amazon produces 20% of all the oxygen generated by land plants on Earth. Without the climate moderation of the forest, the greenhouse effect—rising temperatures and plummeting rainfall—may be greatly accelerated.

RAINFORESTS ARE IN DANGER

The Facts: Over half of the world's rainforests are gone forever—most have disappeared since 1960.

• Loggers, ranchers, miners, and farmers cut or burn the Amazon jungle down at the rate of 40 to 50 million acres annually.

• A 2.5-acre tract of healthy, growing rainforest loses about three pounds of soil through erosion annually. Cut the trees, and the same forest can lose up to 34 tons in a year.

• As settlers clear the forest to make room for agriculture or livestock, they discover the land supports them for only a few years.

• Once the forest is cleared, the only nutrients left are in the ashes. When the soil disappears, the rainfall diminishes, and the forest is gone for good. The damage is irreversible.

• Today, an area the size of the state of Washington is bulldozed every year. At that rate, it will take less than 50 years to destroy the remaining jungle. Some ecologists estimate that the Amazon will be completely gone by the year 2040.

• Scientists fear species are becoming extinct before they are even discovered—a scary prospect since roughly 25% of all prescription drugs contain ingredients originating in the rainforest.

In Japan, the James Bond film *Dr. No* was originaly translated as *We Don't Want a Doctor*.

LARGEST RAINFOREST ON EARTH: THE AMAZON

The Facts: The Amazon contains half the world's tropical forests, spread over an area the size of the continental United States.

• While North American forests rarely have more than 15 species of trees in their entire ecosystem, the Amazon can contain between 100 and 250 different species in a five-acre plot. You can sometimes travel a mile or more before finding two trees of the same species in the Amazon.

• More than 100 types of plants and 1,700 kinds of insects can be found in the branches of a single mature tropical tree.

• The Amazon has more than a million interdependent—and exotic—species of plant and animal life. A few examples:

trees with 6-foot-long leaves

flowers with 3-foot-long petals

plants that can cradle 10 gallons of water in reservoirs formed by their leaves

rodents that weigh up to 100 lbs.

slugs the size of small snakes

butterflies the size of dinner plates

bees the size of birds

tarantulas so big they eat birds

catfish so big they've been known to eat children

*   *   *

MORE ON THE AMAZON

Why is the Amazon so diverse?

Thirty million years ago, the area that is now the Amazon jungle entered a dry period lasting thousands of years. The drought wiped out most of the region's tropical forests—only isolated pockets of jungle survived. Over time, each jungle followed its own evolutionary course.

Then, following the last ice age (10,000 years ago), the climate became warm and wet again, and the different types of jungle grew together, each contributing many different plant and animal species.

MYTH-CONCEPTIONS

"Common knowledge" is frequently wrong. Here are some examples of things that many people believe... but that according to our sources, just aren't true.

Myth: Dry cleaning is *dry* cleaning.

Fact: Dry cleaning isn't really dry. The clothes are put in a large washing machine and treated with a variety of chemical solutions, such as perchloroethylene, after which a drier removes the solvents. Cleaned, yes. Dry, no. It's called "dry" cleaning because no water is used.

Myth: If you stop exercising, your muscle will turn into fat.

Fact: Muscle and fat are different tissues; one can't turn into the other. If you used to be muscular, but are getting fat, it's probably either because you're exercising less...or eating more.

Myth: Snake charmers "charm" snakes with their hypnotic music.

Fact: This art form dates back to the third century B.C. But the charmers don't work their magic with music...because snakes can't hear it. It's the wind from the charmer's flute—as well as various hand and head gestures—that capture the snake's attention.

Myth: New York is the largest city in the United States.

Fact: The largest city isn't New York or even Los Angeles. It's Juneau, Alaska. The city covers 3,108 square miles, making it nearly *seven* times larger than Los Angeles. The largest city in the contiguous 48 states is Jacksonville, Florida, which is 841 square miles—nearly twice the size of Los Angeles.

Myth: Jockey shorts (men's briefs) make men sterile.

Fact: This idea has haunted Jockey shorts since they were introduced in the 1930s. They don't.

Myth: The word *dinosaur* means "terrible lizard" in Latin.

Fact: Richard Owen coined the term in 1842. He used the word *deinos*, which is Greek—not Latin. It means ("fearfully great.")

PHONE PHUNNIES

Feast on a few fun forays from our fantastic phone files.

DON'T CALL ME...

"When someone stole his wife's purse early in 2002, Steve O'Brien decided to call her cell phone, which was inside the stolen purse. A woman answered the phone and said hello, at which point O'Brien demanded the purse and the phone back. The woman hung up. O'Brien dialed again—and again the thief answered, but this time said nothing. Then O'Brien heard someone ordering a Big Mac in the background, so he immediately headed for the nearest McDonald's. Standing inside the restaurant, he dialed and heard his wife's phone ringing and traced it to a woman who was calmly eating a burger. He called the police. She got arrested. Said O'Brien, 'You should have seen her face.'"

—*Ananova.com*

COW-A-RING-A

"In a town in Belgium, Caroline Lenaert became frustrated and frightened at the high number of prank phone calls she received on her cell phone over a two week period early in 2002. When she answered the calls, she heard nothing—only static. The calls came at all hours, even waking her in the middle of the night. She asked the telephone company for help, and they traced the calls... to a cow. It seems a farmer in a nearby town had rigged his cow's milking machine to automatically dial his cell phone whenever a malfunction occurred. Unfortunately, he accidentally programmed Ms. Lenaert's number into the machine."

—*Het Laatste Nieuws*

CALLER I.D.OT

"A Spokane contractor isn't humoring people with his cellphone prank. He registered his phone as Osama bin Laden, whose name pops up on caller ID when the man makes a call. The FBI said it's received complaints about the bin Laden impersonator, but there's no law prohibiting him from using the terrorist's name."

—*USA Today*

Crushed cockroaches, when applied to a stinging wound, are said to ease the pain.

THE "AMERICAN SYSTEM"

In Part 1 of our story (page 93), we told you how Eli Whitney's invention of the cotton gin in 1792 built the pre-Civil War Gone-with-the-Wind *South. Here's the story of Whitney's other invention—the one that destroyed it.*

LIKE MONEY IN THE BANK

Even before Eli Whitney ginned his first handful of upland cotton, he believed that he was on his way to becoming a wealthy man. "Tis generally said by those who know anything about [the cotton gin], that I shall make a Fortune by it," Whitney wrote in a letter to his father. His friend Phineas Miller certainly agreed—Miller became Whitney's business partner, providing money that Whitney would use to build the machines. They would both grow rich together...or so they thought.

COPYCATS

Things didn't work out quite as planned. There were two problems with Whitney and Miller's dreams of grandeur:

First, just as Whitney had intended, his cotton gin was so simple and so easy to make that just about anyone who was good with tools could make one. So a lot of planters did, even though doing so violated Whitney's patent.

Second, Whitney and Miller were too greedy for their own good. They knew that even if they had enough cash to build a cotton gin for every planter who wanted one (they didn't), the planters didn't have enough cash to buy them. So rather than build gins for sale, Whitney and Miller planned to set up a network of gins around the South where *they* would do the ginning in exchange for a share of the cotton they ginned. A *big* share—40%, to be exact. That was more than the planters were willing to part with, least of all to a Yankee. The planters fought back by ginning their cotton in machines they made themselves or by buying illegal copycat machines made by competitors.

And there were rumors: that Whitney himself had stolen the idea for the cotton gin from a Southern inventor; that the copycat gins were actually "improved" models that didn't infringe on

Oldest major U.S. sporting event: The Kentucky Derby, first held in 1875.

Whitney's patents; and, worst of all, that Whitney's machines damaged cotton fibers during the ginning process. That last rumor stuck: By the end of 1795, the English were refusing to buy cotton ginned on Whitney & Miller machines; only cotton ginned on illegal (and usually inferior) machines would do. "Everyone is afraid of the cotton," Miller wrote in the fall of 1795. "Not a purchaser in Savannah will pay full price for it."

COURT BATTLES

Whitney and Miller spent years battling the copycats in court and convincing the English textile mills that their cotton was still the best. The stress may have contributed to Miller's death from fever in 1803, when he was only 39. Whitney carried on, and finally won his last court fight in 1806. But the victory came too late to do any good, because the patent on the cotton gin expired the following year. Now copying Whitney's cotton gin wasn't just easy, it was also perfectly legal.

So how much money did Whitney make on the invention that created huge fortunes for Southern plantation owners? Almost none. In fact, some historians estimate that after his several years of legal expenses are taken into account, he actually *lost* money.

The cotton gin would clothe humanity, but in the process of inventing it, Whitney had lost his shirt. "An invention can be so valuable as to be worthless to the inventor," he groused.

THIS MEANS WAR

But Whitney was already working on another invention—one that would establish his fortune and transform the world again... even more than the cotton gin had.

In March of 1798, relations between France and the United States had deteriorated to the point that it seemed a war might be just around the corner. This presented a problem, because France was the primary supplier of arms to the United States. Where would the country get muskets now?

Congress had established two national armories beginning in 1794, but they had produced only 1,000 muskets in four years, and the government estimated that 50,000 would be needed if a war with France did come. Private contractors would have to supply the rest. Whitney, facing bankruptcy, was determined to be one of them.

Who needs a Stairmaster? There are 898 steps in the Washington Monument.

ONE THING AT A TIME

Until then, all firearms were made by highly skilled artisans who made the entire weapon, crafting each part from scratch and filing and fitting them by hand. Each part, and by extension each musket, was one of a kind—the trigger made for one gun wouldn't work on any other because it fit only that musket. Broken muskets could only be repaired by expert craftsmen. If the weapon broke in the middle of a military campaign, you were out of luck. Armorers capable of such skill were scarce, and new ones took forever to train, which was why the U.S. arsenals were having such a hard time making muskets.

IF YOU'VE SEEN ONE, YOU'VE SEEN THEM ALL

Whitney proposed a new method of making muskets, one he'd been thinking about since trying to speed up production of his cotton gins:

• Instead of using one expert craftsman to make an entire gun, he would divide the tasks among several workers of average skill. They'd be easier to train, and easier to replace if they quit.

• Each worker would be taught how to make one part. They would use special, high-precision machine tools, designed by Whitney.

• The tools would be so precise that the parts would be virtually identical to each other. Each part would fit interchangably in any of the muskets made in Whitney's factory.

• Once the pieces for a musket had been made, assembling them into the finished weapon would be—literally—a snap.

• Ready-made interchangeable spare parts would make it possible for any soldier to fix his musket himself.

BETTER LATE THAN NEVER

On June 14, 1798, Whitney signed a contract with the U.S. government to deliver 10,000 muskets within two years. But the war with France never came. Good thing, too, because Whitney missed his deadline by eight years. Supply shortages and yellow fever epidemics disrupted the schedule, so it took him longer to make his machine tools than he originally thought.

Whitney's reputation as a genius helped him to get extensions and advances against his government contract. But more than anything, what gave Whitney freedom to take the time necessary to perfect his new system was a demonstration he gave to President-elect Thomas Jefferson and other high officials in 1801. Dumping a huge pile of interchangable musket parts onto a table, Whitney invited them to pick pieces from the pile at random and assemble them into complete muskets. For the first time in history, they could.

THE AMERICAN SYSTEM

It may not sound like a big deal, but it was. Whitney had devised a method of manufacturing more muskets of higher quaility, in less time and for less money, than had ever been possible before. And he did it without the use of highly skilled labor. Once again, Whitney had invented something that would change the world.

What worked with muskets would also work with clothing, farm equipment, furniture, tools, bicycles, and just about anything else people could manufacture. Whitney called his process "the American system." Today it's known as *mass production*. In time it would overshadow even the cotton gin itself in the way it would transform the American economy.

Only this time, the transformation would be felt most in the North...and it would bring the South to its knees.

For Part III of the Eli Whitney story, turn to page 456.

*　*　*

Q&A: ASK THE EXPERTS

Q: *How do those luminous light sticks work?*

A: "You mean those plastic rods full of liquid chemicals that are sold at festivals and concerts, and that start glowing with green, yellow, or blue light when you bend them, and that gradually lose their light after an hour or so? When you bend the stick, you break a thin glass capsule containing a chemical, usually hydrogen peroxide, that reacts with another chemical in the tube. The reaction gives off energy, which is absorbed by a fluorescent dye and reemitted as light. As the chemical reaction gradually plays itself out because the chemicals are used up, the light fades." (From *What Einstein Told His Barber*, by Robert L. Wolke)

Not b-a-a-a-d: According to scientists, sheep can remember 50 faces for two years.

WONTON? NOT NOW

Palindromes are words or phrases that are spelled the same way backward and forward. Here are some of the best we've found.

Oozy rat in a sanitary zoo.

Rats paraded a rap star.

Too hot to hoot.

No. It is opposition.

Won't I panic in a pit now?

Panic in a *Titanic*? I nap.

Damn! I, Agassi, miss again! Mad!

O, Geronimo—no minor ego!

Boston ode: Do not sob.

Gateman sees name, garageman sees name tag.

Wonton? Not now.

"Red?" "No." "Who is it?" "'Tis I." "Oh, wonder!"

Todd erases a red dot.

I saw a Santa—at NASA was I.

Mad, a detail of Eden: one defoliated Adam.

Amy, must I jujitsu my ma?

Trapeze part.

No, sir! Away! A papaya war is on!

Men, I'm Eminem.

Satan, oscillate my metallic sonatas!

Snot or protons?

On a clover, if alive, erupts a vast, pure evil: a fire volcano.

Nurses run.

A six is a six is a six is a...

No lava on Avalon; no lava, no Avalon.

Egad! A base tone denotes a bad age.

Lapses? Order red roses, pal.

And finally, there's a town called Yreka near the Bathroom Readers' Institute. You can buy bread at the... Yreka Bakery.

Daily salary of a U.S. senator in 1789: $6. Daily salary in 2001: $580.

PET ME!

Some people have pet peeves.
Uncle John has pet trivia.

• Sir Isaac Newton invented the swinging door...for the convenience of his cats.

• Most dogs run an average of 19 mph.

• Ancient Egyptians could be put to death for mistreating a cat.

• Does your dog seem wary of going out in the rain? It's not because it's afraid to get wet. Rain amplifies sound... it hurts dogs' ears.

• Total Dog is an L.A. health club... for dogs. It has treadmills, masseuses, and an aerobics course. Cost: $800/year.

• Toy-breed dogs live an average of 7 years longer than large breeds. (Tibetan Terriers live up to 20 years.)

• In ancient Rome, it wasn't officially dark until you could no longer tell the difference between a dog and a wolf howling in the distance.

• Average cat bill at the veterinarian: $80/year for life.

• Most popular dog names in Russia: Ugoljok (Blackie) and Veterok (Breezy).

• In Japan, you can rent a dog as a companion for $20/hour.

• John Candy once paid $19,000 for a German Shepherd. (He didn't know the average price for a Shepherd was $1,500.)

• In 1997 a member of Australia's parliament proposed that all cats be eradicated from the country by 2002.

• Why do dogs try to mate with human legs? It's nothing personal. In an excited state, a dog will mount almost anything.

• A schoolteacher in Kansas was ordered not to feed his pet python in class. Why? He wanted to feed it puppies.

• A Persian cat named Precious survived 18 days without food. She was found when rescue crews heard her cries—across the street from the site of the World Trade Center.

• The heaviest (and longest) dog ever recorded was an Old English Mastiff named Zorba: 343 lbs (and 8 feet 3 inches from nose to tail).

• Julius Caesar hated cats.

Frogs drink through their skin.

FUNNY BUSINESS

Big corporations play by a different set of rules: their own.

DEATH AND NO TAXES

The Wall Street Journal reported in May 2002, that hundreds of U.S. companies have life insurance policies on millions of their workers—without the workers' knowledge. The beneficiaries? The companies themselves. The employees' families don't receive anything. In some cases, the companies can collect upon the death of an employee even if the person hadn't worked for them for years. One company, Mellon Financial Corporation, said that if all their covered employees and former employees were to die, Mellon Financial would collect $3.2 billion, and added that they had already collected $75 million. Tax free.

BROUGHT TO YOU BY THE LETTER $

PBS, the Public Broadcasting System, famous for TV shows like *Sesame Street* and *NOVA*, cannot, according to FCC regulations, air commercials. In place of commercials, they regularly show "messages" from corporate underwriters that some say are looking more and more like commercials all the time. One of the "messages" that brought out the critics: Pharmaceutical giant Pfizer, Inc. sponsored *Sesame Street* with its product Zithromax, an antibiotic often used to treat children. After the episode, kids and parents were told that *Sesame Street* was brought to you "by the letter Z, as in Zebra...and Zithromax."

YOU'RE FIRED! HERE'S A ZILLION DOLLARS

A CEO who runs his company into bankruptcy (and sometimes himself into prison) is a loser, right? Not always.

- In April 2002, Bernard Ebbers resigned "under pressure" as CEO of WorldCom after accounting irregularities were revealed and earnings were adjusted downward by an amazing $4.5 billion. In July the company filed for bankruptcy, the biggest in U.S. history. Ebbers's severance package: $1.5 million a year for life (his wife gets $750,000 a year if she outlives him).
- Richard McGinn was forced out as CEO of Lucent Technologies

Don't let the fancy title fool you—a *pulicologist* is someone who studies fleas.

in October 2000 after Lucent missed several financial targets. A month later, the company admitted that earnings had been grossly overstated, spurring a still-ongoing investigation by the SEC, and in January 2001, the company announced that 16,000 employees were going to be laid off. What did McGinn get? $12.5 million in cash and stocks. (He was also able to keep his other job—on the audit committee of American Express.)

• In 2001, as his company's stock prices were tumbling, CEO John Roth of Nortel Networks Corp. in Ontario, Canada, announced that he would retire in April 2002. By March 2002, the stock's price had fallen from its high of $124 (Cdn.) to less than $7 and some 50,000 employees had been laid off. What was Roth's retirement present? $700,000 (U.S.) a year for life. (In 2000, at the company's peak, he had cashed in over $91 million (U.S.) in stock options.)

TAKE ME OUT TO THE CLEANERS

Washington taxpayers paid 75% of the $425 million tab for the construction of the Seattle Seahawks' new football stadium, which opened in 2002. According to *Forbes* magazine in 2001, Seahawks owner Paul Allen was the fourth richest person in the world, worth an estimated $30 billion.

TAKE THE MONEY AND RUN...TO BERMUDA

Most everybody has heard about big corporations moving their headquarters to faraway places like Bermuda to avoid paying income taxes. In fact, the IRS estimates that as much as $70 billion is lost every year. So how does the U.S. government punish these tax dodgers?

• Construction firm Foster Wheeler moved its address from New Jersey to Bermuda in May 2001. Government response: Wheeler got more than $600 million in federal contracts in 2001. (That's taxpayer money.)

• Tyco International moved to Bermuda in 1997. Government response: Tyco has gotten more than 1,800 contracts (and avoided more than $400 million in taxes every year) since then.

• The offices of consulting firm Accenture (an offshoot of Arthur Andersen) set up headquarters in Bermuda in July 2001. U.S. government response: Accenture received $1 billion in federal contracts in fiscal year 2001. One of them was to redesign a website...for the IRS.

3% of U.S. motorists worry about forgetting where they parked.

OLD HISTORY, NEW THEORY

Here's another example of new findings that may change history books.

The Event: On May 6, 1937, the German blimp *Hindenburg* exploded over a New Jersey airfield, killing 36 people, and effectively ending the age of passenger airships.

What the History Books Say: The explosion was caused when the highly volatile hydrogen gas that kept the airship afloat was ignited, most likely by a static electric charge.

New Theory: Two boards of inquiry couldn't explain how the hydrogen escaped from sealed gas cells, which it had to do before it could explode. Yet investigators still determined that hydrogen was the cause of the explosion. According to Dr. William Van Vorst, a chemical engineer at UCLA, they were wrong.

A frame-by-frame analysis of film footage suggests that whatever it was that first ignited, it wasn't the hydrogen. "The picture indicates a downward burning. Hydrogen would burn only upward," Van Vorst says, "with a colorless flame." Eyewitnesses described the explosion as more like "a fireworks display."

So what caused the explosion? Van Vorst says it was the *Hindenburg*'s skin. The ship's cotton shell was treated with chemicals so volatile that they "might well serve as rocket propellant," he says. And the way it was attached to the frame allowed for the buildup of large amounts of static electricity, which, when discharged, were enough to ignite the fabric.

Smoking Gun: It turns out that the Zeppelin Company quietly conducted its own investigation after the disaster...and concluded the same thing. The *Hindenburg*'s sister ship, *Graf Zeppelin*, was reconstructed using new methods and materials, and went on to fly more than a million miles without incident.

Publicly, however, the company blamed hydrogen. Why? Politics. The United States controlled the world supply of helium, which is nonflammable, but refused to sell any to Nazi Germany. So Zeppelin had to use explosive hydrogen gas...which made the United States look bad when the *Hindenburg* went down in flames.

Ohio had 161 horse-and-buggy crashes in 1999, the last year that statistics were kept.

PATENTLY ABSURD

Here's proof that the urge to invent something—anything—is more powerful than the urge to make sure the invention is something that people will actually want to use.

THE INVENTION: Musical Baby Diaper Alarm
WHAT IT DOES: Three women from France marketed this alarm to mothers in 1985. It's a padded electronic napkin that goes inside a baby's diaper. When it gets wet, it plays "When the Saints Go Marching In."

THE INVENTION: The Thinking Cap
WHAT IT DOES: Improves artistic ability by mimicking the effects of autism. The cap uses magnetic pulses to inhibit the front-temporal, or "left brain" functions. This, say the two Australian scientists behind the project, creates better access to extraordinary "savant" abilites. They reported improved drawing skills in 5 of 17 volunteers in a 2002 experiment.

THE INVENTION: Pantyhose x3
WHAT IT DOES: Patented in 1997, they are three-legged panty hose. No, they're not for three-legged people, they're for women who know what it's like to get a run in their stockings. Instead of having to carry spares, you just rotate the legs. The extra leg is hidden in a pocket in the crotch; the damaged leg rolls up to take its place.

THE INVENTION: The Breath Alert
WHAT IT DOES: This pocket-sized electronic device detects and measures bad breath. You simply breathe into the sensor for three seconds, then the LCD readout indicates—on a scale of 1 to 4—how safe (or offensive) your breath is.

THE INVENTION: Weather-Reporting Toaster
WHAT IT DOES: Robin Southgate, an industrial design student at Brunel University in London, hooked up his specially made toaster to the Internet. Reading the day's meteorological stats, the toaster burns the day's predictions into a slice of bread: a sun for

40% of Americans say the theory of evolution is "probably not true."

sunny days, a cloud with raindrops for rainy days, and so on. "It works best with white bread," says Southgate.

THE INVENTION: Separable Pants
WHAT IT DOES: You don't take them off, you take them apart. The zipper goes all the way around the crotch, from the front to the back. That way, you can mix and match the legs with other colors and styles, making your own artistic, customized pants.

THE INVENTION: Vibrating Toilet Seat
WHAT IT DOES: Thomas Bayard invented the seat in 1966. He believed that "buttocks stimulation" helps prevent constipation.

THE INVENTION: Automatic-Response Nuclear Deterrent System
WHAT IT DOES: A relic from the Cold War era, this idea was patented by British inventor Arthur Paul Pedrick in 1974. He claimed it would deter the United States, the USSR, and China from ever starting a nuclear war. How? Put three nuclear warheads on three orbiting satellites. If sensors on the satellites detected that nuclear missiles had been launched, they would automatically drop bombs: one each on Washington, Moscow, and Peking.

THE INVENTION: Lavakan
WHAT IT DOES: It's a washing machine...for cats and dogs. This industrial-strength machine soaps, rinses, and dries your pet in less than 30 minutes. One of the inventors, Andres Díaz, claims that the 5-by-5-foot, $20,000 machines can actually reduce pet stress. "One of the dogs actually fell asleep during the wash," he said. Cats weren't quite as happy about being Lavakanned. "But it's better than having a cat attach itself to your face, which is what can happen when you try to wash one by hand."

* * *

MILITARY INDUSTRIAL SIMPLEX

Andorra is a small country between Spain and France. In the 1970s it reported an annual defense budget of $4.90. The money was used to buy blanks to fire on national holidays.

WHAT AM I?

What's white and black and read all over? This page of riddles. Here are some BRI favorites. Answers are on page 517.

1. Just two hairs upon her head
But she wears a flowered gown
And dances in the flower bed
The prettiest creature in town.

2. I am a word of letters three.
Add two, and fewer there will be.

3. My life is measured in hours,
I serve by being devoured.
Thin, I am quick...
Thick, I am slow...
A gust of wind is my greatest foe.

4. When I am filled
I can point the way,
When I am empty
Nothing moves me,
I have two skins—
One without and one within.

5. I appear once in a minute, twice in a moment, but never in a thousand years.

6. I am placed on the table, then cut, then passed around to everyone present, but I am never eaten.

7. We are identical twins who see everything in front of us, but never each other.

8. I am the only place where you will find yesterday after today.

9. To use me you must throw me away, but you will retrieve me when I am no longer needed.

10. I can circle the globe while never leaving a corner.

11. I am lighter than the lightest feather, but no matter how much strength you have, you couldn't hold me for more than a few minutes.

12. Without wings I fly,
Without eyes I cry.

13. I am only a head; I have nothing within. I've got no mouth; I speak with my skin.

14. Red and blue, purple and green, no one can touch me, not even a queen.

15. I go up and down the hill, yet I'm always standing still.

16. Two bodies have I
Though both joined as one
The stiller I stand
The faster I run.

The word *navel* gets its name from *nave,* which means "hub of a wheel."

AFTER THE QUAKE: THE FIRE WAR

In Part I of the story of the Great San Francisco Earthquake of 1906 (page 45), we told you how the quake set off massive fires around the city. Here's how the flames were fought.

BLASTING THE BLAZE

Within hours after the San Francisco earthquake, fires had broken out all over the city. The fires had many allies: the San Francisco hills, a steady breeze, the slow-burning redwood that composed 75% of the city's structures, numerous aftershocks, and insufficient water to fight them. So as a last resort, Mayor Schmitz decided to fight fire with fire.

What San Franciscans *did* have a lot of was dynamite—so they used it to build firebreaks, the theory being that disintegrating a building before the flames could reach it would cut off the fire's fuel supply. But this plan only partly worked; new fires sprouted up from the explosions. By noon much of downtown was engulfed in flame.

The destruction continued: The Army Medical Supply Depot went up in flames, taking with it material that could have been used in the disaster. One of the city's highest skyscrapers, the Call Building—which had withstood the quake—was reduced to ashes. Also leveled were the St. Ignatius Church (which housed a priceless pipe organ), the Examiner building, the Emporium department store, the Hall of Justice, Chinatown, the Columbia Theater, the California Academy of Sciences, and the Opera House, where world-famous Italian tenor Enrico Caruso had sung the previous night. One by one, San Francisco's most beloved buildings, including more than 30 schools, were destroyed. By midnight on Wednesday, most of the downtown district was in ruins, and there was more destruction to come.

ONE STEP FORWARD...

Wherever firefighters stopped the path of the fires, other avenues of fire opened up. The city streets were so narrow and the buildings so close together that there was more than enough fuel for the flames. One place where firefighters almost got the upper hand was Powell Street. Because it was very wide, the flames couldn't reach both sides and couldn't create the dangerous tunnels of fire that were spreading elsewhere in the city. And the massive St. Francis Hotel formed a huge firebreak. Surrounded by vacant lots, it gave the firefighters room to work and the flames no place to go. It looked like the fire might run out of real estate.

It would have, too, if it hadn't been for a few tired and hungry soldiers on the other side of the firebreak. They went into the empty Delmonico Restaurant to rest and find something to eat. They decided they wanted hot food, so they built a small fire to cook with. Bad idea. The "Ham and Eggs Fire," as it was later called, got out of hand and quickly spread. Soon the entire restaurant was in flames, followed by the Alcazar Theater next door, followed by every building on Geary Avenue. Then it headed toward Powell Street, scattering enraged firefighters and forcing them to regroup elsewhere.

TWO STEPS BACK

At this point, Mayor Schmitz decided the next fire line would be drawn at Van Ness Avenue. He ordered troops to start dynamiting homes to form another firebreak—an unpopular decision because many of the town's wealthiest and most influential people lived there. While one Army officer was sent to begin evacuation procedures, another was sent to take the fastest boat to the nearest city to replenish the town's exhausted stock of dynamite.

But somehow the message was misconstrued and the boat never left. With Van Ness Avenue completely evacuated and firefighters forming a line, they waited for the arrival of the dynamite...and waited...and waited. In disgust, Brigadier General Funston finally commandeered another boat and sent it on its way—but by then it was too late. In desperation, some firemen tried to set a backfire, but it failed to stop the advance of the flames, and Van Ness was on fire before the boat returned.

Next, the firefighters fell back to Franklin Street. It was narrow, but it was their only hope. Once again, residents were evacuated and firefighting forces were gathered. Demolition teams detonated home after home. Then the wind changed and it appeared that the fire was stopped. Bystanders rejoiced—until

What a drag: Each puff of smoke inhaled from a cigarette contains 4 billion particles of dust.

they realized the flames were just being pushed in a new direction. The exhausted firefighters had to drum up the energy to make yet another stand.

On the other side of the city, 20th Street was chosen as a firebreak. It was a fairly wide street with some open ground downhill from a large cistern that still had some water in it. Buildings on the north side of the street were quickly dynamited, and the engines pulled by horses were taken up the hill to the cistern. When the horses gave out, dozens of citizens pushed the engines up the hill themselves to get the water. Their efforts worked. The fire was stopped at 20th street.

After four days of battling the blazes, the firemen slowly began to get the upper hand. By Saturday, only remnants of the great fire were left smoldering in pockets around the city. Late that night a much-needed rain began to fall, and the smoke finally began to clear.

AFTERMATH

About 700 people died as the result of the quake and the fires, but countless more were saved by General Funston, Mayor Schmitz, and all of the brave men and women who stayed to fight the fires and help others. Property losses topped $500 million. Some 497 city blocks covering 2,831 acres lay in ruins. Twenty-eight thousand buildings were gone. Half of the city's population, amounting to a quarter of a million people, were homeless. But San Franciscans were determined to save their city; rebuilding began almost immediately.

Secretary of War Taft rushed a bill through Congress requesting half a million dollars in relief funds for the city. It was passed the same day. He ordered 200,000 rations sent from the Vancouver, Washington, Army Base, and ordered every military post in the nation to send all tents without delay. Then he sent another bill through Congress increasing his request for financial aid to $1 million. It was approved. In addition, $10 million more poured in from 14 nations.

Fundraisers for San Francisco were held all over the nation. Songwriter George M. Cohen sold souvenir newspapers for $1,000 per copy, and boxing champion Jim Jeffries sold oranges for $20 each. Relief distribution centers provided aid—the Red Cross served over 313,000 meals on April 30 alone.

China has a longer border than any other country on Earth (13,700 miles).

GETTING BACK TO NORMAL

Ten days later, water service was restored. Soon after came the lights along the main streets and the trolley cars. And the rebuilding continued nonstop. Within three years, 20,000 of the 28,000 ruined buildings had been replaced, and this time most of the buildings were made of brick and steel—not wood.

In 1915 San Francisco hosted the World's Fair, and by then there was barely any evidence left of the Great San Francisco Earthquake and fires.

A TRAGIC LEGACY

San Franciscans got a rude reminder of the big quake on October 17, 1989. An earthquake hit the area, and although it was much smaller, it was still big enough to cause extensive damage.

Way back in 1915 when they were still rebuilding, many new structures were built in the Marina District. Engineers used rubble, mud, and sand to fill in the shallow bay. But the new land wasn't properly compacted before the buildings went up. After the Exposition ended, homes and other buildings were constructed on top of this unstable base. Without solid ground to stand on, the Marina District was severly damaged in the 1989 quake.

Schmitz and Funston weren't the only heroes. Turn to page 349 for some of the other stories.

* * *

FUZZY MATH

Here's a U.S. Postal Service ad from 1996, defending its policy to raise the price of stamps:

"In 1940, a one-pound loaf of bread cost 8 cents, and in 1995 cost 79 cents; a half-gallon of milk went from 25 cents to $1.43 in the same period; and a first-class postage stamp went from 3 cents to 32 cents. Which, bottom line, means that first-class postage stamps remained well below the rate of inflation."

Do the math: Actually, those figures prove that the price of stamps rose 9% faster than the price of bread and 105% faster than the price of milk.

Raised-bump reflectors on U.S. roads are called "Botts dots." (Elbert Botts invented them.)

BENCHED!

Remember the saying "Judge not, lest ye be judged?" These men in black would have done well to follow that advice.

THE HONORABLE A. HITLER PRESIDING

Douglas County judge Richard Jones was suspended by the Nebraska Supreme Court after an investigation into 17 complaints concerning his conduct, both on and off the bench. Among the findings: Judge Jones had taken to signing court documents with names like A. Hitler and Snow White (he says he did it to keep court personnel on their toes), and setting bail amounts in the form of "a gazillion pengoes" and other imaginary currencies (he says it's "a matter of opinion" whether the fines are nonsensical or not). He was also accused of urinating on courthouse carpets, making an anonymous death threat against another judge (he says it was a "prank that went wrong"), and throwing firecrackers into the same judge's office. Judge Jones contested a number of the charges but admitted he threw the firecrackers. "I was venting," he explained.

GARDEN-VARIETY CRIMINALS

In August 1998, a Missouri judicial commission found Associate Circuit judge John A. Clark guilty of misconduct. The charge "most likely to be remembered," according to the *National Law Journal:* sentencing defendants to community service...and then allowing them to "do their time" by working in his yard.

WHERE'S YOUR LAWYER?

Dogged by a California state investigation into claims that he was abusive to defendants who appeared in his court without an attorney, San Bernardino County judge Fred Heene announced in 1999 that he would not seek reelection. The commission later concluded he had indeed been abusive.

An example of Judge Heene's conduct: A woman convicted of a traffic violation asked for more time to complete her community service because she'd been bedridden—on doctor's orders—during the final weeks of her pregnancy. The judge denied her request

In Atlanta, it's illegal to tie a giraffe to a streetlight or telephone pole. (Dogs are OK.)

and then sentenced her to 44 days in jail. When she protested that she had a seven-day-old baby at home, the judge replied, "Ma'am, you should have thought about that a long time ago."

TAKING A BITE OUT OF CRIME

In 1997 Judge Joseph Troisi spent five days in jail after he bit defendant William Witten on the nose hard enough to make it bleed. The incident came about when Troisi—until then a "highly regarded member" of the West Virginia bench and former member of the state committee that investigates judicial misconduct—denied Witten's bail request, prompting Witten to mutter an insult under his breath. Troisi then "stepped down from the bench, removed his robe, and there was a confrontation," said state police captain Terry Snodgrass. Judge Troisi pled no contest to criminal battery, served his five days, and then resigned from the bench. He also agreed to seek counseling for "impulse control."

TO TELL THE TRUTH

In 1995 the Texas state bar reprimanded newly elected criminal appeals court judge Steven Mansfield for lying about his personal background during his campaign for office. Mansfield claimed he was born in Texas—a big plus for voters in the Lone Star State—when he was actually born in Massachusetts. He also presented himself as a political newcomer when in fact he'd run for Congress twice in New Hampshire (he lost both times). He claimed to have handled more than 100 criminal cases, but about the only case he'd really handled was his own—when he was charged in Florida for practicing law without a license. (He lost, and had to pay a $100 fine.)

Amazingly, Mansfield managed to hang onto his job in Texas's highest criminal court and kept a low profile until 1999, when he was caught trying to scalp complimentary tickets to a Texas A&M football game and received six months' probation. He left office in 2000 but announced the following year that he wanted to come back because the judiciary was becoming too liberal without him. "I feel that I can be a more effective and more consistent conservative vote on the court," he explained. (He lost.)

Some species of Australian earthworms can grow to more than 10 feet in length.

MY END IS NEAR

Uncle John predicts that his death will come…on the last day of his life. As creepy as it sounds, some people have actually been able to predict their deaths much more accurately than that. Take these folks…

ARNOLD SCHOENBERG

Claim to Fame: Austrian composer…and a man obsessed with the number 13

Prediction: Schoenberg was born on September 13, 1874 and believed he would probably die on the 13th as well. Which month and year? Probably, he decided, on a Friday the 13th, and most likely in 1951, when he was 76 (7 + 6 = 13).

What Happened: That year, July 13 fell on a Friday, and Schoenberg stayed in bed all day, awaiting death. Late that night, his wife went to his room to check on him and scold him for wasting the day so foolishly. When she opened the door, Schoenberg looked up at her, uttered the single word "harmony," and dropped dead. Time of death: 11:47 p.m.…13 minutes before midnight.

FRANK BARANOWSKI

Claim to Fame: Host of "Mysteries Around Us," a radio show that dealt with issues of the paranormal

Prediction: Early in January 2002, Baranowski announced to his listeners that he expected to die on January 19.

What Happened: As advertised, Baranowski became an eerily suitable topic for his own show by dying on January 19—exactly as he said he would. Cause of death: congestive heart failure. "It's like he just produced his last show," a co-worker told reporters.

DAVID FABRICIUS

Claim to Fame: German astronomer and Protestant minister

Prediction: For some reason, Fabricius became fixated on the idea that he would die on May 7, 1617. Rather than tempt fate, when the day came, Fabricius decided to play it safe and stay home.

What Happened: About two hours before midnight, he decided that the danger had passed. He stepped outside to get some air…and was promptly murdered by a man from his own church.

THE REVEREND FREDDIE ISAACS

Claim to Fame: Founder of the Reformed Apostolic Church in Cradock, South Africa

Prediction: In January 2002, Reverend Freddie told his followers that he would soon be "going home." He had received a message from the Lord to join Him in Heaven, he said, and God had set the date for Saturday, February 2. He had his grave dug in advance and even booked the town hall for the funeral, busing in hundreds of "mourners" from all over South Africa. He also went on a shopping spree of Biblical proportions, sure that the Creator would take care of the bills after he was gone. "We will miss his earthly body," one church member told reporters, "but we know that he will be sitting at the right hand of the Father."

What Happened: February 2 came and went…and Freddie didn't die. A spokesperson explained to his enraged and humiliated followers that there had been a misunderstanding, saying, "His actual announcement was, 'I am going home.' That is why it is important for us to sit down and clarify certain words and terms, such as the difference between death and going home."

FELIPE GARZA, JR.

Claim to Fame: A 15-year-old high school student living in Patterson, California, in 1985

Prediction: Felipe had a crush on a classmate named Donna Ashlock, who had a degenerative heart disease and was only weeks away from death when Felipe's mother saw a newspaper article about her condition and read it to Felipe. "I remember his voice in the next room," Mrs. Garza remembered. "He said, 'I'm going to die, and I'm going to give my heart to Donna.'"

What Happened: Although Felipe seemed to be in perfect health, he died a few days later when a blood vessel in his brain suddenly burst. His family donated his heart to Donna the following day.

Final Chapter: Unfortunately, the ending was not a happy one. Donna's body rejected Felipe's heart a few years later, and she died in March 1989 before another suitable donor could be found. She and Felipe are buried in the same cemetery.

TOM SWIFTIES

This classic style of pun was originally invented in the 1920s. Here's a modern collection that was sent to us by BRI member Bryan Henry. They're atrocious, but we couldn't resist including them.

"Welcome to Grant's Tomb," Tom said cryptically.

"Smoking is not permitted in here," Tom fumed.

"Your boat is leaking," Tom said balefully.

"I prefer to press my own clothes," Tom said ironically.

"It's the maid's night off," Tom said helplessly.

"You're burning the candle at both ends," Tom said wickedly.

"I hope I can still play the guitar," Tom fretted.

"They pulled the wool over my eyes," Tom said sheepishly.

"Someone removed the twos from this deck," Tom deduced.

"Like my new refrigerator?" asked Tom coolly.

"I'll have to send that telegram again," Tom said remorsefully.

"The criminals were escorted downstairs," said Tom condescendingly.

"I haven't caught a fish all day!" Tom said, without debate.

"A thousand thanks, Monsieur," said Tom mercifully.

"I'd love some Chinese soup," said Tom wantonly.

"I forgot what to buy," Tom said listlessly.

"I need a pencil sharpener," said Tom bluntly.

"I punched him in the stomach three times," said Tom triumphantly.

"...and you lose a few," concluded Tom winsomely.

"I was removed from office," said Tom disappointedly.

"I wonder what it was like being one of Zeus's daughters," Tom mused.

"He only likes whole grain bread," Tom said wryly.

"I'm definitely going camping again," said Tom with intent.

"Oh no! I dropped my toothpaste," said Tom, crestfallen.

...were "the maximum a woman could safely carry."

LORD STANLEY'S CUP

The Stanley Cup, awarded annually to the best team in the National Hockey League, is the oldest trophy in professional sports. And whether you like hockey or not, we bet you'll find the cup's history fascinating.

THE FATHER AND SONS OF HOCKEY

Lord Arthur Frederick Stanley of Preston, England, son of the 14th Earl of Derby, was appointed Governor-General of the Dominion of Canada in 1888. When he arrived in the country he brought his seven ice-skating sons with him. They fell in love with the rough-and-tumble game of hockey and went on to become some of the best players of their time.

Nineteen-year-old Arthur Stanley and his brother Algy nagged their father for support in organizing the game into teams and leagues, and for a trophy to show as "an outward and visible sign of the ice hockey championship." Dad finally came through. At a dinner for the Ottawa Amateur Athletic Association on March 18, 1892, a member of the Governor-General's staff, Lord Kilcoursie (also a hockey player), made this announcement on behalf of Lord Stanley:

> I have for some time been thinking that it would be a good thing if there were a challenge cup which should be held from year to year by the champion hockey team in the Dominion. There does not appear to be any such outward sign of a championship at present, and considering the general interest which matches now elicit, and the importance of having the game played fairly and under rules generally recognized, I am willing to give a cup which shall be held from year to year by the winning team.

THE TROPHY

Lord Stanley instructed an aide in England to order a gold-lined silver bowl to be used as the trophy. The bowl measured 7½ inches high and 11½ inches in diameter, and cost about $50. Original name: Dominion Hockey Challenge Cup. But everyone called it the Lord Stanley Cup.

Stanley appointed two trustees and outlined some conditions:

- The winners are to return the Cup promptly when required by the trustees in order that it may be handed over to any other team which may win it.

• Each winning team is to have the club name and year engraved on a silver ring fitted on the Cup.

• The Cup is to remain a challenge competition and not the property of any one team, even if won more than once.

• The trustees are to maintain absolute authority in all disputes over the winner of the Cup.

• A substitute trustee will be named in the event that one of the existing trustees drops out.

GOING HOME

The boys got their trophy, and the game of hockey grew in popularity. But, ironically, they never got to play for it, and Lord Stanley, the father of organized hockey, never saw a Stanley Cup game. In July 1893, Stanley's brother died and Stanley was called back to England to become the 16th Earl of Derby. He never returned to watch a game for the trophy that bore his name.

Lord Stanley had the trustees present the trophy the first year, 1893, to the Montreal Amateur Athletic Association, which had won an ameteur tournament. Then they arranged for an actual championship game between his hometown Ottawa team and Toronto. But the game never took place.

Ottawa was considered the best team, but the trustees insisted they play a "challenge game" since it was a "challenge cup." They also insisted that the game be played in Toronto. Ottawa refused to do it. So the trustees declared the Montreal AAA the first Stanley Cup champions in 1893 without a playoff.

PLAYOFFS BEGIN

The first official Stanley Cup playoff game took place on March 22, 1894, when Ottawa challenged Montreal in the Montreal Victoria Arena before 5,000 fans. Montreal got to keep the Cup, winning the game 3–1.

Lord Stanley's announcement and his order of a small silver cup would mark the beginning of what would become Canada's national sport...and a game still played internationally more than a century later.

THE STRANGE TRAIL OF THE STANLEY CUP

Okay you just read about the origin of the Stanley Cup... but that's only the beginning. The Stanley Cup has an unusual history.

STANLEY CUP FACTS

• In 1919 the Spanish flu struck the Montreal Canadiens. They offered to play the last scheduled game with substitutes, but their opponents, the Seattle Metropolitans, declined, and for the only time in history, nobody won the Cup.

• In 1924 the trustees started putting more than just the team names on the cup. Today it is the only trophy in professional sports that has the names of winning players, coaches, management and club staff engraved on it.

• In 1927, after decades of being a multi league championship, the cup came under the exclusive control of the NHL.

• It got bigger: With each winner, a new ring was added to the lower portion of the cup. By the 1940s, it was a long, tubular trophy nearly three feet high. In 1948 it was reworked into a two-piece trophy with a wider base. In 1958 it was reworked again and got the five-ring, barrel-like shape it has today. It now weighs 35 pounds.

• In 1969 the original bowl was retired to the Hockey Hall of Fame in Toronto because of its fragile state. A silversmith in Montreal made an exact replica—down to scratches, dents—and bite marks—which is awarded today.

• There's one name crossed out. Peter Pocklington, the owner of the 1984 champion Edmonton Oilers, put his dad's name on it. The NHL wasn't amused, and covered it with "XXXXXXX."

• There were 2,116 names on the Stanley Cup as of May 2002.

• Seven women have their names engraved on the Stanley Cup.

• The cup is actually out of compliance with Lord Stanley's wishes—he wanted it to be a trophy for amateur athletes only.

ROWDY GAME, ROWDY TROPHY

Since each winning player and even the management gets to take the Stanley Cup home for a day, it has seen its share of wild times. Here are a few of the more notorious escapades:

• After the Ottawa Silver Seven won the Stanley Cup in 1905, one of the partying players boasted he could kick it across the Rideau Canal. The drunken group went home and groggily remembered the incident the next day. Luckily, the canal was frozen over. When they went back, the cup was sitting on the ice.

• In 1907 the Montreal Wanderers wanted their team picture taken with the Cup. After the photo session, the team left the studio—and forgot the Cup. It stayed there for months until the photographer's housekeeper took it home and grew geraniums in it.

• In 1924 the cup-winning Montreal Canadiens went to Coach Leo Dandurand's house for a late-night party. The car carrying the Cup got a flat, and the players put the Cup on the side of the road while they changed the tire. Then they drove off...without it. When they got to Dandurand's house, Mrs. Dandurand asked, "Where's the Cup?" They realized what they'd done and went back. Incredibly, the Cup was right where they'd left it.

• Muzz and Lynn Patrick found the Cup in their basement in Victoria, B.C., in 1925. (Their father was the coach of the championship Victoria Cougars.) The boys etched their initials onto the Cup with a nail. Fifteen years later, they got their names on it for real—as members of the 1940 champion New York Rangers.

• When the New York Rangers won the Cup in 1940, the players celebrated by urinating in it.

• The Cup was stolen from the Hockey Hall of Fame twice in the late 1960s. One of the thieves threatened to throw it into Lake Ontario unless the charges against him were dropped.

• In 1962 the Montreal Canadiens were playing the defending champions, the Chicago Blackhawks. During one of the games, a Montreal fan went to the Chicago Stadium lobby display case where the Cup was kept, took the Cup out of the case, and walked away. He almost made it to the door when he was stopped by a security guard. Later, he said he "was taking the Cup back to Montreal, where it belongs."

... a bear, in 1962. (It parachuted safely to Earth.)

• Chris Nilan of the 1986 champion Montreal Canadiens photographed the Cup with his infant son in it. He said, "His butt fit right in."

• A player on the 1987 champion Edmonton Oilers (purported to be Mark Messier) took it to a strip joint across the street from the rink and let everybody drink out of it. (It happened again in 1994 when the New York Rangers won. Mark Messier was also on that team.)

• In 1991 the Cup turned up at the bottom of Pittsburgh Penguin Mario Lemieux's swimming pool.

• In 1994 Mark Messier and Brian Leetch took the cup on *The Late Show with David Letterman*. There it was used in a sketch called "Stupid Cup Tricks."

• In 1996 Sylvain Lefebvre of the Colarado Avalanche had his daughter baptized in it.

• Rangers Brian Noonan and Nick Kypreos brought the Cup on MTV *Prime Time Beach House*, where it was stuffed with raw clams and oysters.

• The Rangers took the Cup to fan Brian Bluver, a 13-year-old patient awaiting a heart transplant at Columbia-Presbyterian Medical Center. According to his father, Brian "smiled for the first time in seven weeks."

• The Cup was once used as a feed bag for a Kentucky Derby–winning racehorse.

* * *

UNCLE JOHN'S DUBIOUS ACHIEVEMENT AWARD

Winner: Dr. Jukka Ammondt, professor of literature at Finland's University of Jyväskylä

Achievement: Not content with translating several of the King's greatest songs into Latin ("It's Now or Never" became "Nunc Hic Aut Numquam") Dr. Ammondt recorded an album of Elvis Presley songs in ancient Sumerian—a language spoken in Mesopotamia around 4000 B.C. ("Layoff of my blue suede shoes" translated as "My sandals of sky-blue, do not touch.")

Brace yourself: Orthodontic braces were invented in 1728.

SALMAN RUSHDIE

Words of wisdom from one of the world's great writers, Salman Rushdie.

"If somebody's trying to shut you up, sing louder and, if possible, better."

"Reality is a question of perspective; the further you get from the past, the more concrete and plausible it seems—but as you approach the present, it inevitably seems incredible."

"What is freedom of expression? Without the freedom to offend, it ceases to exist."

"I do not envy people who think they have a complete explanation of the world, for the simple reason that they are obviously wrong."

"The idea of the sacred is quite simply one of the most conservative notions in any culture, because it seeks to turn other ideas—uncertainty, progress, change—into crimes."

"Most of what matters in your life takes place in your absence."

"Free societies are societies in motion, and with motion comes tension, dissent, friction. Free people strike sparks, and those sparks are the best evidence of freedom's existence."

"Fundamentalism isn't about religion. It's about power."

"In the world of prophecy, angels bring you messages, they bring you the news. And I suggest that what we have now instead of angels is television. We watch television to get the message."

"It is very, very easy not to be offended by a book. You just have to shut it."

"When thought becomes excessively painful, action is the remedy."

"The only way to stop terrorism is to say 'I'm not scared of you.'"

"Free speech is the whole thing, the whole ball game. Free speech is life itself."

Stiff as a board: Wood frogs freeze solid in winter and thaw back to life in spring.

FOR SALE BUY OWNER

We're back with one of our favorite features. More proof that some of the funniest things in life aren't necessarily meant to be funny.

In an office: "Would the person who took the step ladder yesterday please bring it back or further steps will be taken."

On the door of a photographer's studio: "Out to lunch: If not back by five, out for dinner also."

Outside a new town hall: "The town hall is closed until opening. It will remain closed after being opened. Open tomorrow."

Outside a London disco: "Smarts is the most exclusive disco in town. Everyone welcome."

In a safari park: "Elephants Please stay in your car"

Outside a photographer's studio: "Have the kids shot for Dad from $24.95."

At a railroad station: "Beware! To touch these wires is instant death. Anyone found doing so will be prosecuted."

In a department store: "Bargain Basement Upstairs"

In an office building: "Toilet out of order. Please use floor below."

Outside a Burger King: "Now Hiring Losers"

In Cape Cod: "Caution Water on Road During Rain"

In Pennsylvania: "Auction Sunday—New and Used Food"

Next to a red traffic light: "This light never turns green"

Outside a house: "For Sale Buy Owner"

At a McDonald's: "Parking for Drive-Thru Service Only"

In Massachusetts: "Entrance Only Do Not Enter"

Also in Massachusetts: "Lake Chargoggagoggmanchauggagoggchaubunagungamaugg"

Seven thousand U.S. troops invaded Grenada in 1983. They...

AN EXPLOSIVE IDEA

The Nobel Prizes are perhaps the most respected awards on Earth. They're awarded every December 10, the anniversary of the death of their creator and namesake, Alfred Nobel. Here's a look at the man and his medals.

STRONG STUFF

In 1846 an Italian chemist named Ascanio Sobrero stumbled onto the formula for a powerful liquid explosive that he called *pyroglycerine*. Soon to become known as *nitroglycerine*, the substance was several times more powerful than black powder or any other explosive known to scientists at the time.

But nitroglycerine was also terribly unstable. It was difficult to make the stuff without blowing yourself up in the process, and it was just about impossible to transport it safely. A bump in the road, a change in air temperature, even prolonged exposure to sunlight was enough to trigger an explosion. Yet there was no easy way to detonate nitroglycerine in a controlled, predictable fashion. As far as Sobrero was concerned, nitroglycerine was more trouble than it was worth, a laboratory curiosity with no practical value.

WORTH A TRY

But nitroglycerine was *powerful*—and there was a lot of money to be made if someone could work the bugs out. So, in the late 1850s, a bankrupt Swedish munitions manufacturer named Immanuel Nobel decided to try in the hope that nitroglycerine would restore his family fortune.

Success would come at a terrible price: In 1864 Nobel's 20-year-old son, Emil, died in an explosion while experimenting with nitroglycerine. In spite of setbacks, though, Nobel's older son, Alfred, kept plugging away, moving his workshop to a barge in the middle of a lake after the Swedish government forbade him from rebuilding the one that had blown up. In 1865 the 32-year-old Alfred made a breakthrough—he invented the detonating cap. Instead of trying to set off the nitroglycerine directly, he got the idea of detonating a small amount of explosives—usually gunpowder or fulminate of mercury—and using the shock waves from that explosion to set off the nitroglycerine.

DOWN TO EARTH

That took care of the detonation problem, but nitroglycerine was still very unstable and dangerous to work with. Nobel solved that problem in 1866, when he came upon the idea of mixing nitroglycerine with an inert, porous type of earth called *kieselguhr.* The kieselguhr soaks up the nitroglycerine and forms a malleable, puttylike "plastic" explosive that can be molded into any shape—sticks, for example—and dried into solid form, which is much stabler than liquid nitroglycerine. Nobel named his new explosive *dynamite*, after *dynamis*, the Greek word for "power."

BACK IN BUSINESS

Nobel's timing could not have been better. The mid to late 1800s was an era of unprecedented public works projects, as countries all over the world constructed bridges, tunnels, dams, roads, railroads, mines, harbors, and canals. Dynamite was up to eight times more powerful than black powder, so wherever there was solid rock to be blasted through, it became the explosive of choice.

The military applications of dynamite were obvious, and although Nobel had pacifist tendencies, where profits were concerned, he was decidedly apolitical; he gladly sold explosives to just about any combatant who asked for it. During the Franco-Prussian War (1870–1871), for example, he made a killing—both figuratively and literally—selling explosives to both sides.

NOBEL'S SUR-PRIZE

Nobel became one of the wealthiest men in Europe, and his name became a household word. But if he assumed that wealth and fame would also bring him respect, he received what must have been a rude awakening when his brother Ludwig died in 1888. As we told you in *Uncle John's Absolutely Absorbing Bathroom Reader*, many newspapers mistakenly assumed that *Alfred* was the one who had died and wrote scathing obituaries attacking him as a merchant of death and "bellicose monster" whose contributions to science "had boosted the bloody art of war from bullets and bayonets to long-range explosives in less than 24 years."

Makes sense: Jersey cows come from Jersey, an island in the English Channel.

When Alfred Nobel died—this time for real—from a cerebral hemorrhage on December 10, 1896, the world was shocked to learn the details of his will: With the exception of a few small personal bequests, all of his assets were to be liquidated and the resulting cash invested in interest-bearing securities. Each year, the interest earned would be divided into five equal amounts and "awarded in prizes to those persons who shall have contributed most materially to benefit mankind during the year immediately preceding." The awards would be presented in five categories: Physics, Chemistry, Medicine, Literature, and Peace.

So, why did Alfred Nobel, "merchant of death," instruct that his estate be used to fund a Peace Prize? "Most of Nobel's biographers," writes Burton Feldman in *The Nobel Prize*, "feel that he was greatly influenced by his brother Ludwig's death—or rather, the inaccurate obituaries that followed it."

PRIZE FIGHTERS

Today the annual award of the Nobel Prize is taken for granted, but in 1896 the picture was far less clear. For one thing, Nobel's relatives were determined to fight his will so that they could claim a share of the estate. Not only that, the French government wanted to claim Nobel as a legal resident so that it could tax the estate. Either contest to Nobel's bequest would have left little money remaining for prizes. Both the Nobel family and the French government were eventually beaten back, but other questions remained.

The will stipulated that the prize winners would be chosen by the Swedish Academy of Sciences (Physics and Chemistry); the Karolinska Medical Institute (Medicine); and the Swedish Academy (Literature). The Peace Prize winner would be chosen by a committee of five persons appointed by the Norwegian Parliament. Would these organizations even agree to take up the tasks Nobel assigned them? The will said that all of the money would go toward prizes, but made no mention of how the organizations would be compensated, if at all, for their work. If even one of the parties balked, the entire will would be voided and the Nobel Prizes would never come to pass.

In 1897 it was finally decided that 20% of the interest income would go toward expenses; the remaining 80% would be awarded as prizes. That did the trick—on June 11, 1898, the last holdout,

No wonder the lines are so long: 14 of the world's 20 busiest airports are located in the U.S.

the Swedish Academy of Sciences, approved Nobel's will. The first Nobel Prizes were awarded in 1901, on the fifth anniversary of Nobel's death.

BAD PRESS IS GOOD PRESS

So how did the Nobel Prizes become so famous? They were the most valuable prizes of the day, but that alone isn't responsible for their fame. The credit goes to Marie Curie.

Marie Curie and her husband, Pierre, shared the 1903 Nobel Prize for Physics for their pioneering work in the discovery and study of radioactivity. When Pierre died in an accident in 1906, Marie carried on their work. A few years later, in 1911, she was being considered for a second Nobel Prize, this time in Chemistry, for discovering the radioactive elements radium and polonium.

At the same time, Curie was caught up in a public scandal involving her affair with French physicist Paul Langevin, who was married and had four children. All of the tawdry details of the romance—including death threats, duels, and steamy passages from the couple's stolen love letters—were published in newspapers across Europe for the world to see. And then she won her second Nobel Prize.

"Because of Curie," Feldman writes, "newspapers around the globe changed their way of reporting the Nobel Prize, generating endless publicity, and thereby finally changing the meaning of the awards."

It was tabloids as much as talent, that made the Nobel Prizes as popular as they are today.

Want to win a Nobel Prize? Turn to page 312 to find out how.

* * *

MONKEY BUSINESS

The Swedish newspaper *Expressen* gave 10,000 kronor ($1,250) each to five stock-market analysts and one chimp named Ola. They were free to play the market as they wished, the goal being to make the biggest profit. The humans used their expertise; Ola picked his stocks by throwing darts at the financial page. A month later, Ola was 1,541 kronor ($190) richer and the winner of the competition.

Poll: 68% of teenage girls said if they could change one body part, it would be their stomach.

THE SAGA OF SILLY PUTTY

What's stretchy and bouncy and comes in an egg? Silly question. Here's one of Uncle John's favorite toy stories: the origin of Silly Putty.

THE WRIGHT STUFF

During World War II, Japanese invasions of rubber-producing countries in the Far East vastly reduced the availability of rubber in the U.S. In the early 1940's, the U.S. War Production Board asked General Electric for help in developing a cheap substitute that could be used in the production of boots and tires. G.E. hired an engineer named James Wright to head the project.

In 1943 Wright accidentally dropped some boric acid into silicone oil. Result: he created an unusual compound that stretched further and bounced higher than rubber. Not only that, it was impervious to mold, didn't decay the way rubber did, and stayed stretchy and bouncy in extreme temperatures. The only problem was that neither scientists nor the military could find a good use for the stuff. In 1945, G.E. mailed samples to scientists all over the world, to see if they could figure out what to do with it.

GETTING SILLY

An advertising copyrighter named Paul Hodgson was at a party where one of the samples was being passed around. No one was coming up with any scientific uses for it, but they sure were having fun playing with it. To Hodgson it was clear: This was a toy.

It just happened that Hodgson was in the process of creating a catalog for a local toy store. He convinced the owner of the shop to feature what he dubbed "Bouncing Putty." It outsold everything else in the catalog (except a 50-cent box of crayons). Still, the store owner wasn't interested in manufacturing or marketing it, so Hodgson bought the rights and went into business himself. He renamed the product Silly Putty.

In 1950 Hodgson bought 21 pounds of the putty for $147 and hired a Yale college student to cut it up into one-ounce balls and put it into plastic eggs. Sales were slow at first, but Silly Putty's big break came several months later when it was mentioned in *The New Yorker* magazine. Hodgson's phone started ringing off the hook. He received 250,000 orders in only four days. A few years later, Silly Putty was racking up sales of over six million dollars annually—Hodgson was a millionaire.

Today, Binney & Smith, makers of Crayola, own the rights to Silly Putty and produce about 500 pounds of it every day. Over 300 million eggs have been sold since its inception—enough to form a ball of Silly Putty the size of the Goodyear Blimp. It now comes in 16 different colors including glow-in-the-dark, glitter, and hot flourescent colors. In 2000 Metallic Gold Silly Putty was introduced to celebrate the toy's 50th anniversary. There's even Silly Putty that changes color depending on the temperature of your hands. In 2001 Silly Putty was inducted into the National Toy Hall of Fame, taking its place beside such classics as G.I. Joe, Lincoln Logs, and Monopoly.

SILLY PUTTY FACTS

• In 2000 Binny & Smith sponsored a "Silliest Uses for Silly Putty Contest." The winner: replace your stockbroker by throwing a ball of Silly Putty at the stock page in the newspaper and investing in whatever stock it lifts from the newsprint. (Second place went to the woman who suggested it could be used to form a fake swollen gland to get out of an unwanted date.)

• One of the original Silly Putty eggs is on display at the Smithsonian Institution's National Museum of American History.

• Silly Putty cost a dollar in 1950 when it was first introduced, and still cost a dollar in 1976 when Hodgson died. Price in 2002: still under $2.

• Why did Hodgson pack Silly Putty in eggs? It was Easter.

• In 1968 Apollo 8 astronauts used a new adhesive to fasten down tools during their voyage into weightlessness: Silly Putty.

• In 1989 a grad student at Alfred University wanted to find out what would happen to a ball of Silly Putty dropped from a roof. He dropped a 100-lb. ball from the top of a three-story building. The ball first bounced about eight feet into the air, but it shattered into pieces on the second bounce.

In 2001 Indian railroads cited 14 million people for riding without a ticket.

UNCLE JOHN'S MEDICINE CABINET

There's a story behind every item in your medicine cabinet. Here are a few.

• Before World War I, "Aspirin" was a registered trademark of the German company, Bayer. When Germany lost the war, Bayer gave the trademark to the Allies as a reparation in the Treaty of Versailles.

• Why do men wear fragrances? Isn't that a little "girly?" It used to be. But thanks to some clever marketing during World War II, Old Spice aftershave became part of the soldier's standard-issue toiletry kit and changed the smell of things.

• Hate taking care of your contact lenses? It could be worse. Early contacts were made from wax molds (wax was poured over the eyes). The lenses, made of glass, cut off tear flow and severely irritated the eyes. In fact, the whole ordeal was so painful that scientists recommended an anesthetic solution of cocaine.

• On average, each person uses 54 feet of dental floss every year. That may sound like a lot, but dentists recommend the use of a foot and a half of dental floss each day. That's equal to 548 feet a year.

• In the late 1940s, aerosol hairspray was a growing fad among American women. The only problem was that it was water insoluble, which made it hard to wash out. Why? The earliest fixative was shellac, more commonly used to preserve wood.

• Women ingest about 50% of the lipstick they apply.

• Ancient Chinese, Roman, and German societies frequently used urine as mouthwash. Surprisingly, the ammonia in urine is actually a good cleanser. (Ancient cultures had no way of knowing that.)

• Almost half of all men who have dyed their hair were talked into it the first time by a woman.

A recent check of 62 police cars in Atlanta, Georgia, found that 27 had expired tags.

SORRY, CHARLIE

A whole page of gossip about famous people named Charles.

Charlie Sheen. When he was engaged to actress Kelly Preston, he accidentally shot her in the arm. She left him and married John Travolta.

Prince Charles. As a child, he was teased so much about the size of his ears that his great-uncle Lord Mountbatten told the queen to surgically fix the "problem." The queen declined. The prince's ears remain big to this day.

Charles Lindbergh. His father was a U.S. congressman. During a visit to the Capitol as a boy, he locked the doors of the bathroom and threw lightbulbs onto the street below.

Charlie Brown. If he were a real person, he'd be four and a half feet tall: his head would take up two of those feet, his body another two feet, and his legs six inches. Also, his head would be two feet wide.

Charles Barkley. After Tonya Harding called herself the "Charles Barkley of figure skating," Barkley said this: "My initial response was to sue her for defamation of character, but then I realized that I had no character."

Charles Darwin. Born on the same day as Abraham Lincoln, Darwin originally wanted to be a doctor, but had to give it up because he "wasn't smart enough."

Charlie Chaplin. His mansion was next door to notorious Hollywood rake John Barrymore's. Chaplin installed a telescope to spy on his neighbor's nightly exploits.

Charlie Chan. From 1925 to 1949, there were 47 movies made about the fictional Chinese detective. Six actors played Chan—not one was Chinese.

Q: Why are giraffes highly susceptible to throat infections?

BANANA PEELS

To most people, the banana peel is little more than a convenient wrapper around the fruit. We told you the history of the banana on page 143...but it turns out the peel has a story too.

SLIPPERY SUBJECT

Early 20th-century cities had a huge garbage problem. In those days, litter was a part of urban life—it was everywhere. In the wealthier areas of town, streets were cleaned on a regular basis, but in the poorer neighborhoods, they weren't. The result: the streets were polluted with rotting food, horse manure, and trash.

And then came the banana. By the late 1890s, better transportation methods made the banana so cheap that it became a common snack food, particularly popular among the working class. What happened to the peel after the banana was eaten? It ended up on the street.

Magazines, such as *Harper's Weekly* warned that "whosoever throws banana skins on the sidewalk does a great unkindness to the public, and is quite likely to be responsible for a broken limb." The *Sunday School Advocate* told the story of a man who slipped and broke his leg, which had to be amputated. Unable to work, he saw his family end up in a poorhouse. "All this sorrow," the *Advocate* said, "was caused by the bit of banana peel which Miss Sweet-tooth dropped on the sidewalk."

Banana peels were certainly no worse than all the other refuse on the street. But they were bright yellow, which made them highly visible, so they quickly became a symbol of a trash problem that was already out of control...and getting worse.

THE BIG APPLE

New York was the first city to seriously address the trash problem. The police department had been responsible for keeping the streets clean, but the men appointed by the police often did little more than just collect their paychecks. In 1895 Col. George E. Waring, Jr. was appointed the new Commissioner of Streets, assigned to overhaul the ineffective street-cleaning system. A mili-

A: 1) Long throats. 2) They can't cough.

tary man, he required his sanitation workers to wear white uniforms and and instilled a sense of pride in them. Parades of the uniformed street cleaners impressed city residents and slowly raised public awareness about the importance of clean streets.

It would be years before anti-littering and "Beautify America" campaigns permanantly changed the national landscape. But the banana was the turning point. The new science of city sanitation spread to other cities, and within a few years the banana peel, once a symbol of filth and ignorance, became synonymous with the movement for clean city streets.

FIVE THINGS TO DO WITH BANANA PEELS

Is the banana peel just trash? Some people claim it has beneficial uses:

• To get rid of a wart, tape a one-inch square of banana peel over the wart, inside part against your skin. Change the dressing every day or so until the wart is gone—probably within a month or two.

• Use the same treatment to get rid of a splinter. Tape a piece of peel over the splinter. By morning the enzymes (or something) in the peel should bring the splinter to the surface.

• To draw the color from a bruise, hold a banana peel over it for 10 to 30 minutes.

• In the late 1960s, a rumor spread that the inner part of the peel contained an hallucinogenic substance called *banadine*. Supposedly one could smoke it and get legally high. It didn't work (trust Uncle John), but *for historical purposes only*, here's the recipe:

> 1. Take 15 pounds of ripe yellow bananas. 2. Peel them. 3. Scrape off the insides of the skins with a knife. 4. Put all scraped material into a large pot and add water. Boil for three to four hours until it gets a pastelike consistency. 5. Spread this paste on cookie sheets and dry it in an oven for about 20 minutes. This will result in a fine black powder (banadine), which you roll into a cigarette and smoke. Supposedly you'll feel something after smoking three or four. (Unfortunately, it's a really bad headache.)

• To relieve the headache you just got from smoking a banana peel, tape or hold the inner side of a banana peel to the forehead and the nape of the neck. Supposedly the peels increase the electrical conductivity between the two spots.

In the 3 weeks that baby sparrows are in the nest, Mom and Dad make 5,000 trips for food.

URBAN LEGENDS

We're back with one of our most popular features. Remember the rule of thumb for an urban legend: if a wild story sounds a bit too "perfect" to be true, then it probably isn't.

THE LEGEND: A young woman who lives near a beach becomes pregnant but swears it's a mistake. It turns out that she accidentally swallowed microscopic octopus eggs while swimming and has a baby octopus growing inside her, spreading its tentacles to various parts of her body.

HOW IT SPREAD: The story was first published in the *Boston Traveler* in the 1940s and is kept alive mainly in coastal towns.

THE TRUTH: No medical records have ever been found to verify this story, but the universal fear of foreign bodies growing inside us keeps it afloat. Similar legends exist about eating pregnant cockroaches in fast food.

THE LEGEND: The Chevy Nova had dismal sales in Latin American countries because in Spanish the word *Nova* sounds like *no va*, which translates to "doesn't go."

HOW IT SPREAD: It began circulating in business manuals and seminars in the 1980s warning of the follies of failing to do adequate market research before releasing products in foreign markets. It spread from there to newspaper columnists. (Even Uncle John was duped—we included it in *The Best of Uncle John's Bathroom Reader*.)

THE TRUTH: When Chevrolet first released the Nova in Mexico, Venezuela, and other Spanish-speaking countries in 1972, the car sold just fine, even better than expected in Venezuela. According to *www.snopes.com*'s Urban Legends page, the very nature of the tale is absurd:

> Assuming that Spanish speakers would naturally see the word "Nova" as equivalent to the phrase "no va" and think, "Hey, this car doesn't go!" is akin to assuming that English speakers would spurn a dinette set sold under the name "Notable" because nobody wants a dinette set that doesn't include a table.

THE LEGEND: Teenagers drive around looking for open car windows at red traffic lights, yell, "Spunkball!" and throw a gasoline-soaked rag with a lit firecracker connected to it, hoping to start a fire inside the vehicle.

HOW IT SPREAD: Via e-mail, beginning in February 2000.

THE TRUTH: This is another variation on a common urban legend—the "gang initiation" legend. (Like the one about someone who flashed a friendly warning at an oncoming car without lights, only to be shot dead by recently-initiated gang members.) No police reports or news items exist to substantiate either legend. The "spunkball" e-mail looked even more credible when the name Bea Maggio, FCLS, Allstate Insurance Co., began appearing underneath it. After reading it, she supposedly passed it along to some friends—not in a company capacity—but just as a regular concerned (and duped) citizen. Her name stuck with the e-mail, giving it an "official" look, but have no fear, there's nothing official about it.

THE LEGEND: Walt Disney's body was cryogenically stored after he died in 1966, with instructions to reanimate him when the technology is available. He's supposedly stored underneath "The Pirates of the Caribbean" ride at Disneyland.

HOW IT SPREAD: The story began in the early 1970s, but who started it remains unknown. Disney's slow decline in health, his family-only funeral, and the fact that the public was not notified of his death until *after* he was buried all added fuel to the legend. It was given new life when it was reported in two unauthorized—and widely discredited—Disney biographies that were published in the late 1980s.

THE TRUTH: No documented evidence exists anywhere claiming this to be true. Disney's daughter Diane said in 1972, "There is absolutely no truth to the rumor that my father, Walt Disney, wished to be frozen. I doubt that my father had ever heard of cryonics." He wasn't frozen; in fact, he was cremated and buried in the Forest Hills cemetery in Glendale, a suburb of Los Angeles. Disney's very private life, along with his cult status, has put him in the same league with Elvis and Marilyn as a target for urban legends.

GOLF FLUBS

Uncle John was always embarrassed by his golf game...until he read these stories of big-time blunders made by big-time golfers.

Golfer: Bobby Cruickshank

Flub: Cruickshank was leading by two strokes in the final round of the 1934 U.S. Open. At the 11th hole, he looked on in dismay as his drive plopped into a creek. But to his surprise, the ball bounced off a submerged rock and rolled onto the green less than 10 feet from the hole. Cruickshank was so happy he tossed his club in the air and shouted thanks to God. The club came down and hit him in the head, knocking him flat on the ground. He got up after a few moments, but never quite recovered. He finished third.

Golfer: Gary Player

Flub: Player was in the lead at Huddersfield, England, in 1955, but on the final hole, he needed a par four to win. His second shot landed near the green, a few inches from a stone wall. Because there was no room for a backswing and he didn't want to waste a stroke knocking the ball clear of the wall, Player decided to ricochet the ball off the wall. It didn't work out exactly the way he planned. The ball bounced back and hit him in the face. Player was knocked for a loop and was penalized two strokes for "impeding the flight of the ball." He lost the tournament.

Golfer: Elaine Johnson

Flub: Johnson once drove a ball that hit a tree, bounced back, and landed in her bra. "I'll take the two-stroke penalty," she said, "but I'll be damned if I'm going to play the ball where it lies."

Golfer: Andy Bean

Flub: Bean was playing in the 1983 Canadian Open when his ball came to rest a mere two inches from the cup on the 15th green. Just to be cute, he tapped the ball into the cup using the grip of his putter instead of the head. Oops. He had forgotten about Rule 19, which states that "the ball shall be fairly struck at with the head of the club and must not be pushed, scraped or spooned." Bean was assessed a two-stroke penalty, which came back to haunt him when he lost the match...by two strokes.

...drugs. Cost: $11.7 million. Positive tests: 153. Cost per positive test: $76,470.

MY BODY LIES OVER THE OCEAN

When someone passes away and their remains are buried or cremated, it's said they are being "laid to rest." For some, the journey is just beginning.

DANIEL BOONE

Claim to Fame: 18th-century explorer and American frontiersman

Final Resting Place: Near Charette, Missouri...or maybe Frankfort, Kentucky

Details: If you owned a cemetery and wanted to attract new customers, how would you do it? One trick: a celebrity endorsement. Living celebrity pitchmen are best, but dead celebrities aren't bad either, because they can't complain.

That's how Daniel Boone ended up in Frankfort. When he died in the backwoods of Missouri in September 1820, he was buried in a small graveyard on a farm near Charette, in accordance with his wishes. But in 1845, the Capital Cemetery Company of Frankfort, Kentucky, started looking around for a famous American to bury in its new cemetery in the state capital. Boone was the perfect candidate: he was one of the founders of Kentucky and though he eventually left the state over a land dispute and swore he'd never return, he was still considered a hero.

Boone was also admired in Missouri, so the owners of Capital Cemetery had to act quickly and move the body before anyone could object. They enlisted the support of some of Boone's distant relatives, and then went to the farm and talked the new owner into letting them dig up the body. But the graves were poorly marked, so no one knew for sure which one was Boone's. That didn't matter: they made their best guess, dug up the remains of two bodies—assumed to be Boone and his wife—and spirited them off to Frankfort for reburial.

To this day no one knows for sure whether Boone and his wife are buried in Missouri or Kentucky, and it's doubtful we ever will. After so many years in the ground, there's probably not enough left for a DNA test.

Would a water softener help? 500 Americans are injured in their bathtubs each day.

HUMANS OF THE SEA

Ever since he first saw Flipper *in the 1960s, Uncle John has been fascinated by dolphins. He's not alone—some scientists think dolphins are humans' closest relatives. Whether they are or not, we've still got a lot in common.*

ANIMAL MAGNETISM

Few other animals evoke such mystery and curiosity as the dolphin. The more we study them, the more we want to know about them. We know that dolphins live 30 to 40 years. They have a distinct social structure, traveling in flexible groups of between 6 and 12 called *pods*. Young dolphins stay with their mothers for three years or longer before moving on to a new pod. Yet, remarkably, a daughter will often return to her mother's group to have her first calf.

A dolphin's cerebral cortex—the portion of the brain that plans, thinks, and imagines—is larger than a human's and, indeed, dolphins are adept at planning, thinking, and imagining. According to professional trainers, there is no limit to what a dolphin can learn.

Here are some amazing examples of dolphin intelligence:

• **Dolphins learn quickly.** Two dolphins at Sea Life Park in Hawaii knew entirely different routines. One day the trainer accidentally switched the two dolphins and didn't know why they seemed so nervous about performing the stunts. One dolphin, trained to jump through a hoop 12 feet in the air, refused to jump at all until she lowered it to 6 feet. The other seemed shaky about navigating through an underwater maze while blindfolded. Not until the show was over did the trainer discover the error. The dolphin who had jumped through the 6-foot-high hoop had not been trained to go through a hoop at all. The other dolphin was familiar with the blindfold but had never navigated the underwater maze. Yet, somehow, each one had figured out how to perform the other's tricks before the end of the routine.

• **Dolphins can learn sign language.** They can understand syntax and sentence structure, knowing the difference between "Pipe fetch surfboard" ("Fetch the pipe and take it to the surfboard") and "Surf-board fetch pipe" ("Fetch the surfboard and take it to the pipe"). When asked, "Is there a ball in the pool?" the dolphin is able to indicate yes or no—meaning it has understood the language, formed a mental image of the object referred to, and deduced whether the object is or is not there. This is called *referential reporting* and is otherwise documented only in apes and humans.

• **Dolphins consistently demonstrate imagination and creativity.** At the Kewalo Basin Marine Mammal Lab in Hawaii, two young trainers were working with a pair of bottlenose dolphins named Akeakemai and Phoenix. The trainers got the dolphins' attention and then, together, they tapped two fingers of each hand together, making a symbol for "in tandem." They both threw their arms in the air, the sign language gesture that means "creative."

The instruction was "Do something creative together." The two dolphins broke away and began swimming around the tank together. Then in perfect choreography they leapt high into the air while simultaneously spitting water out of their mouths. Because dolphins don't normally carry water in their mouths, the move had to be planned and synchronized before they left the water, proving that this was not a matter of two dolphins playing follow-the-leader. When other games of "Tandem Creative" were played, the dolphins did such things as backpedaling and then waving their tail flukes, or doing simultaneous back flips. The trainers were always surprised.

• **Dolphins have a sophisticated language of their own.** Dr. Jarvis Bastian, a University of California psychologist, taught a game to two dolphins named Doris and Buzz. They were instructed to press one lever (on the left) when they saw a flashing light and another lever (on the right) when they saw a steady light. Then he taught them a new twist: when the light came on, Doris had to wait until Buzz pressed his lever, then she could press her lever. When they had this down pat, Dr. Bastian placed a barrier between the two dolphins so they couldn't see each other and only Doris could see the light. When the light flashed, Doris waited for Buzz to press his lever. Buzz, not knowing the light was on, did nothing. Doris then gave off a burst of whistles and clicks, and Buzz immediately pulled the correct lever. And he pulled the cor-

Like parrots, captive dolphins can imitate human voices.

rect lever every time the test was repeated.

• **Dolphins play jokes.** Dolphins in a San Francisco oceanarium were taught to "clean house," receiving a reward of fish for each piece of trash they brought to their trainer. A dolphin named Mr. Spock kept bringing in soggy bits of paper, getting reward after reward. The trainer finally discovered that the dolphin had hidden a big brown paper bag in a corner of the pool and was earning dividends by tearing off tiny pieces, one at a time.

At Busch Gardens in Florida, scuba diving "janitors" periodically entered the dolphin tank with large underwater vacuum cleaners to pick up debris from the bottom of the pool. On one occasion, the divers were puzzled because they were unable to find any garbage. Only the observers above the tank could see that a dolphin named Zippy was going in front of the divers, just out of their sight, picking up pieces of trash and transferring them to the area behind the divers, which had already been swept.

• **Dolphins enjoy playing games.** They have been observed playing catch, tag, and keep-away. They've been known to sneak up on birds resting on the surface of the ocean and grab them by the feet, pulling them under before releasing them. They intercept swimming turtles, turning them over and over. Once, two dolphins in an aquarium wanted to play with a moray eel, but the eel was hiding in a crevice under a rock where they couldn't reach it. One dolphin picked up a dead scorpionfish and poked at the eel with the spines. The eel swam into the open, where it was caught by the dolphins and teased until being released.

• **Dolphins are affectionate.** Researchers observing them in the wild have noted that a large part of a dolphin's day is spent in physical contact with other dolphins. They swim belly to belly or side by side, sometimes looking like they're holding "hands." They rub their bodies together, pet each other with their fins and flukes, and enjoy sex for the pleasure of it.

• **Dolphins echo the worst of human nature.** The world of dolphins is not all sweetness and light. Just as with humans, there seems to be a wide variation in dolphins' behavior toward members of their own species. Some dolphins exhibit violent aggression and fight with others by ramming and biting them, sometimes

Four most common names for popes: John, Gregory, Benedict, and Clement, in that order.

to the point of death. Male dolphins occasionally build harems, and one researcher even documented a case of a male kidnapping a female and holding her captive. Groups of strong males may gang up on young, smaller dolphins, harassing them. Adult males will sometimes kill infants fathered by another male. They are also consummate predators, ruthless in their kills, and have been known to kill for reasons other than hunger.

• **Dolphins also echo the best of human nature.** There are documented instances of dolphins coming to the aid of other dolphins. Healthy dolphins will support a sick or injured dolphin to the surface, helping it breathe. If one member of a pod becomes entangled in a fishing net, others will come to its assistance, often becoming entangled themselves. Female dolphins will guard another female who's giving birth. There are also many instances on record of dolphins coming to the aid of humans in trouble.

In November 1999, twelve Cubans boarded a small boat in an attempt to escape to the United States. Rough seas sank the boat, drowning most of the people on board. The mother of five-year-old Elian Gonzales stuck him inside an inner tube. When rescuers found him, he was surrounded by dolphins who had broken waves for him and driven away sharks for the two terrible days he had floated alone on the ocean.

* * *

SPARE CHANGE

• Coin collecting was so popular in the late 19th century that the U.S. government issued two coins just for collectors: the Columbian half-dollar of 1892 and the Isabella quarter of 1893. Both coins marked the 400th anniversary of the discovery of America by Columbus. The portrait of Queen Isabella of Spain was the first foreign monarch on an American coin.

• According to experts, only one country in modern times never issued coinage: the Republic of Texas. In 1836 Texas broke away from Mexico and became an independent nation. From 1836 to 1845, when it became the 28th state in the U.S., Texas issued paper money, but no coins. For small change it used U.S. cents and Mexican reals.

Cheesy fact: The holes in Swiss cheese are technically called "eyes."

LOONEY LAWS

Believe it or not, these are real laws.

Tightrope walking is illegal in Winchester, Massachusetts (unless you're in church).

It's against the law in Los Angeles to bathe two babies in the same tub at the same time.

In Margate City, New Jersey, it's illegal to surf in the nude or with a sock over the male genitalia.

If you live in Garfield County, Montana, you can't draw funny faces on window shades—it's illegal.

In Fruithill, Kentucky, any man who comes face to face with a cow on a public road must remove his hat.

It's illegal to sleep in a garbage can in Lubbock, Texas.

You're breaking the law in South Dakota if you fall asleep in a cheese factory.

It's illegal in Roanoke, Virginia, to advertise on tombstones.

In Idaho it's against the law to fish for trout while sitting on the back of a giraffe.

In Tennessee it's illegal to drive a car while you're asleep.

It's against the law to feed margarine instead of real butter to prisoners in Wisconsin.

In Hartford, Connecticut, it's illegal to walk across the street on your hands.

In Oxford, Ohio, a woman may not remove her clothing while standing in front of a picture of a man.

It's illegal in Oak Park, Illinois, to cook more than 100 doughnuts in one day.

It's against the law in South Bend, Indiana, to make a monkey smoke a cigarette.

It's illegal in California to peel an orange in your hotel room.

In Hawaii it's against the law to put coins in your ears.

In Hillsboro, Oregon, it's illegal to let your horse ride in the backseat of your car.

In Carmel, California, it's against the law for a woman to take a bath in a business office.

Deep fat: Americans eat enough ice cream each year to fill the Grand Canyon.

I WANT TO RIDE MY BICYCLE! PART II

In Part I (page 101), we saw the bike go from a modified toy to a useful mode of transportation. But even with all of the improvements, by the middle of the 19th century, bikes were still thought of by most as curious—and dangerous—monstrosities. Here's Part II.

MOVING ON UP

The pedals on Kirkpatrick MacMillan's improved "hobby horse" gave the rider a lot more control, but pedaling required brute strength. In 1862 a French carriage maker named Pierre Lallement improved on MacMillan's design by switching the iron rods and pedals from the rear wheel to the front wheel (technology that's still used in children's tricycles). The result: the *veloce.* Now the rider could crank the wheel and create motion with much less effort. As Lallement rode his veloce through the streets of Paris, creating a stir among townsfolk, he knew had something special, so he moved to the land of opportunity: America.

LOOK OUT BELOW!

Lallement arrived in Ansonia, Connecticut, in 1865. With little money to his name, he got a job in a carriage shop and in his spare time built what historians consider to be the first American bicycle.

He arranged to exhibit his new machine by staging a four-mile ride from Ansonia to the neighboring town of Derby and back. The first leg was mostly uphill, which was difficult. The ride back, however, was disastrous. At first, spectators were amazed to see Lallement speeding down the hill, but their excitement turned to horror when they realized he had no control over his machine—the veloce hit a rut, stopped, and the Frenchman went flying over the handlebars.

Undeterred, Lallement earned an American patent in 1866, but the rough New England roads and even rougher winters made the veloce a tough sell. So Lallement finally gave up and returned to France. When he got to Paris, what he saw amazed him: Parisians were riding around on veloces!

Stall tactic: John McEnroe once tied his shoelaces seven times during a match at Wimbledon.

Lallement's former employer, carriage maker Pierre Michaux, had copied Lallement's design and renamed it the *velocipede* (rough translation: "speed through feet"). With the help of his son, Ernest, Michaux built the first velocipede in 1863. In 1867 they displayed it at the Paris World's Fair and it attracted so much attention that Michaux decided to dedicate all of his resources to producing them. Soon velocipedes—"boneshakers" as they were nicknamed because of their lack of suspension and adequate brakes—became popular all over Europe.

THE PENNY-FARTHING

English mechanics came up with the next big innovation in bicycles—they increased the size of the front wheel. Because the pedals were attached directly to the axle, the larger the wheel, the farther a person could go with one rotation of the pedals. In some instances, the front wheel was four or five feet in diameter. At the same time, the rear wheel shrunk in size to give the bicycle better balance. The new machine became known as the "penny-farthing" because of the drastic disparity between the size of the front and rear wheels (it resembled two British coins, the penny and the farthing, placed next to each other). Now the rider had to carefully climb up the bike to get it going—not an easy task. But thankfully, penny-farthings were the first bikes with brakes.

The penny-farthing was introduced to America at the 1876 Philadelphia World's Fair, and people loved it. To cash in on the public interest, a Boston architect named Frank W. Weston founded a company to import penny-farthings from England. They were a big hit, but because they cost well over $100 each ($1,670 in today's dollars), they were only available to the rich. Aristocrats formed exclusive "riding clubs" in upscale neighborhoods with indoor tracks and private riding instructors. Middle-class people wanted to join in on the fun, but few could afford the expensive import.

Colonel Albert Pope, however, was about to change all that.

For Part III of the story, turn to page 366.

PHONING IT IN

Some stupid criminals actually go someplace to commit their crimes and get caught. These three lazy guys figured they could just phone it in. They were right.

NO SUCH THING AS A FREE RIDE

"In August of 1996, 19-year-old Donterio Beasley got stranded in Little Rock, Arkansas, and called police to request a ride downtown. When informed that it was against police policy, he hung up, waited a few minutes, and called back again. This time he reported a suspicious looking person loitering near a phone booth...and then he gave a complete description of himself. He thought he'd get a free ride downtown to the station, where he'd be questioned and released. Instead he got a free ride downtown and was charged with calling in a false alarm."

—Dallas Morning News

BOREDOM IN A BOOTH

"Ron Vanname was 21 years old in 1992 when he decided to make some prank obscene phone calls from a phone booth in Port Charles, Florida. He decided to make the calls to the 911 operator, and phoned nine times in sixteen minutes with new vulgarities each time. He was unaware that the 911 phone system automatically showed the address of every incoming phone call. Squad cars surrounded him before he'd even hung up the phone. He spent a week in jail."

—The Wolf Files

A BOMB FOR THE BOMBED

"Thirty-nine-year-old Ronnie Wade Cater of Hampton, Virginia, was arrested in 1997 after phoning in a bomb threat. Cater was at a bar, drunk, and wanted to drive home without being nabbed for DUI. So he phoned in his bomb threat saying there was a bomb at another local bar, hoping to divert police attention. The call was traced and he was arrested."

—News of the Weird

National religion of Haiti (unofficially): voodoo.

HOUDINI'S SECRETS

From 1896 to 1926, Harry Houdini was the world's most famous escape artist. He could get out of anything. There was no lock or latch that could hold him. How'd he do it? We'll never tell. Okay, you talked us into it.

THE TRICK: Escaping from a locked container
THE SECRET: Hidden tools
EXPLANATION #1: Houdini often hid tools by swallowing them. He learned the trick while working for a circus, when an acrobat showed him how to swallow objects, then bring them up again by working the throat muscles. Houdini practiced with a potato tied to a string...so he could be pull it back up if needed.
EXPLANATION #2: Houdini would ask several men from the audience come up onstage, first to search him to for hidden tools, and second, to examine whatever he was about to be locked up in: a safe or a coffin or a packing crate. He would then solemnly shake hands with each man. But the last man was a shill—someone who had been planted in the audience. And during the handshake, a pick or a key would be passed from hand to hand.
EXPLANATION #3: Houdini sometimes hid a slim lockpick—like a thin piece of wire—in the thick skin of the sole of his foot.

THE TRICK: One of his greatest—escaping from a water-filled milk can...without disturbing the six padlocks that secured the lid
THE SECRET: A fake can
EXPLANATION: Houdini folded himself into the cylinder (or body) of an old-fashioned milk can. But the neck of the can wasn't really attached to the body. It appeared to be held together by rivets, but the rivets were fake. The two sections actually came apart. Houdini could easily break the neck from the cylinder, step out of the milk can, and then reattached it. And because the can was placed inside a box, the audience never knew how it was done.

THE TRICK: Escaping from handcuffs
THE SECRET: Sleight of hand
EXPLANATION: If he couldn't pick the lock, Houdini had

another trick: he'd insist the handcuffs be locked a little higher on his forearm, then simply slip them over his wrists.

THE TRICK: Mind reading
THE SECRET: Secret stage code (and a clever assistant)
EXPLANATION: Houdini's wife, Bess, often participated in the show. For mind-reading tricks, they worked out a secret code where one could tip off the other using words that stood for numbers: pray = 1, answer = 2, say = 3, now = 4, tell = 5, please = 6, speak = 7, quickly = 8, look = 9, and be quick = 0.

If Houdini was divining the number from a dollar bill, Bess would say, "Tell me, look into your heart. Say, can you answer me, pray? Quickly, quickly! Now! Speak to us! Speak quickly!" Then Houdini the "mind reader" would correctly reply: 59321884778.

THE TRICK: Escaping from a straitjacket
THE SECRET: There was no trick—he did it in plain sight using a combination of technical skill and brute strength
EXPLANATION: From his 1910 book *Handcuff Escapes*:

> The first step is to place the elbow, which has the continuous hand under the opposite elbow, on some solid foundation and by sheer strength exert sufficient force at this elbow so as to force it gradually up towards the head, and by further persistent straining you can eventually force the head under the lower arm, which results in bringing both of the encased arms in front of the body.
>
> Once having freed your arms to such an extent as to get them in front of your body, you can now undo the buckles of the straps of the cuffs with your teeth, after which you open the buckles at the back with your hands, which are still encased in the canvas sleeves, and then you remove the straitjacket from your body.

ONE LAST SECRET: Often Houdini would escape quickly from his entrapment, then sit quietly out of sight of the audience, calmly playing cards or reading the paper while waiting for the tension to grow: "Is he dead yet?" "He's never going to get out alive!" Then, when the audience's murmurings and accompanying music had grown to a fever pitch, he would drench himself in water to make himself look sweaty before stepping triumphantly out in front of the curtain to humbly accept the raucous cheers.

Three words pulled from Microsoft Word's thesaurus in 2000: idiot, fool, and nitwit.

THE INCREDIBLE SHRINKING HEADS

There have been many head-hunting cultures in the world—even the French had the guillotine—but only one made shrunken heads. Here's the story.

THE JIVARO

The Jivaro (pronounced "hee-var-o") tribes live deep in the jungles of Ecuador and Peru. They don't do it anymore as far as anyone knows but as recently as 100 years ago they were ardent head shrinkers. The Jivaro tribes were constantly at war with other neighboring tribes (and with each other), and they collected the heads of their fallen enemies as war trophies. The head, once shrunk, was called *tsantsa* (pronounced "san-sah"). For the Jivaro the creation of tsantsa insured good luck and prevented the soul of the fallen enemy from seeking revenge.

As Western explorers came in increasing contact with the Jivaro tribes in the late 19th century, shrunken heads became a popular souvenir. Traders would barter guns, ammo, and other useful items for shrunken heads; this "arms-for-heads" trade caused the killing to climb rapidly, prompting the Peruvian and Ecuadorian governments to outlaw head shrinking in the early 1900s. If you buy a head today, it's guaranteed a fake.

THE JOY OF COOKING...HEADS

Here's the Jivaro recipe for a genuine shrunken head (Kids, don't try this at home): Peel skin and hair from skull; discard skull. Sew eye and mouth openings closed (trapping the soul inside, so that it won't haunt you). Turn inside out and scrape fat away using sharp knife. Add jungle herbs to a pot of water and bring to a boil; add head and simmer for one to two hours. Remove from water. Fill with hot stones, rolling constantly to prevent scorching. Repeat with successively smaller pebbles as the head shrinks. Mold facial features between each step. Hang over fire to dry. Polish with ashes. Moisturize with berries (prevents cracking). Sew neck hole closed. Trim hair to taste.

Second grossest fact in this entire book: You inhale about 700,000 of your own skin flakes daily.

GOOD DOG

Can a dog be a hero? These people sure think so.

GOOD DOG: Blue, a two-year-old Australian Blue Heeler

WHAT HE DID: One evening in 2001, Ruth Gay of Fort Myers, Florida, was out walking her dog when she accidentally slipped on some wet grass and fell. The 84-year-old woman couldn't get up, and no one heard her cries for help—except a 12-foot alligator that crawled out of a nearby canal. Gay probably would have been gator food if Blue hadn't been there to protect her. The 35-pound dog fought with the gator, snarling and snapping until the reptile finally turned tail. Then Blue ran home barking, alerting Gay's family that she was in trouble. Gay was saved. And Blue? He was treated for 30 puncture wounds. "It's amazing what an animal will do in a time of need," said the vet. "He's a pretty brave dog."

GOOD DOG: Trixie, a six-year-old mixed breed

WHAT SHE DID: In 1991, 75-year-old Jack Fyfe of Sydney, Australia, was home alone when he suffered a paralyzing stroke. Unable to move, he lay helpless, waiting for someone to discover him as the temperature outside climbed to 90 degrees. Fyfe was crying for water—and that's just what Trixie brought him. She found a towel, soaked it in her water dish, then laid it across Fyfe's face so he could suck out the moisture. She repeated this every day until her water dish ran dry, then she dipped the towel in the toilet. After nine days, Fyfe's daughter stopped by and found him—still alive...thanks to Trixie.

GOOD DOG: Sadie, an English Setter

WHAT SHE DID: Michael Miller was walking Sadie when he had a massive heart attack. He was unconscious, but his hand was still wrapped around Sadie's leash. Sadie tried to revive him by licking his face. When that failed, the 45-pound dog began pulling the 180-pound man toward home. For an hour and a half the dog labored to pull his body homeward, a third of a mile away. Finally reaching the back door, the dog howled until Miller's wife came out. Because of the dog's heroism, Miller recovered.

Poll result: 38% of teenage girls in the U.S. say they "think about their weight constantly."

BAD DOG

Can a dog be a pain? These people think so.

BAD DOG: Bear, a Newfoundland

WHAT HE DID: Glen Shaw, a trash collector in New Hampshire occasionally brought Bear along on his route. On December 20, 2001, Shaw got out of his 10-wheeled compactor truck to load some garbage into the back and Bear somehow released the hand brake. As the truck began to roll downhill, Shaw ran after it but it was no use. The runaway truck plunged into the Souhegan River, and Shaw plunged in behind it to rescue the dog. Good news: the dog survived. Bad news: it took a hazardous waste crew more than two hours to clean up the mess.

BAD DOG: Jake, a three-month-old Rottweilier

WHAT HE DID: The Dodson family of Norman, Oklahoma, went out and left Jake in the same place they always left him: the utility room. They returned hours later to find Jake...and a smoking pile of rubble where their home used to be. Evidently Jake had flipped the gas line switch, filling the room with natural gas and when the hot water heater kicked on, the gas exploded. Jake was hurled clear of the explosion...and escaped unharmed.

BAD DOG: a boxer

WHAT HE DID: Muammer Guney, 46, of Denizli, Turkey, had a heart attack while he was walking his dog in the park. The animal stood guard over his fallen master, barking and keeping would-be helpers at bay. By the time relatives arrived on the scene to pull the dog away, it was too late; doctors pronounced Guney dead.

BAD DOG: Stinky, a six-year-old mongrel

WHAT HE DID: In December of 2000 Stinky and his master, Kelly Russell, were out hunting near their New Zealand home. Russell set down his rifle for a moment and Stinky jumped on it. The gun went off, hitting Russell in the foot. At the Waikato hospital, doctors were unable to save his foot. Russell was also fined $500 for hunting illegally in an exotic forest.

No ump-dump rule: In pro baseball, you can't replace an umpire unless he's injured or sick.

REDUNDANCIES

We are all guilty of using 'em. We just can't tolerate a noun or verb standing alone, so we give it an adjective or adverb for company. That doesn't make them harmfully wrong—just doubly redundant. Here are a few sparkling gems we recently uncovered not long ago.

capitol building
baby calf
circle around
slippery slime
hollow tube
illegal poaching
old adage
NFL football team
merge together
sandwiched between
reflect back
very unique
strangled to death
successful escape
3 a.m. in the morning
old fossil
fellow countrymen
old geezer
new beginning
illegal scam

awkward predicament
appreciated in value
disappear from view
total extinction
violent explosion
knots per hour
temporary reprieve
cluster together
hoist up
free of charge
recur again
enclosed herewith
excessive overharvesting
swivel around
new recruits
fellow colleagues
first priority
invited guest
completely satisfied
sink down

Where do they all go? About 200 million tires are discarded every year in the U.S.

BATHROOM NEWS

Here are a few choice bits of bathroom trivia we've flushed out over the years.

ARTSY FARTSY

In 2001 a new work of art by Alphonse Gradant appeared in the Museum of European Art in Paris. Praised as "art in its rawest form...an expression of 21st-century angst, comparable to the best work of Picasso and Salvador Dali," the work later sold for $45,000.

Who is Alphonse Gradant? The museum janitor.

Someone swiped one of his diagrams, had it framed, and hung it in the museum as a joke. Is it art? "No," says Gradant. "It's the layout of the men's toilet," which he colored in with red and black pens to make it easier to understand. "I needed a simple diagram that the contractor could follow," he explains. "All I was trying to do was make his work easier, not create a work of art." Museum officials refunded the $45,000. "If it was meant as a joke," says a spokesperson, "It wasn't a very funny one."

SANITATION ACROSS THE NATION

In March 2002, Parrot Products introduced the Enable Kit, designed for drivers who are grossed out by bathrooms in highway truck stops and rest areas. Each $3.79 kit comes complete with hand wipes, "area and fixture wipes," rubber gloves, toilet paper, a paper seat cover, and even a face mask to protect against "any particulates floating around." Company founder Joe Gawzner says he invented the kit after years of experiencing "negative restroom conditions." "Why suffer when nature calls?" he asks.

WIPE AWAY THE CRACKS

In 2000 the city of St. Louis, Missouri, started using a new material to seal freshly tarred cracks in its roads: toilet paper. The paper reduces the tackiness of the tar so that it doesn't stick to people's shoes or to the tires of cars. T.P. offers advantages over traditional materials like sand and leaf mulch: it's cheap, it doesn't clog sewers, it doesn't stink like leaf mulch, and it's easy to apply—just slap

Wide load: Americans ate 15,000 tons of snack food during Super Bowl XXXVI (2002).

some onto a paint roller, attach a broom handle, and unroll it right over the tar. Bonus: As the toilet paper degrades, it adds an optical illusion. "Stoop down and look at it," says Nigel Martin, a city worker assigned to T.P. duty. "It looks like snow, doesn't it?"

TASTES LIKE...SWITZERLAND

In February 2001, a Swiss man named Roger Weisskopf won a lifetime supply of toilet paper after he went on the German television show *Wetten Dass?* and demonstrated his unusual talent: being able to identify the name and country of origin of any brand of toilet paper...by tasting it. More precisely, by "licking, sucking, and chewing" wads of the stuff until it gives up its secrets.

No word on whether Weisskopf ate his prize. It took him a year of practice to develop his skill, which friends and loved ones encouraged by bringing home foreign toilet paper whenever they traveled abroad. According to Weisskopf (and he would know), Swiss paper tastes the best, while Japanese paper tastes the worst. "It tastes like moth balls," he says. "It nearly turned my stomach when I was practicing." Weisskopf is now developing a singing toilet lid to cash in on his fame.

LIKE MONEY IN THE TANK

In the 1960s, the exchange rate for Indonesian currency was 325 *rupiah* to one U.S. dollar. Distressed by the high cost and low quality of Indonesian toilet paper, some western tourists started buying *sen* notes—worth 1/100 of a *rupiah*, or 32,500 to the dollar—and using them for toilet paper.

WHAT GOES DOWN...

Japanese engineers had a problem in 1993 with some of their new high-speed bullet trains. Everything in the trains was high-tech—except the toilets, which were the old, hole-in-the-floor style. The problem: when the train went through a tunnel, it created "compressed atmospheric pressure." In other words, whatever went down the hole came back up, splattering whoever was there. So were the toilets recalled? Not a chance—railroad officials just posted signs warning passengers not to use the toilets while the trains were going through a tunnel. (They also set up a fund to pay for hot baths and laundry service...just in case.)

IF THEY MARRIED

We finally found a use for celebrities... well, not the whole celebrity, just the name. Somebody actually took the time to invent these celebrity marriages, and we salute them.

- If Bo Derek married Don Ho, she'd be **Bo Ho.**

- If Yoko Ono had married Sonny Bono, she would have been **Yoko Ono Bono.**

- If Dolly Parton had married Salvador Dali, she would have been **Dolly Dali.**

- If Oprah Winfrey married Depak Chopra, she'd be **Oprah Chopra.**

- If Olivia Newton-John married Wayne Newton, then divorced him to marry Elton John, she'd be **Olivia Newton-John Newton John.**

- If Sondra Locke married Eliot Ness, then divorced him to marry Herman Munster, she'd become **Sondra Locke Ness Munster.**

- If Bea Arthur married Sting, she'd be **Bea Sting.**

- If Liv Ullman married Judge Lance Ito, then divorced him and married Billy Beaver (game show host), she'd be **Liv Ito Beaver.**

- If Shirley Jones married Tom Ewell, then Johnny Rotten, then Nathan Hale, she'd be **Shirley Ewell Rotten Hale.**

- If Ivana Trump married, in succession, actor Orson Bean, King Oscar of Norway, Louis B. Mayer (of MGM fame), and Norbert Wiener (mathematician), she would then be **Ivana Bean Oscar Mayer Wiener.**

- If Javier Lopez married Keiko the whale, and Edith Piaf married Rose Tu the elephant, they would be **Javier Keiko and Edith Tu.**

- If Tuesday Weld married Hal March III, she'd be **Tuesday March 3.**

- If Snoop Doggy Dogg married Winnie the Pooh, he'd be **Snoop Doggy Dogg Pooh.**

WORD ORIGINS

Ever wonder where these words came from? Here are the interesting stories behind them.

DOOZIE

Meaning: Something wonderful, superior, or classy

Origin: "The word comes from Duesenberg, an eminently desirable motor car of the 1920s and '30s. The Duesenberg featured a chromed radiator shell, gold-plated emblem, hinged louvered hood, stainless-steel running boards, beveled crystal lenses on the instrument panel, Wilton wool carpet, and twin bugle horns. Magazine ads for the luxury car carried the slogan: 'It's a Duesie.'" (From *The Secret Lives of Words*, by Paul West)

TO KOWTOW

Meaning: To show servile deference

Origin: "The word is Chinese and literally means 'knock the head.' It was an ancient Chinese custom to touch the ground with the forehead when worshiping or paying one's respects to an illustrious personage." (From *Why Do We Say It?*, by Frank Oppel)

TO NAG

Meaning: To annoy by constant urging or fault-finding

Origin: "European households of the early Middle Ages had a problem—rats infested every nook and corner; squirrels nested in the roofs. Between the rats and squirrels, the noise of gnawing was very disturbing. The Germans developed the word *nagen*, from an old Scandinavian term meaning 'to gnaw.' Eventually a person who gnawed at another by constant fault-finding was said to *nag*, and the word soon lost its earlier meaning." (From *I've Got Goose Pimples*, by Marvin Vanoni)

MANURE

Meaning: Animal excrement used to fertilize plants

Origin: "From the Latin *manu operati*, 'to work by hand.' Farming was constant manual labor, especially the fertilizing, which required mixing by hand. Genteel folks who objected to the word *dung*, the excrement of animals, were responsible for its euphemistic displacement with the more 'refined' *manure*.

"Even *manure* became objectionable to the squeamish; they preferred *fertilizer*. According to a famous story about Harry S Truman, the president was explaining that farming meant manure, manure, and more manure. At which point a lady said to the president's wife: 'You should teach Harry to say "fertilizer," not "manure."' Mrs. Truman replied, 'You don't know how long it took me to get him to say "manure."'" (From *The Story Behind the Words*, by Morton S. Freeman)

ADMIRAL

Meaning: High-ranking commissioned officer in a navy or coast guard

Origin: "This is an artificial spelling of the French *amiral*. The Arabian word *amir*, commander, is commonly followed by *al*, as in *amir-al bahr*, 'commander of the sea,' from which *amiral* resulted." (From *More About Words*, by Margaret S. Ernst)

BUCCANEER

Meaning: Pirate or adventurer

Origin: "The literal sense of the word was based on a native West Indian word meaning 'one who cures flesh on a barbecue.' Thus the name was initially applied to woodsmen in the West Indies in the 17th century. The word was transferred to pirates of the 'Spanish Main' whose culinary habits were similar." (From *Dunces, Gourmands & Petticoats*, by Adrian Room)

TEMPURA

Meaning: A Japanese dish of deep-fried vegetables or seafood

Origin: "Neither a native Japanese dish, nor a Japanese name. When the Portuguese arrived in the 17th century, the Japanese noticed that at certain 'times' (Portuguese, *tempora*), notably Lent, they switched from meat to fish. With typical subtlety the Japanese concluded that the word meant a variety of seafood." (From *Remarkable Words with Astonishing Origins*, by John Train)

How big would the Earth be if it had no room between its atoms? About as big as a baseball.

CRUEL CRANE OUTWITTED

Here's another Indian fairy tale. This one deals with the beauty of instant karma, or as Uncle John says, "What you flush down comes back around."

Long ago the Bodisat (the highest degree of saint, one incarnation below Buddha) was born to a forest life as the Genius of a tree standing near a certain lotus pond.

Now at that time the water used to run short during the dry season in that pond. It was not overlarge, but there were a good many fish. And a crane thought on seeing the fish: "I must outwit these fish somehow or other and make a prey of them."

And he went and sat down at the edge of the water, thinking how he should do it.

When the fish saw him, they asked him, "What are you sitting there for, lost in thought?"

"I am sitting thinking about you," said he.

"Oh, sir! What are you thinking about us?" said they.

"Why," he replied, "There is very little water in this pond, and but little for you to eat; and the heat is so great! So I was thinking, 'What in the world will these fish do now?'"

"Yes, indeed, sir! What *are* we to do?" said they.

"If you will only do as I bid you, I will take you in my beak to a fine large pond, covered with all the kinds of lotuses, and put you into it," answered the crane.

"That a crane should take thought for the fishes is a thing unheard of, sir, since the world began. It's eating us, one after the other, that you're aiming at."

"Not I! So long as you trust me, I won't eat you. But if you don't believe me that there is such a pond, send one of you with me to go and see it."

Then they trusted him, and handed over to him one of their number—a big fellow, blind of one eye, whom they thought sharp enough in any emergency, afloat or ashore.

Him the crane took with

World leader: One out of five pieces of the world's garbage was generated in the U.S.

him, let him go in the pond, showed him the whole of it, brought him back, and let him go again close to the other fish. And he told them all the glories of the pond.

And when they heard what he said, they exclaimed, "All right, sir! You may take us with you."

Then the crane took the old purblind fish first to the bank of the other pond, and alighted in a Varana tree growing on the bank there. But he threw it into a fork of the tree, struck it with his beak, and killed it; and then ate its flesh, and threw its bones away at the foot of the tree. Then he went back and called out: "I've thrown that fish in; let another one come."

And in that manner he took all the fish, one by one, and ate them, till he came back and found no more!

But there was still a crab left behind there; and the crane thought he would eat him too, and called out: "I say, good crab, I've taken all the fish away, and put them into a fine large pond. Come along. I'll take you too!"

"But how will you take hold of me to carry me along?"

"I'll bite hold of you with my beak."

"You'll let me fall if you carry me like that. I won't go with you!"

"Don't be afraid. I'll hold you quite tight all the way."

Then said the crab to himself, "If this fellow once got hold of fish, he would never let them go in a pond! Now if he should really put me into the pond, it would be capital but if he doesn't—then I'll cut his throat, and kill him!" So he said to him:

"Look here, friend, you won't be able to hold me tight enough; but we crabs have a famous grip. If you let me catch hold of you round the neck with my claws, I shall be glad to go with you."

And the other did not see that he was trying to outwit him, and agreed. So the crab caught hold of his neck with his claws as securely as with a pair of blacksmith's pincers, and called out, "Off with you, now!"

And the crane took him and showed him the pond, and then turned off toward the Varana tree.

"Uncle!" cried the crab, "the pond lies that way, but you are taking me this way!"

"Oh, that's it, is it?" answered the crane. "Your dear little uncle, you very

Q: What weighs more, a hamster or a Goliath beetle? A: They weigh about the same.

sweet nephew, you call me! You mean me to understand, I suppose, that I am your slave, who has to lift you up and carry you about with him! Now cast your eye upon the heap of fish-bones lying at the root of yonder Varana tree. Just as I have eaten those fish, every one of them, just so I will devour you as well."

"Ah! Those fishes got eaten through their own stupidity," answered the crab, "But I'm not going to let you eat me. On the contrary, it is you that I am going to destroy. For you in your folly have not seen that I was outwitting you. If we die, we die both together; for I will cut off this head of yours, and cast it to the ground!" And so saying, he gave the crane's neck a grip with his claws, as with a vice.

Then gasping, and with tears trickling from his eyes, and trembling with the fear of death, the crane beseeched him, saying, "O my Lord! Indeed I did not intend to eat you. Grant me my life!"

"Well, well! Step down into the pond and put me in there."

And he turned round and stepped down into the pond, and placed the crab on the mud at its edge. But the crab cut through its neck as clean as one would cut a lotus-stalk with a hunting-knife, and only then entered the water!

When the Genius who lived in the Varana tree saw this strange affair, he made the wood resound with his praise, uttering in a pleasant voice the verse:

"The villain, though exceeding clever, / Shall prosper not by his villainy. / He may win indeed, sharp-witted in deceit, / But only as the Crane has beaten the Crab!"

* * *

COMIC STRIP WISDOM

Calvin: People think it must be fun to be a super genius, but they don't realize how hard it is to put up with all the idiots in the world.

Hobbes: Isn't your zipper supposed to be in the front of your pants?

Nevada is the name of a town in Missouri.

Q&A: ASK THE EXPERTS

More random questions, with answers from the nation's top trivia experts.

FEELIN' GROOVY

Q: *Who first faded out the music at the end of a record, rather than having a proper ending?*

A: "Fade-outs became widespread in the United States as the result of a trade survey in the early fifties. This showed that when records were played on jukeboxes, people felt more inclined to replay a record that faded out because it left a subconscious feeling that you hadn't completely heard it. The only other innovation to stimulate jukebox plays was pioneered by the Chess Record Company. They developed a groove-cutting technique which ensured that when played on jukeboxes, their records were one-third louder than all other records in the machine." (From *The Best Ever Notes & Queries*, edited by Joseph Harker)

COUNTER CULTURE

Q: *When spilled coffee dries on my kitchen counter, it forms a brown ring, with almost nothing inside. Why does all the coffee go to the edges to dry?*

A: "When a coffee puddle finds itself on a flat, level surface, it tends to spread out in all directions. The liquid will stop spreading when it hits a barrier, any slight irregularity in the surface that it can't cross, such as a microscopic ditch. Depending on where the barriers happen to be, the puddle will take on a certain shape: longer in this direction, shorter in that, like an amoeba.

"As evaporation takes place, the puddle will start to dry first where it's thinnest: at the edges. That has the effect of making the puddle shrink, pulling its edges back, but it can't do that because they're stuck in the ditches. So as water evaporates from the edges, it has to be replenished from somewhere, and the only place it can come from is the interior of the puddle.

"Thus, there's movement of water from the interior of the puddle to the edges, where it evaporates. That water carries along with it the microscopic brown coffee particles which then find themselves stranded at the edges when the puddle finally runs out of water." (From *What Einstein Told His Barber*, by Robert Wolke)

A HAIR OF A DIFFERENT COLOR

Q: *Why does hair turn gray?*

A: "Gray (or white) is the base color of hair. Pigment cells located at the base of each hair follicle produce the natural dominant color of our youth. However, as a person grows older, more and more of these pigment cells die and color is lost from individual hairs. The result is that a person's hair gradually begins to show more and more gray.

"The whole process may take between 10 and 20 years—rarely does a person's entire collection of individual hairs (which can number in the hundreds of thousands) go gray overnight." (From *How Things Work*, by Louis Bloomfield)

CHALK IT UP TO EXPERIENCE

Q: *There is a common scene on TV and in the movies where there has been a murder. The body has been removed, but its outline is preserved on the floor in white tape or chalk. Do the police really do this?*

A: "At one time, maybe, but according to investigators we surveyed, it's really not done anymore. Why? While chalk or tape might make for dramatic TV, they also contaminate the crime scene, and contamination is a major headache for crime scene investigators." (From *The Straight Dope*, by Cecil Adams)

W-A-A-A-H!

Q: *Besides humans, do any other animals cry?*

A: "Only one other land animal cries: the elephant. Marine animals that cry include seals, sea otters, and saltwater crocodiles (the so-called 'crocodile tears'). All of these animals cry only to get rid of salt. However, one scientist, Dr. G. W. Steller, a zoologist at Harvard University, thinks that sea otters are capable of crying emotional tears. According to Dr. Steller, 'I have sometimes deprived females of their young on purpose, sparing the lives of their mothers, and they would weep over their affliction just like human beings.'" (From *The Odd Body*, by Dr. Stephen Juan)

Estimated number of people who could be fed for a year by the...

YOUR FOOD PERSONA

Here are the results of studies that explore our eating habits and how they relate to our behavior. You may think that it's all a bunch of baloney, that we've had one helping too many, but it is something interesting to chew on.

SOUP'S ON

"The foods we eat do say a lot about who we are as people," says Brian Wansink, head of the Food & Brand Lab at the University of Illinois. He conducted a study comparing subjects' soup preferences to their personality types. Here's what he found:

If you prefer...

- **Chicken noodle soup,** you are more likely to be a churchgoing pet owner. You are stubborn and prefer to stay indoors.
- **Minestrone,** you pay attention to nutrition as well as your waistline. Your family is very important to you, your pets are not.
- **Vegetable soup,** you don't get out much. You're not very spontaneous and you'd rather read *Family Circle* than *Time* or *Newsweek.*
- **Tomato soup,** you live life to its fullest. You seek adventure and love to party, but also find time to curl up with your dog or cat and a good book.

Wansink's conclusion: No matter which kind you prefer, soup is the ultimate "comfort food." It's a guilt-free, easy-to-prepare snack that reminds you of Mom. In fact, two-thirds of the test subjects claimed they felt better about themselves after they slurped their soup.

WHICH SPOON DO I USE?

But wait, there's more. According to a separate study conducted by *Food Processing* magazine in 1996, your personality can also be determined by *how* you eat your soup.

- If you drink your soup **straight from the bowl,** then you're a "free-spirited enthusiast." Never needing to please others, the path you follow in life is your own, and you couldn't be happier.
- If you eat your soup with a **large soup spoon,** then you're a "purposeful traditionalist." You know exactly what you want out of

life. When traveling from A to B, you don't meander—you take the direct route to obtain what you desire.

• If you drink your soup **from a mug,** then you're a "care-free independent." No one can tell you how to live your life because you already know what's best for you. You are the master of your world—you are all you need.

• If you eat your soup with a **small spoon,** then you are a "cautious connoisseur." Not one to rock the boat, you're pragmatic and take orders well. You work best behind the scenes. And without you, no project would ever be completed.

LOVE, ICE CREAM STYLE

Looking for that special someone? According to Dr. Alan Hirsch, the neurological director of the Smell and Taste Research and Treatment Foundation in Chicago, knowing someone's dessert preference can help you choose a potential mate. In his book *What Flavor is Your Personality?*, Dr. Hirsch reveals your "Ice Cream Romance Horoscope." Bring it with you to the freezer section of your local grocery store next time you're on the prowl.

• "If your favorite ice cream flavor is **vanilla,** you like to stay busy achieving your goals. Never one to waste time, you'd be happiest with another vanilla, someone as romantic and expressive as you."

• "If **double chocolate chunk** is your first choice, you recognize the need for stability; so you'll be most compatible with a stable, caring butter-pecan type or, if you're feeling adventurous, a chocolate chip lover may motivate you to stay focused."

• "Those who prefer **strawberries and cream** need someone to give them a sense of hope and optimism, so they'd be happy with chocolate chip lovers who can match their high standards, but do so with a lighter touch."

• "If you love **banana cream pie,** you have many choices—you're likely to be compatible with all other flavor favorites. You are such a good listener and so easy to be with that the other types seek your company, so you are never without a date."

• "**Chocolate chip** lovers most enjoy their ice cream in the company of either butter pecan, who will identify with their high standards, or with the double chocolate chunk lovers, who appreciate their charming nature."

Watch your step: There can be more than a million earthworms in a single acre of land.

• "**Butter pecan** lovers are most compatible with other butter pecan lovers because you both set such high standards that you can admire each other's good taste. Besides, another butter-pecan type won't be pestering you to express your feelings all the time."

* * *

POP QUIZ

Radley Balko was studying a map of the United States created by a Caltech student named Alan McConchie when he noticed something strange: The map showed which states refer to carbonated beverages as "soda," which ones call them "pop," and which ones call them "Coke." And it looked eerily similar to a map of the United States showing a breakdown of how each state voted in the 2000 presidential election—for Bush or for Gore.

Balko put the two maps together and made an amazing discovery: with a few exceptions, "pop" or "Coke" states went for Bush, and "soda" states went for Gore.

And even the exceptions make sense:

• Six "pop" states (Iowa, Illinois, Michigan, Minnesota, Oregon, Washington) voted for Gore. Why? They're traditionally liberal.

• Three "soda" states (Virginia, Nevada, Missouri) voted for Bush. Why? The urban "soda" areas went for Gore, but there weren't enough voters to beat out the rural parts of the states—all "Coke" and "pop" country—which went big for Bush.

• Florida is undecided about whether it's a "Coke" state or a "soda" state. Along the panhandle, where they went for Bush, they drink "Coke." But down in Miami, Palm Beach, and retirement areas they drink "soda"—and they voted for Gore. So who did they end up voting for? "Soda"...no, "Coke"...no, Bush.

Anomalies: Three "soda" states (New Hampshire, Alaska, and Arizona) went for Bush, and one "Coke" state (New Mexico) went for Gore. Balko can't explain why, but he predicts the overall trend will become more pronounced by the next election.

"I say look for Bush to be ordering lots of 'pop,' or be seen with many a can of Coca-Cola come 2004," he says, adding, "As for my analysis, go ahead and send my name to the Nobel committee."

As big as they are, ostriches only have two toes on each foot. Most other birds have four.

HARD-BOILED

Here's our tribute to some classic (and not so classic) Hollywood movies.

Burt Lancaster: "Why did you bolt your cabin door last night?"

Eva Bartok: "If you knew it was bolted you must have tried it. If you tried it, you know why it was bolted."

—*The Crimson Pirate*

"My first wife was the second cook at a third-rate joint on Fourth Street."

—Eddie Marr, *The Glass Key* (1942)

"When I have nothing to do at night and can't think, I always iron my money."

—Robert Mitchum, *His Kind of Woman* (1951)

Guy Pearce: "All I ever wanted was to measure up to my father."

Russel Crowe: "Now's your chance. He died in the line of duty, didn't he?"

—*L.A. Confidential* (1997)

"I used to live in a sewer. Now I live in a swamp. I've come up in the world."

—Linda Darnell, *No Way Out*

"He was so crooked he could eat soup with a corkscrew."

—Annette Bening, *The Grifters* (1990)

"It looks like I'll spend the rest of my life dead."

—Humphrey Bogart, *The Petrified Forest* (1936)

Rhonda Fleming: "You drinkin' that stuff so early?"

Bill Conrad: "Listen, doll girl, when you drink as much as I do, you gotta start early."

—*Cry Danger* (1951)

"You're like a leaf that the wind blows from one gutter to another."

—Robert Mitchum, *Out of the Past* (1947)

"I've got an honest man's conscience... in a murderer's body."

—DeForest Kelley, *Fear in the Night* (1947)

"I'd hate to take a bite out of you. You're a cookie full of arsenic."

—Burt Lancaster, *Sweet Smell of Success* (1957)

SNL PART III: EDDIE

When its tumultuous first era finally ended, Saturday Night Live *had no big stars and no producer, but NBC wasn't about to give up on it.* *(Part II is on page 199.)*

SATURDAY NIGHT DEAD

In the summer of 1980, only a few months before the fall season started, associate producer Jean Doumanian was promoted—against Lorne Michaels's departing advice—to executive producer. The remaining cast and writers, who agreed with Michaels that Doumanian wasn't up to producing the show, also left. Could *Saturday Night Live* survive without any of its original talent?

Hundreds of wannabes tried to get on the revamped show. Doumanian's plan, basically, was to "do what Lorne did" and find seven unknowns—three women and four men. She ended up with Gail Matthius, Denny Dillon, Ann Risley, Gilbert Gottfried, Joe Piscopo, and Charles Rocket, whom Doumanian envisioned as the new star. She still wanted an "ethnic"—so dozens of black and Hispanic comics were brought in to audition. One standout was a foul-mouthed, 19-year-old kid named Eddie Murphy. Doumanian had someone else in mind, but talent coordinator Neil Levy talked her into hiring him. Still, she only made him a featured player and limited his on-air time.

The ensuing season was bad, probably *SNL*'s worst. After the first new episode, Tom Shales echoed the public's sentiments when he wrote, "From the 7 new performers and 13 new writers hired for the show, viewers got virtually no good news." As the ratings began to sag for "Saturday Night Dead"—as it was being called—morale at Studio 8H hit an all-time low. No one could stand Doumanian or the show's arrogant star, Charles Rocket, who sealed his fate by saying the F-word on live television. Both were fired in the spring of 1981.

MR. MURPHY'S NEIGHBORHOOD

Few other shows could have rebounded from such a debacle, but NBC still had faith in *Saturday Night Live*. Dick Ebersol replaced Doumanian. Knowing that recurring characters and biting com-

Why is a female shark's skin twice as thick as a male's? Males like to bite during "courtship."

mentary had propelled the show in the 1970s, he set out to recapture that early magic. He fired the entire cast—save Murphy and Piscopo—and brought in new faces. Mary Gross and Tim Kazurinsky were recommended by their friend John Belushi. Young comedians Brad Hall, Julia-Louis Dreyfus (later of *Seinfeld* fame), and Gary Kroeger were brought in. John's younger brother Jim Belushi, also a veteran comedy troupe performer, joined the cast reluctantly in 1983 (he hated being compared to John).

OTAY!

Ebersol's first move: let Eddie loose. Murphy's characters, such as Gumby, Buckwheat, and Mr. Robinson (an urban parody of Mr. Rogers), became as popular as Belushi's samurai warrior and Radner's Roseanne Roseannadanna from the original cast. Ebersol later admitted that "it would have been very difficult to keep the show on the air without Eddie."

But Murphy's growing stardom soon alienated the other performers, especially his friend Joe Piscopo, the show's second-most-famous cast member. After starring in the hit film *48 Hours*, Murphy became too big for the show, even television in general. He left after the 1983 season to make *Trading Places* with fellow *SNL* alum Dan Aykroyd. To this day, Murphy—not Dan Aykroyd or Bill Murray or Mike Myers—holds the record as the highest-earning former *SNL* cast member.

STAR POWER

In 1984, trying to fill the huge void left by Murphy's absence, Ebersol did something new for *SNL*: he hired established names, hoping they would attract viewers. Billy Crystal's Fernando ("You look mahvelous!") and Martin Short's Ed Grimley ("I must say!") were funny, but they weren't Murphy. And viewers wanted Eddie Murphy. In fact, the highest rated episode of the entire 1984–85 season was on December 15, when he returned to host the show. At the end of a difficult season, Ebersol had had enough. He quit.

Here we go again: no producer, low ratings. Would* Saturday Night Live *rebound? Of course it would!
Turn to page 427 to find out how.

A $100,000 computer 20 years ago computed about as much as a $10 chip can today.

FREEDOM'S VOICE

Born a slave in 1817, Frederick Douglass secretly learned to read and write. He escaped slavery in 1838 and went on to become an acclaimed orator, newspaper publisher, abolitionist, and advisor to presidents Lincoln and Grant.

"Find out just what any people will quietly submit to and you have the exact measure of the injustice and wrong which will be imposed on them."

"There is not a man beneath the canopy of heaven that does not know that slavery is wrong."

"A little learning, indeed, may be a dangerous thing, but the want of learning is a calamity to any people."

"Power concedes nothing without a demand. It never did and it never will."

"The soul that is within me no man can degrade."

"I prefer to be true to myself, even at the hazard of incurring the ridicule of others, rather than to be false, and to incur my own abhorrence."

"Men are whipped oftenest who are whipped easiest."

"I know of no rights of race superior to the rights of humanity."

"You are not judged on the height you have risen but on the depth from which you have climbed."

"Liberty is meaningless where the right to utter one's thoughts and opinions has ceased to exist. That, of all rights, is the dread of tyrants."

"Men may not get all they pay for in this world, but they certainly pay for all they get."

"They who study mankind with a whip in their hands will always go wrong."

"The simplest truths often meet the sternest resistance."

"No man can put a chain about the ankle of his fellow man without at last finding the other end fastened about his own neck."

The droplets in a sneeze can travel 12 feet and remain in the air for as long as three hours.

SO YOU WANT TO WIN A NOBEL PRIZE...

*We told you about the history of the Nobel Prize on page 267. Now, how do you win one? Well, it turns out it's not as simple as "make a major contribution to humanity"—*THERE ARE RULES! *Here are a few of them.*

You can't nominate yourself. Anyone who does is automatically disqualified. No exceptions.

• **You must be alive.** Nominating dead people has never been allowed, but until 1974 if you died *after* you were nominated—but *before* the winner was chosen—you could still win, even though you were dead. (Dag Hammarskjöld, for example, won the 1961 Peace Prize after he died in a plane crash.) In 1974 the rules were tightened up—people who die after they are nominated can no longer win, even if they're the only person nominated.

• **There are no runners-up.** People who are alive when they are selected as the winner (usually in October or November) but die before the awards are handed out on December 10, are still considered winners, even though they're dead. So if you come in second behind someone who drops dead before they pick up their medal, you still lose.

• **You can't win by default.** What happens if you come in second behind someone who refuses to accept their Nobel Prize? Do you win...or at least get their prize money? Answer: No and no. When a person declines a Nobel Prize, they are still entered into the official list of Nobel laureates; the only difference is that they just get the annotation "declined the prize," next to their name. The forfeited prize money goes back in the bank. Who says "no" to a Nobel Prize? Vietnamese politician Le Duc Tho declined it in 1973.

• **There's no such thing as a team effort.** With the exception of the Nobel Peace Prize, which can be awarded to entire organizations, such as the International Red Cross (1917) or Doctors Without Borders (1999), no single prize can be awarded to more than three people. That's true no matter how many people contribute to the endeavor. So if you and three of your friends find a cure for cancer next year, one of you is going to be out of luck. Of all the Nobel rules, this one is "probably the most damaging on a personal level," says Dr. Paul Greengard, winner of the 2000 Nobel Prize for Medicine. "The scientific world is full of embittered team members who were left out."

• **Nobel Prize in Economics? What Nobel Prize in Economics?** Alfred Nobel's will stipulated five prizes: Physics, Chemistry, Medicine, Literature, and Peace. In 1968 the Nobel Foundation approved the addition of a prize for Economics, but it is awarded by the Central Bank of Sweden. Its official name is the "Central Bank of Sweden Prize in Economic Sciences in Memory of Alfred Nobel." So even if you win it, Nobel purists will tell you that it's not *really* a Nobel Prize. Only the five original categories are considered true Nobel Prizes. Adding insult to injury: If you do win the Economics Prize, they don't engrave your name on the face of the medal like they do with other prizes—they just inscribe it on the outer rim.

• **Prizes don't necessarily have to be awarded every year.** If war or some other problem makes it impossible for the prize committees to meet (as in World War I and World War II), or if the foundation just decides that nobody deserves an award that year, they don't give them out. The Peace Prize has been withheld 19 times—more often than any other Nobel Prize.

• **You don't get a laurel.** The term "Nobel Laureate" is just an expression. If you win a Nobel Prize, you get a gold medal, a diploma with your name on it, and a cash prize. If you want to wear a crown of leaves, you've got to make it yourself.

• **Good news: If you do win, you will get more prize money now.** Over the years, taxes, inflation, overly cautious investment strategies, two world wars, and the Great Depression ate into the Nobel Foundation's assets. It wasn't until 1991 that the prizes finally recovered their full value and were worth more than they were in 1901. Since then, their value has continued to rise; in 2000 the payout for each prize was about $1 million.

• **More good news (and some bad news):** If your government orders you to decline the Nobel Prize (as Hitler did to German winners after 1936), the Nobel Foundation will hold the award until you're able to accept it—but you won't get the cash prize; that goes back to the Foundation.

Did you hear the one about the guy who invented the door knocker? He won the "No Bell" prize.

LET'S PLAY PONG!

If you know anything about the pop culture of the 1970s, the name Atari is synonymous with video games. So what happened? Where did Atari go? Here's the story.

THE GAMBLER

In the early 1960s, a University of Utah engineering student named Nolan Bushnell lost his tuition money in a poker game. He immediately took a job at a pinball arcade near Salt Lake City to make back the money and support himself while he was at school.

In school, Bushnell majored in engineering and, like everyone else who had access to the university's supercomputers, was a Spacewar! addict. But he was different. To his fellow students, Spacewar! was just a game; to Bushnell, it seemed like a way to make money. If he could put a game like Spacewar! into a pinball arcade, he figured that people would line up to play it.

FALSE START

Bushnell graduated from college in 1968 and moved to California. He wanted to work for Disney but they turned him down, so he took a day job with an engineering company called Ampex. At night he worked on building his arcade video game.

He converted his daughter's bedroom into a workshop (she had to sleep on the couch) and scrounged free parts from Ampex and from friends at other electronics companies. The monitor for his prototype was a black-and-white TV he got at Goodwill; an old paint thinner can was the coin box.

When he finished building the prototype for the game he called Computer Space, he looked around for a partner to help him manufacture and sell it. On the advice of his dentist, he made a deal with a manufacturer of arcade games, Nutting Associates. Nutting agreed to build and sell the games in exchange for a share of the profits, and in return Bushnell signed on as an engineer for the firm.

If you've never heard of Computer Space, you aren't alone. The game was a dud. It *sounded* simple—the player's rocket has to destroy two alien flying saucers powered by the computer—but it

The Caribbean island of St. Barts is named for Bartolomeo Columbus, Christopher's brother.

came with several pages of difficult-to-understand instructions.

The fact that it was the world's first arcade video game only made things worse. Neither players nor arcade owners knew what to think of the strange machine sitting next to the pinball machines. "People would look at you like you had three heads," Bushnell remembered. "'You mean you're going to put the TV set in a box with a coin slot and play games on it?'"

NUTTING IN COMMON

Still, Bushnell was convinced that Nutting Associates, not the game, was to blame for the failure. And he was convinced that he could do a better job running his own company. So he and a friend chipped in $250 apiece to start a company called Syzygy (the name given to the configuration of the sun, the earth, and the moon when they're in a straight line in space).

That's what Bushnell *wanted* to name it...but when he filed with the state of California, they told him the name was already taken. Bushnell liked to play Go, a Japanese game of strategy similar to chess. He thought some of the words used in the game would make a good name for a business, and company legend has it that he asked the clerk at the California Secretary of State's office to choose between *Sente*, *Hane*, and *Atari*.

She picked Atari.

FAKING IT

Bushnell hired an engineer named Al Alcorn to develop games. Meanwhile, Bushnell installed pinball machines in several local businesses, including a bar called Andy Capp's Tavern. The cash generated by the pinball machines would help fund the company until the video games were ready for market.

Alcorn's first assignment was to build a simple Ping-Pong-style video game. Bushnell told him that Atari had signed a contract to deliver such a game to General Electric and now it needed to get built.

According to the official version of events, Bushnell was fibbing—he wanted Alcorn to get used to designing games and wanted to start him out with something simple. Ping-Pong, with one ball and two paddles, was about as simple as a video game can be. In reality, there was no contract with G.E. and Bushnell had no intention of bringing a table tennis game to market. He was convinced that the biggest moneymakers would be complicated games like Computer Space. "He was just going to throw the Ping-Pong game away," Alcorn remembers. But then Alcorn gave him a reason not to.

OUT OF ORDER

Instead of a simple game, Alcorn's Ping-Pong had a touch of realism: if you hit the ball with the center of the paddle, the ball bounced straight ahead, but if you hit it with the edge of a paddle, it bounced off at an angle. With Alcorn's enhancements, video Ping-Pong was a lot more fun to play than Bushnell had expected.

As long as the game was fun, Bushnell decided to test it commercially by installing Pong, as he decided to call it, at Andy Capp's Tavern.

Two weeks later, the owner of Andy Capp's called to complain that the game was already broken. Alcorn went out to fix it, and as soon as he opened the machine he realized what was wrong—the game was so full of quarters that they had overflowed the coin tray and jammed the machine.

That was only half of the story. The bar's owner also told Alcorn that on some mornings when he arrived to open the bar, people were already waiting outside. But they weren't waiting for beer. They'd come in, play Pong for a while, and then leave without even ordering a drink. He'd never seen anything like it.

That was their first indication that Pong was going to be a hit.

JUST A COINCIDENCE?

But did Nolan Bushnell really come up with the idea for Pong... or did he lift it from another video game company? Video history buffs still debate the issue today.

Here's what we do know: In the late 1960s, a defense industry engineer named Ralph Baer invented a video game system that could be played at home on a regular television. The system featured 12 different games, including Table Tennis.

Magnavox licensed Baer's system in 1971 and prepared to market it as Odyssey, the world's first home video game system. The company planned to sell the system through its own network of dealers and distributors. In May 1972, the company quietly began demonstrating the product around the country...and on May 24 it demonstrated it at a trade show in Burlingame, California.

"In later litigation," Steven Kent writes in *The Ultimate History of Video Games*, "it was revealed that Bushnell not only attended the Burlingame show but also played the tennis game on Odyssey."

UNANSWERED QUESTIONS

Did Bushnell have a revelation when he played the Odyssey game? Did it convince him that simple games like Pong would be more popular than complicated games like Computer Space?

Or was it just as he claimed—that he instructed Alcorn to invent a ping-pong game, perhaps inspired by the Magnavox Odyssey, only because it was the simplest one he could think of? We'll probably never know for sure.

As far as the law is concerned, the only thing that really mattered was that, unlike Willy Higinbotham (Tennis for Two) and Steve Russell (Spacewar!), Ralph Baer actually *had* patented his idea for playing video games on a TV screen and had even won a second patent for video Ping-Pong. His patents predated the founding of Atari by a couple of years.

Bushnell never applied for a patent for Pong, and didn't have a case for proving that he'd invented it. And even if he did, he didn't have a chance fighting a big corporation like Magnavox in court.

SMART MOVE

So why did Atari become synonymous with video games instead of Magnavox? It was skillfull maneuvering by Bushnell.

Since he couldn't win in court, Bushnell paid a flat fee of $700,000 for a license to use Baer's patents. That meant that Atari bought the rights free and clear and would never have to pay a penny in royalties to Magnavox. And because Magnavox was now the undisputed patent holder, they *had* to sue Atari's competitors in court whenever competing game systems infringed the patents. Atari didn't even have to chip in for the legal fees.

Magnavox had Odyssey on the market while Atari was still years away from manufacturing a home version of Pong. But Magnavox wouldn't capitalize on their exclusive market. Their first mistake was selling the product exclusively through their own network of dealers, when it would have been smarter to sell them in huge chain stores like Sears and Kmart. Their second mistake was implying in their advertising that Odyssey would only work with Magnavox TVs. That wasn't true, but the company was hoping to increase TV sales. All they ended up doing was hurting sales of Odyssey.

In 1975 they discontinued the 12-game system and introduced a table tennis-only home video game to compete against the home version of Pong. Then in 1977 they introduced Odyssey² to compete against Atari's 2600 system.

Yet in spite of all the effort—and in spite of the fact that they, not Atari, owned the basic video game patents—Magnavox was never more than a me-too product with a marginal market share. Magnavox finally halted production in 1983.

Turn to page 411 for the story of how videogames found their way into the home.

* * *

CELEBRITY GOSSIP

Meryl Streep. After the 1979 Academy Awards, she lost the Oscar statuette she'd won for *Kramer vs. Kramer*. Where was it found? On the back of a toilet in the ladies room, where she had left it.

Thomas Edison. As a boy he tried to invent a way for people to float by feeding his friend "gas-producing powder." It didn't work.

Jimmy Stewart. His father was so disgusted with Stewart's role in *Anatomy of a Murder*, he took out a newspaper ad urging people not to see it.

Richard Burton. "When I played drunks I had to remain sober because I didn't know how to play them when I was drunk."

Tom Cruise. He enrolled in seminary school at age 14 to become a priest. He dropped out when he was 15.

Joan Crawford. She was married five times. Weird habit: Every time she remarried, she replaced all of the toilet seats in her mansion.

A single ounce of gold can be stretched into a wire 65 miles long.

TEE-SHIRT WISDOM

BRI member Eva Perry found this on the internet.

I childproofed my house, but they still get in.

I'm still hot. It just comes in flashes.

At my age, "getting lucky" means finding my car in the parking lot.

Life is short, make fun of it.

I'M NOT 50. I'M $49.95 PLUS TAX.

I NEED SOMEBODY BAD. ARE YOU BAD?

Physically pfffffft!

I'm not a snob. I'm just better than you are.

MY REALITY CHECK JUST BOUNCED.

It's my cat's world. I'm just here to open cans.

Buckle up. It makes it harder for the aliens to snatch you from your car.

KEEP STARING....I MAY DO A TRICK.

We got rid of the kids. The cat was allergic.

My mind works like lightning. One brilliant flash, and it's gone.

EVERY TIME I HEAR THE WORD "EXERCISE," I WASH MY MOUTH OUT WITH CHOCOLATE.

Cats regard people as warm-blooded furniture.

Live your life so that when you die, the preacher won't have to tell lies at your funeral.

(On the front of the shirt)

60 is not old...

(On the back of the shirt)

...if you're a tree

Earth is the insane asylum of the universe.

In God we trust. All others we polygraph.

How do they know? According to lizard experts, iguanas can feel joy.

SAGE OF THE SIXTIES

For anyone who lived through the 1960s, Timothy Leary's name is synonymous with LSD. But this former Harvard psychology professor and counterculture guru had some really far-out wisdom to share.

"Civilization is unbearable, but it is less unbearable at the top."

"Women who seek to be equal with men lack ambition."

"You can't stop the human instinct to think for oneself. You can hold it down, but in every situation it springs forth."

"All suffering is caused by being in the wrong place. If you're unhappy where you are, *move*."

"The critics of the Information Age see everything in the negative, as if the quantity of information can lead to a loss of meaning. They said the same thing about Gutenberg."

"Think for yourself. Know what you're doing. Question authority."

"The problem with the sixties, the problem with most hippies, the problem with television watching, is it's passive consumption. You're just sitting there."

"Our genetic assignment is the receiving, processing, and producing of digital information."

"Man's best friend is his dogma."

"Never before has the individual been so empowered. But in the Information Age you do have to get the signals out. Popularization means making it available to the people."

"The universe is an intelligence test."

"You're only as young as the last time you changed your mind."

"Nobody ever understands what a pioneer is doing."

"We have this incredible brain, 120 billion neurons; the complexity is beyond our ability to conceive. The challenge of the human species is to learn how to operate this wonderful equipment."

"Intelligence is the ultimate aphrodisiac."

If you could drive to the sun at 60 mph, it would take 176 years...not including "pit stops."

THEY WENT THAT-A-WAY

Sometimes the circumstances of a famous person's death are as interesting as their lives. Take these folks, for example.

BUDDHA (SIDDHARTHA GAUTAMA)

Claim to Fame: Founder of Buddhism

How He Died: From indigestion, following a meal of spicy foods

Postmortem: Like many spiritual people who search for enlightenment, Prince Siddhartha Gautama hoped to find it by fasting, eating only mosses and roots. When that didn't work, he went back to eating a normal diet...and soon acquired the huge belly that became as famous as the religion he founded.

He also acquired what modern historians believe were ulcers—he suffered terrible stomach and intestinal pains—and they caught up with him in 483 B.C. when he sat down to a lavish meal of *sukara-maddava* (spicy pork) in the village of Pava, India. While eating, Gautama suffered an attack of stomach pain so severe that he wasn't able to finish the meal. He and his followers promptly left the banquet and began walking to the village of Kusinara. Along the way, Gautama collapsed from dehydration and may have worsened his condition by drinking tainted water. By the time he arrived at Kusinara, the Buddha—or Enlightened One—was bleeding, vomiting, and near death. Fading in and out of consciousness, he finally passed away after instructing his followers, "Try to accomplish your aim with diligence." He was 80.

PRESIDENT JOHN QUINCY ADAMS

Claim to Fame: Sixth president of the United States

How He Died: Shouting the word "No!"

Postmortem: Adams served as president from 1825 to 1829. In 1831 the ex-president was elected to the House of Representatives. He was still there 17 years later, when the House took up the matter of honoring U.S. Army officers who had fought in the Mexican-

Having friends for dinner: Jellyfish eat other jellyfish.

American war. Adams was vehemently opposed to the idea.

When the vote was taken and the House erupted into a chorus of "Ayes" in favor of the idea, Adams stood up and shouted, "No!" Right then and there he suffered a stroke, collapsing into the arms of another congressman. Four of his colleagues carried him out to the capitol rotunda for some air, and he regained consciousness long enough to thank them for their effort. He drifted in and out of consciousness for the next two days before dying on February 23, 1848.

WILLIAM THE CONQUEROR

Claim to Fame: William, Duke of Normandy, conquered England in 1066, in what became known as the Norman Conquest

How He Died: From a riding injury

Postmortem: In 1087 William and his soldiers attacked the French town of Mantes, destroying an enemy garrison and burning the town to the ground. Rather than waiting for the fires to go out, William decided to survey the ruins while they were still burning. Big mistake—his horse stepped on a hot coal and lurched violently, lifting William up off his saddle and plopping him on top of the *pommel*, the hard metal protrusion in the front of the saddle. The injury ruptured William's intestine, causing a severe infection that spread across his entire abdomen. He spent the next five weeks in excruciating pain, finally dying on September 9, 1087.

ELEANOR ROOSEVELT

Claim to Fame: Former First Lady, wife of President Franklin D. Roosevelt, U.S. Ambassador to the United Nations

How She Died: From a stroke, possibly the result of medical errors made while she was being treated for anemia

Postmortem: In April 1960, the 75-year-old Mrs. Roosevelt was found to be suffering from aplastic anemia, which means her bone marrow wasn't producing enough red blood cells. By April 1962, she was also suffering from a shortage of white blood cells and platelets, so doctors prescribed prednisone, a drug that stimulates the bone marrow to produce more blood cells. But prednisone has a side effect: it suppresses the body's ability to fight off infections.

In August 1962, Mrs. Rooselvelt was back in the hospital, this time with a fever and a cough. Her doctors considered the possibility that she was suffering from tuberculosis, but when a chest X-ray showed no signs of the disease, they declined to do any further tests.

Mrs. Roosevelt was discharged from the hospital...but six weeks later she was back again, this time in even worse shape and still suffering from a "fever of unknown origin." On September 27, her doctors finally took a bone marrow sample and sent it to a laboratory to test for tuberculosis, a process that takes four to six weeks.

By October 18, Mrs. Roosevelt was so miserable and so convinced her end was near that she had herself discharged so that she could die at home. Her test results came back on October 26: she had tuberculosis... and months of treatment with prednisone had made it impossible for her body to fight it off. Not only had the doctors' diagnosis been wrong, but the medication was the worst possible thing they could have given her.

Nine days after finally receiving the correct diagnosis, Mrs. Roosevelt, still at home, suffered a stroke and slipped into a coma. She died three days later.

* * *

TWO (VERY) DUMB CROOKS

"Charged with murder in Fort Lauderdale, Florida, Donald Leroy Evans wanted a little respect. Evans filed a motion which would allow him to wear a Ku Klux Klan robe during his court appearance. The motion also requested that Evans's name be officially changed on all court documents to 'the honorable and respected name of Hi Hitler.' Apparently, Evans thought Hitler's subjects were chanting 'Hi Hitler' instead of 'Heil, Hitler.'"

—***Presumed Ignorant***

A man was sentenced to two years in prison yesterday for trying to break *into* the Rideau Correctional Center. Shane Walker, 23, was believed to be bringing drugs to his friends last week when he was foiled by striking corrections workers who heard bolt-cutters snapping the wire fence and apprehended him.

—***National Post***

An astronaut orbiting Earth can see as many as 16 sunrises and sunsets every 24 hours.

A ROOM WITH A FISH

Do you select a hotel for the amenities it offers? Well, forget mints on your pillow. Here are a few examples of how far some hotels will go to get you into their rooms.

HOTEL: Hotel Monaco, Chicago
AMENITY: Goldfish
ROOM SERVICE: The hotel is proud to be pet-friendly—so much so that if you didn't bring one of yours, they'll lend you one of theirs. (On your next visit you can even ask for a specific goldfish by name.)

HOTEL: Hotel Monasterio, Cuzco, Peru
AMENITY: Oxygen
ROOM SERVICE: Cuzco is the home of the famed Inca ruins at Machu Picchu and sits at about 10,890 feet above sea level. For the altitude-weary visitor, oxygen pumps are supplied. Every room has one.

HOTEL: The Clift Hotel, San Francisco
AMENITY: Live music
ROOM SERVICE: If you're having trouble sleeping, this hotel has a string quartet on call. And they'll come to your room at bedtime to play you a lullaby. (Cost: $1,000)

HOTEL: The Jailhouse Inn, Preston, Minnesota
AMENITY: Steel bars
ROOM SERVICE: The old Fillmore County Jail, built in 1869, was converted into a hotel in 1989. For $129 (starting rate) you can spend the night in an actual cell.

HOTEL: A proposed hotel in Bozeman, Montana
AMENITY: Grizzly bears
ROOM SERVICE: Plans for this hotel include rooms in underground caverns—that are also grizzly bear dens. You'll get a TV, a kitchenette, and a one-way window to watch your roommates in their natural habitat.

Down to Earth: Caesar salad used to be known as "aviator's salad."

BOX OFFICE BLOOPERS

We all love bloppers... er... we mean bloopers. Here are some great ones from the silver screen.

Movie: *The Bridge on the River Kwai* (1957)
Scene: The film's opening credits.
Blooper: This blockbuster won seven Oscars, but not for spelling. They misspelled the star's name, Alec Guinness, as "Guiness."

Movie: *Clueless* (1995)
Scene: A close-up shot of Cher's (Alicia Silverstone) report card.
Blooper: The name on the report card is Cher Hamilton, not the character's name, Cher Horowitz.

Movie: *Vanilla Sky* (2001)
Scene: Julie (Cameron Diaz) and David (Tom Cruise) are in the car. Julie goes crazy and drives it off a bridge.
Blooper: The exterior shot reveals there's no one in the car.

Movie: *Die Hard* (1989)
Scene: When Sgt. Al Powell (Reginald VelJohnson) crashes his squad car, his forehead is bleeding pretty badly.
Blooper: Throughout the remainder of the film, no evidence of the wound is present.

Movie: *Double Indemnity* (1944)
Scene: Fred MacMurray plays a bachelor.
Blooper: Then why is he wearing a wedding ring?

Movie: *North by Northwest* (1959)
Scene: In a restaurant, Eve (Eva Marie Saint) pulls a gun on Thornhill (Cary Grant).
Blooper: Just before the shot is fired, a boy sitting at a table in the background puts his fingers in his ears to muffle the sound of a gun he has no way of seeing... but obviously knows is there.

Model president: As a struggling actor, Ronald Reagan once posed nude as an artist's model.

Movie: *Twister* (1996)
Scene: The story chronicles one of the biggest tornadoes in Oklahoma's history.
Blooper: Most of the road signs are from Texas.

Movie: *Shrek* (2001)
Scene: Shrek (Mike Myers) and Fiona (Cameron Diaz) blow up some balloons and let them go.
Blooper: The balloons fly up in the air. (Okay, we know they're fairy tale characters, but that doesn't explain how they could exhale helium.)

Movie: *Independence Day* (1996)
Scene: Inside a tunnel, Jasmine (Vivica A. Fox) and her son, Dylan (Ross Bagley), escape through a service door just before they're overtaken by a wall of fire. Then Jasmine calls the dog.
Blooper: Even allowing Hollywood its usual "artistic license," the fact that Jasmine and Dylan make it out is barely plausible. But the dog? A shockwave is tossing cars like toys, yet somehow superdog manages to jump out of the way barely a few feet in front of it.

Movie: *Kate & Leopold* (2001)
Scene: Spectators on a bridge are waving American flags.
Blooper: The flags have all 50 stars... in 1876.

Movie: *Pulp Fiction* (1994)
Scene: Vincent (John Travolta) and Jules (Samuel L. Jackson) are in an apartment when someone bursts out of the bathroom and starts shooting at them.
Blooper: The bullet holes are in the wall *before* the gunman starts shooting.

Movie: *Cocktail* (1988)
Scene: Tom Cruise goes into the Regency Theatre in Manhattan and gets into a fight.
Blooper: It must have been a long fight—when he went into the theater, *Barfly* appeared on the marquee. When he exited, it was *Casablanca.*

MOTHER NATURE IS OUT TO GET YOU

When you hear the word "danger," you probably think of slippery floors, shifty criminals, or busy intersections. These days, people tend to ignore the threats posed by the natural world. But after reading this article, you may decide not to come out of the bathroom—it's a dangerous world out there.

BEWARE OF: Your backyard
EXPLANATION: Some common garden plants and shrubs can kill you if you eat them. These attractive but potentially fatally toxic plants include rhododendron, daphne, English ivy, foxglove, hemlock, jonquil, mistletoe, morning glory, and yew. The list of plants that can leave you in a coma, paralyzed, or spasmodic is as long as your arm.

BEWARE OF: Golf courses and riverbanks
EXPLANATION: Each year about 100 people are killed in the United States by lightning strikes, and most of these unfortunate victims became targets while out enjoying golf or fishing. A typical lightning flash carries about 15 million volts, so you don't want to be caught swinging a number 5 iron or a 20-foot fishing rod when a storm comes by. The National Weather Service recorded 3,511 deaths and 11,489 injuries from lightning strikes between 1959 and 1999. PGA advice to all golfers is to stop playing and seek shelter as soon as any storm approaches.

BEWARE OF: The woods
EXPLANATION: "Assassin bugs," also known as "kissing bugs," have been known to suck blood from the lips, eyelids, or ears of a sleeping human. There are various species that hang out in the woodlands and bushes of Africa, Central America, South America, and even North America. Most assassin bugs aren't deadly to humans, but the *Triatoma infestans* makes up for it. Found mostly from Mexico to the south of Argentina, it can spread Chagas' disease, which will kill a person in just a few weeks by weakening the

nervous system, eventually causing a heart attack. Five thousand people die from Chagas disease each year.

BEWARE OF: Old baby rattles
EXPLANATION: Toy manufacturers once used castor beans as the noisemakers in baby rattles. They probably didn't know that castor beans contain *ricin*, a protein that's fatal to humans. Scientists estimate that, ounce for ounce, ricin can be 6,000 times more deadly than cyanide. A teeny bit of ricin, weighing no more than just one grain of salt, can kill an adult.

BEWARE OF: Jewelry
EXPLANATION: Not quite as toxic as ricin but still pretty dangerous is *abrin*. Abrin is found in jequirity beans which are used in rosary necklaces. Just one seed can be fatal, yet this bean is often used to make necklaces in Mexico and Central America.

* * *

REST IN PEACE

In 1994 Alexandra Sergeyev and several of her co-workers chipped in to buy three tickets in a lottery to win an automobile. Mrs. Sergeyev gave one to her husband to put in a safe place; soon afterward he dropped dead from a heart attack. It wasn't until after the funeral that she realized that

1) the ticket she gave her husband was the winning ticket
2) he put it in the pocket of his best suit
3) that was the suit he was buried in

Mrs. Sergeyev consented to have Ivan's body exhumed, but when the authorities went to dig him up, they discovered the grave was empty...and that someone had already cashed in the winning ticket.

Police discovered that a ring of grave robbers had looted the grave, sold the casket back to an undertaker, and sold Sergeyev's suit to a thrift shop. Someone apparently bought the suit, found the lottery ticket still in the pocket, and cashed it in. Mrs. Sergeyev was eventually awarded the automobile, but she never recovered her husband's body—the thieves had sold it for animal feed.

Homebodies: 89% of Americans don't have a valid passport.

IN MY EXPERT OPINION

Think the experts and authorities have all of the answers? Well, they do...but they often have the wrong ones.

"Anyone who expects a source of power from the transformation of the atom is talking moonshine."

—Lord Rutherford, *scientist and Nobel laureate, 1933*

"No woman will in my time be prime minister."

—Margaret Thatcher, *1969, 10 years before being elected prime minister*

"I applaud President Nixon's comprehensive statement, which clearly demonstrates again that the president was not involved with the Watergate matter."

—George Bush, *1974*

"No matter what happens, the U.S. Navy is not going to be caught napping."

—Frank Knox, *Secretary of the Navy, Dec. 4, 1941, 3 days before Pearl Harbor*

"We're going to make everybody forget The Beatles."

—Bee Gee Barry Gibb, *on his group's 1976 movie,* Sgt. Pepper's Lonely Hearts Club Band, *which flopped*

"No flying machine will ever fly from New York to Paris."

—Orville Wright, *1908*

"Novelty is always welcome, but talking pictures are just a fad."

—Irving Thalberg, MGM *movie producer, 1927*

"Airplanes are interesting toys but of no military value."

—Maréchal Foch, *French military strategist, 1911*

"I cannot conceive of anything more ridiculous, more absurd, and more affrontive to all sober judgment than the cry that we are profiting by the acquisition of New Mexico and California. I hold that they are not worth a dollar."

—Daniel Webster, *senator of Massachusetts, 1848*

"It will be gone by June."

—Variety, *referring to rock 'n' roll, 1955*

"Sensible and responsible women do not want to vote."

—President Grover Cleveland, *1900*

The longest earthworm ever found was 22 feet from head to tail.

ELVIS BY THE NUMBERS

Elvis may have left the building, but his memory lives on... and on... and on. Here are tidbits from the BRI Elvis file.

Five Foods Served at Elvis' Wedding Breakfast:

1. Suckling pig
2. Fried chicken
3. Oysters Rockefeller
4. Champagne
5. Wedding cake

Nine Songs Elvis Recorded But Never Released:

1. "Also Sprach Zarathustra"
2. "Fool, Fool, Fool"
3. "Funky Fingers"
4. "Love Will Keep Us Together"
5. "Mexican Joe"
6. "Nine-Pound Hammer"
7. "Oakie Boogie"
8. "What a Friend We Have in Jesus"
9. "You Are My Sunshine"

Seven Dogs Elvis Owned:

1. Baba (Collie)
2. Getlo (Chow)
3. Muffin (Great Pyrenees)
4. Sherlock (Basset Hound)
5. Snoopy (Great Dane)
6. Stuff (Poodle)
7. Teddy Bear of Zixi Pom-Pom (Poodle)

Thirteen Songs Elvis Sang in Concert, but for Which There Is No Known Recording:

1. "Bad Moon Rising"
2. "Blowin' in the Wind"
3. "Chain Gang"
4. "Happy Birthday to You"
5. "House of the Rising Sun"
6. "I Can See Clearly Now"
7. "I Write the Songs"
8. "It Ain't Me Babe"
9. "Jingle Bells"
10. "Lodi"
11. "Mr. Tambourine Man"
12. "Susie Q"
13. "That's Amore"

The King's Four Favorite Reading Materials:

1. The Bible
2. *The Prophet*, by Kahlil Gibran
3. *Captain Marvel* comics
4. *Mad* magazine

Three Elvis Aliases:

1. John Burrows
2. Dr. John Carpenter
3. Tiger (his karate name in tae kwon do)

As of 2001, there were 43,429,000 single men in the U.S. and 50,133,000 single women.

FOR POSTERITY'S SAKE

Look around you. What do you see? A toothbrush, some deodorant, a digital watch, an Uncle John's Bathroom Reader. *They may look like everyday items to you, but to an archaeologist in the distant future, they'll tell a fascinating story of what life was like at the beginning of the third millennium. They're perfect for a time capsule.*

TALES FROM THE CRYPT

The modern craze of saving things began when scientists opened the Egyptian pyramids in the 1920s. Dr. Thornwell Jacobs, president of Oglethorpe University in Atlanta, was inspired by all of the valuable information society learned. He decided to create a similar vault of records and items to be opened by "any future inhabitants or visitors to the planet Earth."

Jacobs called his swimming pool–sized container the "Crypt of Civilization." It was sealed on the campus on May 28, 1940, with instructions not to open it until the year 8113. Jacobs didn't just include a few everyday items in the crypt, but a collection he hoped would represent our entire civilization. There are over 640,000 pages of microfilmed material, hundreds of newsreels and recordings, a set of Lincoln logs, a Donald Duck doll, and thousands of other items. There is even a device designed to teach the English language to the crypt's finders.

TIME AND AGAIN

Jacobs's idea, published in a 1936 *Scientific American* article, created a new fad of "keeping time." For the 1939 New York World's Fair, Westinghouse Electric filled a seven-foot-long cylindrical vault with modern amenities and sealed it with instructions that it not be opened for 5,000 years. A company executive named G. Edward Pendray came up with a name for the highly publicized promotion: *time capsule*. The term entered the English language almost overnight. (He also invented the word *laundromat*.)

Westinghouse designed a second capsule for the 1964 New York World's Fair. Here are just a few of the hundreds of included items:

Wishful thinking: The wishbone of the turkey used to also be known as the merrythought.

- a bikini
- a Polaroid camera
- plastic wrap
- an electric toothbrush
- tranquilizers
- a ballpoint pen
- a 50-star American flag
- superconducting wire
- a box of detergent
- a transistor radio
- an electric watch
- antibiotics
- contact lenses
- reels of microfilm
- credit cards
- a ruby laser rod
- a ceramic magnet
- filter cigarettes
- a Beatles record
- irradiated seeds
- freeze-dried foods
- a rechargeable flashlight
- synthetic fibers
- the Bible
- a computer memory unit
- birth-control pills

Also included was a bound "Book of Records." Many scientists and world leaders put messages in the book. Albert Einstein wrote, "I trust that posterity will read these statements with a feeling of proud and justified superiority."

NOW WHERE DID I PUT THAT?

The International Time Capsule Society (ITCS) was formed in Atlanta in 1990. They believe that only a small fraction of time capsules will ever be recovered. Why? Partly because of thievery and partly because of secrecy. But mostly because of poor planning—people just plain forget where they buried it. The ITCS's mission is to document every time capsule to give it a better chance of being opened someday. "People often think that in the future people are going to be more efficient than we are," said ITCS co-founder Knute Berger, adding that it's not so. "If we have incompetent bureaucracy, they will too. You have to plan for that."

The ITCS has created a list of the 10 most-wanted time capsules. (Two have been found—here are the other eight.)

1. Bicentennial Wagon Train Time Capsule. This holds the signatures of 22 million Americans. President Gerald Ford arrived for the sealing ceremony in Valley Forge, Pennsylvania, on July 4,

1976, but someone had already stolen it from an unattended van.

2. MIT Cyclotron Time Capsule. In 1939 a group of MIT engineers placed a brass time capsule beneath an 18-ton-magnet used in a brand-new, state-of-the-art cyclotron. It was supposed to be opened in 1989, but by then the cyclotron had been deactivated and the capsule all but forgotten. When the capsule's existence was discovered, the brains at MIT had no clue how to get a time capsule out from underneath a 36,000-pound lid. They still don't.

3. Corona, California, Time Capsules. The citizens of Corona have lost not just 1, but 17 time capsules since the 1930s. In 1986 they tried, unsuccessfully, to recover them. "We just tore up a lot of concrete around the civic center," said a spokesperson.

4. *M*A*S*H* Time Capsule. In January 1983, the hit TV show wrapped for good. In a secret ceremony, the cast members buried a capsule containing props and costumes from the set. Where it was buried is a mystery—no one will say. But it's somewhere in the 20th Century Fox parking lot. The lot, however, has shrunk somewhat over the last 20 years, so the time capsule may be located underneath a Marriott Hotel.

5. George Washington's Cornerstone. In 1793 George Washington, a Mason, performed the Masonic ritual of laying of the original cornerstone of the U.S. Capitol. Over the years, the Capitol has undergone extensive expansion, remodeling, and reconstruction, but the original George Washington cornerstone has never been found. It is unknown whether there is anything inside it.

6. Gramophone Company Time Capsule. In 1907 in Hayes, Middlesex, England, sound recordings on disk were deposited behind the foundation stone of the new Gramophone Company factory by the opera singer Nellie Melba. During reconstruction work in the 1960s, the container was officially removed, but before it could be reburied, someone stole it.

7. Blackpool Tower. In Blackpool, Lancashire, England, a foundation deposit was interred in the late 19th century with the customary ceremony. When a search was organized recently in preparation for new building work, not even remote sensing equipment or a clairvoyant could find the lost capsule.

...while traveling with it? A: He trained his camels to walk in alphabetical order.

8. Lyndon, Vermont, Time Capsule. The capsule is an iron box containing proceedings of the town's centennial celebration in 1891, scheduled to be opened a century later. But when the time came, the townsfolk couldn't find it. They looked in the town vault, the bank, and the library for clues, to no avail. So they created a new one, which they vowed not to lose.

WANT TO CREATE YOUR OWN TIME CAPSULE?

It's not as easy as you might think. The ITCS has created a list of guidelines to follow:

1. Select a retrieval date. A 50-year or less time capsule may be witnessed by your own generation. The longer the duration, the more difficult the task.

2. Choose an "archivist" or director. Committees are good to share the workload, but one person should direct the project.

3. Select a container. A safe is a good choice. As long as the interior is cool, dry, and dark, artifacts can be preserved. For more ambitious (century or more) projects, there are professional time capsule companies.

4. Find a secure indoor location. It is recommended that time capsules not be "buried"—thousands have been lost in this way. Mark the location with a plaque describing the "mission" of the time capsule.

5. Secure items for time storage. Many things your committee selects will have meaning into the future. Try to have a mix of items from the sublime to the trivial. The archivist should keep an inventory of all items sealed in the time capsule.

6. Have a solemn "sealing ceremony." Christen the time capsule with a name. Invite the media and keep a good photographic record of your efforts, including the inside of your completed project.

7. Don't forget your time capsule! You would be surprised how often this happens, usually within a short time. Try to "renew" the tradition of memory with anniversaries and reunions.

8. Inform the ITCS of your completed time capsule project. The ITCS will add your time capsule to its database in an attempt to register all known time capsules. (They can be reached on the Web at *www.oglethorpe.edu/itcs/*.)

SOME IDEAS TO GET YOU STARTED

Deciding what to include is the most difficult part. There are the obvious choices: a cell phone, a *Bathroom Reader*. But what about things like barbed wire or a Twinkie (don't worry—it'll last). Need suggestions? Here are some of the items the *New York Times* put in their "Millennium" time capsule in 1999:

- a Purple Heart medal from the Vietnam War
- a Beanie Baby
- UPC bar codes
- a firearms registration form
- a pager
- a cellular phone
- a battery
- a friendship bracelet
- an advertisement for an SUV
- food stamps
- a copy of the *The New York Times Magazine*
- an LP record containing sounds of the late 20th century
- a New York Yankees baseball
- greeting cards
- Post-It Notes
- a video rental card
- a phone card
- a David Letterman top 10 list
- a Y2K Bug stuffed toy
- wild apple seeds from Kazakhstan
- a Macintosh mouse
- St. John's Wort capsules
- the Holy Bible in multiple translations
- a *Weight Watchers Magazine*
- a Butt Blaster instruction manual
- the *National Enquirer*
- Alcoholics Anonymous pamphlets
- a Dr. Seuss book
- a *Dictionary of American Slang*
- *The Guinness Book of World Records*
- a reservation list for the Four Seasons restaurant
- an IRS 1040 tax form
- a hair sample from Dolly the cloned sheep
- a Garry Trudeau cartoon sketch

FAMILIAR PHRASES

Here are yet more origins of some common phrases.

IN THE BAG

Meaning: Certain to succeed

Origin: "This term refers to the container in which hunters placed small game, called a 'bag' since the 15th century. It began to be used figuratively for a virtual certainty in the 20th century, at first in America. The *Emporia Gazette* used the phrase in describing Gene Tunney's victory over heavyweight champion Jack Dempsey in 1926: 'After Tunney landed with that terrific right, the fight was in the bag.'" (From *Southpaws & Sunday Punches*, by Christine Ammer)

IN THE BUFF; TO BUFF

Meaning: In the nude; to polish something

Origin: "These expressions are rooted in the buffalo hide craze of the 19th century. *In the buff* is from the soft yellow skins made from buffalo hides, which looked a little like bare human skin. *To buff* comes from the strips of buffalo hide that were used to polish metals." (From *Word and Phrase Origins*, by Robert Hendrickson)

BY HOOK OR BY CROOK

Meaning: To obtain something one way or another

Origin: "In 1100 William Rufus, king of England, was slain by an arrow while out hunting in the New Forest. A charcoal burner named Purkiss found the king's body and took it by cart to Winchester. As a reward Purkiss was allowed to gather wood from the New Forest—all that could be reached by a shepherd's *crook* and cut down with a bill*hook*." (From *Everyday Phrases*, by Neil Ewart)

FLY-BY-NIGHT

Meaning: Unreliable or untrustworthy (often a business)

Origin: "Even as recently as a century and a half ago this meant a witch, one who actually mounted her broom at midnight and went off on her round of appointments, whatever they may have been, or to meet secretly the Old Boy himself." (From *Heavens to Betsy!*, by Charles Earle Funk)

Look out! The continent of Australia is drifting northward at a rate of 2.25 inches per year.

"A GOOD EXAMPLE IS THE BEST SERMON"

Benjamin Franklin: Founding Father, renaissance man, and...world-class hypocrite? His advice in the pages of Poor Richard's Almanack is timeless—but did Dr. Franklin always practice what he preached?

What Poor Richard Said: "God helps those who help themselves."

What Franklin Did: It probably wasn't what he meant, but Franklin wasn't above helping himself to the work of others. One of the things Franklin is best known for is *Poor Richard's Almanack*, which he wrote and published for 25 years. What's less well-known is the extent to which Franklin "borrowed" from the work of others: He appropriated his journal's title from his own brother James, publisher of *Poor Robin's Almanack*, and took the pen name Richard Saunders ("Poor Richard") from a dead astrologer and doctor of the same name.

• Only a handful of Franklin's most famous quotes are truly his ("Experience keeps a dear school, yet fools will learn in no other" is one example); the rest he lifted without permission, compensation, or apology from *Lexicon Tetraglotton*, *Outlandish Proverbs*, and other popular journals of the day. "Why should I give my Readers bad lines of my own, when good ones of other People's are so plenty?" he liked to joke. And with no copyright laws in place to stop him, there was nothing the other writers could do.

• To his credit, whenever possible, Franklin tried to improve upon the writing he stole from others, either by making it more to the point ("God restoreth health and the physician hath the thanks" became "God heals and the doctor takes the fee"), or by adding coarse references to sex, flatulence, or bodily functions. ("He that lives upon hope, dies farting," "The greatest monarch on the proudest throne is obliged to sit upon his own arse," and "Force sh*ts upon reason's back.")

Remember tan-colored M&Ms? They're gone—they were replaced by the blue ones in 1995.

What Poor Richard Said: "Dally not with other folks' women or money."

What Franklin Did: Franklin had a lifelong habit of engaging in "foolish intrigues with low women," as he put it, a tendency that began in his teenage years and continued through his married life. He amazed friends and associates with the number and variety of his conquests; it wasn't unusual for visitors to happen upon Franklin in a compromising state with a parlor maid, cleaning girl, or someone else who had consented to the great man's advances. According to legend, when he was young and short of funds, he got his rent lowered by taking his elderly landlady as a lover.

• Why settle for one woman at a time? When Franklin lived in London, he became close friends with the postmaster general of England, Sir Francis Dashwood, with whom he co-authored a revised edition of the *Book of Common Prayer*. But Sir Dashwood also had a naughty side—he was the founder of the Order of St. Francis, a society of orgiasts better known as the Hellfire Club. The club met regularly at Dashwood's country house in Buckinghamshire, and its proceedings usually began with blasphemy, usually a black mass or some other obscene religious ceremony, before turning to fornication, which usually involved women dressed as nuns.

• To be fair, there's no proof that Franklin ever went to a single Hellfire Club orgy. But "it is certainly known that he was a frequent, not to say eager, visitor to Dashwood's house," Bill Bryson writes in *Made in America*, "and it would take a generous spirit indeed to suppose that he ventured there repeatedly just to discuss postal regulations and the semantic nuances of the *Book of Common Prayer*."

What Poor Richard Said: "One good Husband is worth two good Wives; for the scarcer things are, the more they're valued."

What Franklin Did: Technically speaking, even Franklin's marriage was a form of adultery. He never officially married his "wife," Deborah Read Franklin, who was still legally married to her first husband, a potter named John Rogers. Rogers had left her years earlier and run off to the West Indies, where it was rumored that he had died in a fight. But nobody knew for sure, and that presented a serious problem for Ben and Deborah when they decided to marry: what if Rogers came back? In those days, even unintentional bigamy was punishable by 39 lashes for both husband and wife, along with life imprisonment doing hard labor. Even if Rogers really was dead, if Franklin married Deborah he risked becoming legally obligated to repay Rogers's substantial debts.

• For these reasons, Ben and Deborah never formally married; instead, on September 1, 1730, they simply began presenting themselves to the community as man and wife. Such a "common law" marriage, as it was called, was (barely) formal enough to satisfy community standards and Deborah's family, yet it spared Franklin the risk of being branded a bigamist or having to assume Rogers's debts.

What Poor Richard Said: "He that lieth down with dogs shall rise up with fleas."

What Franklin Did: Not long after he and Deborah were "married," Franklin brought home an infant son, William, that he'd fathered by another woman. Out of that one indescretion would flow years of pain for the Franklin family: Deborah's relationship with her stepson was predictably strained; by the time he reached his twenties they barely spoke and she had taken to calling him "the greatest villain upon earth." Years later William sided with the English during the revolutionary war, opening a breach between father and son that would never heal. When Ben Franklin died in 1790, he disinherited his son, "leaving him no more of an estate he endeavoured to deprive me of."

What Poor Richard Said: "A good Wife and Health is a Man's best Wealth."

What Franklin Did: So what thanks did Deborah get for raising Franklin's illegitimate son as her own? Not much—in addition to cheating on her throughout their long "marriage," Franklin virtually abandoned her in her old age, leaving her alone for five years while he went off to live in London from 1757 to 1762, and again in 1764, this time for more than a decade. He never returned home to visit, not even when Deborah suffered a stroke in the winter of 1768–69. When she died in 1774, she had not seen him in more than 10 years.

Benjamin Franklin was America's first newspaper cartoonist.

THE LEGEND OF GORGEOUS GEORGE

If you like professional wrestling, you've probably already heard of The Rock, The Iron Sheik, and Hulk Hogan. But have you heard of Gorgeous George? He was TV's first big wrestling villain. TV made him a star, and in many ways, he made television. Here's his story.

IN THIS RING, I THEE WED

In 1939 a 24-year-old professional wrestler named George Wagner fell in love with a movie theater cashier named Betty Hanson and married her in a wrestling ring in Eugene, Oregon. The wedding was so popular with wrestling fans that George and Betty reenacted it in similar venues all over the country.

With the sole exception of the wedding stunt, Wagner's wrestling career didn't seem to be going anywhere. After 10 years in the ring, he was still an unknown, and that was a big problem: Nobodies had a hard time getting booked for fights.

THE ROBE OF A LIFETIME

Wagner might well have had to find something else to do for a living had his wife not happened to make him a robe to wear from the locker room to the ring before a fight, just like a prizefighter. Wagner was proud of the robe, and that night when he took it off at the start of his fight, he took such care to fold it properly that the audience booed him for taking so long. That made Betty mad, so she jumped into the crowd and slapped one of the hecklers in the face. That made George mad, so he jumped out of the ring and hit the guy himself. Then the whole place went nuts.

"The booing was tremendous," wrestling promoter Don Owen remembered:

> And the next week there was a real big crowd and everyone booed George. So he just took more time to fold his robe. He did everything to antagonize the fans. And from that point he became the best drawing card we ever had. In wrestling they either come to like you or to hate you. And they hated George.

Girl power: On average, a woman's heart beats faster than a man's.

PRETTY BOY

Out of this hatred, George discovered the shtick he was looking for—and over the next several years gradually changed his look. Where other wrestling villains had always been dirty and ugly, "Gorgeous George," as he began to call himself, set out to become the prettiest, daintiest pro wrestler the sport had ever seen. He grew his hair long, curled it, and bleached it platinum blond. And before each fight, he secured it in place with golden bobby pins and a golden hair net. He amassed a collection of more than 100 frilly, purple robes, made of satin and silk and trimmed with sequins, lace, and fur. He made sure to wear one to every match, and before he would enter the ring, he insisted that his tuxedoed "valet" be allowed to spray the mat, the referee, and his opponent with perfume.

Then, as the lights were dimmed and "Pomp and Circumstance" played over the loudspeaker, George would enter the hall under a spotlight and slowly traipse his way to the ring. He made such a show of climbing into the ring and removing (with the assistance of his valet) his robe, his hair net, and his golden bobby pins, that his entrances sometimes took longer than his fights, giving wrestling's blue-collar fans one more reason to hate him.

FIGHTING DIRTY

Appearances aside, Gorgeous George was no sissy—not out of the ring and certainly not in it. He fought hard and he *always* cheated—gouging eyes, biting ears, butting heads, punching kidneys, kicking crotches, and pulling every other dirty stunt he could think of. He gloated when he was winning, squealed and begged for mercy when he was losing, and bawled like a baby when his opponents mussed his hair, which they did every fight. All of this was fake, of course, but the crowds either didn't know or didn't care. They ate it up, fight after fight.

Gorgeous George's antics may not sound like much compared to the wrestling of today, but at the time, they were mind-boggling. He became famous in the late 1940s, not long after the end of World War II. Many wrestling fans were veterans, and the boys who landed at Omaha Beach on D-Day or battled their way across the Pacific, and raised the flag at Iwo Jima had some pretty rigid ideas about what it meant to be a man. And bobby pins, frilly

There are about 10,000,000,000,000 ways to play the first 10 moves in a game of chess.

bathrobes, and platinum blond hair were definitely *not* considered manly. Gorgeous George broke all the rules, and these guys hated him for it. They *loved* to hate him for it. People got in their cars and drove for hours to see him fight, just so they could hate him in person. Gorgeous George made 32 appearances at the Los Angeles Olympic Auditorium in 1949; he sold it out 27 times.

A BOOB FOR THE BOOB TUBE

But what was most remarkable about Gorgeous George was the impact he had on TV sales. In Los Angeles, wrestling matches—many featuring Gorgeous George—were broadcast on TV as early as 1945, and they proved so popular that by the late 1940s, many TV stations around the country were broadcasting live pro wrestling every night of the week. It was the perfect sport for television—the ring was small and easy to film and the action was larger than life, so viewers had no problem following the fights at home on their tiny black-and-white screens. Baseball and football players looked like ants by comparison.

TV turned Gorgeous George into a national star, even for people who didn't watch wrestling. And in the process, he helped make television the centerpiece of the American living room. Appliance dealers put TVs in their store windows and pasted pictures of Gorgeous George onto their screens. People who'd never owned a TV before came in and bought TVs...just so they could watch Gorgeous George. As Steve Slagle writes in *The Ring Chronicle*,

> In a very real sense, Gorgeous George single-handedly established the unproven new technology of television as a viable entertainment medium that could reach literally millions of homes all across the country. Pro wrestling was TV's first real "hit"...and Gorgeous George was directly responsible for all of the commotion. He was probably responsible for selling more television sets in the early days of TV than any other factor.

YOU'RE MY INSPIRATION

As we told you in *Uncle John's Legendary Lost Bathroom Reader*, a young pro boxer named Cassius Clay, soon to change his name to Muhammad Ali, reinvented his public persona after he happened to meet Gorgeous George on a radio show in Las Vegas in 1961. "That's when I decided I'd never been shy about talking, but if I

Legal capacity of the bar in TV's *Cheers*: 75. How we know: It was posted over the door.

talked even more, there was no telling how much people would pay to see me," Ali remembered. That's when he started calling himself "The Greatest"... just like Gorgeous George.

Muhammad Ali wasn't the only one—Gorgeous George is credited with inspiring Little Richard... and even Liberace. "He's imitating me," George groused to a reporter in 1955.

THE FINAL BELL

There was, however, a limit to how long American TV viewers could stand to watch live pro wrestling every single night of the week, and by the mid-1950s, the craze had died down. George continued to wrestle until 1962, when a liver ailment—brought on by heavy drinking—forced him into retirement. Nearly broke from two expensive divorces, George had a heart attack on Christmas Eve 1963 and died two days later. He was 48.

Ironically, the fame that made Gorgeous George a national celebrity may have also contributed to his death. Believe it or not, he was a reticent person, and for years he had used alcohol to stiffen his spine and give him the courage to be Gorgeous George.

"He really didn't have the nerve to do all those things," his second wife, Cherie, remembered. "That's why he drank. When he was sober, he was shy."

* * *

SIGNATURE WRESTLING MOVES

Lord Blears: The Oxford Leg Strangle

The Leduc Brothers: The Lumberjack Bearhug

Baron Michele Scicluna: The Maltese Hangman

Leo "The Lion" Newman: The Diamond-Drill Neck Twist

Hard-Boiled Haggerty: The Shillelagh Swing

Johnny Valentine: The Atomic Skullcrusher

Cowboy Bob Ellis: The Bulldog Headlock

Danny Dusek: The Filipino Guerrilla Hold

Lord Athol Layton: The English Octopus

The Shiek: The Camel Clutch

Big Mess: The sun spews out more than a million tons of matter every second.

CARTWHEEL KICKS

These wrestling moves have very colorful names, but boy are they violent. In fact, they're so violent that you wonder why wrestlers don't get killed. Oh! It's because THEY'RE FAKE! But just to be safe, please don't try them at home—somebody's brain might get busted.

Forward Russian Leg Sweep. Stand next to your opponent, facing in the same direction. Wrap one arm around his (or her) neck, and step in front of his nearest leg, hooking it. Then fall forward, and cause your opponent to fall face first onto the mat.

Airplane Spin. Lift your opponent over your head and hold him so he is facing up toward the ceiling. Then spin around and around to make him dizzy, and then drop him on the mat.

Brainbuster. Lift your opponent up across your shoulders, hooking one of his legs with one arm, and cradling his neck in your other arm. Then fall to the side that your opponent's head is on, and release his legs, causing him to fall head first onto the mat.

Tilt-a-Whirl Pile Driver. Grab your opponent around the waist, lift him, and spin his body until he is upside down, then wrap your arms around his body to hold him in place. Then sit or kneel, dropping your opponent on his head.

Atomic Drop. Stand behind and to the side of your opponent. Grab his midsection with one arm, and hook one of his legs with the other. Lift him up over your shoulder so that he is parallel with the mat, then drop him tailbone first on your knee.

Gutbuster Drop. Bend your opponent over in a crouch, then grab him by one leg and across his chest. Lift him up so that his body is facing downward, then drop him stomach first across your knee.

Cartwheel Kick. Do a cartwheel in the direction of your opponent, taking care to kick him in the head with the side of your foot as it contacts his body.

Shooting Star Press. Climb up onto the top rope, then do a backflip, landing on your opponent.

By the time you reach age 60, your eyes will have been exposed to more...

WRESTLING LINGO

Had enough of wrestling yet? But wait, there's more. If you want to sound like a pro, you have to know the special lingo. Here's a sample.

Face (noun). A "good guy." (Wrestlers with *pretty faces* are often cast as good guys.)

Heel (noun). A "bad guy." Someone who cheats and breaks the rules to win.

Feud (noun). A grudge match, frequently between a face and a heel.

Turn (noun or verb). When a heel changes his persona and becomes a face, or vice versa.

Potato (verb). Injure a wrestler by hitting them on the head or causing them to hit their head.

Stiff (adjective). A move intended to cause real injury.

Run-in (noun). Intervention in a match by an audience member or other nonparticipant.

Blade (verb). Intentionally cut yourself with a hidden piece of razorblade in order to produce "juice" (see below).

Juice (noun or verb). Blood. Usually caused by blading.

Job (noun). A staged loss.

Post (verb). Run someone into the ringpost.

Hardway juice (noun). Blood from an unintentional injury.

Heat (noun). The level of the crowd's enthusiasm for a fight.

Pop (noun or verb). A sudden rise in the heat of the crowd, such as when a popular wrestler makes his entrance.

Bump (noun). A fall or other move that results in the wrestler falling out of the ring.

Jobber (noun). A wrestler who does a job—he's hired to lose to the featured wrestler. Also known as redshirts or PLs, short for "professional losers."

Clean job (noun). A staged loss that doesn't involve illegal wrestling moves.

Screw-job (noun). An ending that isn't clean—someone, usually the heel, wins by cheating.

Shoot (noun). The opposite of a job—one wrestler really is trying to hurt another.

...light than would be released by detonating a nuclear bomb.

DID YOU KNOW THAT BEES...

Some scientists think that after a nuclear holocaust, bees might become the predominant species on Earth. True? We hope we never find out, but look at some of the astonishing things bees can do.

...COMMUNICATE BY DANCING

Studies show that bees are far more complex than you might think, with a sophisticated system of communication. They report the location of food sources to other bees using a kind of waggling dance. The dances always show the direction of the food in relationship to a reference point—the sun.

In 1919 an Austrian zoologist named Karl von Frisch became one of the first people to study and understand the dancing language of bees. In a series of trials, he found that if the bee's view of the sun was entirely blocked by artificial means, the dances became disoriented. If the view of the sky was replaced with a mirror that reflected the sky's scenery backward, the dances were reoriented to the sun's reflection. When von Frisch moved the hive into a darkened room and provided only the light of a flashlight, the dances were oriented to that artificial sun. Bees raised indoors with only a stationary electric light to guide them became hopelessly lost when their hive was moved outdoors under a constantly moving sun.

...SEE IN COLOR

Popular theory once held that bees could see only in black and white. Von Frisch designed an experiment to test this. First he trained bees to feed at a clear glass container full of sugar water located on a brightly colored card. Then, when the bees left to return to their hive, an array of empty glasses was set out on cards of many different colors, as well as cards that were various shades of gray. Would the returning bees be able to distinguish the container that was sitting on the correct color, or would they be confused and go to the wrong dish? Over and over the bees returned without hesitation to the correct color, proving that they see in color. (The only exception was when the sugar water sat on a red card. Bees would often go to a dark gray card instead, showing that they are unable to distinguish the color red.)

How do they do it? In a test to see whether they could distinguish shades of gray, the experimenter was surprised to find that bees were able to differentiate between two gray cards that looked absolutely identical to him. He eventually discovered that different companies manufactured the cards, and one reflected more ultraviolet light than the other—an important visual clue for a bee. Think of this: If bees were color-blind, flowers would not be so colorful.

...HEAR

One experiment testing the hearing of bees involved rigging a feeding station with an electrical current. A tone sounded three seconds before an electrified current was passed through the station. A different tone sounded when the current stopped, and would sound again periodically until the juice was turned back on. The bees soon learned the meaning of both sounds. They ignored the "safe" noise and reacted immediately to the "warning" noise.

...ANTICIPATE

Princeton University ethologist (animal behavior specialist) James Gould, one of the world's foremost authorities on bee behavior, performed an experiment in which he placed a source of food next to a beehive. Once the bees discovered it, he moved it 164 feet (50 meters) away to see how long it would take the bees to relocate the supply. After only one minute, they found the food. Gould then moved it another 164 feet, and again the bees tracked it down again in less than a minute. Every time Gould moved the food another 164 feet, the bees found it without delay. Then he noticed that the bees were flying on to the next station before he had even moved the food.

In the next experiment, Gould placed a bowl of sugar water near a beehive and then, after it had been discovered by the bees, started moving it. Every few minutes, he moved the dish, but each move was four times longer than the previous move. He moved it 1 inch, then 4 inches, then 16 inches, and so on. Soon he was moving the dish more than 100 feet in a single jump. Amazingly, the bees soon caught on...and were waiting for him when he got there.

...SENSE TIME

Bees like the nectar of the buckwheat flower, which exudes nectar in the morning. Bees know this and visit the flowers only during the morning hours. This led scientists to wonder if bees had a built-in sense of time, so they did some experiments. In the first experiment, they put out a bowl of sugar water from 10:00 a.m. to noon every day. After only a few days, the bees learned exactly what hours to come for the food and didn't waste time coming early or late.

So next time you're at a picnic and are tempted to swat a curious bee, remember how astonishing the honeybee is and leave it...bee.

RANDOM BEE FACTS

- Honeybees are not native to North America. They were introduced here from Europe in the 1600s by the Puritans.
- Different bees have different dialects. A German bee cannot understand an Italian bee.
- Honey never spoils. In fact, honey placed in tombs in Southampton, England, over 400 years ago was still good when the tombs were opened.
- A typical American consumes about a pound of honey per year. A typical worker bee lives for one month and in that time collects enough nectar to make about one-twelfth a teaspoon of honey.
- Bees use ultraviolet vision—a specialized vision that allows them to see which flowers have the largest amounts of nectar.
- Honey comes in different colors and flavors—there are more than 300 unique kinds of honey in the United States alone. Why? Honey is made from diverse flower sources—clover, eucalyptus, or orange blossom, for example—and soil chemistry and honeycomb quality also influence how it tastes and looks.
- Another experiment: Will bees feed from water that's been artificially sweetened with Sweet 'N' Low? No.

AFTER THE QUAKE: THE HEROES

Disasters often bring out the best in people. At 5:13 a.m., April 18, 1906, an earthquake rocked San Francisco (see page 45). For the next four days, fire ravaged the city. City fathers, the army, police, and firefighters all worked together to put the fires out. But the city might not have survived without the extraordinary efforts of ordinary people who stepped up and helped out. Here are some of their stories.

The **Post Office** remained standing after the quake but was soon threatened by the growing blaze. Many brave postal workers risked their lives by beating out the smaller fires with wet mail sacks. As soon as the danger was past, they fervently began sorting the tons of mail city residents needed to get out to worried relatives. Survivors scribbled messages on boards, newspapers, even shirts, and as long as it had a legible address, it was delivered—no stamp needed.

The Western Union lines were down, but the Postal Telegraph office managed to stay open for business, providing a link of communication with the outside world.

• Of the city's five newspapers, one, the ***Daily News***, actually managed to put out an edition Wednesday afternoon. The other four newspapers, long bitter rivals, joined forces with the *Daily News* to put out a combined issue on Thursday. The editors never bothered to ask permission of the owners, knowing it would be denied. The most important task at that moment was to get out the information that citizens needed to find food, shelter, services, and loved ones.

• The **Southern Pacific Railroad Station** depot was saved by brave men with one pumper, a single stretch of hose, some wet gunny sacks, and a few buckets. Volunteers carried water from the bay three blocks away. Through this depot in the next few days passed millions of tons of food, blankets, clothing, and medical supplies—as well as 300,000 refugees fleeing the city. All traveled free of charge.

• The **San Francisco Mint** was built of steel and concrete with metal windows. It was fireproof on the outside, but the rampaging fires blew out the windows and set fires inside. Firemen and employees frantically hauled water from a cistern to put out fires in interior woodwork and on the tarpaper roof. Seven hours later, the mint—and all the money inside—was safe.

• The **Hopkins Art Institute** contained thousands of dollars worth of paintings and statues. Throughout Wednesday, teachers and students removed hundreds of pictures to the lawn, where they were carried in wheelbarrows, wagons, and on shoulders to safe spots around the city. Navy men arrived to help Wednesday night, and a young lieutenant used his service pistol to encourage other folks from the passing crowds to assist.

• **Bank owner Amadeo Giannini** walked 17 miles to inspect the damage of his livelihood, the Bank of Italy. When he arrived, the fire was approaching fast. His clerks swore the fire would never reach that far, but Giannini disagreed. He loaded all the bank's funds into two wagons and hauled them to his house, where he hid the money behind his fireplace. When the fires were out, Giannini hauled the money to a new location in the financial district. Giannini's bank later expanded to become one of the largest in the nation—the Bank of America. Another bank president, **Charles Crocker**, had workers load all of his bank's cash into sacks, stack them in a wagon, and take it to the docks. Then he put the money on a boat, which took it out to the middle of San Francisco Bay until all the fires were out. So why is this important? It meant that survivors would be able to withdraw much-needed funds.

• **Alice Eastwood** made her way downtown to the California Academy of Sciences. She was the curator of botany and managed to save many treasured plants while her own home burned to the ground. She could have saved her own possessions, but decided it was easier for her to buy new furniture than to replace the botanical specimans. All she had left after the fire was the dress she wore.

• **The Ultimate Sacrifice:** Police Sergeant Behan saved much of the city's paperwork by wetting it down with beer collected from nearby stores.

GREETINGS FROM EARTH

We told you about time capsules on page 331. When you see Star Wars *or* Star Trek *you probably think space travel is way off in the future. You're wrong—we're already out there. Here's some information about our time capsule in outer space.*

TO BOLDLY GO

The Voyager mission continues. Launched in 1977, the twin Voyager 1 and Voyager 2 spacecraft will soon leave our solar system and become emissaries from Earth. NASA placed a message aboard Voyagers 1 and 2, a time capsule intended to communicate a story of our world to extraterrestrials.

The Voyager message is carried by a phonograph record—a 12-inch gold-plated copper disk containing sounds and images selected to portray the diversity of life and culture on Earth. A committee led by Dr. Carl Sagan of Cornell University assembled:

- 115 images
- A variety of natural sounds
- Musical selections from different cultures and eras
- Spoken greetings from Earth-people in 55 languages—beginning with Akkadian, spoken in Sumer about 6,000 years ago, and ending with Wu, a modern Chinese dialect.

Each record is encased in a protective aluminum jacket, together with a cartridge and a needle. Instructions, in symbolic language, explain the origin of the spacecraft and indicate how the record is to be played. The images are encoded in analog form. The remainder of the record is in audio, designed to be played at 16⅔ revolutions per minute.

Here's a list of the contents of the record:

THE PHOTOS (PARTIAL LIST)

Earth
DNA structure
Human sex organs
Diagram of conception
Fetus diagram
Diagram of male and female
Birth
Nursing mother
Father & daughter (Malaysia)
Group of children
Family portrait
Seashore

Hibernating, a woodchuck breathes 10 times/hr; awake, 2,100 times/hr.

Ansel Adams' photos of Snake River and Grand Tetons
Forest scene with mushrooms
Sequoia tree
Flying insect with flowers
Diagram of vertebrate evolution
Seashell
Dolphins
Tree toad
Crocodile
Eagle
Jane Goodall and chimps
Page of book (Newton's *System of the World*)
Bushmen hunters
Guatemalan man
Balinese dancer
Supermarket
Turkish man with beard and glasses
Schoolroom
Sunset with birds
Elephant
House (Africa)
Taj Mahal
Sydney Opera House
Rush-hour traffic
Violin
Underwater scene with diver and fish
Demonstration of licking, eating and drinking
Great Wall of China

MUSIC

- Bach's *Brandenburg* Concerto no. 2 in F, first movement
- Bach's "Gavotte en rondeaux" from the Partita no. 3 in E-major
- Mozart's *The Magic Flute*, "Queen of the Night" aria, no. 14
- Stravinsky's *Rite of Spring*, "Sacrificial Dance"
- Bach's *The Well-Tempered Clavier*, Book 2, prelude and fugue in C
- Beethoven's Fifth Symphony, first movement
- Beethoven's String Quartet no. 13 in B-flat, Opus 130, Cavatina
- Holborne, Paueans, Galliards, Almains and Other Short Aeirs, "The Fairie Round" (Ireland)
- Court gamelan (Java)
- Percussion (Senegal)
- Pygmy girls' initiation song (Zaire)
- Aboriginal songs, "Morning Star" & "Devil Bird" (Australia)
- "El Cascabel" (Mexico)
- "Johnny B. Goode" (USA)
- "Melancholy Blues," performed by Louis Armstrong (USA)
- "Dark Was the Night," by Blind Willie Johnson (USA)
- Panpipes and drum (Peru)
- Men's house song (New Guinea)
- "Tchakrulo" (Georgia S.S.R.)
- "Flowing Streams" (China)
- "Tsuru No Sugomori" (Japan)
- "Izlel je Delyo Hagdutin" (Bulgaria)
- Panpipes (Solomon Islands)
- Night Chant (Navajo)
- Wedding song (Peru)
- Raga: "Jaat Kahan Ho" (India)
- Bagpipes (Azerbaijan)

THE SOUNDS OF EARTH

Hyena	Volcanoes	Mother and child	Train
Elephant	Earthquake	Herding sheep	Bus
Wild dog	Thunder	Sawing	Auto
Tame dog	Mud pots	Tractor	F-111 flyby
The first tools	Wind	Riveter	Frogs
Footsteps	Rain	Morse code	Saturn 5 lift-off
Heartbeats	Surf	Ships	Kiss
Laughter	Crickets	Horse and cart	Life signs
Fire	Birds		Pulsar
Speech	Blacksmith		

THE INTERSTELLAR MESSAGE

Speakers were given no instructions on what to say other than that it was to be a greeting to possible extraterrestrials and that it must be brief. Here's a sample:

• "Greetings to our friends in the stars. We wish that we will meet you someday."

—Arabic

• "Hello to everyone. We are happy here and you be happy there."

—Rajasthani (Northwest India)

• "Hello from the children of planet Earth."

—English

• "Friends of space, how are you all? Have you eaten yet? Come visit us if you have time."

—Amoy (Eastern China)

Here are some (not all) of the languages in which they spoke: Sumerian, Urdu, Italian, Ila, Romanian, Hindi, Nguni, Hittite, French, Vietnamese, Sotho, Swedish, Hebrew, Burmese, Amoy, Sinhalese, Akkadian, Ukrainian, Aramaic, Spanish, Greek, Korean, Wu, Persian, Indonesian, Latin, Armenian, Serbian, Portuguese, Kechua, Polish

It will be forty thousand years before the Voyagers make a close approach to any other planetary system.

The spacecraft will be encountered and the record played only if there are advanced civilizations in interstellar space. But the launching of this bottle into the cosmic ocean says something very hopeful about life on this planet.

—Carl Sagan

...justify being there? Gomer—short for "Get out of my emergency room."

NATURE'S REVENGE

What happens when we mess around with nature, trying to get it to do our bidding? Sometimes it works... but sometimes nature gets even. Here are a few instances when people intentionally introduced animals or plants into a new environment—and regretted it.

Import: English sparrows

Background: One hundred sparrows were brought from England to Brooklyn, New York, in 1850. Reason: to control canker worms that were killing trees in city parks.

Nature's Revenge: The sparrows did their job—for a while. Then they got a taste for native insects, then they had a lot of babies, and then they took off. By 1875 the sparrows had made it to San Francisco, stealing nesting sites from native birds and ravaging crops and livestock feed along the way. In 1903 noted ornithologist W. L. Dawson said, "Without question the most deplorable event in the history of American ornithology was the introduction of the English sparrow." Today they number about 150 million in North America. *Note:* They're not even sparrows—they're from the weaverbird family.

Import: Cane toads

Background: The cane toad can grow up 9 to 10 inches long and weigh as much as 4 pounds. Its croak is said to sound like a dog's bark. This bizarre species is native to Central America but was imported to Australia in 1935. Australian farmers wanted it to eat two types of beetle that were damaging their sugarcane crops.

Nature's Revenge: Nobody seemed to notice that the cane toad lives on the ground—so they were only able to eat beetles that fell off the sugarcane. The experiment was a failure, then a disaster. The toads feasted on other native insect species—many to the point of extinction—and spread into neighboring habitats. They are large enough to eat any insect, as well as frogs and other toads, and have even been known to eat from dog and cat food bowls. And, to make matters worse, they're poisonous. Whatever tries to eat them dies—even if they only eat the tadpoles. The situation continues to be dire: people who spot a cane toad are advised to contact toad hotlines and websites.

Import: Rats

Background: In the 16th and 17th centuries, hoards of people were leaving Europe on ships bound for the New World. Tyranny, poverty, horrendous filth, and epidemics drove boatload after boatload of settlers across the Atlantic seeking wide-open spaces, better resources, more freedom, and less disease.

Nature's Revenge: The settlers found a pristine paradise—and quickly infested it with rats. Early ocean-crossing ships were famously rat infested, the vermin often numbering more than the humans onboard. The adaptable rodent made itself at home and spread all over the continent. According to a study by Cornell University, by 1999 there were approximately a billion rats in the United States—on farms alone, and rats do an estimated $19 billion in economic damage every year.

Import: Rabbits, opossums, and stoats

Background: New Zealand's landscape had evolved for 60 to 80 million years with only four mammals—all bats. In this unique ecosystem, exceptionally unique flora and fauna, such as flightless birds, prospered. Then, in the early 1800s, Europeans arrived bringing sheep, pigs, and goats as livestock, and rabbits and opossums as game for sportsmen.

Nature's Revenge: Rabbits multiply... like rabbits. By 1894 more than 17 million rabbit pelts were being exported annually. While that made money for some, the rabbits' effect on the land, competing wildlife, and sheep farmers was devastating. The opossum did similar damage by eating massive amounts of native plant life in the exotic canopy.

Desperate farmers imported the stoat, a weasel-like creature that eats rabbits and opossums. That worked for a while, but birds, insects, and bats were easier for the stoats to catch. They quickly decimated bird populations, especially that of the kiwi. Thanks to the stoat, today several other species are either endangered or already extinct. New Zealand's government spends millions every year trying to stop the continuing rampage. And what of the stoat's intended targets, the rabbit and opossum? As of 2001, they were still the number one and number two pests in the country.

Rice-O-Roni: Italy produces the most rice of any country in Europe.

FAMOUS FOR 15 MINUTES

Here's more proof that Andy Warhol was right when he said that "in the future, everyone will be famous for 15 minutes."

THE STAR: Mark Stutzman, a 34-year-old illustrator living in Mountain Lane Park, Maryland

THE HEADLINE: *Struggling Artist Takes Care of Business*

WHAT HAPPENED: Stutzman was just another artist having trouble making ends meet when one of his clients encouraged him to enter a contest to design a stamp commemorating Elvis Presley. He'd never designed a stamp before, but he entered anyway, creating a portrait of the King in his younger days. "It's the first thing I think of when I think of Elvis," he says, "when he was really young and parents didn't want their kids to listen to his music."

Thirty artists submitted designs to the U.S. Postal Service; only Stutzman's (a young Elvis) and another artist's (an old, fat Elvis) were chosen as finalists. The American public would choose between the two designs by voting at their post office or mailing in a special ballot.

What happened? Millions of people cast their votes...and Stutzman's stamp won overwhelmingly.

THE AFTERMATH: The U.S. Postal Service ordered 300 million of the stamps and then, when those sold out in barely a month, ordered 200 million more, making it the most popular commemorative stamp in U.S. history. Estimated profits: $20 million. How much of that went to Stutzman? Zero—he got the standard design fee of $3,000...nothing more.

THE STAR: James Carter, 76, an ex-convict and retired shipping clerk from Mississippi

THE HEADLINE: *Ex-Con Makes It Big with a Song He Can't Remember, in a Movie He's Never Seen*

WHAT HAPPENED: In September 1959, Carter was chopping wood with a Mississippi prison road gang. He frequently led the men in singing while they worked, and one afternoon he happened to be recorded while singing a song called "Po' Lazarus." Carter served out his sentence and became a shipping clerk when he got out of prison. By 2002 he was retired.

What happened to that recording of "Po' Lazarus" is another story: It was preserved in a music archive, and in 2000 it ended up in the soundtrack of the film *O Brother, Where Art Thou*. The soundtrack was an even bigger hit than the movie: It went on to sell more than five million copies, generating thousands of dollars in royalties for Carter... if anyone could find him, that is: after more than 40 years, nobody knew whether he was even still alive.

It took the record's producer about a year to track Carter down in Chicago. One day two people showed up at his doorstep, told him about the movie (he'd never seen it) and the soundtrack (he'd never heard it), and handed him a check for $20,000, the first of what would likely be hundreds of thousands of dollars in royalties.

THE AFTERMATH: About a week later, Carter flew to the Grammy Awards in Los Angeles, where he saw the album win five Grammies, including Album of the Year. For all that, Carter has trouble remembering the lyrics to the song that made him an instant celebrity. "I sang that song a long time back," he says.

THE STAR: Patrick Singleton, the only athlete representing Bermuda in the 2002 Winter Olympics in Salt Lake City

THE HEADLINE: *Athlete Comes Up Short(s) in Salt Lake*

WHAT HAPPENED: Did you watch the opening ceremony for the 2002 Winter Olympics? If you did, maybe you saw it: In the sea of athletes who participated in the ceremony, all properly outfitted for the bitter cold, Singleton wore shorts. Bright red shorts. *Bermuda* shorts—the one thing (other than the Bermuda Triangle) that the tiny British colony is known for.

Even before the Olympics were over, Switzerland's Olympic Museum (where the International Olympic Committee is headquartered) contacted Singleton to see if he would be willing to donate his outfit to the museum. "I doubt we will ever see again an athlete walk into the opening ceremony of the Winter Olympics wearing shorts," a museum spokesperson told reporters. "Everyone will remember, because it was so cold!"

THE AFTERMATH: Singleton was glad to hand them over. But how'd he do in the Olympics? Not so good—he came in 37th out of 50 in the men's singles luge. Had he worn pants to the opening, he would've been quickly forgotten. But now his legacy—or at least his shorts—will be preserved forever.

THE STAR: Andrea Noceti, representing Colombia in the Miss Universe pageant in 2001

THE HEADLINE: *Ay Colombia! Beauty Queen Puts Letterman in His Place*

WHAT HAPPENED: In May 2001, Noceti participated in the Miss Universe contest and was eliminated in the first round. That might have been it as far as her fame was concerned, had David Letterman not joked a few days later that she competed in the talent competition by "swallowing 50 balloons full of heroin," a reference to the country's troubled past as a haven for drug smugglers.

Outraged by the comment, Noceti (and the Colombian ambassador and consul general) threatened to sue. As Letterman watched helplessly, his simple one-liner mushroomed into an international incident. He quickly invited the beauty queen to come on his show so that he could apologize to her in person.

THE AFTERMATH: Do you remember who won the Miss Universe pageant in 2001? Winners of beauty pageants are fogotten almost as quickly as the losers. But Noceti's dispute with Letterman was covered all over the world, and millions of viewers—probably more than watched the pageant—tuned in to watch Letterman apologize. He did so effusively and then invited her to sing on the show. She reciprocated the gesture by giving Letterman an autographed picture of Colombian coffee pitchman Juan Valdez and a book about her hometown.

"You joke about what you shouldn't joke about," she said to Letterman, "but you're a nice man." And then her 15 minutes of fame were up.

* * *

"According to a new study reported in *USA Today*, three out of four people make up 75% of the population."

—David Letterman

If you took an average shower today, you used about 30 gallons of water.

SECRETS OF THE STRADIVARIUS

The violins made by Antonio Stradivari are considered by many to be the most perfect instruments ever made. Here's the story of these mysterious instruments and the man behind them.

MUSIC MAN

Antonio Stradivari was born in Cremona, Italy, in 1644. As a young man he came under the tutelage of a famous violin maker named Nicolo Amati. He proved a gifted student and, before his training was even completed, began putting his own labels on the violins he made, using the Latin form of his name, *Stradivarius*. He was about 22 years old.

Amati himself was a member of one of the most famous violin-making families in Italy. Of all the members of the Amati family, Nicolo was considered the most gifted craftsman—and yet even *his* violins couldn't compare to those of his pupil Stradivari.

As early as 1684, Stradivari began to experiment with the details of violin making in search of better sound. He found it, of course, and in the process gave the violin its modern form—shallower in construction, less arched in the belly and back, with an improved bridge and a new varnish, deeper and darker than the yellower varnish Amati had used.

In the 19th century, a few more changes were made to the design of violins so that they could be heard more easily in large auditoriums. But for the most part, all modern violins follow the style established by Stradivari more than 300 years ago...only they don't sound nearly as good as the original. When Stradivari died in 1737, he took many of his secrets to the grave with him.

Or did he?

SOLVING THE MYSTERY

It's estimated that Stradivari made more than 1,100 instruments in his lifetime; more than 450 of his violins survive to this day, as do numerous violas, cellos, guitars, and even a few harps. Many of his tools survive too, and so do many of the patterns and molds that

Price of a Stradivarius copy advertised in the 1909 Sears, Roebuck & Co. catalog: $6.10.

he used to fashion his instruments. But without his expert skills and knowledge, they're useless—even when experienced craftspeople use his original equipment, no one, Stradivari's admirers claim, has been able to make a violin as good as an original Stradivarius.

Stradivari has been dead for more than 250 years now, and people are still arguing over what it is that makes his musical instruments sound so beautiful. People have studied Stradivarius violin slivers under electron microscopes and taken violins to the hospital to have them CAT scanned. Some people have even taken these priceless instruments apart to precisely measure every piece and tiny detail of their construction, hoping to learn their secrets.

"You have to put in a thin blunt knife and ease it around to separate the pieces, breaking the glue," explains Sandra Wagstaff, who cracked open her $2.2 million Stradivarius violin in 2001. "You hear, 'Click, click, click,' and if it goes quiet, you stop. *Immediately*, because that means you're cutting into the wood."

What do we have to show for more than two and a half centuries of such efforts? Not much. Music experts still can't agree on anything—what the secret is, whether there really *is* a secret, and if there is, whether Stradivarius even *knew* what it was.

Theory #1: It's in the man. Like Picasso paintings, Stradivarius violins get their beautiful sound from his unique—and unreproducible—techniques. "The real secret," says violin dealer Robert Bein, "is that Stradivari was an artist, and those instruments are imbued with that X-factor that we recognize as art. So the secret died with him."

Theory #2: It's in the varnish. Stradivari apparently used three layers of varnish: the first coat consisted of silica and potash, which was allowed to soak into the bare wood to give it strength; the second coat probably consisted of egg whites and honey or sugar; and the third coat was a mixture of gum arabic, turpentine, and a resin known as Venetian red. But—at least according to this school of thought—the details of Stradivari's varnish recipes may remain a mystery forever.

Theory #3: It's in our heads. "If the audience sees you've got a Strad, you must be good because only good players have Strads," explains Dr. Bernard Richardson, a musical acoustics specialist at the University of Cardiff in the United Kingdom. "There was no secret. We know the tools he used, the techniques he used, and

How many baseball gloves can be made from a single cowhide? Five.

the wood he used, so there's no reason people should not make exactly the same instruments."

Gregg Alf, a Michigan violin maker, agrees. "There's a lot of mumbo-jumbo about the Stradivarius mystique," he says. Alf and his partner, Joseph Curtin, took apart a famous Stradivarius known as the Booth Stradivarius, measured it carefully, and built a precise replica—even down to the scratches—that, like the original, has a beautiful sound. Just *how* beautiful is open to interpretation, but it later sold at Sotheby's for $33,000, the highest price ever paid for a violin made by someone who isn't dead yet. Alf argues that, with practice, he'll be able to make replicas as good as or even better than the originals, especially considering that the originals have been aging and deteriorating for more than 250 years.

Theory #4: It's in the bugs. According to this theory, Stradivari didn't have any secrets at all—tiny microbes in the wood he used are what give his violins their wonderful sound. In Stradivari's day, when trees were cut down the logs were thrown into the river and floated downstream to Venice, where they might soak in a lagoon for two or three years before they were finally sold. In this time the wood became waterlogged, allowing for rich growth of bacteria and fungus. These life forms ate away much of the pectin in the sap and also the hemicellulose, the organic material that holds moisture in wood.

With the hemicellulose gone, the wood became lighter, drier, and 50 times more permeable to varnish than ordinary wood. Stradivari's varnish contained 20 or more different minerals that caused it to dry with a hard gemlike finish that gave the wood excellent sound characteristics, unlike the gummy, oil-based varnishes that are popular today.

"This combination of highly permeable wood and a very hard composite varnish, which happened to be used by all craftsmen of the period, even on furniture, is what accounts for these remarkable acoustic properties," theorizes Dr. Joseph Nagyvary, a biochemist at Texas A&M University. "Stradivari was a marvelous craftsman, but the magnificent sound of his instruments was a lucky accident."

"Do you know why they haven't made any good violins in Italy for a hundred years?" Nagyvary asked in 1986. "In the 1840s, they dammed up the rivers."

Theory #5: Update—The worms helped too. In 2001 Dr. Nagy-

It's the law: If you want to drive in London, England, you must sit in the *front* seat of the car.

vary revised his theories to give some credit for Stradivari's success to woodworms. Actually, the lack of them: Stradivari happened to be in business at a time when the region of Cremona was suffering through a woodworm epidemic. So Stradivari treated his wood with borax, a preservative, to keep the worms out. The borax also bound the molecules of the wood more tightly together, so in using this treatment, Stradivari unknowingly improved the wood's acoustic properties.

The epidemic passed at about the same time that Stradivari died, Nagyvary says, so subsequent violin makers from Cremona stopped treating their wood. When the sound quality of their instruments declined, they mistakenly assumed that Stradivari's "secrets" must have died with him...or so the theory goes.

LUCKY FIND?

If you ever happen to see an old violin at a flea market or a garage sale and notice that the label reads "Stradivarius," go ahead and buy it if you want. But don't pay a lot of money for it and don't get your hopes up—it's probably a fake.

As we said earlier, Stradivari was largely responsible for establishing the standard design for modern violins. Later violin makers followed his standard...and communicated as much by labeling their violins "Stradivarius" too. This was not intended to defraud, it was just a maker's way of stating that the violin's design was inspired by Stradivari and not by Amati or some other master craftsman. Over time, the true intent of these labels was forgotten...and as a result, hundreds if not thousands of unintentionally "fake" Stradivarius violins are still in circulation.

Even the experts have been fooled: In 1999 the Ashmolean Museum in Oxford, England, had to admit that it "might" have a fake in its collection after a violin nicknamed The Messiah, previously described as "a flawless Stradivarius jewel," was found to be made from a spruce chopped down after Stradivari's death.

* * *

"I inherited a painting and a violin which turned out to be a Rembrandt and a Stradivarius. Unfortunately, Rembrandt made lousy violins and Stradivari was a terrible painter."

—Tommy Cooper, comedian

Ratio of American WWII pilots killed in training, to those killed in combat: 2 to 1.

WORD ORIGINS

Ever wonder where words come from?
Here are some more interesting stories.

POSTHUMOUS

Meaning: Something that arises or occurs after one's death

Origin: "*Posthumous* comes from the Latin *postumus*, 'last' or 'last-born,' which, strictly speaking, could be applied to the last child born of a particular mother and father, without reference to death. The *h* crept into *postumus* by association with *humus* (earth or ground) and perhaps with some help from *humare* (to bury). The modern spelling and meaning were fixed by Posthumus Leonatus, hero of Shakespeare's *Cymbeline*, who received this name, as the audience is informed at the start of the play, because he was born after his father died." (From *Devious Derivations*, by Hugh Rawson)

YANKEE

Meaning: A nickname for Americans or New Englanders

Origin: "The exact origin is uncertain, but the idea that enjoys the largest following is that it came from Dutch *Jan Kees*—a variant of *John Kaas*, which literally meant 'John Cheese,' an ethnic insult for a Hollander. Other ideas abound. According to James Fenimore Cooper, Indians sounded the word 'English' as *Yengees*; whence *Yankees*. Or the word may be derived from the Scottish *yankie*, 'dishonest person.'" (From *The Story Behind the Word*, by Morton S. Freeman)

TYCOON

Meaning: A wealthy and powerful business person

Origin: "A trumped-up Japanese title, *taikun* was a word used to magnify the role of the shogun or military commander of the country, especially when he was addressing foreigners, the point being to suggest that he was more potent and important than the emperor himself. The word meant 'emperor' or 'great prince,' borrowed from the Chinese *t'ai kiuen* ('great prince')." (From *The Secret Lives of Words*, by Paul West)

When your dog drags his rear end across your floor, that's known as "sleigh riding."

SABOTAGE

Meaning: To deliberately destroy or obstruct

Origin: "*Sabots* are great, clumsy wooden shoes, worn by French peasants at the time of the Revolution. But *sabotage* was not invented until about 1910, during the great French railway strikes, and meant, figuratively, to throw a wooden shoe in the gears; deliberate destruction of plant and machinery by dissatisfied workers." (From *More About Words*, by Margaret S. Ernst)

SINISTER

Meaning: Evil or ominous

Origin: "In Latin, the word had two meanings: 'on the left side,' and 'unfavorable.' According to Greek tradition people faced north while prophesying, so west—the left side—became the unlucky one. By the early 15th century the interpretation was 'dishonest'; later in the 15th century it became 'evil.' The sense 'threatening' or 'ominous' does not arise until the 18th century." (From *Jesse's Word of the Day*, by Jesse Sheidlower)

LUKEWARM

Meaning: Barely warm

Origin: "*Luke* was a Middle English word, now obsolete, meaning 'warm,' which was based on *lew*, another word for 'warm.' *Lew*, in turn, was derived from the Old English word *hleow*, meaning (guess what?) 'warm.' You have probably realized by now that lukewarm actually amounts to saying 'warm-warm,' but this sort of redundancy is common when obsolete words are carried over into modern usage." (From *The Word Detective*, by Evan Morris)

HAMMOCK

Meaning: A hanging bed of cloth tied between two supports

Origin: "The airiness and cleanliness of Taino (Native American) houses impressed the Europeans. The people slept in *hamacas*, hanging beds which Columbus described as 'nets of cotton.' By the 17th century, these practical beds were being used by sailors onboard ship. The spelling *hammock* did not prevail until the 19th century." (From *The Chronology of Words and Phrases*' by Linda and Roger Flavell)

A tree planted near a streetlight will keep its leaves longer into the fall than other trees.

OOPS!

More tales of outrageous blunders.

TAKE YOUR BEST SHOT

"A Ghanaian man was shot dead by a fellow villager while testing a magic spell designed to make him bulletproof, the official Ghana News Agency reported. Aleobiga Aberima, 23, and 15 other men from Lambu village had asked a witch doctor to make them invincible to bullets.

"After smearing his body with a concoction of herbs every day for two weeks, Aberima volunteered to be shot to check if the spell had worked. It didn't. Villagers then beat the witch doctor."

—*Fate* magazine

EIGHT IS ENOUGH

"In Coventry, England, nine police officers got onto an elevator on their way to a drug bust on the ninth floor of an apartment building. Unfortunately, the elevator was designed for eight people. The extra weight caused it to stop—trapping the officers between floors. For the next 45 minutes they screamed for help. Finally a neighbor heard them and announced, 'I'll call the police.' The officers screamed back, 'We are the police! Get the fire department!'"

—*Pantograph*

CUT ALONG THE DOTTED LINE

"A surgeon at Rhode Island Hospital operated on the wrong side of a man's brain after a CT scan was placed backward on an X-ray viewing box. The patient was fine, but the error occurred one year after a surgeon at the same hospital removed the tonsils and adenoids of a girl who was supposed to get eye surgery."

—Associated Press

YOU PUT YOUR RIGHT LEG IN...

"A Rockettes performance in New York Ciy ended abruptly when a dancer's prosthetic appendage flew into the audience. Gina Chalmers, who lost her foot in a 1999 auto accident, had been fired but was rehired after threatening a lawsuit."

—*Maxim*

Dolphins can fish in complete darkness, using sonar to find their prey.

I WANT TO RIDE MY BICYCLE! PART III

Toward the end of the 19th century, America was in the middle of an Industrial Age. Factories everywhere were mass-producing products using Eli Whitney's revolutionary "American System." *(See page 239.)* *It was only a matter of time before somebody would apply it to bicycles.* *(Part II is on page 286.)*

MADE IN THE USA

Why import a product when you can build it yourself? That was the thinking of Colonel Albert Pope, a wealthy Civil War veteran. He saw the obvious demand for the penny-farthing bicycle from England and decided that he would be the one to supply it.

First he studied the mechanics of an entire fleet of European bicycles, and then hired engineers to copy their style and design. Pope's first bicycle, which he named the "Columbia," was a durable, lightweight penny-farthing with wire spokes and rubber tires. In 1878 he rented a sewing-machine factory and started production.

The true genius behind Pope's Columbia was his use of "interchangeable parts" technology. The bicycles that were produced in Europe were handmade and welded by individual mechanics—a costly, time-consuming process that produced a slightly different bike every time. Pope standardized bicycle parts so they could be used interchangeably, making bikes easy to build and easy to repair. Soon thousands of mass-produced bicycles started rolling off Pope's assembly line. Now all he had to do was sell them.

GETTING THE WORD OUT

Pope began spending money to promote the bicycle—a lot of money. He started a publication called *The Wheelman* and paid well-known journalists to write encouraging articles about the bicycle; he paid doctors to write about the health benefits associated with riding; and he helped start riding clubs. He hired Charles Pratt, a lawyer and popular author, to write a set of guidelines for the clubs. Pratt referred to bicycling as "manly" and composed a set of rules that included proper dress, position, and responsibilities. He also established a national organization called the League of American Wheelmen.

It worked. By the 1880s, the bicycle industry was flourishing. But in creating a demand for bikes, Pope's success sparked competition—and Pope didn't like competition. So he and Pratt purchased as many bicycle patents as they could. The patents ranged from Lallement's original design for the veloce (Lallement was then back in America working as a mechanic at one of Pope's factories) to various patent improvements on wheels, spokes, and pedals. Then Pope sent Pratt across the country charging retailers licensing fees for selling Pope's products and threatening lawsuits if they refused to pay. Since most small-time shop owners couldn't afford to go to court against a big-time baron like Pope, they paid up.

But while Pope and Pratt were busy fighting to keep their newly acquired patents alive, a British engineer named James Starley was developing a breakthrough that would make Pope's high-wheeled bicycles obsolete.

BACK ON THE CHAIN GANG

In 1884 Starley developed a special chain that could connect the pedals to the axle of the bicycle's rear wheel. This development, known as "gearing," allowed manufacturers to shift the pedals of the bicycle from the front wheel to the middle of the crossbar, eliminating the need for a high front wheel. In fact, now both wheels could be the same size—about three feet in diameter—lowering the risks to the rider. Starley dubbed his new machine the "Rover," but the public called it the "safety bike."

This innovation would soon combine with another: In 1888 Scottish veterinarian John Dunlop invented rubber pneumatic (air-filled) tires, making bicycles ride much smoother than ever before. The entire industry was changed overnight, and the modern bicycle was born.

CATALYST FOR CHANGE

The 1890s were known as the "Golden Age of Bikes." On both sides of the Atlantic, the "miracle machine" provided people freedom they'd never before known. And the world hasn't been the same since.

...animal in the entire animal kingdom? A: The housefly.

• Now that the crossbar was lower, women were able to ride (the bike had been primarily designed by men...for men). But now, women had a means of escaping the house. The bike would soon become an excuse for women everywhere to shed their more restrictive clothing—such as corsets and dresses—in the pursuit of more comfortable riding. These seemingly small social changes would soon help pave the way for women's suffrage.

• In 1892 two brothers bought a pair of safety bikes. They loved them so much that they opened up a shop and started building and repairing bikes for a living. But they wouldn't be dabbling in bikes for long—Wilbur and Orville Wright would, however, incorporate the bicycle's design into their new invention: the airplane.

• The new bicycles also caught the attention of another young man. Many of their features intrigued him: interchangeable parts, assembly line production, chain-propelled gear shifts, inflatable rubber tires. In 1896 he teamed them up with a new design for a gasoline engine, added two more wheels, and called it the "Quadricycle." The man's name: Henry Ford.

* * *

BATHROOM MISCELLANY

• In medieval Europe, wedding ceremonies often took place in baths. Participants stood in a large tub as food was passed around on small boats.

• Some 19th-century chamber pots were decorated with portraits of popular enemies on the inside. One popular target: Napoleon.

Smelly even when washed: Some people in Siberia make clothes out of halibut skins.

A FAMOUS PHONY

Another story of one of history's boldest—and funniest— imposters.

BACKGROUND: In 1906 shoemaker and career criminal Wilhelm Voigt was released from a German prison after a 15-year sentence for robbery. His identity card and passport had been taken away, he was nearly broke, and his prospects weren't good. He was desperate. Then he remembered how he had learned to mimic the speech and mannerisms of the self-important Prussian officers whose boots he had mended when he was young. It gave him an idea.

MOMENT OF "TRUTH": He bought a secondhand army uniform, went to a local army barracks, and waited for the right opportunity. When a corporal and five privates came marching by, he stepped in, started barking orders, and instantly became the leader of a tiny army. Their mission: To take over the town of Kopenick on the outskirts of Berlin.

They marched down the road, got five more men along the way, and commandeered a bus. Once in Kopenick, Voigt marched his men into the town hall. There, after pretending to inspect the accounts, he had the mayor arrested, took over the telegraph and telephone lines, and helped himself to 4,000 marks from the treasury. The mayor was sent in custody to military headquarters in Berlin, and "Captain" Voigt quietly disappeared.

UNMASKED: Nine days later, Voigt was captured and arrested. But the story made headlines around the world and unintentionally brought world attention to the abuses of the German prison system. Whether it was because of this, or as some believe, simply because he thought the ruse was funny, Kaiser Wilhelm pardoned the lifelong crook—who had already spent 27 of his 57 years in prison for petty crimes—and sent him on his way.

IMMORTALITY ACHIEVED: The story inspired a 1932 German movie, *Der Hauptmann von Köpenick* (*The Captain of Köpenick*), which wickedly lampooned the bumbling Prussian officers. A 1956 remake won the 1957 Academy Award for the Best Foreign Language Film.

Whiskey gets its name from *uisce beathadh,* a Gaelic phrase that means "water of life."

GANDER

Far too few people know the heartwarming story about what happened in a small town on a remote island in the North Atlantic on September 11, 2001. Canadian air traffic controller (and BRI member) Terry Budden told us about it, and we decided to share it with you.

THE TOWN OF GANDER

Gander is located in Newfoundland, Canada's easternmost province. The town is central to Newfoundland Island, and the home of Gander International Airport. The decision to build an airport on Gander was made in 1935 because aircraft couldn't make the long flight from New York to London without stopping to refuel. Newfoundland falls on the Atlantic Ocean right under the flight path between these two points, making it the ideal stopover location. The town itself formed around the airport and was mostly populated by people who worked in support of the aviation industry. They referred to Gander as "the crossroads of the world."

Today, of course, aircraft can fly farther without refueling, making Gander an unnecessary stop. With the exception of local and cargo flights, very little international traffic stops there anymore. Gander has since become a quiet town. Until September 11, 2001.

GROUNDED

Less than an hour after the terrorist attacks of September 11, the U.S. Federal Aviation Administration grounded all flights and closed their airspace for the first time in history. Transport Canada (Canada's equivalent to the FAA) followed suit, ordering all aircraft to the ground. There were approximately five hundred planes arriving over the east coast of Canada with nowhere to go. Air traffic controllers quickly started directing these flights to the closest airports. Before long, 38 planes were parked wingtip to wingtip on Gander's taxiways and runways—and more than 6,500 passengers and crew suddenly found themselves stranded.

THE LOGISTICAL NIGHTMARE

Town officials and coordinators immediately scrambled to assess the situation thrust upon them, still reeling from the images on CNN. The Emergency Coordination Center at the airport and the Emergency Operations Center at the town hall were activated, and the situation was discussed. Gander has many contingency plans for all sorts of different situations—there is even a contingency plan for an emergency space-shuttle landing at the airport—but no plan for accommodating and feeding so many people for an undetermined amount of time. The town's 500 hotel rooms were no match for 6,500 unexpected visitors.

Des Dillon of the Canadian Red Cross was asked to round up beds. Major Ron Stuckless of the Salvation Army became the coordinator of a mass collection of food. Murray Osmond, the only Citizenship and Immigration officer on site, began the arduous task of processing thousands of passengers. "There was also the issue of security," Osmond told reporters. "We didn't know which planes out there might have individuals aboard like the ones who attacked the World Trade Center." He worked with a planeload of U.S. soldiers who had arrived to help maintain order.

While airport officials made preparations to process everyone, the passengers had to remain on board—some for as long as 30 hours—worried, confused, and cut off from the outside world. They couldn't see the attacks that kept the rest of the world glued to their televisions and still had no idea why they had been forced to land. Before long, though, passengers with cell phones and portable radios began spreading the word that the United States was under attack. If so, what would be the passengers fate? Were they war refugees? How long would it be until they saw home again?

JUST PLANE FOLKS

When the passengers finally disembarked, they received a warm welcome. Although Newfoundland is the poorest province in Canada, everyone helped out:

• It was quickly decided that the majority of the rooms would go to the flight crews so they would be well rested and ready to travel on short notice. The decision as to where to house everyone else had to be faced next: the town of Gander, even with all its residents, churches, schools, and shelters opening their doors, could

Frequent fly-er: A common housefly beats its wings about 20,000 times per minute.

handle only about half of the stranded passengers. The rest would have to be transported to the surrounding communities of Gambo, Lewisporte, Appleton, Glenwood, and Norris Arm. But transporting these people seemed to be a problem as well—the local bus drivers had been on strike for weeks. They weren't for long: the striking bus drivers put down their picket signs and manned 60 buses to drive the passengers to their destinations.

• Families were kept together. Many places set up special rooms for families with babies and small children where portable cribs were assembled, and boxes were filled with toys and games. Diapers, bottles, and formula were provided, all free of charge.

• When calls went out for food and bedding, people emptied their cupboards, refrigerators, and closets and went to the airport. "They were there all night long, bringing food and standing at the tables, passing it out," said Captain Beverly Bass from American Flight 49. Asked who was manning the tables, a passenger from Air France Flight 004 responded, "They were the grocer, the postman, the pastor—everyday citizens of Gander who just came out."

• The passengers weren't allowed to take their luggage off the flights; they were there with just the clothes on their backs. So, responding to radio announcements, the residents and businesses of Gander supplied deodorant, soap, blankets, spare underwear, offers of hot showers and guestrooms—even tokens for the local laundromat and invitations to wash their clothes in people's homes.

• A lot of the guests didn't speak English and had no idea what was happening. Locals and U.S. soldiers were put to work as translators.

• The local phone company set up phone banks so that all the passengers could call home. They strung wires and cables so those staying in schools, churches, and lodges would also have access to television and the Internet. Passengers participated, too—those who had cell phones passed them around for others to make calls until the batteries ran dead.

• Hospitals added extra beds and sent doctors to the airport, just in case. Anyone with a medical background worked with the local doctors and pharmacies to tend to those with special needs. People in need of prescriptions received what they required at no cost.

• Residents of Twillingate, a tiny island off the northeast coast of

Newfoundland, prepared enough sandwiches and soup for at least 200 people, then delivered them to the mainland.

• To keep their spirits up, the passengers were given a choice of excursion trips, such as boat cruises of the lakes and harbors, while others went to see the local forests and memorials. Whale and iceberg watching were also popular activities. Newfoundlanders brought in entertainers who put on shows and grief counselors to talk to those who needed it.

After the airspace reopened, with the help of the Red Cross the passengers were delivered to the airport right on time. Not a single person missed a flight. Many of the "plane people," as they were sometimes called, were crying and sharing stories with each other. Many people exchanged phone numbers and addresses with newfound friends.

THE AFTERMATH

Many travelers have since shown their thanks with donations to local churches, libraries, and charitable organizations.

• Lufthansa Airlines was so moved by the townspeople's reaction that they named one of their new aircraft after the town, an honor never before given to any place outside of Germany.

• The passengers from Delta Flight 15 started a scholarship fund and raised more than U.S. $30,000 for the school that housed them.

• The Rockefeller Foundation, which had used a small computer lab at a school in Lewisporte as the nerve center for their philanthropic activities, supplied the school with a brand new state-of-the-art computer lab.

• Gander Academy, which housed the passengers of Sabena Flight 539, Lufthansa Flight 416, and Virgin Flight 21, has received $27,000 in donations from the passengers that stayed there. The school is using the funds to finance a new six-year global peace awareness program.

• On the one-year anniversary, Canadian Prime Minister Jean Chretien traveled to Gander to honor the townsfolk. "You did yourselves proud," he told a crowd of 2,500 people who had gathered on the tarmac. "And you did Canada proud."

In a typical diamond mine, you have to dig 23 tons of ore to find a single one-carat diamond.

A NOTE FROM GANDER

Here is a great letter we found posted on the Internet from Gander resident Scott Cook, reprinted with his permission.

"It's been a hell of a week here in Gander. The stories are amazing. We had 38 aircraft with a total of 6,656 people drop by for coffee. They stayed for three or four days. Our population is just under 10,000, so you can imagine the logistics involved in giving each of these people a place to sleep and a hot meal three times a day.

"Many of us spent our time bringing people home so they could get a shower or, once the rain started on the third day, driving them to the mall or sightseeing to relieve their boredom. The diversity of the people who have been in my car and in my shower over the past few days is pretty wild.

"You should have seen the look on my little girl's face when three Muslim women came home with me for a shower. With their robes, she could only see their faces, hands and feet. Their hands and feet were covered with henna paint and two of them didn't speak English. There was a king from the Middle East here, a British MP, the Mayor of Frankfurt, Germany, etc., etc.

"There were also immigrants from all over the world, some of whom didn't have two pennies to rub together. They all slept side by side in schools and church halls. Except the Irish, of course! A flight from Ireland was put up at a couple of local drinking establishments! The Royal Canadian Legion and the Elks Club. One woman here gave a driving tour to a fellow from the U.S. When she brought him back to his gymnasium cot, they exchanged cards. She looked at his and said, 'So you work with Best Western?' He replied, 'No, I own Best Western.'

"You should have been here, but of course, there wouldn't have been room."

* * *

"We make a living by what we've got, but we make a life by what we give." —**Winston Churchill**

"OH MY GOD, THEY KILLED KENNY!"

More of our all-time favorite TV catchphrases. There are so many good ones that we can't list every one. (If we left your favorites out, let us know and we may add them to next year's book.)

Catchphrase: "Yadda yadda yadda."
From: *Seinfeld* (1990–98)
Here's the Story: The phrase has been around since the 1940s; but then it showed up on *Seinfeld* in the 1990s and, yadda yadda yadda, now it's in the dictionary.

Catchphrase: "I've fallen and I can't get up!"
From: TV commercials selling LifeCall personal emergency response systems in the 1980s
Here's the Story: Advertisers also try to come up with catchy catchphrases (remember the "Where's the beef?" lady from the Wendy's ads?). The "I've fallen..." plea, however, was never intedned to be catchy—or funny. But somehow it outlasted the company that advertised it (bankrupt) and the woman who said it (died). More than a decade after its debut, "I've fallen and I can't get up!" is still being used by comedians from Jay Leno to Carrot Top.

Catchphrase: "Oh my God, they killed Kenny!"
From: *South Park* (1997–)
Here's the Story: A big part of what made *South Park* a hit was the tasteless but innovative routine of killing off the same character in nearly every episode. Asked why, the show's creators Trey Parker and Matt Stone admitted, "We just like to kill him.... And we really like the line 'Oh my God, they killed Kenny!'" A few years later, Stone retracted: "We got sick of figuring out ways to kill him.... It was funny the first 38 or 40 times we did it. Then it turned into, 'OK, how can we kill him now?'" So in December 2001 they killed Kenny for good... but the phrase lives on.

box, he gets a dime... and the farmers who grew the wheat get a nickel.

Catchphrase: "Yabba-dabba-doo!"

From: *The Flintstones* (1960–66)

Here's the Story: Just like Homer's "D'oh!" (see page 105) this one came from the man who voiced the character, Alan Reed. *Flintstones* co-creator Joe Barbera tells the story: "In a recording session, Alan said, 'Hey, Joe, where it says "yahoo," can I say "yabba-dabba-doo?"' I said yeah. God knows where he got it, but it was one of those terrific phrases." Reed later said that it came from his mother, who used to say, "A little dab'll do ya."

Catchphrase: "Just the facts, Ma'am."

From: *Dragnet* (1952–59/1967–70)

Here's the Story: Sergeant Joe Friday's (Jack Webb) deadpan delivery made this statement famous...sort of. He actually never said it. Friday's line was "All we want are the facts, Ma'am." Satirist Stan Freberg spoofed the popular show on a 1953 record called "St. George and the Dragonet," which featured the line: "I just want to get the facts, Ma'am." The record sold more than two million copies, and Freberg's line—not Webb's—became synonomous with the show. According to Freberg: "Jack Webb told me, 'Thanks for pushing us into the number one spot,' because after my record came out, within three weeks, he was number one."

Catchphrase: "Let's get ready to... (something that rhymes with 'mumble' but starts with an 'R')."

From: Sports announcer Michael Buffer

Here's the Story: This one wins out over many other famous TV sports sayings because of the controversy it created. After hearing others imitating his famous battle cry, Michael Buffer and his brother Bruce decided to trademark it, a decision that made them both millionaires. Michael now charges $15,000 to $30,000 just to show up, say it, and leave. But if you feel like yelling the "rumble" phrase out loud, do it quietly; the Buffer brothers will sue the pants off of you if you say it at an event without paying them. (They even sued Ollie North.) Why such big safeguards on such a trite saying? "It's probably the most famous phrase said by a human being in history," Michael explains.

Hey, we've all had crummy jobs: When Confucius was 16, he worked as a grain inspector.

NAPOLEON'S CODE

Although he stood only 5'6", Napoleon Bonaparte was one of the most important figures in history. Emperor of France and conqueror of Europe, he created new standards for civil law, the French educational system, and much more. Here are some snippets of his wisdom.

"History is the version of past events that people have decided to agree upon."

"There is no place in a fanatic's head where reason can enter."

"The best way to keep one's word is not to give it."

"The most dangerous moment comes with victory."

"In politics...never retreat, never retract...never admit a mistake."

"In politics stupidity is not a handicap."

"A man will fight harder for his interests than for his rights."

"From sublime to ridiculousness there is only one step."

"If you wage war, do it energetically and with severity. This is the only way to make it shorter and consequently less inhuman."

"Public morals are the natural complement of all laws: they are by themselves an entire code."

"An order that can be misunderstood will be misunderstood."

"If you wish to be a success in the world, promise everything, deliver nothing."

"Ten people who speak make more noise than ten thousand who are silent."

"Adversity is the midwife of genius."

"The word 'impossible' is not in my dictionary."

"Men are moved by only two levers: fear and self-interest."

"Governments keep their promises only when they are forced, or when it is to their advantage to do so."

"He who fears being conquered is sure of defeat."

What do Swiss steak and Russian dressing have in common? Both were invented in the U.S.

IT'S A WEIRD, WEIRD WORLD

More proof that truth really is stranger than fiction.

FAMILY FEUD

"Philip Buble, 44, was denied permission to bring his 'wife' into a main courtroom because she is a dog. Buble wanted the dog, who he calls Lady Buble, to sit with him in the courtroom while his father was being sentenced for attempted murder (the elder Buble tried to kill the younger Buble when he learned his son had married a dog). In Buble's plea to the court, he said, 'I'd like my significant other to attend by my side, as she was in the house during the attack, though not a witness to it, thank goodness.'"

—*FHM*

DIRTY POLITICS

"The African country of Swaziland has been thrown into a political crisis after Mgabhi Dlamini, the speaker of parliament, stole a piece of royal cow dung out of the royal corral. Dlamini's opponents say he wanted to use the stuff in a ritual that would improve his standing with the king. The theft was detected by witch doctors who had foreseen it in a vision. Dlamini admits to having taken a handful of dung but insists he did not intend to use it for personal profit."

—The London *Telegraph*

GNOME, SWEET GNOME

"In July 2001, political activists in France 'liberated' 105 garden gnomes and put them in the middle of a traffic circle. The gnomes were discovered after being stolen from the gardens of several homes in Chavelot during the night. Police say the French Liberation Front for Garden Gnomes is responsible.

"The activist group—which in French is called the *Front de libération des nains de jardin*—has undertaken similar stunts in the past. Its stated aim is to free all garden gnomes and 'return them to the wild.'"

—Ananova.com

An onion by any other name: Onions are members of the lily family.

THEY WENT THAT-A-WAY

So how did the Spanish master painter Francisco de Goya die? Modern analysis suggests that he literally painted himself to death.

FRANCISCO DE GOYA (1746–1828)

Claim to Fame: Art historians consider Goya a master painter—one of the greatest who ever lived. He became a "court" painter for Spanish royalty in 1786. But after an illness in 1792 he abandoned his conventional portrait-painting style and his work became cynical and dark; it is this later work that made him famous and inspired later painters like Edouard Manet and Pablo Picasso.

How He Died: He was killed by his own paints.

Postmortem: In 1792 Goya, 46, was struck by a sudden mysterious illness that manifested itself in symptoms including convulsions, paralysis of the right side of his body, poor balance, alternating giddiness and chronic depression, ringing in his ears, hallucinations, mental confusion, blindness (temporary), deafness (permanent), and impaired speech.

He almost died. In fact, he was so incapacitated that he had to give up painting for a time. Then, after a period of convalescence, the symptoms disappeared just as mysteriously as they had appeared, and he was able to resume his work.

Thus began a pattern that plagued Goya for the rest of his life: He would paint until he became too ill to work; then he'd rest and the symptoms would disappear. He'd start painting again, and the symptoms would return. The cycle continued for more than 30 years until 1828, when his illness is believed to have triggered the stroke that finally killed him.

For generations, historians assumed that Goya was felled by syphilis or some similar illness, but with syphilis the symptoms don't usually go away. In the early 1970s, a physician, Dr. William Niederland, concluded that Goya most likely died from exposure

Wide load: If a walrus eats enough food, it can grow wider than its own length.

to the lead and mercury in his paints.

But why did *he* die from poisoning when so many of his contemporary artists did not? One reason is that Goya's luminous, mother-of-pearl painting style required huge amounts of white paint, which contained lead. He also used it to prime his canvases. Not only that, Goya had to mix all of his paints himself. In those days, artists couldn't buy their paint ready made, so Goya ground lead white and a mercury compound called cinnabar into his paints.

And because Goya was one of the fastest of the great portrait painters, he used *a lot* of paint, thus inhaling as much as triple the amount of mercury and lead as his contemporaries, Niederland speculates. His contemporaries didn't inhale enough to even become ill, but Goya inhaled enough to kill himself.

Final Irony: The poisonous paint that killed him may also have been what turned Goya into one of the greatest painters in history. The 1792 attack was so severe that Goya never painted the same again—and it was this later painting style that made him famous. "In terms of artistic greatness," Charles Panati writes in *The Browser's Book of Endings*, "had the painter's career ended prior to his major 1792 ailment, it would have survived with only passing mention, the work of a gifted artist, popular in his day, who missed greatness by a wide margin."

*   *   *

RULES OF LIFE THEY DON'T TEACH IN SCHOOL
(But you can learn on the Internet)

1. Never give yourself a haircut after three margaritas.

2. You need only two tools. WD-40 and duct tape. If it doesn't move and it should, use WD-40. If it moves and shouldn't, use the tape.

3. Everyone seems normal until you get to know them.

4. If he or she says that you are too good for him or her—believe them.

5. Never pass up an opportunity to pee.

6. Be really nice to your friends. You never know when you are going to need them to empty your bedpan.

THE MAGIC SCREEN

"As new as 1960!" That was the slogan on Uncle John's first Etch A Sketch. It provided hours of mindless fun (just like TV), even though he couldn't figure out how it worked (he still can't).

A HUMBLE BEGINNING

In 1958 a 37-year-old Parisian garage mechanic named Arthur Granjean invented an amazing new toy. He called it *L'Ecran Magique*—Magic Screen.

The Magic Screen was an unusual toy for its time—it didn't have a lot of little pieces that could get lost and didn't need batteries. Granjean felt sure his creation would interest someone at the International Toy Fair in Nuremberg, Germany. But everyone passed on it...until executives from a small American toy firm, the Ohio Art Company, convinced their boss to take a second look. That did it. Ohio Art bought the rights for $25,000 and renamed it Etch A Sketch. Then they advertised it on TV—just in time for the 1960 Christmas season—and sales took off. The response was so great that they kept the factory open until noon on Christmas Eve desperately trying to fill orders.

A CLASSIC TOY

How does Etch A Sketch work? There's a stylus, or pointer, mounted on two rails behind the screen. Using a system of wires and pulleys connected to the knobs on front, one rail moves back and forth, and the other moves up and down. The gray stuff is powdered aluminum mixed with tiny plastic beads. The powder sticks to the glass screen because aluminum powder sticks to *everything*. The beads help the powder flow easily. When the stylus moves, it touches the glass and scrapes the aluminum powder off. Shake it, and the aluminum is redistributed evenly. To prevent it from breaking, a clear plastic film covers the glass.

The basic Etch A Sketch design hasn't changed since 1960, although variations have been introduced:

• Pocket-sized models, travel-sized models, and glow-in-the-dark

Cockfighting is still legal in three states: Oklahoma, Louisiana, and New Mexico.

models (only the frame glows).

• The new Zooper model makes weird noises—beeps, boops, squeaks, and squawks—as the knobs turn.

• There's also an Etch A Sketch "action pack," which offers various puzzles and games printed on overlays placed on top of the screen.

• To celebrate the toy's 25th anniversary in 1985, Ohio Art came out with an Executive model made of silver. The drawing knobs were set with sapphires and topaz. Price: $3,750.

ETCH A SKETCH TRIVIA

• **How many?** Eight thousand Etch A Sketches are sold every day.

• **World's largest Etch A Sketch.** Steve Jacobs created it at the Black Rock Arts Festival in California in 1997. He placed 144 regulation-sized Etch A Sketches in a huge square and surrounded them with a huge red Etch A Sketch frame, including huge white knobs. It qualified for a Guinness World Record.

• **Robot Etch A Sketch.** A Canadian computer programmer named Neil Fraser pulled the knobs off a standard Etch A Sketch and hooked it up to two motors that were attached to the port of his computer. The motors worked by remote control, enabling Fraser to draw pictures without ever touching the toy. Other robotic components tilt the Etch A Sketch upside down and shake it.

• **Extreme Etch A Sketch.** George Vlosich was ten years old in 1989 when, on a long drive from Ohio to Washington, D.C., he brought along his Etch A Sketch. On the way home, he drew a sketch of the Capitol that was so good his parents photographed it. An artist was born. He soon began sketching portraits of his favorite sports heroes, then waited after games to get them to autograph his Etch A Sketch. The "Etch A Sketch Kid" started getting so much media attention that in 2000, Ohio Art sent someone to his home to see if he lived up to his reputation. They were so impressed by his talent that they've been supplying him with free Etch A Sketches ever since.

It takes George between 40 and 60 hours to complete a single Etch A Sketch masterpiece. After it's done, he carefully unscrews the back and removes the excess aluminum powder to preserve the picture forever. His Etch A Sketch artworks sell for up to $5,000 each.

Cost of a ticket to a Beatles' concert in 1966 (corrected for inflation): $31....

HOW TO TOILET TRAIN YOUR CAT

This how-to article was sent to us by a reader who thought it was right up our...er...alley. We agree. Sure, the idea of toilet-training a cat is far-fetched, but who is Uncle John to say anything is impossible? We salute the author, Karawynn Long, for giving the meaning of "domesticated animal" new meaning.

BACKGROUND

There have been more books and articles about toilet training your cat than you'd think. In the summer of 1989, when Misha was a small kitten with big ears and enough meow for five cats, I searched out and read a half-dozen of them. And then tried it myself and discovered there were a few things they all failed to mention. Here's what worked for me and Misha.

The central idea is that the transition from litter box to toilet be accomplished in a series of stages. Make a small change and then give your cat time to adjust before you make another small change. If at any time Felix gives the whole thing up and pees on the rug instead, you're pushing him too far too fast; back up a stage or two and try again, slower.

In the following instructions, I've used the word "rest" to mean: do nothing for a period of between a day and a week, depending on how flappable your cat is. Misha caught on fast and was completely trained in under two weeks, far in advance of what the books led me to expect, but every cat is different.

LID UP, SEAT DOWN

The very most important thing to remember is: Lid Up, Seat Down. Post a note on the back of the door or the lid of the toilet if you think you or your housemates or guests might forget. (If I have a guest who leaves the lid down, Misha will usually come and ask me to fix it, but you can't expect every cat to go to this much trouble. Besides, he's been using the toilet for more than six years now; when the whole idea was new to him he'd just as soon pee in the bathtub instead.) And if you're accustomed to closing the bathroom door when it's vacant, you'll have to break that habit too.

Begin by moving the cat's litter box from wherever it is to beside the toilet. Make sure he knows where it is and uses it. Rest. Next put something—a stack of newspapers, a phone book, a cardboard box—under the litter box to raise it, say, about an inch. (Magazines are too slick; you don't want the litter box sliding around and making Felix feel insecure. Tape the litter box down if you need to.) Rest. Get another box or phone book and raise it a little higher. Rest. Continue this process until the bottom of the litter box is level with the top of the toilet seat. For Misha I raised it about two inches per day.

IN THE CATBIRD SEAT

At the beginning of this process, your cat could just step into the box; later he began jumping up into it, until at some point he probably started jumping up onto the toilet seat first and stepping into the box from there. You've been diligently keeping the lid up and the seat down, of course, so by now your cat is thoroughly familiar with tromping around on the open toilet.

Lift the seat on your toilet and measure the inside diameter of the top of the bowl at its widest point. Venture forth and buy a metal mixing bowl of that diameter. Do not (I discovered this the hard way) substitute a plastic bowl. A plastic bowl will not support the cat's weight and will drop into the toilet bowl, spilling litter everywhere, not to mention scaring the hell out of the cat.

Now you move the litter box over so that it's sitting directly over the toilet seat. If your cat has shown reluctance over previous changes, you might want to split this into two stages, moving it halfway onto the seat and then fully over. Then take away the stack of phone books or whatever. Rest.

Here's the cool part. Take away the litter box entirely. (Ta da!) Nestle the metal mixing bowl inside the toilet bowl and lower the seat. Fill the bowl with about two inches of litter. And note that this is much easier if you have the tiny granules of litter that can be scooped out and flushed.

AVOIDING CAT-ASTROPHE

Naturally, any humans using the toilet at this point will have to

Very thin, weak ice is known as "cat ice." Why?

remove the metal bowl prior to their own use and replace it afterward. The next week or two the whole process is likely to be something of an annoyance. But if you begin to think it's not worth it, just remember that when you're done, you will never have to clean a litter box again.

Watch your cat going in the metal bowl. Count the number of feet he gets up on the toilet seat—as opposed to down in the bowl of litter. The higher the number, the luckier you are and the easier your job is going to be...

PURR-FECT POSITION

Because next you have to teach him proper squatting posture. Catch him beginning to use the toilet as often as possible and show him where his feet are supposed to go. Just lift them right out of the bowl and place them on the seat, positioned so kitty is facing forward. If he starts out with three or, heaven forbid, all four feet in the bowl, just get the front two feet out first. Praise him all over the place every time he completes the activity in this position.

Misha is very doglike in that he craves approval and praise. If your cat is indifferent to this sort of thing, you can also reward him with small food treats and wean him from them later when the toilet behavior has "set." Just keep the treats as small and infrequent as possible—half a treat per occasion should be plenty.

FANCY FOOTWORK

When he is regularly using the toilet with his front feet out of the bowl (and some cats naturally start from this position), begin lifting a hind foot out and placing it on the seat, roughly halfway between the front and the back. Your cat will probably find this awkward at first and try to replace the foot in the litter. Be persistent. Move that foot four times in a row if you have to, until it stays there. Praise and/or treat.

Repeat with the other hind foot, until your cat learns to balance in that squat. Note, too, that there will actually be two different squats, a low one for urine elimination and a high one for bowel movements. Once he's getting all four feet regularly on the seat, it's all downhill from there.

That's fortunate, because the last bit is also the most unpleasant. I suggest you postpone this stage until you have at least a weekend,

Because it can't even support the weight of cats.

and preferably several days, when you or another responsible party will be at home most of the time. I skipped through this part in about two days; I only hope that your cat allows you to move along that fast.

ARE WE THERE YET?

Begin reducing the litter in the bowl. Go as fast as he's comfortable with, because as the litter decreases, the odor increases. You'll want to be home at this point so that you can praise him and dump out the contents of the bowl immediately after he's finished, to minimize both the smell and the possibility that your cat, in a confused attempt to minimize the smell on his own, tries to cover it up with litter that no longer exists and ends up tracking unpleasantness into the rest of the house.

By the time you're down to a token teaspoonful of litter in the bottom of the bowl, your next-door neighbors will probably be aware of the precise instant your cat has used the toilet. This is as bad as it gets. The next time you rinse out the metal bowl, put a little bit of water in the bottom. Increase the water level each time, just as you decreased the litter level. Remember—if at any point Felix looks nervous enough about the change to give the whole thing up and take his business to the corner behind the door, back up a step or two and try the thing again more slowly.

Once the water in the mixing bowl is a couple of inches deep and your cat is comfortable with the whole thing, you get to perform the last bit of magic. Take the mixing bowl away, leaving the bare toilet. (Lid Up, Seat Down.)

Voilà! Your cat is now toilet trained.

* * *

BIRD VIOLATES CANADIAN LANGUAGE LAWS

"According to a Canadian Press report in September, a customer at a Napierville, Quebec, pet shop threatened to report the shop to the government's French language monitoring office because she was shown a parrot that spoke only English."

—*News of the Weird*

AMAZING COINCIDENCES

We're constantly finding stories about amazing coincidences. Here are a few more of Uncle John's favorites.

MESSAGE IN A BOTTLE

Charles Coghlan was born on Prince Edward Island in 1841. He became a successful stage actor and toured the world, but the island was always his home. In 1899, during an appearance on Galveston Island, Texas, he fell ill and died, and was buried in a Galveston cemetery. On September 8, 1900, a hurricane struck Galveston, washing away most of the town and swamping all the cemeteries. Seven years later, a fishermen from Prince Edward Island noticed a large box in the water. He towed it to shore, chipped off the barnacles, and discovered the coffin of Charles Coghlan, beloved native son. It had floated into the Gulf of Mexico, been caught by the West Indian current, carried into the Gulf Stream, and deposited on shore only a few miles from his Canadian birthplace.

MONSTER TRUCK

Christina Cort lived in Salvador, Brazil, in 1966 when an out-of-control truck crashed into her house. In 1989, she was still living in the same house when another out-of-control truck crashed into it. It was the same truck driver who had barreled into her home 23 years earlier.

TELL-TALE SKULL

In 1983, a man cutting peat for fuel near Cheshire, England, uncovered a human skull, which he took to the police. Forensic scientists examined the remains and announced they belonged to a European middle-aged woman who had been buried for not less than five but not more than 50 years. After investigating, the police found that a Mrs. Malika Reyn-Bardt had mysteriously disappeared from the area in 1961. When police confronted Peter Reyn-Bardt with the evidence, he broke down and confessed to

Holy molar! In its lifetime, an alligator will go through as many as 3,000 teeth.

murdering her and burying pieces of her body at various locations. Before the trial, however, the skull was sent to Oxford University's lab for additional testing. Those tests revealed that the skull actually belonged to a woman who had died around 410 A.D. Reyn-Bardt pleaded not guilty, but was convicted and sentenced to life imprisonment. No trace of his dead wife has ever been found.

THE LONG WAY HOME

Actor Anthony Hopkins, while playing a role in a movie based on a book called *The Girl from Petrovka* by George Feifer, looked all over London for a copy of the book but was unable to find one. Later that day he was waiting in a subway station for his train when he noticed someone had left a book on a bench. Picking it up, Hopkins found it was... *The Girl from Petrovka.* Two years later Hopkins was filming another movie in Vienna when he was visited on the set by author George Feifer. Feifer complained that he no longer had even a single copy of his own book because he'd loaned his last one to a friend who had lost it somewhere in London. Feifer added that it was particularly annoying because he had written notes in the margins. Hopkins, incredulous, handed Feifer the copy he had found in the subway station. It was the same book.

* * *

THREE STRANGE COINCIDENCES FROM INSIDE THE BRI

• We once printed a fact that said: "Moo. Country star Lyle Lovett is afraid of cows." Not long after the book was released, Lyle Lovett was attacked by a bull.

• Our 2002 Page-A-Day calendar was written in 2001. The page for March 27, 2002, had a funny story about Milton Berle, who just so happened to die on... March 27, 2002.

• Sad coincidence: In 2000, we put together a page of odd holidays for our *All-Purpose Extra Strength Bathroom Reader.* We found a great one called "No News is Good News Day." The date of the holiday: September 11.

That's gotta hurt: Actor Jackie Chan once dislocated his cheek bone filming an action movie.

ONE GOOD TURN DESERVES ANOTHER

Here's a gut-wrenching story with a happy ending.

TOOL TIME

One day in 1964, an 18-year-old high school kid named Peter Roberts was tinkering around in his dad's garage. His father repaired lawn mowers in his spare time to earn pocket money and sometimes Peter helped him. Repairing lawn mowers would be a lot easier, he thought, if his socket wrench had a button that would release the socket from the grip of the wrench. So he kept tinkering and by the end of the day he had invented the ratchet wrench.

Peter worked part-time at the local Sears-Roebuck, so he took his new wrench to his boss...who showed it to his boss...who showed it to all the execs at Sears headquarters in Chicago.

GETTING SCREWED

Nearly a year went by and Roberts never heard back from them, so he assumed no one was interested in his invention. Then one day a lawyer showed up and informed him that Sears was prepared to offer him two cents for every one of his ratchet wrenches they sold—with the stipulation that they wouldn't owe him any further royalties after he reached the $10,000 mark. The lawyer said it was going to be difficult and time consuming for Sears to manufacture the wrenches, so it might take Roberts years to collect the maximum amount of royalties. He signed over the patent to Sears.

A year later, he was amazed to receive the entire $10,000 in a single check. Suspecting that he'd been had, Roberts hired his own lawyer and took Sears to court in 1969. They argued that Sears was guilty of fraud—they'd led Roberts to believe that they'd only be able to sell a few wrenches a year when in reality they'd already sold more than a million. More importantly, Roberts had been a minor (under 21) when he'd signed the contract. After 20 years of legal wrangling, they finally settled...and Roberts collected $8.2 million.

Staying in shape: Trash in landfills keeps its original weight, volume, and form for 40 years.

A LIGHT IN THE NIGHT

Before radio, sonar, and GPS, lighthouses provided the only way for sailors to visually locate the shore at night or in foul weather. Here are a few facts about a forgotten piece of history.

No one knows for sure when or where the very first lighthouse was built. Early lighthouses were too simple to be recorded; some were little more than candles placed in the windows of tall buildings at night. Others were hilltop structures on which large fires could be built. The earliest *known* lighthouses were built on the Mediterranean Sea in the seventh century B.C.

• The Great Lighthouse at Alexandria, Egypt, was one of the Seven Wonders of the ancient world. Completed around 280 B.C., it stood about 450 feet high on the island of Pharos in the Alexandria harbor. Still in operation as late as 1115, it was destroyed by earthquakes in the 1300s.

• The oldest American lighthouse is the Boston Light, in Boston's outer harbor. Built in 1716 on Little Brewster Island, it was destroyed by the British during the American Revolution. It was rebuilt in 1783 and still stands today.

• The oldest working lighthouse in the world is Spain's Tower of Hercules, built by the Romans in 20 B.C.

• Before electricity, lighthouses provided light via wood or coal fires, or even candles. These were replaced by whale-oil lanterns, which gave way to kerosene lanterns in the 1800s. Keeping such a light continually lit wasn't easy. In the United States, most lighthouses had a full-time keeper (nicknamed "wickies" because they kept the lantern wicks trimmed), who lived at the lighthouse and made sure it stayed lit.

• No more—now every working lighthouse in the United States is automated. The last manned lighthouse, Maine's Goat Island Light, became automated in 1990.

• First American lighthouse to use electricity: the Statue of Liberty, which served as a lighthouse in New York Harbor until 1902.

Michigan borders no ocean...but has more lighthouses than any other state.

STRANGE LAWSUITS

These days, it seems that people will sue each other over practically anything. Here are more real-life examples of unusual legal battles.

THE PLAINTIFF: Toshi Van Blitter
THE DEFENDANT: Harrah's casino
THE LAWSUIT: After losing $350,000 playing blackjack, Van Blitter decided to sue the Las Vegas casino. She filed to have her debts canceled, claiming that Harrah's was negligent—they should have told her that she was an incompetent blackjack player.
THE VERDICT: The gamble didn't pay off. A federal judge dismissed her claim.

THE PLAINTIFF: Timothy Ray Anderson, an armed robber
THE DEFENDANT: John Hobson, a security guard at a McDonald's restaurant
THE LAWSUIT: Anderson was robbing a McDonald's at gunpoint; Hobson ordered him to drop the weapon. Anderson spun around, aiming his gun at Hobson, but Hobson shot first, hitting Anderson in the stomach. Anderson was subsequently convicted of armed robbery and sentenced to 15 years.

Anderson then sued Hobson, the firm Hobson worked for, and the owner of the McDonald's, claiming "excessive force" was used against him. His argument: "The mere fact that you're holding up a McDonald's with a gun doesn't mean you give up your right to be protected from somebody who wants to shoot you."
THE VERDICT: The case was thrown out of court.

THE PLAINTIFF: Boomer, a golden retriever
THE DEFENDANT: Invisible Fence Co.
THE LAWSUIT: According to a petition filed in Common Pleas Court in Dayton, Ohio, in May (2001), Boomer, is suing the fence company because the electrical charge to his collar, triggered when he attempts to leave his guardians' yard, was too strong and, according to an Associated Press dispatch, caused him severe emotional distress, for which he asks $25,000. Boomer's guardians,

In 1920 Detroit became the first U.S. city to put in a stoplight.

Andrew and Alyce Pacher, who purchased the "invisible fence" and permitted the electrical charge, were not sued.
THE VERDICT: Unknown.

THE PLAINTIFF: Robert Lee Brock
THE DEFENDANT: Robert Lee Brock
THE LAWSUIT: Brock, an inmate serving 23 years for grand larceny at the Indian Creek Correction Center in Chesapeake, Virginia, filed a $5 million lawsuit against himself. He claimed that he violated his own religious beliefs and his own civil rights by forcing himself to get drunk—and because of this self-induced drunkennes, perpetrated several crimes. Brock wrote, "I partook of alcoholic beverages in 1993. As a result I caused myself to violate my religious beliefs." He went on to claim, "I want to pay myself $5 million for violating my own rights but ask the state to pay it in my behalf since I can't work and am a ward of the state."
THE VERDICT: Judge Rebecca Smith dismissed the claim.

THE PLAINTIFF: Ned Searight
THE DEFENDANT: State of New Jersey
THE LAWSUIT: In a $14 million lawsuit, Searight claimed he had suffered injuries while in prison in 1962. He charged he was injected with a "radium electric beam" against his will. As a result of the injection, Searight claimed he began hearing voices in his head.
THE VERDICT: The U.S District Court dismissed the claim... not on the grounds that it was frivolous, but because the statute of limitations had run out. In his opinion, the judge also offered this strange lesson in physics: "Taking the facts as pleaded... they show a case of presumable unlicensed radio communication, a matter of which comes within the sole jurisdiction of the FCC.... And even aside from that, Searight could have blocked the broadcast to the antenna in his brain simply by grounding it...Searight might have pinned to the back of a trouser leg a short chain of paper clips so that the end would touch the ground and prevent anyone from talking to him inside his brain."

* * *

Misnomer: The tit**mouse** is actually a **bird**.

DISRAELI, REALLY

Ever heard of Benjamin Disraeli? He was British Prime Minister (1868, 1874–80), a staunch supporter of Queen Victoria, and the British Empire...and very wise.

"Justice is truth in action."

"The palace is not safe when the cottage is not happy."

"The greatest good you can do for another is not just to share your riches but to reveal to him his own."

"It is much easier to be critical than to be correct."

"What we anticipate seldom occurs: but what we least expect generally happens."

"Nobody is forgotten when it is convenient to remember him."

"We should never lose an occasion. Opportunity is more powerful even than conquerors and prophets."

"Man is only truly great when he acts from passion."

"There is no act of treachery or meanness of which a political party is not capable; for in politics there is no honor."

"You will find as you grow older that courage is the rarest of all qualities to be found in public life."

"Everyone likes flattery; and when you come to Royalty you should lay it on with a trowel."

"Youth is a blunder, manhood a struggle, old age a regret."

"Let the fear of a danger be a spur to prevent it; he that fears not, gives advantage to the danger."

"One secret of success in life is for a man to be ready for his opportunity when it comes."

"To be conscious that you are ignorant of the facts is a great step to knowledge."

"Desperation is sometimes as powerful an inspirer as genius."

"Action may not always bring happiness; but there is no happiness without action."

THE VIDEO GAME HALL OF FAME

Today most video games are played in the home, but in the 1970s and 1980s, if you wanted to play the newest, hottest games, you went to an arcade. Here are the stories of a few of the classics we played back in the golden age of arcade games.

SPACE INVADERS (Taito, 1978)

Object: Using a laser cannon that you scroll back and forth across the bottom of the screen, defend yourself from wave after wave of aliens descending from the top of the screen.

Origin: Space Invaders started out as a test that was used to measure the skill of computer programmers, but someone decided that it might also work well as an arcade game. They were right—the game became a national craze in Japan.

Introduced to the U.S. market by Midway in October 1978, Space Invaders became the biggest hit of the year. It made so much money—a single unit could earn back its $1,700 purchase price in as little as four weeks—that it helped arcade games break out of arcades and smoky bars into nontraditional venues like supermarkets, restaurants, and movie theaters.

TEMPEST (Atari, 1981)

Object: Shoot the moving shapes—red brackets, green spikes, yellow lines, and multicolored balls, before they climb up and out of the geometrically shaped "well" they're in and get you.

Origin: Atari game designer Dave Theurer needed an idea for a new video game, so he went to the company's book of potential themes compiled from brainstorming sessions. The idea he chose to develop was "First Person Space Invaders"—Space Invaders as seen from the perspective of the laser cannon at the bottom of the screen.

Theurer created a game and showed it to his superiors...and they told him to dump it unless he could "do something special with it." Theurer told them about a nightmare he'd had about monsters climbing out of a hole in the ground and coming to get him. "I can put it on a flat surface and wrap that surface around to

Theater spotlights used to burn lime for light. That's where the term *limelight* comes from.

make a cylinder, and rotate the cylinder," Theurer suggested. As he conceived it, the cylinder would move while the player stood still... but he abandoned that idea when the rotating cylinder started giving players motion sickness. "I switched it so the player moved around," Theurer says. "That fixed it."

PAC-MAN (Namco, 1980)

Object: Maneuver Pac-Man through a maze and eat all 240 dots without getting caught by one of the four "ghosts"—Inky, Blinky, Pinky, and Clyde.

Origin: In 1979 a game designer named Toru Iwatani decided to make a game that would appeal to women, who were less interested in violent, shoot-the-alien games like Space Invaders. Iwatani thought that eating things on the computer screen would make a good nonviolent alternative to shooting them. He came up with the idea for the Pac-Man character over lunch. "I was having pizza," he says. "I took one wedge and there it was, the figure of Pac-Man." Well, almost: Pac-Man was originally supposed to be called Puck-Man, because the main character was round like a hockey puck... but the name was changed to Pac-Man, because Namco officials "worried about American vandals changing the 'P' to an 'F'."

DONKEY KONG (Nintendo, 1980)

Object: Get the girl.

Origin: One of Nintendo's first video games was a Space Invaders knockoff called Radarscope. It flopped in the United States, nearly bankrupting the distributor—who wanted to stop doing business with Nintendo. What could Nintendo do? They promised to ship new chips to American distributors so the unsold Radarscope games could be turned into new games.

There was just one problem—they didn't have any new game chips. So Nintendo president Hiroshi Yamauchi told the company's staff artist, Shigeru Miyamoto, to come up with something, *fast*.

Miyamoto had never made a game before, and he hated tennis games, shooting games, and most games that were popular at the time. So he invented a game about a janitor who has to rescue his girlfriend from his pet ape, who has taken her to the top of a construction site. Miyamoto wanted to name the game after the ape,

If you plant bamboo today, it may not sprout flowers and produce seeds for 100 years.

so he looked up the words for "stubborn" and "ape" in his Japanese/English dictionary...and found the words "donkey" and "Kong." Donkey Kong went on to become one of the most successful video games in history, giving Nintendo the boost it needed to build itself into a multibillion-dollar company and an international video game juggernaut. And it might never have succeeded if Radarscope hadn't failed.

DEFENDER (Williams Electronics, 1980)

Object: Use your spacecraft to shoot hostile aliens while saving humanoids from being kidnapped and turned into mutants.

Origin: Another game helped along by a dream: Defender was supposed to make its debut at the 1980 Amusement & Music Operators of America (AMOA) convention, but less than two weeks before his deadline, creator Eugene Jarvis had only the rough outlines of a game—the name, Defender, and a spaceship attacking aliens, all against a planetary backdrop dotted with humanoids who didn't really do anything. What was the defender defending?

"The answer came to him in a dream," Nick Montfort writes in *Supercade*. "Those seemingly pointless little men, trapped on the surface below, *they* were the ones to be defended."

Jarvis made his deadline, but the AMOA was afraid the game was too complicated. They were wrong. Defender became one of the most popular games of the year and made so much money that in 1981 the AMOA voted it Video Game of the Year.

LEGENDARY FLOP: LUNAR LANDER (Atari, 1979)

Object: Find a flat spot on the lunar surface and use your booster engines to slow your spaceship (without running out of fuel) and land it safely on the moon.

Origin: The game was adapted from a computer simulation used in college physics courses to teach students about lunar gravity. Atari had high hopes for the game, even designing a special two-handled lever that controlled the booster engines. It flopped. So did the special lever: "Springs on the lever made it snap back in place when it was released," Steven Kent writes in *The Ultimate History of Video Games*. "Unfortunately, some younger players got their faces too close to the lever, resulting in complaints about children being hit in the face."

DUMB CROOKS

More proof that crime doesn't pay.

THE RIGHT TO REMAIN STUPID

"An Illinois woman, when asked to walk a straight line after being pulled over for weaving across a highway divider, told the state trooper, "You'll have to give me a little longer. This is tougher when you've been drinking."

—Bloomington-Normal *Daily Pantograph*

OVERNIGHT SENSATION

HELSINGBORG, Sweden—"A 20-year-old man developed what he thought to be a foolproof robbery plan. He hid in a store, waited for employees to leave for the night, and proceeded to rob the place. All was going according to plan until, as he was stuffing items in a sack, he realized he was locked in the store. He tried using a crowbar to open the front door and then attempted to break through a wall in the restrooms, but to no avail. He finally gave up and called the police."

—Bizarre News

OUT OF THE FRYING PAN...

SAN JOSE, California—"According to the Department of Corrections, Arnold Ancheta, 25, apparently escaped from Elmwood Correctional Facility by squeezing through the bars on the roof of his cell, breaking out through the skylight, and jumping down from the roof. But then, instead of heading toward the fence that leads to the road, he jumped a smaller fence and ended up on the women's side of the facility. Female inmates saw Ancheta running around the yard and alerted correctional officers. He was taken to a hospital and then back to jail."

—San Diego *Union-Tribune*

PATIENCE IS A VIRTUE?

"A bank robber in Fresno, California, made a withdrawal from his own account, then demanded all the money in the bank vault. When they told him it would take 15 minutes to empty the vault, he went outside to wait patiently on the curb, according to police, who found him sitting there, still waiting."

—*Fresno Bee*

JUST DESSERTS

"In Lafayette, Louisiana, a man robbed a bank with his head covered in whipped cream. His disguise melted before he could collect the loot, however, and he was later arrested."

—"The Edge," *The Oregonian*

PISTOL-PACKIN' IDIOT

"Gilbert MacConnell went to the West Hartford, Connecticut, police station in February 2002 for a job interview. He wanted to become a cop. MacConnell, age 35, had already passed the written exam, the oral exam, and the physical agility test. But during an interview with police chief James Strillacci, MacConnell admitted owning an unlicensed gun. Officers found the .45-caliber handgun in his car. 'Does this mean I'm not getting the job?' he asked as he was booked and charged with carrying a pistol without a permit and having a concealed weapon in a car. He didn't get the job."

—*Hartford Courant*

YOU REAP WHAT YOU SEW

"Los Angeles sheriff's deputies investigating the break-in of a sewing shop discovered the theft of a large industrial sewing machine, then noticed a thick thread snagged on the floor. They followed the thread out the door, down the alley, across the street, through a backyard, up some steps, and under a door. After kicking in the door, they discovered the sewing machine in the kitchen and nabbed three surprised thieves."

—*Maxim*

PRINTS CHARMING

"When John Michell's home was broken into, he did what anyone would do—he called the police. To distinguish his prints from the crook's, citizen Michell allowed investigators to fingerprint him. Police quickly discovered that Michell himself had been wanted for burglary for three years. Michell is now serving a 12-month sentence."

—*Fortean Times*

The glue that barnacles use to stick themselves to ship hulls is twice as strong as epoxy resin.

THE DEATH OF A PRINCESS

She was called the "people's princess." Beautiful, kind, and caring, Princess Diana captured the hearts of people around the world. But she was also outspoken and, in the eyes of some very powerful people, a troublemaker. Her worst "offense" may have been her love affair with Egyptian millionaire Dodi Al-Fayed. When the princess and her lover died in a tragic car crash, many were quick to wonder whether it was really an accident.

The Deceased: Diana, Princess of Wales

How She Died: In the early hours of Sunday, August 31, 1997, a black Mercedes S280 carrying Princess Diana and her soon-to-be fiancé Dodi Al-Fayed left the Paris Ritz Hotel. The pair were on their way to Dodi's Paris apartment. In the front seat Dodi's bodyguard, Trevor Rees-Jones, sat beside the driver, Henri Paul, deputy chief of security at the Ritz. As usual, Diana's vehicle was pursued by "paparazzi"—tabloid photographers with the reputation of doing anything to get a lucrative photograph. At least one photographer was snapping pictures from the back of a high-powered motorcycle.

Minutes later the Mercedes entered the Place de L'Alma tunnel. Some eyewitnesses report hearing an explosion, then a crash. Many of the first people to arrive after the crash described a grisly scene—photographers crowding within inches of the crumpled car, which had hit a support pillar, shooting pictures of the dying princess and the other bloodied victims.

Dodi and Henri Paul were killed instantly. Diana was taken by ambulance to a hospital, where she died three and a half hours after the crash. The only survivor was Trevor Rees-Jones—the one person in the car who had fastened his seatbelt.

Early reports blamed the crash on the paparazzi. According to stories, Henri Paul was driving at high speeds trying to evade them. Or perhaps he was blinded by a flash and swerved into the pillar. An outraged public accused the photographers not only of causing the crash, but also of interfering with the efforts of rescue

The first American cookbook, *The Compleat Housewife,* was published in 1746.

personnel. (A doctor who came upon the wreck about a minute after the crash says those reports are false—the photographers were not obstructing efforts to help the victims.)

Several photographers and a motorcyclist were detained for investigation. The photographers admitted to the chase but denied any responsibility for causing the crash. According to them, the Mercedes had outrun them before they got to the tunnel. They were quickly released.

A blood test on the driver, Henri Paul, raised other possibilities. He had more than three times the legal limit of alcohol in his blood, as well as the antidepressant Prozac. Inexplicably, there were also high levels of carbon monoxide.

Was the crash caused by a mix of zealous photographers and a drunk driver? For some, including French officials who concluded their investigation two years later, it was simply a tragic accident. But others remain convinced there's more to the story.

UNANSWERED QUESTIONS

✔ **Was Diana pregnant?** Almost immediately after the crash, rumors began to circulate that Diana had been six weeks' pregnant with Al-Fayed's child. She had hinted to the press earlier that she was going to "surprise" them. Could she have been planning to announce her engagement or her pregnancy—or both? One person who believes both is Dodi's father, billionaire businessman Mohamed Al-Fayed. He has charged that the CIA has tapes from phone taps indicating that Diana was pregnant, and that she and Dodi intended to marry.

An autopsy, which may have revealed the truth, was not performed until her body was returned to England. When asked if Diana had been pregnant, the coroner replied, "No comment."

✔ **Why was there no traffic-camera video of the Mercedes?** Paris has one of the most sophisticated video traffic surveillance systems in the world. When Mohamed Al-Fayed asked to see the tapes from the 17 cameras that covered the route the Mercedes took from the Ritz to the tunnel, French officials told him no tapes existed for those cameras at that time. What would the video have shown?

✔ **Why did the Mercedes take an indirect route to Dodi's apartment?** The tunnel where the Mercedes crashed was not on the most direct route between the Ritz and Dodi's apartment. An eyewitness reports seeing a car blocking an exit, forcing the Mercedes to take the road through the tunnel.

✔ **Was Henri Paul hired to keep Diana and Al-Fayed under surveillance?** A former British intelligence agent claims Henri Paul was an informant for MI6, the British equivalent of the CIA. There are reports that Paul had multiple bank accounts with balances that are hard to explain, based on his salary as a security officer at the Ritz. Was Paul an expendable part of the network keeping track of Diana and Al-Fayed?

✔ **Was Henri Paul really drunk?** According to one expert, to account for the amount of alcohol reportedly in Paul's blood, he would have had to drink the equivalent of 10 ounces of whisky (eight shots) within a few hours of leaving the hotel—uncharacteristic behavior according to friends and co-workers. On security camera tapes recorded just before the Mercedes left the hotel, Paul does not appear drunk. His co-workers have also testified that he was not drunk, nor did he have a reputation for heavy drinking.

The sole survivor of the crash, Rees-Jones, received head injuries and claims the last thing he remembers was leaving the Ritz. He told investigators that Paul did not act drunk at the hotel. As Al-Fayed's bodyguard, Rees-Jones would have had the responsibility to note whether the driver was in a condition to drive safely.

Was the blood test rigged? Was Henri Paul a scapegoat?

✔ **Did Rees-Jones expect trouble?** Rees-Jones was the only person in the Mercedes wearing a seatbelt. Did the former British paratrooper know something?

✔ **Was another car involved?** Investigators found evidence that the Mercedes had been grazed by another vehicle just before the crash. Pieces of a taillight and flecks of white paint embedded into the front bumper of the Mercedes probably belonged to a white Fiat Uno, according to their investigations.

Witnesses report seeing a small car cut in front of the Mercedes moments before the crash. Some speculate that the car intentionally slowed down in front of the fast-moving Mercedes as it rounded a slight corner in the tunnel, causing Henri Paul to swerve. The white Fiat has never been found.

✔ **Was there an explosion in the tunnel *before* the crash?**

26% of American men say their workplace filing system consists of "putting things in piles."

Eyewitnesses report hearing a loud bang in the tunnel just before the crash. Others say they saw a bright light, much brighter than that made by a photographer's flash. Was someone trying to disorient or blind the driver of the Mercedes?

✔ **Why did it take so long to get Diana to the hospital?** The doctor who arrived at the site about a minute after the crash quickly noted the conditions of the passengers, then called emergency services. The first ambulance didn't arrive until 15 minutes later. Diana was treated at the scene for more than 30 minutes after rescue personnel pulled her from the car. The closest hospital with 24-hour emergency service was only a few miles away, normally a 5- to 10-minute drive. The ambulance carrying Diana took 40 minutes to reach the hospital, finally arriving almost two hours after the crash.

CONSPIRACY THEORIES

✔ **Diana was killed by British intelligence.** Richard Tomlinson, a former British intelligence agent, claims British intelligence had the expertise to fake Diana's crash. He knew of a British plan to assassinate Serbian leader Slobodan Milosevic by faking a car crash similar to the one that killed Diana. According to that plan, the crash would take place in a tunnel and the driver would be disoriented with a powerful strobe light.

Mohamed Al-Fayed has said he is "99.9% certain" Diana and his son were murdered. According to Al-Fayed, British and American intelligence agencies had Diana under surveillance for years and were following her and Dodi for three months before the crash.

Al-Fayed has stated that he believes British intelligence killed Diana and Dodi, and that the CIA has documents directly implicating Prince Philip, Queen Elizabeth's husband. According to Al-Fayed, a document quotes Philip as saying of the relationship between Diana and Dodi, "Such an affair is racially and morally repugnant and no son of a Bedouin camel trader is fit for the mother of a future king."

In many ways Diana was an annoyance to the Royal Family and its supporters. After the end of her "fairy tale" marriage to Prince Charles, she aired her uncomplimentary views of the queen, her former husband, and the rest of the Royal Family in the press. And the public took Diana's side against the Royals. Some felt Diana was a real threat to the monarchy. Maybe her intent to marry Dodi Al-Fayed was the last straw.

✔ **Diana was killed by the CIA.** Mohamed Al-Fayed claims the CIA has a secret dossier of more than 1,000 pages on Diana. The princess personally campaigned against the use of landmines, visiting injured victims in Angola and Bosnia. Her high-profile involvement led to an international treaty banning landmines that has been ratified by 125 nations. The United States, a major producer of landmines, has not signed the treaty. Diana was a nuisance to the American arms industry... but would she have been targeted for assassination?

✔ **Diana was killed by Israeli agents.** England, along with the United States, has been a strong supporter of Israel in the ongoing conflicts between that country and its Arab neighbors. If Diana—mother of a future king of England, Prince William—married an Egyptian, gave birth to half-Arab children, or even converted to Islam, public opinion and official policy may have turned against Israel.

ONE OTHER POSSIBILITY

Diana faked her own death. In spite of overwhelming evidence that Diana died in the crash, some observers believe that she wanted to escape the pressures of her public life so badly that she staged her own death.

✔ Could the driver of the Mercedes have dropped Diana and Al-Fayed off somewhere before entering the tunnel? The army-trained bodyguard, Rees-Jones, may have had the expertise to make a switch. Is Diana really living somewhere in blissful anonymity?

✔ Still other people believe Diana planned to set up the accident... but something went wrong and the plan backfired.

Because the princess was so beloved and died under such strange circumstances, some people will always question the official reports of what happened. Whether Diana faked her death, was murdered, or was actually the victim of a tragic accident, the world may never know.

DESPERATELY SEEKING APPROVAL

Some people will do anything to look good. Even something stupid.

SEEKING APPROVAL: Douglas Altman of Florida
FROM WHOM: His mom
HOW: By keeping a huge stockpile of weapons stashed in his condo. In 2000 Altman was arrested for impersonating a Navy officer. Cops then searched his home and found rifles, swords, and 17,000 rounds of ammunition. Asked why he had all that artillery, his attorney explained, "He was trying to impress his mother."

SEEKING APPROVAL: A 31-year-old Chicago basketball fan
FROM WHOM: Dennis Rodman of the Chicago Bulls
HOW: Trying to "be like Dennis." The fan got several body piercings to emulate his heavily spiked hero. Unfortunately, they resulted in a severe bacterial infection—from which he barely survived.

SEEKING APPROVAL: Police Chief John Tuchek of Lanesboro, Minnesota
FROM WHOM: His ex-girlfriend
HOW: By burning down her apartment building. He had hoped to be her hero by setting fire to some cardboard behind her building and beating the fire department to the rescue. But the fire got out of control, destroying two century-old buildings and causing an estimated $500,000 in damage.

SEEKING APPROVAL: South Korea
FROM WHOM: The world community
HOW: By treating dogs in a kinder and gentler way. After becoming official hosts of the 2002 World Cup, South Korea took a lot of heat for one of their traditional foods—dog. Trying to polish their image, South Korean officials vowed to improve the conditions in which the specially bred canines are raised. They would not, however, promise to stop eating them.

Per capita, Canadians buy more diamonds than anyone on Earth.

PAY AS YOU GO

Ever wandered a strange city looking for someplace to answer the call of nature? Finding a clean, safe public restroom can be a trying experience. Good news: Someone's doing something about it.

MADE IN FRANCE

Jean-Claude Decaux was in advertising—he worked as a poster-and-paste man, running around Paris slapping advertising bills on buildings, walls, and anyplace else he could find. Then one day in 1964 he happened to notice some people waiting for a bus in the rain and it gave him an idea: he could build bus shelters at his own expense and provide them to the city free of charge. In return he would get the right to sell advertising on the shelters.

Decaux began building and installing bus shelters all over the city. And he used his success in Lyons to get the attention of officials in Paris and other cities; soon the shelters were popping up in cities all over France.

Why stop at bus shelters? Decaux expanded into other forms of "street furniture,"—clocks, newsstands, bicycle stands, telephone booths, drinking fountains, vending machines, subway ticket dispensers, and just about anything else he could think of. Everything was provided free of charge in exchange for the right to provide space for advertising. On the strength of this single concept, over the next 20 years, Decaux built his business, JCDecaux, into the world's largest outdoor advertising company.

THAT'S NO PHONE BOOTH

Building drinking fountains and ticket dispensers was easy compared to the task that the mayor of Paris presented JCDecaux in 1979: come up with a better design for the *pissoir*.

What's a pissoir? Exactly what it sounds like. Picture a phone booth without a door, erected in the middle of a sidewalk on a busy street...only instead of a phone, the booth contains a urinal. French cities were full of pissoirs well into the 1980s.

In theory, pissoirs were supposed to be the answer to the prob-

In ancient Greece, tossing an apple to a girl was a marriage proposal; catching it meant "yes."

lem of public urination, and in some respects they were successful. But no matter how much money cities spent trying to keep them clean, it never seemed to be enough. The pissoirs of Paris were invariably smelly and dirty, and every bit as disgusting as they sound. They were only marginally less offensive than the problem they were supposed to solve. And besides, only men could use them. The mayor of Paris wanted something better, and JCDecaux agreed to see what they could come up with.

In 1980, after spending a fortune on research, the company introduced what it called the Automatic Public Convenience, a public toilet unlike any other.

OPEN FOR BUSINESS

For starters, the toilets are built like M1 tanks to protect against vandalism. The entire exterior is made of stainless steel, and the interior is indestructible as well.

When the user deposits the correct amount of coins, an automatic door glides open to reveal a bathroom that's not much bigger than one on an airplane, complete with a toilet, sink, mirror, and coat hook. (Why so cramped? To discourage sleeping in the restroom and other illegal activity.)

When you finish your "business," the toilet flushes itself; when you stick your hands under the faucet, they're automatically sprayed with soap and water and then blown dry. You don't have to touch a thing—the bathroom is designed to work automatically, so that there aren't any handles for vandals to destroy.

LATHER, RINSE, REPEAT

But the most interesting feature of the restroom is one that most people will never see, because it takes place after you leave and the steel door shuts behind you. This is when the room switches into self-cleaning mode, functioning more like a big dishwasher with a toilet in it than the restroom you just used.

Both the sink and the toilet bowl retract into the wall, where they are scrubbed, disinfected, and blown dry before returning to their in-use position. While this is happening, a wave of disinfectant and water sweeps across the floor, flushing any accumulated dirt and debris into a drain. The restroom receives this thorough cleaning after each use, leaving it spotless for the next

Fathead: The sperm whale's brain weighs 20 pounds, the largest in the animal kingdom.

person who needs to use it. The whole process takes less than a minute.

FRIENDS IN NEED

JCDecaux's toilets cost a lot more to build and operate than the company's simple bus shelters and other street furniture, and it isn't possible to offer them to the public for free. These are *pay* toilets—in France they usually cost two francs (about 40¢) to use, and in the United States they cost a quarter. But the company also works with city governments and nonprofit agencies to distribute free tokens to the homeless, so that the facilities are available to anyone who needs them.

The company also manufactures a much larger version of the restroom that's wheelchair-accessible, but since toilets with this much space are more prone to abuse, they are restricted to disabled people only and are accessible only via special magnetic cards.

In the United States, it's still an open question as to whether the federal Americans with Disabilities Act will allow such "separate-but-equal" toilet facilities. Some cities, like San Francisco, have opted to install only the wheelchair-accessible versions, and to make them available to the public. And just as JCDecaux predicted, they are having trouble with vandalism. Other cities that try to install both standard and wheelchair-accessible versions face the threat of lawsuits from disabled groups.

WAITING TO GO

So when are self-cleaning toilets coming to your area? Don't hold your breath. So far, only a handful of major American cities like Boston, San Francisco, and Los Angeles have them, and unless you live in a big city, chances are it'll be a while...if you ever get them at all.

JCDecaux can only afford to offer the restrooms free of charge to cities where it can make enough money on advertising revenue to justify the $250,000 per-toilet expense. And the only places that have that much foot traffic are big cities. Smaller cities that want them are going to have to pay for them out of public coffers, which is unlikely. So the next time you're in San Francisco, Los Angeles, Paris, or any other large city that has them, pop in a coin or two and treat yourself to a magic toilet ride. Trust us, you'll be glad you did.

1% to 2% of Americans have an extra nipple somewhere on their body.

SMART ALECKS

One of the privileges of fame is you get to say nasty things about other people and get away with it. Here's a few of our favorite zingers.

"Do you mind if I smoke?"

—*Oscar Wilde* to Sarah Bernhardt

"I don't care if you burn."

—*Sarah Bernhardt*

"Do you mind if I sit back a little? Because your breath is very bad."

—*Donald Trump,* to CNN host Larry King

"Michael Jackson's album was only called *Bad* because there wasn't enough room on the sleeve for "Pathetic."

—*Prince*

"Ernest Hemingway has never been known to use a word that might send a reader to a dictionary."

—*Author William Faulkner*

"Poor Faulkner. Does he really think emotions come from big words?

—*Ernest Hemingway*

"He's racist, he's homophobic, he's xenophobic, and he's a sexist. He's the perfect Republican candidate."

—*Commentator Bill Press,* on Pat Buchanan

"Boy George is all England needs: another queen who can't dress."

—*Joan Rivers*

"What other problems do you have besides being unemployed, a moron, and a dork?"

—*Tennis pro John McEnroe,* to a spectator

"McEnroe was as charming as always, which means that he was about as charming as a dead mouse in a loaf of bread."

—*Journalist Clive James*

"Never trust a man who combs his hair straight from his left armpit."

—*Alice Roosevelt Longworth,* on Gen. Douglas MacArthur

"He has so many fish hooks in his nose, he looks like a piece of bait."

—*Bob Costas,* on Dennis Rodman

"Why, this fellow don't know any more about politics than a pig knows about Sunday."

—*Harry S Truman,* on Dwight Eisenhower

Bad old days: Dentures used to be made with teeth pulled from the mouths of dead soldiers.

BENCHED!

Remember the saying, "Judge not, lest ye be judged?" Here are a few more stories about men in black who would have done well to follow that advice.

SEE YOU IN (MY) COURT

In 1999 Delaware County Municipal Court judge Michael Hoague was convicted of misdemeanor coercion and fined $250 after he mailed a threatening letter to a woman and her fiancé following a traffic altercation. Hoague had become upset at the way Jenny Panescu and Walter Russel Brown were driving. So he chased them—tailgating at speeds of up to 80 mph, and screaming obscenities. Afterward, Hoague (illegally) used a police computer to obtain Panescu's address from her license plate number and wrote her the letter threatening to arrest her and impound her vehicle if she failed to appear in his court, even though she was not the driver and had not been charged with a crime. When the Ohio Supreme Court's Office of Disciplinary Counsel learned of the incident, it slapped Judge Hoague with a six-month suspension from the bench. Justice? Not quite—they also suspended the suspension.

WHAT'S WRONG WITH THAT?

In December 1997, the Texas Commission on Judicial Conduct suspended Judge James Barr from the 337th District Court for his "lack of social graces." Among the incidents cited: making obscene comments to the three female prosecutors, whom he refers to as his "all-babe court," and telling an unnamed lawyer, "I feel like coming across the bench and slapping the crap out of you."

JUDGE BREWSKI

While presiding over deliberations in a drunk-driving case, Lakewood, Washington, Municipal Court judge Ralph H. Baldwin disappeared into his chambers and returned a short time later with a 12-pack of beer, inviting the attorneys, jurors, and court staff to "stay for a cool one," but admonishing them not to tell anyone, promising them, "I'll deny it if you repeat it." Afterward, he carried an open container of beer to his car, telling onlookers, "I

High pressure: A pumping human heart can squirt blood as far as 30 feet.

might as well drink and drive. I do it all the time anyway." Judge Baldwin admitted he made the statement but claimed he was joking and that the can he carried to his car was empty. He said he regrets making the mistakes. "When I thought about it later, I thought, 'Oh, my God, you fool!'" he explained.

IT'S ENOUGH TO MAKE YOU SICK

One week after the city of Potosi, Missouri, discontinued paying for his health insurance, Judge Ronald Hill announced that he was lowering all municipal fines to $1. Hill insisted that he was just trying to clear up a backlog of nonviolent cases, not retaliating against the city. But at its next meeting, when the board again voted down health insurance for elected officials, an angry Judge Hill reportedly muttered, "It's a good thing I left my gun at home because I might have shot the mayor." Not long after that, Judge Hill was scheduled to hear a case in which the mayor's daughter was the victim of an assault. He subpoenaed her four days before trial and when she failed to appear, had her arrested. By that time the Missouri Supreme Court had had enough...and removed him from the bench.

FAILURE TO APPEAR

In February 1998, the Supreme Court of Texas removed Justice of the Peace Bill Lowry from the bench in Irving. Among the infractions cited: making an ethnic slur against a parking attendant who refused to let the judge park his car for free, and holding court in an auto repair shop (the judge said that since all concerned parties were present, he swore them all in and went to work). The final straw: faking attendance at a course aimed at correcting his behavior.

TAKING NOTES

In 1997 Manhattan Supreme Court justice Salvador Collazo was removed from the bench for covering up an incident that had occurred five years earlier. In 1993 Judge Collazo had written a lurid note about an intern's "knockers" and passed it to a law clerk. Then, when the intern complained about the heat, he suggested she remove her top. The offensive incident might never have come to light except that the law clerk, Ralph Silverman, kept the note... and then gave it to investigators in 1993 after Collazo fired him.

If you kiss an average amount over a lifespan, you'll spend about two weeks kissing.

THE RISE AND FALL OF ATARI

On page 314 we told you the story of how Atari "invented" Pong, the first commercially successful video game. Here's the story of how they came to dominate the American home video game industry... and then lost it all.

KING PONG

From the moment it was introduced in 1972, Atari's arcade game, Pong, was a money maker. Placed in a busy location, a single Pong game could earn more than $300 a week, compared to $50 a week for a typical pinball machine. Atari sold more than 8,000 of the machines at a time when even the most popular pinball machines rarely sold more than 2,500 units.

Atari would have sold a lot more machines, too, if competing game manufacturers hadn't flooded the market with knockoffs. But there was no way that Atari could fight off all the imitators.

Instead, Atari founder Nolan Bushnell managed to stay one step ahead of the competition by inventing one new arcade game after another. (One of these games, Breakout, in which you use a paddle and a ball to knock holes in a brick wall, was created by an Atari programmer named Steve Jobs and his friend Steve Wozniak, an engineer at Hewlett-Packard. Do their names sound familiar? They should—a few years later, they founded Apple Computer.)

THE ATARI 2600

In 1975 Atari entered the home video game market by creating a home version of Pong. Selling its games through Sears Roebuck and Co., Atari sold 150,000 games that first season alone.

Bushnell was ready to introduce more home versions of arcade games, and he'd decided to do it by copying an idea from a competing video game system, Channel F. The idea: game cartridges. It was a simple concept: a universal game system in which interchangable game cartridges plugged into a game player, or "console."

There was just one problem: inventing a video game cartridge system from scratch and manufacturing it in great enough volume to beat out his competitors was going to cost a fortune. The only way that he could come up with the money was by selling Atari to Warner Communications (today part of AOL Time Warner) for $28 million in 1976. Bushnell stayed on as Atari's chairman and continued to work on the cartridge system.

Introduced in mid-1977, the Atari Video Computer System (VCS)—later renamed the Atari 2600—struggled for more than a year. Atari's competitors didn't do much better, and for a while it seemed that the entire video game industry might be on its last legs—the victim of the public's burnout from playing too much Pong.

ALIEN RESURRECTION

Then in early 1979, Atari executives hit on the idea of licensing Space Invaders, an arcade game manufactured by Taito, a Japanese company. The game was so popular in Japan that it actually caused a coin shortage, forcing the national mint to triple its output of 100-yen coins.

Just as it had in Japan, Space Invaders became the most popular arcade game in the United States, *and* the most popular Atari game cartridge. Atari followed up with other blockbuster cartridges like Defender, Missile Command, and Asteroids; by 1980 it commanded a 75% share of the burgeoning home video game market. Thanks in large part to soaring sales of the VCS system, Atari's annual sales grew from $75 million in 1977 to more than $2 billion in 1980, making Atari the fastest growing company in U.S. history. But it wouldn't stay that way for long.

THE BEGINNING OF THE END

Within months of bringing the VCS to market, Bushnell was already pushing Warner to begin work on a next-generation successor to the system, but Warner rejected the idea out of hand. They had invested more than $100 million in the VCS and weren't about to turn around and build a new product to compete with it. Warner's determination to rest on their laurels was one of the things that led to Bushnell's break with the company.

By the time Space Invaders revived the fortunes of the VCS, Nolan Bushnell was no longer part of the company. Warner Com-

The Three Stooges appeared in more movies than any other comedy team in U.S. film history.

munications had forced him out following a power struggle in November 1978.

If Bushnell had been the only person to leave the company, Atari's problems probably wouldn't have gotten so bad. But he wasn't—Warner also managed to alienate nearly all of Atari's best programmers. While Atari made millions of dollars, Warner paid the programmers less than $30,000 a year, didn't share the profits the games generated, and wouldn't even allow them to see sales figures.

The programmers didn't receive any public credit for their work, either. Outside of the company, few people even knew who had designed classic games like Asteroids and Missile Command; Warner was afraid that if it made the names public, the programmers would be hired away by other video game companies.

BREAKOUT

So Atari's top programmers quit and formed their own video game company, called Activision, then turned around and began selling VCS-compatible games that competed directly against Atari's own titles.

Activision dealt a huge blow to Atari, and not just because Activision's games were better. Atari's entire marketing strategy was based around pricing the VCS console as cheaply as possible—$199—then reaping huge profits from sales of its high-priced game cartridges. Now the best games were being made by Activision.

Atari sued Activision several times to try to block it from making games for the VCS but lost every time, and Activision kept cranking out hit after hit. By 1982 Activision was selling $150 million worth of cartridges a year and had replaced Atari as the fastest growing company in the United States.

THE ATARI GLUT

Activision's spectacular success encouraged other Atari programmers to defect and form *their* own video game companies, and it also prompted dozens of other companies—even Quaker Oats—to begin making games for the VCS.

Many of these games were terrible, and most of the companies that made them soon went out business. But that only made things worse for Atari, because when the bad companies went out

Partly foggy? The first TV weather chart was broadcast in Britain on November 11, 1936.

of business, their game cartridges were dumped on the market for as little as $9.99 apiece. If people wanted good games, they bought them from Activision. If they wanted cheap games, they pulled them out of the discount bin. Not many people bought Atari's games, and when the cheap games proved disappointing, consumers blamed Atari.

Meanwhile, just as Bushnell had feared, over the next few years, new game systems like Mattel's Intellivision and Coleco's ColecoVision came on the market and began chiseling away at Atari's market share. With state-of-the-art hardware and computer chips, these game systems had higher-resolution graphics and offered animation and sound that were nearly as good as arcade video games...and vastly superior to the VCS. Adding insult to injury, both ColecoVision and Intellivision offered adapters that would let buyers play the entire library of VCS games, which meant that if consumers wanted to jump ship to Atari's competitors, they could take their old games with them.

EATEN BY PAC-MAN

But what really finished Atari off was Pac-Man. In April 1982, Atari released the home version of Pac-Man in what was probably the most anticipated video game release in history. At the time, there were about 10 million VCS systems on the market, but Atari manufactured 12 million cartridges, assuming that new consumers would buy the VCS just to play Pac-Man.

Big mistake—Atari's Pac-Man didn't live up to its hype. It was a flickering piece of junk that didn't look or sound anything like the arcade version. It wasn't worth the wait. Atari ended up selling only 7 million cartridges, and many of these were returned by outraged customers demanding refunds.

ATARI PHONE HOME

Then Atari followed its big bomb with an even bigger bomb: E.T., The Extra-Terrestrial. Atari guaranteed Steven Spielberg a $25 million royalty for the game, then rushed it out in only six weeks so that it would be in stores in time for Christmas (video games typically took at least six *months* to develop). Then they manufatured five million cartridges without knowing if consumers would take any interest in the game.

Q: What do you get when you cross a sheep with a goat?

They didn't. The slap-dash E.T. was probably the worst product Atari had ever made, worse even than Pac-Man. Nearly all of the cartridges were returned by consumers and retailers. Atari ended up dumping millions of Pac-Man and E.T. game cartridges in a New Mexico landfill and then having them crushed with steam-rollers and buried under tons of cement.

TOO LITTLE, TOO LATE

That same year Atari finally got around to doing what Nolan Bushnell had wanted to do since 1978: they released a new game system, the Atari 5200.

But in the face of stiff competition from ColecoVision, which came out with Donkey Kong (the 5200 didn't) and had better graphics and animation, it bombed. Staggering from the failures of Pac-Man, E.T., and the 5200, Atari went on to lose more than $536 million in 1983.

THE LAST BIG MISTAKE

In 1983 Atari had what in retrospect might have been a chance to revive its sagging fortunes...but it blew that opportunity, too. Nintendo, creators of Donkey Kong, decided to bring its popular Famicom (short for Family Computer) game system to the United States. The Famicom was Nintendo's first attempt to enter the American home video game market, and rather than go it alone, the company wanted help. It offered Atari a license not just to sell the Famicom in every country of the world except Nintendo's home market of Japan, but also to sell it under the Atari brand name. Consumers would never even know that the game was a Nintendo. In return, Nintendo would receive a royalty for each unit sold and would have unrestricted rights to create games for the system.

Atari and Nintendo negotiated for three days, but nothing ever came of it. Nintendo decided to go it alone—and it was a good choice.

Free replay. Turn to page 499 for more video game history: "Let's Play Nintendo!"

* * *

"When things go wrong...don't go with them." **—Anonymous**

A: A geep or a shoat. (We're not kidding.)

THE GRANNY QUIZ

Put on your knitted thinking caps for this quiz about some unusual old ladies. (*Answers on page 516.*)

1. In 2002, 89-year-old Sylvia Mandell of Naples, Florida, spent a night in...
a) A sewage canal under New York City
b) Jail for punching a cop
c) An Anheuser-Busch brewery restroom
d) A coma after an Ex-lax overdose

2. What did 88-year-old Viola Meckel of Texas, win in 2001?
a) A death penalty reprieve
b) The lottery
c) A deer-hunting contest
d) A date with Clint Eastwood

3. In 2002, 94-year-old Ruby Barber of Duston, England, was ordered by police to take down what from outside her home?
a) Razor wire
b) Naked statues of the Royal Family
c) A billboard advertising her "vital statistics"
d) Her Christmas lights

4. In 2001 Amy Hulmes of Manchester, England, passed away at 114. To what did she attribute her long life?
a) Four beers a day
b) Four decades without a husband
c) Four cigars a week
d) Four decades as a vegetarian

5. At Miami International Airport in 2002, 81-year-old, wheelchair-bound Stella Michetti was...
a) Refused entry to the U.S. for allegedly being a mafia matriarch
b) Found with 10,000 Ecstasy tablets in her suitcase
c) Dragged 20 feet by a luggage rack that caught her coat.
d) Arrested for indecent exposure in a men's room

Average age of a first-time U.S. bride in 1970: 20.8 years. In 2000: 25.1.

ELVIS BY THE NUMBERS

We're not superstitious at the BRI, but we always try to include at least one Elvis page. Last year we forgot...and we were all shook up. We hope this makes up for it.

TWELVE VITAL STATISTICS

1. Driver's license number (Tennessee): 2571459

2. Waistline, 1950s: 32 inches

3. Waistline, 1970s: 44 inches

4. Blood type: O

5. Shoe size: 11D (he wore size-12 combat boots)

6. Social Security Number: 409-52-2002

7. Draft number: 53310761

8. Checking account number: 011-143875

9. Length of his wedding to Priscilla Beaulieu: eight minutes

10. Phone number (Memphis): 397-4427

11. Phone number (Beverly Hills): 278-3496

12. Phone number (Palm Springs): 325-3241

NICKNAMES OF SIX GIRLFRIENDS AND MISTRESSES

1. Ann-Margret: "Bunny," "Thumper," "Scoobie"

2. Malessa Blackwood: "Brown Eyes"

3. Margrit Buergin: "Little Puppy"

4. Dolores Hart: "Whistle Britches"

5. Ursula Andress: "Alan"

6. Ginger Alden: "Gingerbread," "Chicken Neck"

FIVE CODE NAMES FOR THE "MEMPHIS MAFIA" (ELVIS' HANGERS-ON)

1. James Caughley: "Hamburger"

2. Joe Esposito: "Diamond Joe"

3. Lamar Fike: "Bull"

4. Marvin Gamble: "Gee Gee"

5. Charlie Hodge: "Slewfoot," "Waterhead"

Fore! 18% of all money spent on sporting goods in the U.S. is used to buy golf equipment.

FIVE ADVANTAGES TO BEING IN THE "MEMPHIS MAFIA"

1. Salary of $250 a week (1950s) to $425 a week (1960s)

2. Cadillacs, jewelery, women, and down payments on homes given as gifts

3. Free lodging (mobile homes on the grounds of Graceland)

4. Gold TCB ("Taking Care of Business") necklaces and .38-caliber pistols provided free of charge

5. Elvis never leaves Graceland without you

SIX DRAWBACKS TO BEING IN THE MEMPHIS MAFIA

1. Elvis never leaves Graceland without you.

2. On call 24 hours a day

3. No paid vacations

4. No pensions

5. No matter how stupid or dangerous the request that Elvis makes of you, if you don't fulfill it, you're out of a job.

6. Outsiders disparage you as Elvis' "fart catchers."

ELVIS' FAVORITE BIBLE PASSAGE

Matthew 19:24, "It is easier for a camel to go through the eye of a needle than for a rich man to enter the kingdom of God." (The passage haunted Elvis toward the end of his life.)

THREE TIPS FROM ELVIS FOR STAYING HEALTHY

1. "I eat a lot of Jell-O. Fruit Jell-O."

2. "The only exercise I get is on the stage. If I didn't get that, I'd get a little round around the tummy, as much as I eat."

3. "I have never tasted alcohol."

SIX WOMEN WHO CLAIM TO BE ELVIS' WIFE, DAUGHTER, OR THE MOTHER OF HIS CHILDREN

1. Lucy deBarbin: Claims Elvis fathered her daughter Desiree on August 23, 1958.

2. Ann Farrell: Claims she married the King in Alabama in 1957, after refusing to sleep with him "unless they were man and wife."

23% of the Earth's land mass is buried under snow at least part of the year.

3. Candy Jo Fuller: Claims to be Elvis' daughter after he had an affair with her mother in the 1950s. Claims Elvis paid child support for many years.

4. Zelda Harris: Claims the King married her in Alabama in 1960, "after just one date."

5. Barbara Jean Lewis: Claims she and Elvis dated for a year in the mid-1950s and that she gave birth to Elvis' daughter, Deborah Delaine Presley, in 1955. (In 1988 Deborah sued the Presley estate demanding her "fair share." She lost.)

6. Billie Joe Newton: Claims Elvis married her and fathered three children by her, the first when she was only nine years old. Claims Elvis divorced her in 1956 "because Colonel Tom Parker demanded it."

Note: None of these women have any proof to back up their claims. Most claim that the documentation—marriage certificates, birth certificates, divorce papers, etc.—has been lost or destroyed.

SIX FORGOTTEN MOMENTS IN ELVIS HISTORY

1. December 30, 1970: Tours FBI headquarters in Washington, D.C.; sought and obtained permits to carry firearms in every state.

2. July, 1971: Spends $55,000 on a stretch limousine that matched the one he saw in the movie *Shaft*.

3. January 2, 1972: Buys a $10,000 robe inscribed "The People's Champion" and gives it to Muhammad Ali.

4. March 31, 1973: Ali wears the robe that Elvis gave him for his fight against Ken Norton. Ali loses the fight.

5. September 1, 1975: Elvis is sworn in as deputy sheriff (honorary) of Shelby County, Tennessee.

6. December 18, 1975: Elvis spends the day obsessing over (1) the supernatural, (2) the occult, (3) his weight, (4) his fear of becoming impotent. Loved ones describe him as "a physical and mental wreck."

* * *

"Ambition is a dream with a V8 engine."

Elvis Presley

Three states with the highest per-capita credit card debt: Alaska, Vermont, South Dakota.

NO CAN(ADA) DO

Many of our Canadian readers have sent us items about life in the Great White North... including some strange Canadian laws. Here are a few examples.

In Canada, it's illegal to jump from a flying airplane without a parachute.

In Nova Scotia, you're not allowed to water the lawn when it is raining.

In Toronto, it's illegal to drag a dead horse along Yonge Street on Sunday.

A maritime law in Canada specifies that two vessels cannot occupy the same space at the same time.

In Quebec, margarine must be a different color from butter.

The city of Guelph, Ontario, is classified as a "no-pee zone."

In Montreal, you may not park a car in such a way that it is blocking your own driveway.

It's illegal to ride a Toronto streetcar on Sunday if you've been eating garlic.

In Alberta, wooden logs may not be painted.

It is illegal to kill a Sasquatch in British Columbia.

An Etobicoke, Ontario, bylaw states that no more than 3.5 inches of water is allowed in a bathtub.

In Charlottetown, Prince Edward Island, you can only buy liquor with a doctor's prescription.

Burnaby, BC, has a 10 p.m. curfew—for dogs.

An anti-noise ordinance in Ottawa makes it illegal for bees to buzz.

Pedestrians on Toronto sidewalks must give a hand signal before turning.

In Vancouver, BC, it's illegal to ride a tricycle over 10 mph.

It is illegal to sell antifreeze to Indians in Quebec.

Tightrope walking over the main streets of Halifax is prohibited. (Side streets are okay.)

40% of the world's newspapers are printed on paper that comes from Canadian forests.

THE WORLD'S FIRST DISPOSABLE DIAPER

With everything we've sent through the pipeline in 15 years of Bathroom Readers, *it's amazing that we've never gotten around to telling the story of the disposable diaper. Here it is at last.*

NOT AGAIN

One afternoon in the late 1940s, a young mother named Marion Donovan changed her daughter's cloth diaper.. only to see the baby wet the new diaper, her clothes, and her crib bedding all over again just a few minutes later. Traditional cloth diapers weren't like modern disposable diapers—the wetness and goo immediately soaked through, soiling everything the baby came in contact with. Rubber baby pants could be used to hold in the moisture, but they caused terrible diaper rash because they didn't allow the baby's skin to breathe.

CURTAIN CALL

There weren't any other solutions... until Donovan glanced over at her waterproof shower curtain and something clicked. She realized the curtain material would make an excellent outer cover for cloth diapers. If the cover was made properly, it would hold in moisture but would also breathe better than rubber, preventing diaper rash. She cut out a piece of the shower curtain, took it to her sewing machine, and started sewing.

It took Donovan three years (and a lot of shower curtains) to perfect her design for waterproof diaper covers. She ended up switching to nylon parachute cloth instead of shower curtains. She also added snaps, so that mothers didn't have to worry about sticking their babies with safety pins.

Donovan jokingly named her diaper covers Boaters—since the covers didn't leak they kept babies "afloat"—and she convinced Saks Fifth Avenue to begin carrying them in 1949. They were an immense hit, and in 1951 Donovan sold the rights to her diaper covers for $1 million.

Trying to call a ship in the eastern Atlantic? Use area code 871. Western Atlantic? Try 874.

SO CLOSE...AND YET SO FAR

But she wasn't done yet. Donovan then came up with the idea that turned out to be the Holy Grail of modern motherhood: diapers made from absorbant paper instead of cloth, allowing them to be thrown away instead of washed and reused.

So are today's disposable diapers direct descendants of Donovan's idea? Nope—when Donovan went around to the big paper companies and tried to get them interested in paper diapers, they all thought she was nuts.

Disposable diapers had to wait until 1959, when a Procter & Gamble employee named Vic Mills invented his own disposable diaper for his grandson, apparently without even knowing that Donovan had beaten him to the task by nearly a decade. It was Mills's diaper, not Donovan's, that P&G introduced as "Pampers" in 1961.

No matter—Donovan was number one, and she's the person historians credit as the inventor of the world's first disposable diaper.

* * *

THE OLD REVOLVING-TROOPS TRICK

In September 1864, Civil War General Nathan Forrest was leading his Confederate troops north from Alabama toward Tennessee. He planned to attack the Union post in Athens, Alabama, having heard that Union reinforcements were approaching and wanted to take the fort before they arrived. The problem: the post was well manned and heavily fortified. Forrest was greatly outnumbered, but he had a plan.

He sent a message to Union commander Campbell requesting a personal meeting. Campbell agreed to the meeting. Forrest then escorted Campbell on a tour of the Confederate troops, during which Campbell silently calculated the number of troops and artillery surrounding his fort. What he didn't realize was that Forrest's men—after being inspected and tallied—were quietly packing everything up and quickly moving to a new position, to be counted again. Campbell was seeing the same troops over and over again. Assuming he was vastly outnumbered by the Confederates, he returned to his fort, pulled down the Union flag and gave up without a fight.

IT'S A WEIRD, WEIRD WORLD

More proof that truth really is stranger than fiction.

SPICE UP YOUR LIFE

"A 40-year-old ex-drug dealer named Kenny Carter finally found his calling in 1997. Carter says, 'I was crying out in the middle of church: "Oh, God! Oh, God!" And suddenly I heard an audible male voice that said, "You will be a vegetable."' That was all he needed to hear. He made a costume—a vegetable persona called 'Peppy the Pepper.' Now he greets customers and sings his 'Peppy the Pepper' song at the Super Fresh market, where he is a community relations manager."

—*Baltimore Sun*

GOING POSTAL

"Istvan Beki of Budapest needed to see his ill mother 150 miles away but didn't have enough money for train fare. So he got a large cardboard box and mailed himself home. Beki poked air holes in the box and took it to the post office, then climbed in with a bottle of water and some sandwiches and told the postal clerk to seal up the box. He arrived the next day."

—*BoneheadoftheDay.com*

PSYCHO-BIBLE

"Samson exhibited almost all the symptoms of 'Anti-Social Personality Disorder,' says Dr. Eric Altschuler in *Archives of General Psychiatry*. Although the biblical hero is credited with extraordinary strength and remarkable exploits—such as the slaying of a lion and moving the gates of Gaza—he was also apparently a bully, a thief, and a liar. Altschuler's evidence: failure to conform to social norms by burning the Philistines' fields; repeated involvement in physical fights; reckless disregard for the safety of others by having killed 1,000 Philistines; and his lack of remorse, shown by his gloating after killing them.

"'It should be noted that Samson also displayed many of the

behaviors listed in the criteria for "Conduct Disorder,"' added Altschuler, 'such as cruelty to animals, bullying, and using a weapon (the jawbone of ass).'"

—*The Jerusalem Post*

CLOSE TO HER HEART

"A grieving Australian widow has had her husband's ashes injected into her breast implants, a British newspaper has reported. Sydney woman Sandi Canesco, 26, took the bizarre step after her husband Dustin was killed in a car accident, the *Daily Star* reported. 'It dawned on me that if I carried Dustin's cremated remains in my breast implants, I'd never really have to part with him at all,' the paper quoted Canesco as saying, under the headline 'Dust to Bust.'"

—*News.com*

IN COLD BLOOD

"When Chamlong Taengniem's 13-year-old son died in a motorcycle accident, she had no idea he would revisit her. As a lizard. The Thai mother claims a lizard followed her home after her son's cremation and sleeps in his mattress and drinks his favorite drinks. Flocks of people have journeyed to the woman's home to catch a glimpse of the lizard, even stroking its stomach in the hopes of finding clues to future lottery numbers."

—"The Edge," *The Oregonian*

TYRANNOSAURUS RETCH

"London's Natural History Museum is home to a new animatronic *Tyrannosaurus rex*. Not content with having another boring dinosaur display, the museum decided to re-create the exact odor that would have come out of T-Rex's mouth, a mixture of dead flesh and rotting meat. 'The smell was found to be so offensive it would have put people off,' says a museum spokesperson. 'So we've gone for a smell that was found in the environment instead.'

"Officially named *Maastrichtian miasma*, the reformulated scent is a concoction of jaguar urine, cesspit, boiler room, brewery, wild stag, machine oil, garbage, Thai curry, smoked fish, and ozone. Bottles of dinosaur smell are available for purchase in the museum gift shop."

—*The Times* (London)

How're you doing so far? The average American will eat 35,000 cookies in their lifetime.

D.C. FOLLIES

Some people say the best comedy is on TV.
We say it's in Washington, D.C.

BUT IT'S DEFINITELY NOT BRAIN SURGERY

"At a press briefing last Friday, **Senate Majority Leader Thomas Daschle (D-S.D.)** lit into President Bush's plans for a space-based missile-defense system, saying that committing billions of dollars 'to a concept that may or may not be practical or doable is something that I am mystified by.'

But as his mystification intensified, Daschle slipped up a bit. 'It just seems like common sense,' he said. 'I mean, this isn't—this isn't rocket science here.'

Daschle quickly caught his mistake, as the room erupted in laughter. 'Yes, it is rocket science,' he said to more laughter, 'now that I think about it.'"

—*Roll Call*

IN THE DOGHOUSE

Maryland Sen. Barbara Mikulski (D-Md.) "stood in front of the cameras and assembled reporters in a Senate gallery Tuesday, eagerly flapping her arms and belting out a stadium favorite of Baltimore Ravens fans: 'Who let the dogs out? Who, who? Who, who?'

"Why? She was celebrating. She had just won a Super Bowl bet with New York Senators Charles Schumer and Hillary Clinton."

—Capital News Service

POLITICAL THEATER OF THE ABSURD

"House Speaker Dennis Hastert (R-Ill.) held a press conference surrounded by a group of hard hat-wearing 'working Americans.' But the 'workers' were really lobbyists in disguise. The conference was called to pass off the trillion-dollar Bush tax cut as a boon for the working class.

"According to a memo sent to the lobbyists, 'the Speaker's office was very clear in saying that they do not need people in suits. If people want to participate, they must be DRESSED DOWN, and appear to be REAL WORKER types.'"

—*Common Dreams*

Me, me, me: Rembrandt painted more self-portraits (62) than any other world-famous artist.

MAN OF THE PEOPLE

"Three security guards filed complaints accusing **Bob Barr (R-Ga.)** of cursing and yelling racial slurs after he was denied entry to a private parking lot at Atlanta's Hartsfield International Airport.

"Guard Ramona Phenix, who is black, reported that Barr cursed at her and used racial slurs when she told him the van could not enter the lot. Supervisor Alicia S. Gordon, who is also black, said Barr became more angry after they decided to let the van into the lot, but not until the driver filled out a form. While the driver was working on the form, Barr became angry again.

"'This time he yelled, "When are you going to open the gate you stupid black idiot,"' Gordon wrote."

—Associated Press

TICKLE ME, ELMO

"**Rep. Duke Cunningham (R-Calif.)** summoned Elmo, the Sesame Street character made of red felt, to the Capitol to testify on the importance of music education. Said one political analyst who witnessed the event, 'Elmo has higher poll ratings than most members of Congress. They like to be in his reflective glory.'"

—Mother Jones

DON'T QUIT YOUR DAY JOB

"**Orrin Hatch (R-Utah)** has written several gospel and love songs and released several CDs. But nothing tops the 68-year-old conservative's most recent composition, featured in the movie *Rat Race*. Says Hatch, it's a 'patriotic rock song for children.'

"A sample of his lyrics: 'America rocks! America rocks! / From its busy bustling cities / To its quiet country walks / It's totally cool, it's totally hot / I mean it's like right there at the top / America rocks! America rocks! America rocks!'"

—St. Petersburg Times

LOVE BOAT

"**Rep. James Traficant (D-Oh.)** was convicted of selling a boat to a businessman at an inflated price in return for favors. Responding to an ethics subcommittee on why he kept the boat docked in the Potomac River, he said: 'I wanted to have Playboy bunnies come on at night to meet me. I wanted to be promiscuous with them.'"

—Washington Post

Coincidence? The average single man is one inch shorter than the average married man.

SNL PART IV: "WELL ISN'T THAT SPECIAL"

Part III of our history of Saturday Night Live *(page 309) ended with the show once again in shambles—no producer, low ratings, an unhappy cast. It needed a lot of help. Who better to save it then the man who created it?*

NEW BEGINNING

Lorne Michaels returned to NBC in 1984 to develop a new show for Friday nights called...*The New Show*. He was having trouble trying to make it as good as *SNL* without copying his original show—and it showed. *The New Show* limped along for 12 weeks getting low ratings and poor reviews. Michaels decided he'd had enough of television. A film that he co-wrote with Randy Newman and Steve Martin, *The Three Amigos*, had just started filming when NBC president Brandon Tartikoff called and offered him his old job back at *SNL*. Michaels initially turned him down, but when Tartikoff threatened to cancel the show instead, he relented and moved back into his old office on the 17th floor of Rockefeller Plaza. The first order of business: hiring a new cast.

SATURDAY NIGHT DEAD #2

NBC called the 1985–86 season a rebuilding year—most fans and critics called it a disaster. Michaels experimented with established Brat Pack stars Robert Downey, Jr., Anthony Michael Hall, and Joan Cusack, as well as veteran actor Randy Quaid. Everyone else he added was a no-name. Nothing seemed to click.

What went wrong? Among other things, NBC executives had decided that the show was too important to leave alone, so the 17th floor was invaded by "strange men with clipboards" scribbling secret notes to take back upstairs. The writers now had to get network approval for any even slightly taboo subject. They blamed their unfunny scripts on an un-funny cast.

Was it the scripts or the cast? Either way, what resulted was a string of shows met with dead silence from the studio audience and shrinking ratings from the television audience. Toward the

Dust storms in Arizona will cause about 40 traffic accidents this year.

season's end, Tartikoff couldn't take it anymore—he decided to put *Saturday Night Live* out of its misery. Michaels flew to Los Angeles to reassure Tartikoff that the show would rebound, that there were bright spots emerging. Tartikoff agreed to give him one more season to turn it around.

The bright spots Michaels was referring to were the only three cast members who would survive that season: Nora Dunn, Jon Lovitz and Dennis Miller.

BACK TO THE DRAWING BOARD

Having learned his lesson of hiring names over talent, Michaels returned to his 1975 tactics and once again scoured the improv circuit. Now his main goal was to see not only who was funny, but also who worked well with others.

The first new cast member hired for the the 1986 season was stand-up comedian Dana Carvey. Michaels was impressed by Carvey's talent for impressions, as well as his brain full of ideas and characters. Michaels also found Jan Hooks, Victoria Jackson, Kevin Nealon, and a young Canadian comic named Mike Myers. (As a boy in 1972, Myers had starred in a TV commercial—his mother was played by Gilda Radner.)

The cast was completed by Phil Hartman. His versatility in front of the camera is well documented, but what was even more important for the show's renewed success was what he added backstage. "Phil was a rock," remembers Jan Hooks. Jon Lovits called him a "big brother." "He was my mentor," said Mike Myers. Now Studio 8H had something it had sorely been lacking: a family atmosphere—and it showed in front of the camera.

SCHWING!

As in the past, memorable recurring characters and political satire propelled the show, and *Saturday Night Live* enjoyed its third golden age. A few standouts:

• Dana Carvey's Church Lady, Garth, and George Bush. On Bush: At first, "I couldn't do him at all...but then one night I just sort of hooked it, and it was that phrase 'that thing out there, that guy out there, doin' that thing,' and from there on it was easy."

• Mike Myers's Simon, Sprockets, and *Wayne's World*. Conan O'Brien, a writer for the show from 1988 to 1991, recalls Myers's

Kryptonite tights? Actor George Reeves needed three men to help him out of his Superman suit.

first week: "He came to us and said he had this character named Wayne who had a cable show in his basement. We politely told him that we didn't think it was his best idea…I felt sorry for him. I thought, 'This poor kid is going to have to learn the hard way.'" But Michaels liked the character and later worked with Myers in 1992 to produce a feature film based on it. *Wayne's World* was the only movie derived from an *SNL* sketch to earn over $100 million.

• John Lovitz's compulsive liar Tommy Flannagin and Master Thespian. He created the character when he was 18 but never thought it would work on *SNL*. "I was just goofing around," he remembers, "saying 'I'm Master Thespian!' And now they've built an entire set for it."

• Phil Hartman's Frank Sinatra. Joe Piscopo, who'd done Sinatra on the show 10 years before, says that the Sinatra family hated Hartman's impression. "I think there's some kind of law: Don't even attempt to do Sinatra unless you're Italian."

TOO MANY PEOPLE

In his quest to create stars, Michaels continued packing the stage with featured players. He struck gold in 1990 and 1991 by adding a slew of comics who had grown up watching *SNL*: Tim Meadows, Adam Sandler, Rob Schneider, David Spade, Chris Rock, Chris Farley, Ellen Cleghorne, and Julia Sweeney. The opening credits in 1991 seemed to go on forever, and there were more people backstage than ever before.

In fact, viewers barely noticed when Carvey, Lovitz, and Hartman left the show because the new, younger performers were catering to a new, even younger audience, taking on subjects such as shopping malls, frat parties, and MTV.

Sandler, Rock, and Farley emerged as the new big stars. In addition to bringing back much of the rebellious anything-can-happen comedy that recalled the early days, the young cast members brought back another backstage tradition: drugs. Especially Farley, who did everything in excess. (Unfortunately for him, his hero was John Belushi. Both died of drug overdoses at the age of 33.)

Most critics called *SNL* in the early-1990s a "juvenile" show, but that was fine by NBC. The 18 to 34 demographic brought in the highest advertising dollars—and the show remained high in the ratings…for a while.

When you do something on the "Q.T." you are using an abbreviation of the word quiet.

SATURDAY NIGHT DEAD #3

By 1995 the writers were finding it increasingly tough to find new material for overused characters, which resulted in yet another a succession of seemingly endless and pointless skits. Once again, the show had become difficult to watch. The network pressured *SNL* to clean house one more time, and Michaels agreed:

> No one anywhere was saying, "*SNL* is doing what it's supposed to be doing," or "These people are funny." So we had to let Adam Sandler go with two years on his contract, and Farley with a year. And Chris Rock had gone on to do *In Living Color.*

It was time for a new cast.

The roller-coaster ride continued. To read about SNL's long crawl back to the top, go to page 490.

*   *   *

DEEP THOUGHTS BY JACK HANDEY

• The face of a child can say it all, especially the mouth part of the face."

• "For mad scientists who keep brains in jars, here's a tip: Why not add a slice of lemon to each jar, for freshness."

• "I wish I had a kryptonite cross, because then you could keep both Dracula and Superman away."

• "Can't the Marx Brothers be arrested and maybe even tortured for all the confusion and problems they've caused?"

• "The crows were all calling to him, thought Caw."

• "Why do the caterpillar and the ant have to be enemies? One eats leaves, and the other eats caterpillars....Oh, I see now."

• "Consider the daffodil. And while you're doing that, I'll be over here, looking through your stuff."

• "Instead of a Seeing Eye dog, what about a gun? It's cheaper than a dog, plus if you walk around shooting all the time, people are going to get out of the way. Cars, too."

FUTURE IMPERFECT

Uncle John predicts that you won't believe some of the ridiculous things people use to tell fortunes. How does he know? His Ouija board told him.

Scarpomancy: Predict someone's future by studying their old shoes.

Tiromancy: Study the shape, holes, mold, and other features on a piece of cheese.

Scatomancy: Predict your future by studying your own poop. (Not to be confused with *spatulamancy,* the study of "skin, bones, and excrement.")

Bibliomancy: Open the Bible and read the first passage you see—that's your fortune. (In some Christian denominations, this is grounds for excommunication.)

Stichomancy: Read the first passage of *any* book you see.

Pynchonomancy: Throw darts at a paperback copy of *Gravity's Rainbow,* by Thomas Pynchon, then read the sentence on the deepest page penetrated by the dart.

Uromancy: Predict someone's future by studying their urine.

Dilitiriomancy: Feed African *benge* poison to a chicken. Ask the gods a question, being careful to end the question with, "if the chicken dies, the answer is yes," or "if the chicken dies, the answer is no." Then wait to see if the chicken dies.

Haruspication: Study the guts of an animal, preferably a sacred one.

Hepatoscopy: Study only the animal's liver; ignore the rest of the guts.

Alphitomancy: Feed a special cake to an alleged wrongdoer. An innocent person will be able to eat and digest the cake, a guilty person will gag on the cake or become ill.

Alepouomancy: Draw a grid in the dirt outside your village. Each square represents a different question. Sprinkle the grid with peanuts, wait for a fox to eat them, then study the fox's footprints to see how the questions are answered.

...2) call the police when they hear a car alarm.

NAME THAT CITY

Here's a game: a lot of American cities have had other names throughout their histories. Can you guess which are which?

FORMER NAME

1. Fort Dallas
2. Hot Springs
3. Yerba Buena
4. Fort Dearborn
5. Lancaster
6. Terminus
7. Cole's Harbor
8. Waterloo
9. Willingtown
10. Quinnipiac
11. Assunpink
12. Rumford
13. Oyster Point
14. New Netherland
15. St. Charles
16. Fort Pontchartrain
17. All Saints
18. Juneautown
19. Lake Crossing
20. New Connecticut

PRESENT NAME

a. Austin, TX
b. Cleveland, OH
c. New York, NY
d. Baltimore, MD
e. Charleston, SC
f. Atlanta, GA
g. Chicago, IL
h. Miami, FL
i. Minneapolis, MN
j. Truth or Consequences, NM
k. Reno, NV
l. Milwaukee, WI
m. Lincoln, NE
n. San Francisco, CA
o. Denver, CO
p. Wilmington, DE
q. Concord, NH
r. Detroit, MI
s. Trenton, NJ
t. New Haven, CT

Answers

1. h; 2. j; 3. n; 4. g; 5. m; 6. f; 7. d; 8. a; 9. p; 10. t; 11. s; 12. q; 13. e; 14. c; 15. o; 16. r; 17. i; 18. l; 19. k; 20. b

In St. Louis, Missouri, it's illegal to drink beer from a bucket when you're sitting at the curb.

WORD ORIGINS

Ever wonder where words come from?
Here are some more interesting stories.

FIASCO

Meaning: A complete and humiliating failure

Origin: "The making of a fine Venetian glass bottle is a difficult process—it must be perfect. If the slightest flaw is detected the glassblower turns the bottle into a common flask—called in Italian, *fiasco*." (From *Why Do We Say It?*, by Frank Oppel)

ASSASSIN

Meaning: One who carries out a plot to kill a prominent person

Origin: "In the 11th and 12th centuries, the *Hashashin* ("hashish eaters") were a secret murder cult of the Ismaili sect of Muslims. Their leader, Hasan ben Sabah, offered them sensual pleasures, including beautiful maidens and hashish, so that they supposed they were in heaven. He then sent them on gangland-style missions to rub out prominent targets, assuring them of a quick trip to paradise if things went sour. The Hashashin survived in our word *assassin*." (From *Remarkable Words with Astonishing Origins*, by John Train)

SEEDY

Meaning: Somewhat disreputable; squalid

Origin: "During the seasons when rye, barley, oats, and other grains were being planted, a fellow who spent his days in the fields was likely to be covered with seeds. Once the derisive title entered common usage, it came to mean anything run-down—from shacks to individuals." (From *Why You Say It*, by Webb Garrison)

BOO

Meaning: An exclamation used to frighten or surprise someone

Origin: "The word *boh!*, used to frighten children, was the name of Boh, a great general, the son of the Norse god, Odin, whose very appellation struck immediate panic in his enemies." (From *Pulleyn's Etymological Compendium*, by M. A. Thomas)

Americans stand about 14 inches apart when they converse; Russians, about 10 inches.

TRIVIAL

Meaning: Of little or no consequence/value

Origin: "The Latin *triviu*—from *tri* (three) and *via* (way)—means 'a place where three roads meet.' In Medieval schools the *trivium* were three roads of learning—grammar, logic, rhetoric. With the passage of time the 'academic' *trivium* was forgotten but not the 'inconsequential' *trivial.* It has long been felt that gossips and idlers gather where roads intersect. What was usually discussed at these congregations was the commonplace, matters of little value, the gosssip that one might expect to hear at *tri-viae*—the trivial." (From *The Story Behind the Word*, by Morton S. Freeman)

GALORE

Meaning: A great deal of something

Origin: "The term was brought into our speech by sailors. It is from the Irish *go leor* ('in abundance')." (From *War Slang*, by Paul Dickson)

TATTOO

Meaning: A permanent mark on the skin made by ingraining an indelible pigment

Origin: "When Captain Cook sailed to Tahiti in 1769, he unwittingly introduced tattoos to sailors. Upon studying the island's inhabitants, Cook described how '*both sexes paint their bodys.*' Cook called it '*tattow,*' his rendition of the Tahitian term *tatau.* The word was derived from the Polynesian *ta,* 'to strike,' a reference to the puncturing of the skin '*with small instruments made of bone, cut into short teeth.*'" (From *The Chronology of Words and Phrases*, by Linda and Roger Flavell)

ATCHOO!

Meaning: The sound you make when you sneeze

Origin: "Excluded from dictionaries, this imitative word corresponds oddly with the French *a tes souhaits* (pronounced 'a tay soo-eh'), their version of 'God bless.' It even sounds like it, though *à tes souhaits* follows the sneeze. Is this overlap a mere fluke, or has somebody really been listening?" (From *The Secret Lives of Words*, by Paul West)

MEMORABLE MOMENTS IN MARKETING

All those advertising gimmicks that clutter our lives didn't simply materialize out of thin air. There's a story behind each one...

MEMORABLE MOMENT: First mail solicitation
THE PRODUCT: National Cash Register
THE STORY: In the late 1800s, John Patterson's store had a problem with employee theft. There was no reliable method of making sure clerks didn't simply help themselves to the cash that came in. When Patterson heard about a saloonkeeper in Dayton named James Ritty who had solved the problem, he investigated.

Ritty had invented a "cash register," a machine that kept a running tab of all the money received during the day. Patterson ordered two, and they ended his employee theft problem. Patterson was so impressed that he bought the cash register company for $6,500 in 1884 and renamed it National Cash Register.

Convinced that cash registers would make him rich, he mailed out 90,000 brochures—one to every major retailer in the Midwest. It was the nation's first serious direct-mail campaign—and it was a complete failure. Patterson discovered that the brochures had been intercepted by the same salesclerks who were stealing cash. The brochures were destroyed before they could be seen by the business owners.

He changed his strategy and sent out hand-addressed envelopes marked "highly confidential." Inside, store owners found fancy invitations asking them to come to the best hotel in town for a demonstration of a foolproof method of ending employee theft. That year he sold over 15,000 machines. By 1922 he had sold two million cash registers. Today National Cash Register (NCR) is still a thriving corporation, all because of America's very first junk mail campaign.

MEMORABLE MOMENT: First service contract
THE PRODUCT: Coleman lanterns
THE STORY: William (W. C.) Coleman was a typewriter sales-

man in 1900 who was partially blind. One evening he walked into a drugstore in Alabama that was illuminated by a pressurized gas lantern. It was so much brighter than the standard wick-burning oil lamps that for the first time Coleman could see well at night. He immediately quit his job selling typewriters so he could sell the gas lamps instead. Sixty sales calls later, he'd sold only two lanterns. He discovered people were so used to inferior lamps that they refused to believe Coleman's were better.

So he decided to *rent* the lanterns for $1 per month, promising that any lamps that quit working would be immediately repaired free of charge. "No light, no pay," he said. Four days later, he had sold every lantern he had. In 1901 he bought the patents for the lamp and named it after himself. Today Coleman products are available worldwide, all because of a bright idea: the first service contract.

MEMORABLE MOMENT: First use of the phrase "new and improved"

THE PRODUCT: Toni Home Permanent

THE STORY: The "permanent wave" style of curling hair was invented in 1906. And for close to 40 years, the only way a woman could get a "perm" was to go to a beauty salon and sit underneath a large, cumbersome machine. In 1943 Richard Harris became the first person to offer a "home permanent." His product, called Noma (because it used No Machines) used chemicals to curl hair. Unfortunately, it also *damaged* hair. Harris reformulated the product and changed the name to Toni ("tony" was slang for "classy"). He came up with the slogan "new and improved" and was back in business again. Ten years after his disastrous Noma experience, Harris sold Toni to Gillette for $20 million, and his slogan went down in advertising history.

MEMORABLE MOMENT: First premium

THE PRODUCT: Quaker Oats

THE STORY: As we told you in *Uncle John's All-Purpose Extra Strength Bathroom Reader*, in 1881 Henry Parsons Crowell bought a small bankrupt oat mill called the Quaker Mill in Ravenna, Ohio. In those days oats were sold in 180-pound barrels, which were kept in the back of store. Crowell decided to sell his oats in two-pound packages, advertising that his resealable cartons kept his

Only 20% of diamonds are considered high enough quality to be classified as a "gem."

oats free from dirt, disease, animals, and insects. Crowell also added another new gimmick: premiums. Each box contained a free spoon or a dish. Boxtops could be redeemed for kitchen items or a radio. In 1888 Crowell, Schumacher, and five other oatmeal processors merged their companies to form the American Cereal Company, later renamed Quaker Oats. When Crowell died in 1943, he was one of the wealthiest men in Chicago, due in large measure to the fact that he was the first person to put a free prize in the bottom of a box of cereal.

MEMORABLE MOMENT: First money-back guarantee
THE PRODUCT: Sherwin-Williams paint
THE STORY: Henry Sherwin and Edward Williams formed a paint company in 1866. Their paint was so cheap that it washed off in the rain and peeled in the sun. Dissatisfied customers refused to buy any more paint from them.

So they reformulated the product, improving the quality. But they couldn't convince people to buy it because of their bad reputation. So to overcome this resistance, Sherwin-Williams offered to refund cusomers' money if they weren't completely satisfied with the paint. It worked. Today Sherwin-Williams is the largest producer and distributor of paints and varnishes in the United States, and the third largest worldwide, thanks to the invention of the money-back guarantee.

*   *   *

UNCLE JOHN'S POLICE LOG

In February 2000, an accountant named John Brady was using a restroom in East Memphis, Tennessee, when a man reached under the stall, grabbed his pants leg, and demanded that Brady hand over his wallet. When Brady, 55, refused, the robber, 29-year-old Oscar Reynolds, grabbed Brady's ankles and tried to pull him out of the stall. All he managed to do was tear off half of Brady's pants—the half that contained his wallet. Luckily, though, Brady's screams alerted security guards, who nabbed the thief and held him until police arrived. It took a jury just 15 minutes to convict Reynolds of robbery; a judge later gave him the maximum sentence: 10 years... in the can.

"Researchers" in Washington State claim to have taken a plaster cast of Bigfoot's butt.

TRUST ME...

Call it doublespeak, call it spin, call it "a different version of the facts." The truth is—it's still a lie.

TRUST ME... "All the waste in a year from a nuclear power plant can fit under a desk."
SAID BY: Presidential candidate Ronald Reagan, 1980
THE FACT: It would have to be a pretty big desk—the average nuclear plant yields 30 tons of waste per year.

TRUST ME... "If you don't start crying right now, I'm gonna have that dog shot!"
SAID BY: Director Norman Taurog. Taurog said this to his 10-year-old nephew Jackie Cooper, while filming the movie *Skippy* in 1931. Cooper was having trouble crying on cue, so his dog was removed from the set and a gunshot rang out. Cooper started sobbing profusely while the cameras rolled.
THE FACT: After Taurog was satisfied with the footage he brought the un-shot dog back on the set. He won an Oscar for best director.

TRUST ME... "Though neutral during WWII, Switzerland favored the Allied cause."
SAID BY: The inscription on a watch given to President Truman in 1946 by the city of Geneva
THE FACT: The Swiss government helped finance the Nazi movement.

TRUST ME... "I wasn't lying, Senator. I was presenting a different version of the facts."
SAID BY: Oliver North at the Iran-Contra Hearings, 1987
THE FACT: No comment.

TRUST ME... "I have never had my cheeks altered or my eyes altered. I did not have my lips thinned, nor have I had dermabrasion or a skin peel."
SAID BY: Michael Jackson
THE FACT: Again, no comment.

MORE OPENING LINES

Here are more winners of the Bulwer-Lytton Fiction Contest, a literary challenge to compose the opening sentence to the worst of all possible novels. (See page 75 for the rules.)

The lovely woman-child Kaa was mercilessly chained to the cruel post of the warrior-chief Beast, with his barbarous tribe now stacking wood at her nubile feet, when the strong, clear voice of the poetic and heroic Handsomas roared, "Flick your Bic, crisp that chick, and you'll feel my steel through your last meal."

—Steven Garman, Pensacola, Florida (1984 winner)

• **The corpse exuded the irresistible aroma** of a piquant, ancho chili glaze enticingly enhanced with a hint of fresh cilantro as it lay before him, coyly garnished by a garland of variegated radicchio and caramelized onions, and impishly drizzled with glistening rivulets of vintage balsamic vinegar and roasted garlic oil; yes, as he surveyed the body of the slain food critic slumped on the floor of the cozy, but nearly empty, bistro, a quick inventory of his senses told corpulent Inspector Moreau that this was, in all likelihood, an inside job.

—Bob Perry, Milton, Massachusetts (1998 winner)

• **Sultry it was and humid,** but no whisper of air caused the plump, laden spears of golden grain to nod their burdened heads as they unheedingly awaited the cyclic rape of their gleaming treasure, while overhead the burning orb of luminescence ascended its ever-upward path toward a sweltering celestial apex, for although it is not in Kansas that our story takes place, it looks godawful like it.

—Judy Frazier, Lathrop, Missouri (1991 winner)

• **Through the gathering gloom** of a late-October afternoon, along the greasy, cracked paving-stones slick from the sputum of the sky, Stanley Ruddlethorp wearily trudged up the hill from the cemetery where his wife, sister, brother, and three children were all buried, and forced open the door of his decaying house, blissfully unaware of the catastrophe that was soon to devastate his life.

—Dr. David Chuter, Kingston, Surrey, England (1999 winner)

...of Egypt three miles south in 4,500 years.

• **The notes blatted skyward** as the sun rose over the Canada geese, feathered rumps mooning the day, webbed appendages frantically peddling unseen bicycles in their search for sustenance, driven by Nature's maxim, "Ya wanna eat, ya gotta work," and at last I knew Pittsburgh.

—Sheila B. Richter, Minneapolis, Minnesota (1987 winner)

• **"Ace, watch your head!"** hissed Wanda urgently, yet somehow provocatively, through red, full, sensuous lips, but he couldn't you know, since nobody can actually watch more than part of his nose or a little cheek or lips if he really tries, but he appreciated her warning.

—Janice Estey, Aspen, Colorado (1996 winner)

• **Professor Frobisher couldn't believe** he had missed seeing it for so long—it was, after all, right there under his nose—but in all his years of research into the intricate and mysterious ways of the universe, he had never noticed that the freckles on his upper lip, just below and to the left of the nostril, partially hidden until now by a hairy mole he had just removed a week before, exactly matched the pattern of the stars in the Pleiades, down to the angry red zit that had just popped up where he and his colleagues had only today discovered an exploding nova.

—Ray C. Gainey, Indianapolis, Indiana (1989 winner)

• **Paul Revere had just discovered** that someone in Boston was a spy for the British, and when he saw the young woman believed to be the spy's girlfriend in an Italian restaurant he said to the waiter, "Hold the spumoni—I'm going to follow the chick an' catch a Tory."

—John L. Ashman, Houston, Texas (1995 winner)

• **A small assortment of astonishingly** loud brass instruments raced each other lustily to the respective ends of their distinct musical choices as the gates flew open to release a torrent of tawny fur comprised of angry yapping bullets that nipped at Desdemona's ankles, causing her to reflect once again (as blood filled her sneakers and she fought her way through the panicking crowd) that the annual Running of the Pomeranians in Liechtenstein was a stupid idea.

—BRI member Sera Kirk, Vancouver, B.C. (2001 winner)

58% of Americans say that when their finances improve, their sex life does too.

IT'S GREEK TO ME

Εϖερ ηεαρ σομεονε σπεωινγ φαργον ανδ ωονδερ "Ωηατ τηε ηελλ αρε τηεψ ταλκινγ αβουτ?" Σο ηασ Υνχλε ϑοην. Ηερε∏σ α παγε φορ ανψονε ωηοσε εϖερ σαιδ "Ιτ∏σ Γρεεκ το με."

Γαρβαγε: 400,000 πουνδσ οφ "πιζζα σλυδγε" (φλουρ, τοματο παστε, χηεεσε, πεππερονι, ετχ.)

Λοχατιον: Ωελλστον, Οηιο

Σουρχε: Α ϑενο'σ, Ινχ., φροζεν πιζζα πλαντ

Προβλεμ: ϑενο'σ προδυχεδ σο μυχη ωαστε ιν τηειρ πιζζα φαχτορψ τηατ τηε λοχαλ σεωαγε σψστεμ χουλδν't αχχομμοδατε ιτ. Τηεψ χουλδν't βυρψ ιτ ειτηερ, βεχαυσε ενϖιρονμενταλ εξπερτσ σαιδ ιτ ωουλδ "μοϖε ιν τηε γρουνδ" ονχε τηεψ πυτ ιτ τηερε. Τηεψ ηαδ το τρυχκ ιτ ουτ.

Γαρβαγε: 27 ψεαρσ' ωορτη οφ ραδιοαχτιϖε δογ ποοπ

Λοχατιον: Υνκνοων

Σουρχε: Δεπαρτμεντ οφ Ενεργψ εξπεριμεντσ. Φορ αλμοστ τηρεε δεχαδεσ, τηε ΔΟΕ στυδιεδ τηε εφφεχτσ οφ ραδιατιον βψ φεεδινγ 3,700 βεαγλεσ ραδιατιον–λαδεν φοοδ. Εαχη ατε τηε φοοδ φορ α ψεαρ ανδ α ηαλφ, ανδ ωασ τηεν λεφτ το λιϖε ουτ ιτσ λιφε.

Προβλεμ: Νο ονε αντιχιπατεδ τηατ ωηιλε τηε εξπεριμεντ ωασ γοινγ ον, τηε δογ–δοο ωουλδ βε δανγερουσ ανδ ωουλδ ηαϖε το βε τρεατεδ ασ ηαζαρδουσ ωαστε. Τηεψ σαϖεδ ιτ φορ δεχαδεσ... and φιναλλψ τοοκ ιτ το α ηαζαρδουσ ωαστε φαχιλιτψ.

Γαρβαγε: 1,000 πουνδσ οφ ρασπβερρψ γελατιν ανδ 16 γαλλονσ οφ ωηιππεδ χρεαμ

Λοχατιον: Ινσιδε α χαρ ιν Προϖο, Υταη

Σουρχε: Εϖαν Ηανσεν, α στυδεντ ατ Βριγηαμ Ψουνγ Υνιϖερσιτψ. Ηε ωον α ραδιο χοντεστ φορ "μοστ ουτραγεουσ στυντ" βψ χυττινγ τηε ροοφ οφφ α στατιον ωαγον ανδ φιλλινγ τηε χαρ ωιτη τηε δεσσερτ.

Προβλεμ: Ηανσεν χουλδν't φινδ α ωαψ το γετ ριδ οφ τηε ϑελλ–Ο. Ηε φιναλλψ δροϖε το α μαλλ παρκινγ λοτ, οπενεδ ηισ χαρ δοορσ, ανδ δυμπεδ ιτ δοων α δραιν. Ηε ωασ φινεδ $500 φορ ϖιολατινγ Υταηεσ Ωατερ Πολλυτιον Χοντρολ Αχτ.

The Latin word for "dust" is *pollen*. (It can also mean "fine flour.")

AS SEEN ON TV

It wasn't long ago that when you saw a product advertised on TV, you went to the store to buy it. Then came the infomercial. Here's the quintessential infomercial success story, the true tale of a washed-up producer who paired a washed-up product with a washed-up celebrity...and made a fortune.

THE WANDERER

For most people it isn't easy figuring out what to do with your life. For Peter Bieler, a Canadian who graduated from college in the mid-1960s, it was next to impossible.

First he wanted to devote his life to spiritualism and lived a monk-like existence of prayer, meditation, and self-denial. But he got tired of that after a couple of years, so he found a job with the consumer products giant Procter & Gamble. He tired of that a few years later, so he went to film school, then managed a rock concert hall in Los Angeles, then landed a job with a TV producer.

After that he got a job at the American Film Institute, after which he decided to become an independent film producer. That turned out to be harder than he thought it would be, so he tried out a job with a company making specialty videos. VCRs were still pretty new, and he was hoping to cash in on the boom.

By now it was 1986. Bieler had spent about 20 years figuring out what to do with his life, and he still hadn't figured it out.

DOWN THE HALL

Bieler struggled at making videos, too; even his most successful production, *The Eight-Week Cholesterol Cure*, hosted by Larry King, was a dud. His whole division was losing money. "I had no budget for promotion or marketing," Bieler writes in his book *This Business Has Legs*. "All this hard work, and the videos just sat on the shelf and collected dust. It was frustrating."

The company where Bieler worked also had its own production studio that it rented to outside producers. It was constantly buzzing with activity, and one day Bieler went to see what was going on.

EASY MONEY

The studio was being rented by a man named Tony Hoffman to produce a two-hour infomercial called *Everybody's Money Matters*. Hoffman and his co-host Bob Braun sold their own books and also interviewed other authors selling the same kinds of get-rich-quick books and tapes: how to buy property with no money down, how to get low-interest loans from the government, etc. The show aired on cable at night when airtime was cheap, so it cost only about $7,500 to broadcast the two-hour show nationwide.

And on a good night the show generated more than $80,000 in cash sales of books and tapes direct to the public through the show's 800 number—a heck of a lot more than Bieler's division was making by selling videos to retail outlets.

Bieler went to his boss and suggested that the company itself get into the infomercial business instead of just renting out the studio to outside producers. His boss wasn't interested, so Bieler formed his own company, which he named Ovation. But what would he sell?

Rather than try and invent something on his own, Bieler went to county fairs, home and garden shows, any place where he thought pitchmen might be demonstrating new products to live audiences. He finally settled on a chemical powder that turned spilled liquids into dried slush, which could then be vacuumed or scooped up by hand. He named the product "Gone." It was interesting stuff, but it couldn't do anything that paper towels couldn't do for a lot less money. The infomercial bombed.

THE V-TONER

Bieler looked around for another product to sell. He found it with help from an entrepreneur named Josh Reynolds, who had made a fortune in the 1970s inventing the "mood ring," a ring that changed colors according to changes in body temperature, supposedly revealing your mood.

Reynolds wasn't having much luck with a new product he was trying to market, an exerciser invented by a Los Angeles chiropractor to help skiiers with broken legs maintain the tone in their good leg while the broken one healed. Called the "V-Toner," the product was little more than two foam-padded triangular handles extending from a central steel spring to form a V-shaped angle.

The swine flu vaccine of 1976 caused more sickness and death than the flu itself did.

When you squeezed the two handles together, the spring in the center provided resistance, which helped build muscle tone.

The original inventor had managed to sell a few V-Toners, but Reynolds's advertising campaign, which marketed it as a "gym-in-a-bag," was a dud. Even though the product was an old dog, he still thought it had potential. Looking for new investors and new ideas, he found Bieler, who agreed to give it a shot.

THE MAIN SQUEEZE

Bieler took home the commercials that Reynolds had already made and watched them to figure out what had gone wrong. They weren't bad, but they weren't great, either. Bieler decided to make some changes.

• Rather than pitch it as an all-in-one, gym-in-a-bag product, he decided to emphasize one particular benefit: the fact that women could use it to tone and improve the appearance of their hips and thighs. (He also thought that video footage of sexy women exercising their thighs would make for compelling television.)

• The product's new name: ThighMaster.

• Its new spokesperson: Suzanne Somers. Somers was a familar face who would get the channel-surfers to stop and pay attention. He wanted someone in her mid-forties, the same age as the customers he was targeting. Somers was famous for her role as Chrissy on the TV show *Three's Company*. She was written out of the show in 1980 over a pay dispute, and since then her TV career had been struggling. Her sitcom *She's the Sheriff* had failed miserably, and by 1986 it was questionable whether she would ever get another shot at primetime again. Still, for Bieler's purposes she was the right age, the viewers knew who she was, and she was in great shape. She was perfect, and she took the job.

UP, UP AND AWAY

Two measures are used to gauge the success of an infomercial: 1) the number of broadcasting markets in which it earns more money than it costs to put the infomercial on the air, and 2) how well it works in different time slots. "ThighMaster was a colossal hit by both definitions," Bieler says. "It worked everywhere. All the time." ThighMasters started out selling at a rate of 2,000 units a week, then grew to 7,500 a week. But Bieler wanted more.

OFF THE SHELF

Bieler knew from his research that only a fraction of viewers who see an infomercial will actually want to buy the product, and only 20% of these willing buyers will actually order the product over the phone. The rest—80%—wait until the product arrives in retail stores... and if it never arrives, they never buy.

Bieler wanted that 80%, so he took his infomercial profits and set up a nationwide sales force that would help to place the ThighMaster in stores like Wal-Mart, Kmart, and Target. The job was made easier by the fact that infomercial viewers all over the country were walking into retailers asking to purchase ThighMasters, only to go home empty-handed... and disappointed. When the salespeople came knocking, the retailers jumped at the chance to stock ThighMasters.

LARGER THAN LIFE

Sales soared again—this time to 75,000 units per week. The product broke sales records at Wal-Mart, Kmart, Target, and Woolworths, and in the process it became a cultural phenomenon: David Letterman and Jay Leno joked about it in their monologues, and it began popping up as a pop-culture reference in movies and sitcoms. Suzanne Sommers became a popular guest on talk shows again; even President George H. W. Bush joked to reporters that his chubby press secretary, Marlin Fitzwater, should use the ThighMaster.

DISASTER-MASTER

In its first two years in business, Bieler's company sold more than $100 million worth of ThighMasters, an unprecedented success.

• So where's Bieler now? In 1993 he had a falling-out with his business partner and left Ovation forever.

• Where's Suzanne Somers now? She never did get another hit TV series, but she's done very well with infomercials for products like the Torso Track and the Facemaster.

• And where's Ovation now? It's gone. In 1995 the company, which launched one of the most successful infomercial products in history, closed its doors and filed for bankruptcy. How did *that* happen? Your guess is as good as ours... or Bieler's.

"I don't know," he laments. "I wish I did."

Celebritv sighting: Drew Carey once worked in Las Vegas. He was a waiter at Denny's.

DOMINO THEORY

Uncle John recently learned that dominoes were invented in 12th-century China. What he found most interesting is that they were first used for fortune telling, not gaming. So he did some research and put together these basic tips for fortune telling with dominoes. (First tip: don't try this in the bathroom.)

GETTING STARTED

Sort through a standard set of dominoes and remove any pieces with no dots. Then spread the rest face down on a table.

Next, draw three dominoes with your left hand and turn them face up. If two people are telling their fortunes, take turns drawing the dominoes. It's also a good idea to make a wish.

BY THE NUMBERS

Here are what the numbers on your draw represent:

Six: Luck (may apply to granting your wish)

Five: Work and career

Four: Money

Three: Love

Two: Friends and social relationships

One: Travel

CONNECTING THE DOTS

Now combine the numbers on each domino to tell your fortune. Drawing a six-one, for example, means you'll have good luck when you travel. Warning: Two specific dominoes are unlucky: four-two (expect a disappointment) and three-one (temporary bad news).

"Double" dominoes have special meanings:

Six-six: You're getting married or (if you're already married) will have very good luck at a wedding.

Five-five: You'll get a promotion at work or a new job.

Four-four: Money will come to you from a surprising source.

Three-three: You'll have a "new and important" love affair.

Two-two: You'll make new friends and have fun with them.

One-one: You'll visit a place you've never been before.

Gladys Knight would know: What do you call the spots on dice and dominoes? The "pips."

WHERE THERE'S A WILL...

Ben Franklin is famous for the maxim "A penny saved is a penny earned." But for Ben, that was a lot easier in death than it had been in life.

DO AS I SAY, NOT AS I DO

For all his preaching about the importance of frugality, Franklin never practiced it. As U.S. ambassador to France in the late 1700s, he was living in Paris at taxpayer expense. And that expense ran to an astonishing $12,000 per year, including a collection of more than 1,000 bottles of the finest French wines and lavish gifts of carpets, fine china, and other luxuries that he sent to friends and loved ones back home. Spending money wisely, Franklin admitted in 1782, was "a virtue I never could acquire myself."

...at least not while he was alive.

INVESTING IN THE FUTURE

In 1785 a French mathematician named Charles-Joseph Mathon de la Cour wrote *The Testament of Fortunate Richard,* a parody of the folksy American optimism in Franklin's *Poor Richard's Almanack.* In the parody, Fortunate Richard sets aside a small amount of money in his will with instructions that it be put to good use only after it has collected interest for 500 years.

When Franklin read the story, rather than being offended, he wrote back to Mathon de la Cour *thanking* him for the idea. Sure enough, when the 83-year-old Franklin updated his will in 1789, he left £1,000 (about $4,400) to his hometown of Boston, and another £1,000 to Philadelphia, where he'd worked as a printer and made much of his fortune. (Why British pounds? They were still the most popular currency in the United States in the 1780s.)

In the will, Franklin gave these specific instructions as to how his money should be managed over the next 200 years:

- For the first 100 years, each city was supposed to lend the

Only 1% of Americans say they are "much worse" at raising kids than their parents were.

money out to apprentice tradesmen "under the age of twenty-five years," to assist them in setting up their own businesses. (Franklin had set up his own printing business with money borrowed from two benefactors, and he wanted to repay the favor by doing the same thing for other tradesmen.)

• The loans were to be repaid over 10 years with interest and the money lent right back out again.

• Franklin estimated that after a century of earning interest, the Boston and Philadelphia funds would grow to £131,000 ($576,400) each.

• For the second 100 years, Franklin's will directed each city to spend 75% of the fund (about £100,000 or $440,000) on public works, and continue to lend out the remaining 25% as before.

ROUND TWO

Franklin estimated that over the second 100 years, the £31,000 ($136,400) in each fund would grow to £4 million at which point he wanted each city to turn over 75% of the money to its respective state—Boston to Massachusetts, and Philadelphia to Pennsylvania—to spend without restriction. Each city could keep the remaining 25% also to spend without restriction.

Franklin died on April 17, 1790, at the age of 85. That would mean that the money came due in the 1990s...so what happened to it?

WILL-POWER

Both Boston and Philadelphia accepted Franklin's money, but things didn't go as Franklin had hoped. The will specified that the money had to be lent to apprenticed tradesmen. But the apprentice system faded away during the Industrial Revolution, and tradesmen increasingly went to work for large industrial companies instead of setting up their own shops.

The number of loan applicants dropped sharply, even when the program was expanded to include tradesmen who *weren't* apprentices. And the loans they did make were seldom repaid. By 1831 the Boston fund was averaging only one new loan a year.

By the end of the first 100 years, nothing had worked out according to Franklin's plan. The Boston fund was worth only

70% of what Franklin had expected, and the funds shrank even further because politicians were dipping in it to pay for "business trips." In 1904, 75% of the fund was used to found a trade school called the Franklin Union, now known as the Benjamin Franklin Institute of Technology. The rest was loaned out and reinvested.

Philadelphia's fund fared even worse—it was only worth $173,000, less than half the value of the Boston fund. The city spent $133,000 on a museum called the Franklin Institute and continued lending the balance out for another 100 years, just as Franklin had instructed.

STILL, NOT BAD

A hundred years later, in 1991, the money in the Boston fund had grown to $5 million. The Philadelphia fund wasn't as lucky: its investments had only grown to $2.2 million. Since the term of Franklin's will had expired, all the money was to be divided up and spent. What happened to it?

• After a legal fight, nearly all of the Boston funds—both the state's share and the city's—were donated to the Franklin Institute of Technology.

• The state of Pennsylvania distributed its share of the money to community foundations and gave $165,000 to the Franklin Institute Museum.

• Philadelphia Mayor Wilson Goode proposed spending his city's share of the money on a huge party celebrating Franklin's contributions. But so many people attacked that idea as being against the spirit of Franklin's bequest that he backed off and appointed a panel of Franklin scholars to think of something better. They set up a scholarship program for graduating Philadelphia high school graduates who want to study crafts, trades, and applied sciences.

Ultimately, Franklin got a lot of bang for his buck, and 200 years after his death, he finally proved that a penny saved really *is* a penny earned.

* * *

A TALE OF TWO PRESIDENTS

President Jimmy Carter had solar panels installed to heat water in the White House. President Ronald Reagan had them taken out.

... and 3) income. More bad news: The prettier the date, the more likely the man will lie.

DEMOCRACY IN ACTION

A democracy is only as weird as the people who participate in it—and you know what that means: anything can happen in an election. Here's proof.

DO OR DYE

"During the 2002 campaign for Chancellor of Germany, the DDP news agency quoted an image consultant suggesting that Gerhard Schroeder, aged 58, should admit that he dyed his hair to keep it looking dark. It would be better, she suggested, for his 'credibility.' It became a campaign issue when members of the opposition Chistian Social Union party demanded a scientific test of his hair. 'Someone who touches up his hair,' said CSU leader Karl Josef Laumann, 'also touches up statistics.'"

—*BBC News*

NAME CALLING

"In 2001, the ruling Alliance of Democratic Forces party tried to manipulate the Bulgarian parliamentary election by having all parties using the name 'Bulgaria' banned from the election. Since the word 'Bulgaria' is a national symbol, they said, it should not be used for political purposes. Among their opposition: Bulgarian Socialist Party, Civic Party of Bulgaria, Empire of Bulgaria, and Forward Bulgaria! Common sense prevailed—the idea was later modified to pertain only to parties which have the designation 'for Bulgaria' as part of their name."

—*AIM*

FLIP CITY

"In Sultan, Washington, in 2001, Rob Criswell was trying to unseat incumbent Cindy Broughton in a very close race. Even after two recounts the result was still a 501–501 tie. So how did they determine the winner? State law dictates that tied races be called 'by lot.' Legally, they could have rolled dice, picked cards or drawn straws to determine the winner, but they flipped a coin. Broughton called heads. She lost."

—*Seattle Times*

In 1995 Kellogg paid $2,400 to a man whose kitchen was damaged by a flaming Pop-Tart.

SELLING OUT

"What's the value of a vote these days? If it's a Canadian Alliance party leadership vote, the answer is $42. That's what the bidding got up to on eBay after Montrealer Charlie McKenzie, alias 'deep toke,' put his first-round Alliance party leadership ballot up for auction. EBay stopped the sale, saying it is against the rules to buy or sell anything that could determine the outcome of an election.

"McKenzie originally paid $10 to join the party, with the intention of voting for a fringe candidate. But when party finance rules forced drag queen Enza out of the race, McKenzie decided to follow 'the Dow of democracy' and sell his vote to the highest bidder."

—*Montreal Gazette*

DEAD HEAT

"Incumbent U.S. Senator from Missouri, John Ashcroft (R), was left running against a dead man after his opponent, Governor Mel Carnahan (D), died in a plane crash three weeks before election day. By that time, it was too late to remove Carnahan's name from the ballot.

"Ashcroft held the lead in polls until Carnahan's death threw the race into turmoil. On election day, no one could predict how the sympathy factor would play at the polls. The late governor's wife, Jean Carnahan, used ads to make emotional appeals for 'the values and beliefs that Mel Carnahan wanted to take to the United States Senate.'

"Her ads worked. Ashcroft lost; Carnahan beat him by 41,000 votes."

—CNN

UNION MAID

"In 2002, workers in a Miami nursing home voted 49–37 to unionize. But the nursing home immediately filed an appeal with the National Labor Relations Board, claiming a series of voodoo signs may have spooked the facility's large Haitian-American workforce into voting to organize. Workers testified at a hearing that they were frightened by seeing lines of pennies, half-empty water cups, and a pro-union empolyee twisting black beads in her hand before the vote."

—*Bradenton Herald*

Better name? Greenwich mean time is also known as "Zulu time."

THE PROFESSOR'S "INVENTIONS"

It's one of TV's eternal mysteries: Here he was stranded on Gilligan's Island with no tools and no power. Yet the Professor was such a genius that he could invent virtually anything... except a boat. Stupefying. Well, here's a list of some of the things he did *invent.*

- Lie detector (made from the ship's horn, the radio's batteries, and bamboo)
- Bamboo telescope
- Jet pack fuel
- Paralyzing strychnine serum
- "Spider juice" (to kill a giant spider)
- Nitroglycerine
- Shark repellent
- Helium balloon (rubber raincoats sewn together and sealed with tree sap)
- Coconut-shell battery recharger
- Xylophone
- Soap (made from plant fats, it's not really so far-fetched)
- Roulette wheel
- Geiger counter (*that's* far-fetched)
- Pedal-powered bamboo sewing machine
- Pedal-powered washing machine
- Keptibora-berry extract (to cure Gilligan's double vision)
- Pedal-powered water pump
- Pedal-powered telegraph
- Hair tonic
- Pedal-powered generator
- Various poisons and antidotes
- Pool table (for Mr. Howell)
- Lead radiation suits and lead-based makeup (protection against a meteor's cosmic rays)

WHAT'S ALL THE BUZZ ABOUT?

Most people are afraid of bees—hey they sting. But bees aren't merely pests—they're an essential part of the ecosystem. Consider this: One-third of the average human diet comes from plants that depend on insects to pollinate them, and honeybees perform 80% of that pollination.

BUSY AS A BEE

Honeybees are real workhorses. A typical bee visits—and pollinates—between 50 and 100 flowers in a single foraging trip from the hive...and never visits the same flower twice. On average, a honeybee flies 500 miles over the course of its lifetime at an average speed of 15 mph—the human equivalent to traveling twice around the circumference of Earth. And they carry loads up to half their body weight while doing it. There's one simple reason for all that activity: They're collecting food.

MOTHER NATURE'S PLAN

Here's how it works: Honeybees fly from flower to flower to collect nectar. At a flower, they use their proboscis, or long sucking mouth, to drink the flower's nectar. They store the nectar in a special "honey stomach," which sits next to their regular stomach, then fly back to their hive. Once back in the hive, they spit the nectar into one of the honeycomb cells. Other bees then suck it up and regurgitate it—a process that gets repeated up to 50 times. The combination of water evaporation and enzymes from the bees' saliva creates honey.

In the process of collecting nectar, honeybees also collect pollen. They do this by rubbing up against the flower's *anther*—its male apparatus. Their body hairs brush the pollen into pollen "baskets," which sit on the bees' hind legs; some of the pollen also gets stuck to their body hair. Back in the hive, the pollen that's stuck on their hair gets mixed with different types of pollen by brushing against other bees; outside the hive, it gets mixed by entering different flowers. Either way, the process contributes to

32% of managers say being "too young-looking" can make a salesperson's job more difficult.

cross-pollination—the fertilizing of one flower with pollen from another flower... which produces fruit.

THINKING AHEAD

It also contributes to the bees' diet. Honeybees eat both the pollen and the nectar they collect from flowers. The pollen provides their protein, fat, vitamins, and minerals for growth and reproduction; the nectar provides sugar for energy. Adult bees convert some of the pollen into a milk that they secrete from glands in their heads to feed to their larvae.

And what do the bees do with their honey? They store it for use as food during seasons when flowers don't bloom—winters in temperate climates; rainy spells or droughts in tropical climates. When lots of nectar-producing flowers blossom, bees store much more honey than they could ever eat.

SWEET HARVEST

Honey harvested by beekeepers is collected in at least two ways: liquid honey is extracted from honeycombs by machine; comb honey is collected while it's still in the original wax combs made by the bees (this honey is less adaptable to cooking but is preferred by connoisseurs).

* * *

I WANNA BEE AN ENGINEER

Bees collect not only nectar and pollen but also water. They don't drink the water—they use it to air-condition the hive on hot days by spreading it on every surface and fanning it with their wings. When a worker bee arrives back at the hive bearing a load of food, house bees meet it and take the food from him to be stored. Generally, returning bees bearing food are relieved of their loads immediately; those carrying only water have to wait. However, researchers once deliberately turned up the heat under a hive. As the temperature slowly and steadily rose, bees bringing water were greeted at once while those bringing food were ignored. So effective is the evaporative method of air-conditioning that a bee colony on a lava field kept their hive at a constant temperature of 97°F as the surrounding air temperature soared to 140°F.

In 2002 runner Tom Johnson ran an 80-km. race against a horse... and beat it by 10 seconds.

YAH-HAH, EVIL SPIDER WOMAN!

Until recently, law required all movies made in Hong Kong had to have English subtitles. But producers spent as little on translations as possible... and it shows. These gems are from the book Sex and Zen & a Bullet in the Head, *by Stefan Hammond and Mike Wilkins.*

"Take my advice, or I'll spank you without pants."

"Fatty, you with your thick face have hurt my instep."

"You always use violence. I should've ordered glutinous rice chicken."

"Who gave you the nerve to get killed here?"

"This will be of fine service for you, you bag of the scum. I am sure you will not mind that I remove your toenails and leave them out on the dessert floor for ants to eat."

"A normal person wouldn't steal pituitaries."

"That may disarray my intestines."

"The bullets inside are very hot. Why do I feel so cold?"

"Beware! Your bones are going to be disconnected."

"I am darn unsatisfied to be killed in this way."

"If you don't eat people, they'll eat you."

"She's terrific. I can't stand her."

"Darn, I'll burn you into a BBQ chicken."

"I'll cut your fats out, don't you believe it?"

"Sex fiend, you'll never get reincarnated!"

"How can I make love without TV?"

"I got knife scars more than the number of your leg's hair!"

"Yah-hah, evil spider woman! I have captured you by the short rabbits and can now deliver you violently to your doctor for a thorough extermination."

"What is a soul? It's just a toilet paper."

As of 2001, 2% of Americans still don't have 911 service.

THE COTTON WAR

Here's Part III of our story on Eli Whitney.
(Part II starts on page 239.)

NOT GONNA HAPPEN

Eli Whitney's cotton gin played a pivotal part in creating the pre–Civil War south as an economic power. Cotton had transformed the South from an underdeveloped, underpopulated wilderness into the home of America's largest cash crop. It enriched not only the South, which grew it, but also the North, which had its own fledgling textile industry, and whose merchants shipped it to England.

One of the ironies of the invention is that the wealth it helped create ultimately led to the Civil War and doomed the South to defeat. King Cotton gave Southerners a false sense of security. The North *needed* cotton, the thinking went, so how could it go to war against the South?

THE BRITISH ARE COMING...AGAIN

And what about England, which imported 90% of its cotton from the South? Cotton fueled its economy too, and Southern leaders like Jefferson Davis (who would become president of the Confederacy in 1861), were convinced that if war did come, England would side with the South. England would have little choice but to use the Royal Navy to keep Southern ports open, so that its access to cotton would be guaranteed. The North knew this as well, the Southerners reasoned, and that made it even less likely that the Northern states would ever go to war over slavery. Fighting the South was one thing; fighting England *and* the South was another.

"You dare not make war upon our cotton," South Carolina Senator James Henry Hammond proclaimed in 1858. "No power on Earth dares make war on it. Cotton is King."

But when the war finally did come in April 1861, England didn't hesitate—it immediately declared its "strict and impartial neutrality" and then sat on the sidelines. Why? England didn't have to worry about cotton—the long, slow buildup to the Civil War had given English mills plenty of time to stockpile extra cotton. When that ran out, they would make do with what they could buy from countries like Egypt and India. And unemployment resulting from cotton shortages was tolerated, because many English textile workers opposed slavery and were willing to go without jobs to help end it.

SLIP-SLIDING AWAY

Another nail in the coffin: The South's failure to expand its economy beyond a single cash crop left it vulnerable. The invention of the cotton gin had encouraged cotton cultivation not just in the southern United States, but all over the world, and as cotton plantations sprang up in other countries, the price of cotton began a long, steady slide throughout the 1850s.

For decades, Southern planters had reinvested their profits into expanding cotton production instead of diversifying into factories, textile mills, or anything else. As the price of cotton fell, plantations lost money. By the late 1850s, there was little cash available to diversify the Southern economy, even if the South had wanted to. It was too late.

MASS PRODUCTION

In the North, things were different. Manufacturers of everything from doors and windows to nuts, bolts, shoes, plows, and grandfather clocks had adopted the principles of Eli Whitney's "American system," and were now using machine tools to mass-produce their wares. Soaring profits encouraged further investment and growth; from 1840 to 1860, the 100-mile-long region between Delaware and New York was the most rapidly industrializing region on Earth.

With the growth of industry came increased economic and military strength. By the start of the Civil War, factories in the North were producing goods at a rate of 10 times that of the South. For every ton of iron produced in the South, the North produced 15; for every firearm the South produced, the North manufactured 32. Northern states had more than twice the population of Southern states, and three times the wealth.

And though the South grew 24 times as much cotton as the North, the North had 14 times as many textile mills. So when war

A: So bad that as many as 4,000 people died from it.

came in April 1861, it was the Union soldiers, not the Confederates, who were best outfitted for battle. Though the Civil War dragged on from 1861 to 1865, its outcome was a virtual certainty from the very beginning.

ELI WHITNEY'S LEGACY

For a person who had never discovered a continent, never commanded an army, and never served as president, Eli Whitney had about as big an impact on American history as anyone. And unlike his fellow inventors Henry Ford and Alexander Graham Bell, *two* of his inventions altered the course of history, not just one.

Cotton gave the South its wealth and strengthened the institution of slavery, sparking the tensions that would lead to the Civil War. At the same time, cotton convinced Southerners that if war did come, its importance guaranteed that the South would never lose. And that made the South all the more willing to fight.

With the invention of mass production, Whitney gave the North the military might and economic strength that it used to destroy the South that the cotton gin had built.

"If Whitney's cotton gin enabled the slave-system to survive and thrive," writes historian Paul Johnson, "his 'American System' also gave the North the industrial muscle to crush the defenders of slavery in due course.... He is a fascinating example of the complex impact one man can have on history."

* * *

SPECIAL DELIVERY

"Rome post-office workers were confronted by a group of men delivering a very big package, too big for the security hole that packages are normally slipped through. Ignoring security rules, employees asked the group to go to a service window behind the counter. As soon as they brought the package inside, a robber burst out of the carton, waved a gun, and shouted, 'It's a holdup.' The criminals escaped with 115,000 lira."

—*Townsville Bulletin* (Australia)

Two most dangerous countries for journalists between 1992 and 2001: Algeria and Colombia.

THE REST OF THE REST OF THE UNITED STATES

On page 211, we gave an overview of the commonwealths and territories owned by the United States. Here are some of the smaller, uninhabited islands and their stories. (Well, they may have a few inhabitants, but no natives.)

UNINHABITED U.S. TERRITORIES

Wake Island

Location: North Pacific Ocean, between Hawaii and the Northern Mariana Islands

Size: Two and a half square miles

Population: 300

Background: Wake Island is an atoll made up of three islets around a shallow lagoon. It was discovered in 1796 by British sea captain William Wake. The United States annexed it in 1899 for a telegraph cable station. An airstrip and naval base were built in late 1940, but in December 1941 the island was captured by the Japanese and held until the end of World War II. Today the facilities are under the administration of the Federal Aviation Agency.

Kingman Reef

Location: North Pacific Ocean, between Hawaii and American Samoa

Size: Less than one-half square mile

Population: Uninhabited

Background: The U.S. annexed this reef in 1922. There's no plant life on the reef (which is frequently under water) but it does support abundant and diverse marine life. In 2001 the waters surrounding the reef were designated a National Wildlife Refuge.

Midway Islands

Location: North Pacific Ocean, north of Hawaii

Size: Less than two and a half square miles

Population: 150 U.S. Fish and Wildlife Service personnel

When asked to name the odor that best defines America, 39% of Americans said "barbecue."

Background: Part of the Hawaiian island chain, Midway was first discovered by a Hawaiian sea captain in 1859. At the urging of the North Pacific Mail and Steamship Company, which was looking for a coal depot for its Asian mail run, the U.S. Navy claimed the atoll for the United States in 1867. Midway is best known as the site of a U.S. naval victory over the Japanese fleet in 1942, one of the turning points of World War II. The naval station closed in 1993. Today the island is a wildlife refuge open to eco-tourists.

GUANO ISLANDS

What is guano? Bird droppings. Fish-eating birds have been dropping their poop in the same spots for thousands of years. The result: huge deposits of guano, rich in nitrogen and phosphorous and highly valued as an agricultural fertilizer.

The Guano Act was enacted by the U.S. government in 1856. It authorized Americans to take "peaceable possession" of any uninhabited, unclaimed islands for the purpose of mining the guano. Nearly 100 islands were claimed for the United States under the act, mostly in the South Pacific. The U.S. still owns a half dozen—the others were abandoned or given up to other countries that claimed them. They're not really anybody's idea of paradise, so don't expect to see any postcards from these tiny islands. But some of these poop-covered rocks have interesting histories.

Navassa Island

Location: Caribbean Sea, between Haiti and Jamaica

Size: Less than two and a half square miles

Population: No permanent residents

Background: The Baltimore-based Navassa Phosphate Company began mining guano in 1865, using convicts at first, then former slaves. In deplorable living conditions, the ex-slaves were forced to mine one and a half tons of guano per day for a daily wage of 50 cents. In 1889 they revolted, killing 15 white overseers. Forty workers were taken to Baltimore for trial. Acknowledging the basis for the uprising, the court sentenced only one worker to death—the rest were given life imprisonment. The Navassa Phosphate Company continued to mine guano until 1898.

In 1998 a California entrepreneur named Bill Warren filed a

How small is a newborn Chinese water deer? Small enough to hold in your hand.

claim under the Guano Act, obtained a deed from heirs of the Navassa Phosphate Company, and claimed ownership of the island. Predictably, the U.S. government denied his claim.

There is also a dispute between the U.S. and Haiti, which maintains that the island lies within its territorial boundary.

Howland Island

Location: North Pacific Ocean, between Hawaii and Australia

Size: A little more than one-half square mile

Population: Uninhabited

Background: Claimed by the American Guano Company in 1858. Its other claim to fame: in 1937 an airstrip was built on the island as a stopover for aviation pioneer Amelia Earhart on her round-the-world flight. Earhart and her navigator took off from Lae, New Guinea, but never reached Howland. (The unexplained disappearance still intrigues conspiracy buffs.) Today Howland Island is a National Wildlife Refuge.

Baker Island

Location: North Pacific Ocean, between Hawaii and Australia

Size: One-half square mile

Population: Uninhabited

Background: Named by an American whaler, Michael Baker, who found the island in 1832. Presently, it is a National Wildlife Refuge run by the U.S. Department of the Interior.

Johnston Atoll

Location: North Pacific Ocean, 800 miles southwest of Hawaii

Size: One square mile of dry land; 50 square miles of shallow water

Population: 1,000 military and support personnel

Background: The four tiny islands were discovered in 1796 by an American sea captain.

During World War II, the military used Johnston Island, the largest of the four outcroppings, as a refueling point for aircraft and submarines. A few days after the attack on Pearl Harbor, Japanese submarines fired on military facilities there but caused no casualties.

The U.S. Air Force took over in 1948 and used the site for

Snoring is legal in Massachusetts *only* when all bedroom windows are closed and locked.

high-altitude nuclear tests in the 1950s and 1960s. In 1964 a series of open-air biological weapons tests were conducted near the atoll using several barges loaded with rhesus monkeys. Chemical weapons have been stored on Johnston Island since 1971, but the U.S. Army began destroying them in 1981. Munitions destruction is reportedly complete, and the Army plans to turn over the atoll to the U.S. Fish and Wildlife Service in 2003.

Jarvis Island

Location: South Pacific, between Hawaii and the Cook Islands

Size: Less than two square miles

Population: Uninhabited

Background: Discovered by the British in 1821; claimed by the American Guano Company in 1858; abandoned in 1879; annexed by Britain in 1889; abandoned soon after. Reclaimed by the United States in 1935. The island is currently a National Wildlife Refuge; a small group of buildings are occasionally occupied by scientists and weather researchers.

Palmyra Atoll

Location: North Pacific Ocean, 1,000 miles south of Hawaii

Size: Four and a half square miles

Population: Uninhabited

Background: This group of 54 islets is known for its lush natural beauty and biological diversity.

The first to land on the atoll were sailors from the American ship *Palmyra*, which was blown ashore during a storm in 1852. Though the American Guano Company claimed it, guano was never mined there. In 1862 King Kamehameha IV of Hawaii took possession of the atoll, which is actually a part of the Hawaiian archipelago. The United States included it when it annexed Hawaii in 1898, but when Hawaii became a state in 1959, Palmyra was excluded.

The 1974 murder of a yachting couple on Palmyra became the subject of a 1991 novel by Vincent Bugliosi (and a subsequent TV movie) entitled *And the Sea Will Tell.* Today the atoll is privately owned by the Nature Conservancy, which is managing it as a nature preserve.

Only 16% of the able-bodied males in the 13 American...

MR. GAME BOY

You've probably never heard of Gumpei Yokoi, but if you've ever played a Game Boy, a Color Game Boy, Donkey Kong, or just about any other Nintendo product made between 1970 and 1996, you have him to thank for it. Here's his story.

IN THE CARDS

In the mid-1960s, an electronics student named Gumpei Yokoi graduated from Doshisha University in Kyoto, Japan, and got a job as a maintenance engineer with the Nintendo company, a manufacturer of playing cards.

Keeping the playing card printing machines in good working order must have been boring work, because Yokoi started passing the time building toys—with company materials, using company machines and equipment, on company time.

That didn't exactly fit into his job description, so when Nintendo's president, Hiroshi Yamauchi, found out what he was up to and called him into his office, Yokoi figured that he'd soon be looking for a new job.

Not quite—Nintendo was making so much money selling children's playing cards that it had decided to create an entire games division. Yamauchi transferred Yokoi to the new division, and told him to come up with a game that Nintendo could manufacture in time to sell for Christmas.

Yokoi went home and got one of the toys he'd already made: an extendable grabbing "hand" that he made out of crisscrossing pieces of wooden latticework When you squeezed its handles together like a pair of scissors, the latticework extended and the hand closed its grip.

YOU'VE GOT TO HAND IT TO HIM

Yamauchi was impressed, and production on the Ultra Hand, as they named it, began right away. The company ended up selling more than 1.2 million of the hands at a price of about $6 apiece—the games division's first toy was also its first big hit.

Yokoi's team followed with a series of other toys, including the Ultra Machine (an indoor pitching machine), the Ultra Scope (a periscope), and a "Love Tester" that supposedly measured how much love existed between a boy and a girl. All the Love Tester really did was give people an excuse to hold hands, but that was enough—it was a huge success too. So was the Beam Gun, a gun that shot beams of light at optical targets.

Nintendo spent a fortune converting old bowling alleys and shooting galleries into Beam Gun shooting galleries...and nearly went bankrupt. But it recovered after Yamauchi noticed how much money Atari, Magnavox, and other companies were making in the video game business. He licensed their technology and came out with Color TV Game 6, the company's first video game.

GAME & WATCH

As video games were becoming more successful, Yamauchi started pressing Yokoi for a competing product. So the design team came up with the Game & Watch, a series of dozens and eventually hundreds of pocket-sized video games that also displayed the time at the top of the screen.

The games used simple calculator technology—LCD screens and tiny buttons that served as game controllers—and they weren't much bigger than credit cards. Kids could play them anywhere: in cars, at school during recess, or in their rooms before bedtime. Nintendo ended up selling more than 40 million of the devices all over the world between 1980 and 1989.

GAME BOY

As we told you on page 415, Nintendo introduced the Famicom (short for Family Computer)—its first cartridge-based videogame system—in 1983 and then released it in the United States as the Nintendo Entertainment System (NES) in 1985. The system established the company as the dominant world player in the video game business. By 1988, however, the NES was getting a little old and Nintendo's rival Sega was preparing to launch a new system called the Mega Drive. Nintendo's new Super NES system was still in the works, so the company needed a product that would generate revenue and keep fans of the company's products occupied until Super NES was ready.

Lucky for Nintendo, Yokoi had one. Called the Game Boy, it sought to combine the best that the Game & Watch series and

It takes 10,000 pounds of roses to make one pound of rose essence.

the NES had to offer. The Game Boy was portable, about the size of a transistor radio, and it was a cartridge-based system like the NES. With the Game & Watch series, anytime you wanted to play a new game, you had to buy a whole new Game & Watch. With a Game Boy, all you had to do was buy a new cartridge. Better yet, Game Boys could be linked together so that two players could compete against each other.

LOW TECH

The Game Boy wasn't exactly state of the art. It didn't have a color screen or a backlight, because those drained the batteries too quickly and added too much to the cost. You couldn't play it in the dark. The screen was so crude, in fact, that when Atari's engineers saw it for the first time, they laughed. Over at Sony, the response was different. "This Game Boy should have been a Sony product," one executive complained.

The Game Boy went on to become hugely successful, thanks in large part to the fact that the game appealed to adults in a way that the NES didn't. The original Game Boy was packaged with Tetris, an adult-friendly, maddeningly addictive game in which the player has to maneuver and interlock blocks that fall from the top of the screen. Game Boys became a fixture on subways, on airplanes, in company lunchrooms, any place adults had a few free moments. When President George H. W. Bush went into the hospital in May 1991, the leader of the free world was photographed playing a Game Boy. Kids liked to play Game Boys too...whenever they could pry them away from their parents.

NEW AND IMPROVED

Yokoi led the effort to keep the Game Boy product line fresh and profitable over the years. In 1994 his design team came up with an accessory that allowed Game Boy cartridges to be played on the Super NES system. That was followed by the Game Boy Pocket and the first Pokémon (short for Pocket Monsters) cartridge in 1996.

Pokémon was the first game that allowed players to exchange items from one linked Game Boy to another, and though Nintendo's expectations for the game weren't particularly high, the game became an enormous industry unto itself, spawning other toys, trading cards, clothing, an animated TV series, a movie, and even

Food claim: Four tablespoons of ketchup contain as much nutrition as a medium-sized tomato.

food. It's estimated that Pokémon merchandise has racked up more than $20 billion worth of sales for Nintendo since 1996, *not including* the video games. As for the Game Boy product line (which saw the addition of the Game Boy Color in 1998), by 2001 it had sold more than 115 million units and 450 million cartridges, making it the most popular game system of all time.

DOWN AND OUT

Needless to say, Yokoi made Nintendo a lot of money over the years. What did he have to show for it? Not much—in 1995 his Virtual Boy, an addition to the Game Boy line that was kind of like a 3D View-Master—bombed. The red LED display gave so many players headaches and dizziness that when the product was released in the United States it came with a warning label. One reviewer called it a "Virtual Dog."

Nintendo lost a lot of money on the Virtual Boy, and Yamauchi apparently decided to humiliate Yokoi publicly by making him demonstrate the game system at the company's annual Shoshinkai trade show, even though it was all but dead. "This was his punishment, the Japanese corporate version of Dante's Inferno," Steven Kent writes in *The Ultimate History of Video Games*. "When employees make high-profile mistakes in Japan, it is not unusual for their superiors to make an example out of them for a period of time, then return them to their former stature."

EARLY EXIT

Yokoi must have decided not to wait around for his restoration. He left the company in August 1996 after more than 27 years on the job, and founded his own handheld game company called Koto (Japanese for "small town"). It produced a game system similar to the Game Boy, only with a bigger screen and better speakers. We'll never know what kind of gains he might have made against the Game Boy, because on October 4, 1997, he was killed in a car accident. He was 56.

* * *

"When you come to a fork in the road, take it."

—Yogi Berra

One giant leap for lefties: Astronaut Neil Armstrong stepped on the moon with his left foot.

THE EXTENDED SITTING SECTION

A Special Section of Longer Pieces

Over the years, we've had
numerous requests from BRI members
to include a batch of long articles—
for those leg-numbing experiences.
Well, the BRI aims to please…
So here's another great way
to pass the uh…time.

A RESTLESS NIGHT

Mark Twain is one of Uncle John's heroes—a humorist whose writing is still funny a hundred years after his death. We found this in Mark Twain's Library of Humor *from 1888. It's a chapter from his novel* A Tramp Abroad.

EARLY TO BED

We were in bed by ten, for we wanted to be up and away on our tramp homeward with the dawn. I hung fire, but Harris went to sleep at once. I hate a man who goes to sleep at once; there is a sort of indefinable something about it which is not exactly an insult, and yet is an insolence; and one which is hard to bear, too. I lay there fretting over this injury, and trying to go to sleep; but the harder I tried, the wider awake I grew. I got to feeling very lonely in the dark, with no company but an undigested dinner. My mind got a start, by and by, and began to consider the beginning of every subject which has ever been thought of; but it never went further than the beginning; it was touch and go; it fled from topic to topic with a frantic speed. At the end of an hour my head was in a perfect whirl and I was dead tired, fagged out.

The fatigue was so great that it presently began to make some head against the nervous excitement; while imagining myself wide awake, I would really doze into momentary unconsciousnesses, and come suddenly out of them with a physical jerk which nearly wrenched my joints apart—the delusion of the instant being that I was tumbling backwards over a precipice. After I had fallen over eight or nine precipices, and thus found out that one half of my brain had been asleep eight or nine times without the wide-awake, hard-working other half suspecting it, the periodical unconsciousnesses began to extend their spell gradually over more of my brain-territory, and at last I sank into a drowse which grew deeper and deeper, and was doubtless on the very point of becoming a solid, blessed, dreaming stupor, when—what was that?

CREATURES IN THE NIGHT

My dulled faculties dragged themselves partly back to life and took a receptive attitude. Now out of an immense, limitless distance, came something which grew and grew, and approached, and

The shoe size of the "average" American has increased 1.5 sizes in 25 years.

presently was recognizable as a sound—it had rather seemed to be a feeling, before. This sound was a mile away, now—perhaps it was the murmur of a storm; and now it was nearer—not a quarter of a mile away; was it the muffled rasping and grinding of distant machinery? No, it came still nearer; was it the measured tramp of a marching troop? But it came nearer still, and still nearer—and at last it was right in the room: it was merely a mouse gnawing the woodwork. So I had held my breath all that time for such a trifle!

A MOUSE IN THE HOUSE

Well, what was done could not be helped; I would go to sleep at once and make up the lost time. That was a thoughtless thought. Without intending it—hardly knowing it—I fell to listening intently to that sound, and even unconsciously counting the strokes of the mouse's nutmeg-grater. Presently I was deriving exquisite suffering from this employment, yet maybe I could have endured it if the mouse had attended steadily to his work; but he did not do that. He stopped every now and then, and I suffered more while waiting and listening for him to begin again than I did while he was gnawing.

Along at first I was mentally offering a reward of five—six—seven—ten—dollars for that mouse; but toward the last I was offering rewards which were entirely beyond my means. I close-reeled my ears—that is to say, I bent the flaps of them down and furled them into five or six folds, and pressed them against the hearing-orifice—but it did no good: the faculty was so sharpened by nervous excitement that it was becoming a microphone, and could hear through the overlays without trouble.

IF THE SHOE FITS

My anger grew to a frenzy. I finally did what all persons before have done, clear back to Adam—resolved to throw something. I reached down and got my walking shoes, then sat up in bed and listened, in order to exactly locate the noise. But I couldn't do it; it was as unlocatable as a cricket's noise; and where one thinks that is, is always the very place where it isn't. So I presently hurled a shoe at random, and with a vicious vigor. It struck the wall over Harris's head and fell down on him; I had not imagined I could throw so far. It woke Harris, and I was glad of it until I found he

Because of the weight of its face, a penny is slightly more likely to land "heads" than "tails."

was not angry; then I was sorry. He soon went to sleep again, which pleased me; but straightaway the mouse began again, which roused my temper once more.

A GNAWING PROBLEM

I did not want to wake Harris a second time, but the gnawing continued until I was compelled to throw the other shoe. This time I broke a mirror—there were two in the room—I got the largest one, of course. Harris woke again, but did not complain, and I was sorrier than ever. I resolved that I would suffer all possible torture, before I would disturb him a third time.

The mouse eventually retired, and by and by I was sinking to sleep, when a clock began to strike. I counted till it was done, and was about to drowse again when another clock began; I counted; then the two great Rathhaus clock angels began to send forth soft, rich, melodious blasts from their long trumpets. I had never heard anything that was so lovely, or weird, or mysterious—but when they got to blowing the quarter-hours, they seemed to me to be overdoing the thing. Every time I dropped off for a moment, a new noise woke me. Each time I woke I missed my coverlet, and had to reach down to the floor and get it again.

EARLY TO RISE

At last all sleepiness forsook me. I recognized the fact that I was hopelessly and permanently wide awake. Wide awake, and feverish and thirsty. When I had lain tossing there as long as I could endure it, it occurred to me that it would be a good idea to dress and go out in the great square and take a refreshing wash in the fountain, and smoke and reflect there until the remnant of the night was gone.

I believed I could dress in the dark without waking Harris. I had banished my shoes after the mouse, but my slippers would do for a summer night. So I rose softly, and gradually got on everything—down to one sock. I couldn't seem to get on the track of that sock, any way I could fix it. But I had to have it; so I went down on my hands and knees, with one slipper on and the other in my hand, and began to paw gently around and rake the floor, but with no success. I enlarged my circle, and went on pawing and raking. With every pressure of my knee, how the floor creaked! And every time I

Mark Twain liked to say he only smoked once a day—"all day long."

chanced to rake against any article, it seemed to give out thirty-five or thirty-six times more noise than it would have done in the daytime. In those cases I always stopped and held my breath till I was sure Harris had not awakened—then I crept along again.

I moved on and on, but I could not find the sock; I could not seem to find anything but furniture. I could not remember that there was much furniture in the room when I went to bed, but the place was alive with it now—especially chairs—chairs everywhere—had a couple of families moved in, in the meantime? And I never could seem to *glance* on one of those chairs, but always struck it full and square with my head. My temper rose, by steady and sure degrees, and as I pawed on and on, I fell to making vicious comments under my breath.

SPUN AROUND IN CIRCLES

Finally, with a venomous access of irritation, I said I would leave without the sock; so I rose up and made straight for the door—as I supposed—and suddenly confronted my dim spectral image in the unbroken mirror. It startled the breath out of me for an instant; it also showed me that I was lost, and had no sort of idea where I was. When I realized this, I was so angry that I had to sit down on the floor and take hold of something to keep from lifting the roof off with an explosion of opinion. If there had been only one mirror, it might possibly have helped to locate me; but there were two, and two were as bad as a thousand; besides, these were on opposite sides of the room. I could see the dim blur of the windows, but in my turned-around condition they were exactly where they ought not to be, and so they only confused me instead of helping me.

I started to get up, and knocked down an umbrella; it made a noise like a pistol-shot when it struck that hard, slick, carpetless floor; I grated my teeth and held my breath—Harris did not stir. I set the umbrella slowly and carefully on end against the wall, but as soon as I took my hand away, its heel slipped from under it, and down it came again with another bang. I shrunk together and listened a moment in silent fury—no harm done, everything quiet. With the most painstaking care and nicety I stood the umbrella up once more, took my hand away, and down it came again.

I have been strictly reared, but if it had not been so dark and

Forgotten first: On February 18, 1930, a cow flew in an airplane for the first time.

solemn and awful there in that lonely vast room, I do believe I should have said something then which could not be put into a Sunday-school book without injuring the sale of it. If my reasoning powers had not been already sapped dry by my harassments, I would have known better than to try to set an umbrella on end on one of those glassy German floors in the dark; it can't be done in the daytime without four failures to one success. I had one comfort, though—Harris was yet still and silent; he had not stirred.

FUTILE EFFORTS

The umbrella could not locate me—there were four standing around the room, and all alike. I thought I would feel along the wall and find the door in that way. I rose up and began this operation, but raked down a picture. It was not a large one, but it made noise enough for a panorama. Harris gave out no sound, but I felt that if I experimented any further with the pictures I should be sure to wake him. Better give up trying to get out. Yes, I would find King Arthur's Round Table once more—I had already found it several times—and use it for a base of departure on an exploring tour for my bed; if I could find my bed I could then find my water pitcher; I would quench my raging thirst and turn in.

So I started on my hands and knees, because I could go faster that way, and with more confidence, too, and not knock down things. By and by I found the table—with my head—rubbed the bruise a little, then rose up and started with hands abroad and fingers spread, to balance myself. I found a chair; then the wall; then another chair; then a sofa; then an alpenstock, then another sofa; this confounded me, for I had thought there was only one sofa. I hunted up the table again and took a fresh start…found some more chairs.

BUMP IN THE NIGHT

It occurred to me now, as it ought to have done before, that as the table was round, it was therefore of no value as a base to aim from so I moved off once more, and at random, among the wilderness of chairs and sofas—wandered off into unfamiliar regions, and presently knocked a candlestick off a mantel-piece; grabbed at the candlestick and knocked off a lamp; grabbed at the lamp and knocked off a water-pitcher with a rattling crash, and thought to myself, "I've

Ha-ha: Researchers claim men laugh longer, more loudly, and more often than women.

found you at last—I judged I was close upon you." Harris shouted "murder," and "thieves," and finished with "I'm absolutely drowned."

The crash had roused the house. Mr. X. pranced in, in his long night garment, with a candle, young Z. after him with another candle; a procession swept in at another door, with candles and lanterns; landlord and two German guests in their nightgowns, and a chambermaid in hers.

ENLIGHTENED

I looked around; I was at Harris's bed, a Sabbath day's journey from my own. There was only one sofa; it was against the wall; there was only one chair where a body could get at it—I had been revolving around it like a planet, and colliding with it like a comet half the night.

I explained how I had been employing myself, and why. Then the landlord's party left, and the rest of us set about our preparations for breakfast, for the dawn was ready to break. I glanced furtively at my pedometer, and found I had made forty-seven miles. But I did not care, for I had come out for a pedestrian tour anyway.

* * *

A FEW MORE WORDS FROM MARK TWAIN

- "Name the greatest of all inventors. Accident."
- "Sometimes too much to drink is barely enough."
- "Familiarity breeds contempt—and children."
- "A man who carries a cat by the tail learns something he can learn in no other way."
- "A round man cannot be expected to fit in a square hole right away. He must have time to modify his shape."
- "Always acknowledge a fault. This will throw those in authority off their guard and give you an opportunity to commit more."
- "Always do right. This will gratify some people and astonish the rest."

Q: By what name is the fictional character Princess Aurora known as? A: Sleeping Beauty.

REDISCOVERED TREASURE: BUSTER KEATON

Any list of the greatest movie comedians has to include Buster Keaton. Never heard of him? You don't know what you're missing. Here's the story of one of Hollywood's comic treasures.

THE GREAT STONE FACE

Today filmmakers have nearly a century of history to build on. But that wasn't always the case—in the early days of Hollywood, directors had to invent their craft as they went along. How do you film a romantic scene? A car chase? An Old West shootout? An invasion from Mars? Somebody had to do it first—and they had to figure it out for themselves.

One such innovator was the silent film star Buster Keaton, one of the three most popular comedians of the 1920s (Charlie Chaplin and Harold Lloyd were the other two). His unsmiling "Great Stone Face" was said to be as recognizable at the time as Abraham Lincoln's, but his work behind the camera made a larger contribution to the art of filmmaking than his brilliant performances in front of it.

WHAT MADE HIM DIFFERENT

• Before Keaton, the standard practice for filming a comedian was to set up a camera in a fixed position and then have them perform in front of it, just as they had performed before live audiences in vaudeville. Keaton made the camera his partner in the action of storytelling, instead of just a passive, immobile recorder of events.

• In his silent short film *The Playhouse* (1921), for example, Keaton figured out how to film a dream sequence where he plays every role in a vaudeville theater—the orchestra members, the performers onstage, and all the men and women in the audience. Nine characters on screen at the same time, all of them played by Buster Keaton himself.

• In his 1924 film *Sherlock Jr.*, Keaton plays a movie theater projectionist who—literally—walks into the movie screen and becomes a participant in the film being shown there.

• Audiences were thrilled with Keaton's work—and so were filmmakers. They went to see his movies over and over again, just to try to figure out how he filmed his scenes.

• Like Chaplin and Lloyd, Keaton routinely risked his life performing virtually all of his own stunts. He nearly drowned while filming a river scene in *Our Hospitality* (1923) when a safety line broke, and he actually broke his neck filming a scene in *Sherlock Jr.* (1924), when he fell onto a railroad track while dangling from a water tower. Both of these scenes were used in the final films. (Keaton didn't even realize he'd broken his neck until 11 years later, when he finally got around to having it X-rayed.)

• Keaton had a very distinctive onscreen persona—he *never* smiled on camera. His legendary "Great Stone Face" was something that dated back to his childhood in vaudeville. "If I laughed at what I did, the audience didn't," he told an interviewer in the 1960s. "The more serious I turned the bigger laugh I could get. So at the time I went into pictures, that was automatic. I didn't even know I was doing it."

IN THE BEGINNING

Keaton spent nearly his entire life in show business, first in vaudeville and then in film and television. He was born Joseph Frank Keaton, Jr. in Piqua, Kansas, on October 4, 1895, while his parents were performing in a traveling medicine show with magician Harry Houdini. His father, Joe Keaton, Sr., was a dancer and acrobatic comic; his mother Myra played the saxophone.

Joe Jr. got his nickname from Houdini, following an accident in a hotel when he was only six months old. "I fell down a flight of stairs," Keaton told an interviewer in 1963. "They picked me up… no bruises, didn't seem to hurt myself, and Houdini said, 'That's sure a Buster.'" (In vaudeville, pratfalls were known as "busters.")

The name stuck and so did Buster's ability to survive accidents. Family legend has it that he also lost his right index fingertip (true), nearly lost an eye (unknown), and was sucked out of a hotel room window by a cyclone (unlikely) in three separate incidents all on the same day. True or not, three-year-old Buster got into enough trouble backstage that his parents decided the safest

Longest railway on Earth: the Transiberian Railway (Russia), nearly 6,000 miles long.

thing to do was to put him in their act, so they could keep an eye on him when they were working.

SO *THAT'S* WHY THEY CALL IT SLAPSTICK

It wasn't long after they added little Buster to the act that they realized *he* was getting all the laughs. So they reworked the act. In one skit, Joe would demonstrate how to make children obey their parents while Buster tripped his dad up and hit him with a broom. Joe would pretend to lose his temper and then hit, kick, and throw little Buster all over the stage—into the scenery, into the orchestra pit, and even into the audience—using a hidden suitcase handle and a harness sewn into Buster's costume. The Keatons billed their son as "The Human Mop" and "The Little Boy Who Can't Be Damaged."

SCHOOL OF HARD KNOCKS

Keaton claimed that in all his years of performing in vaudeville, he was rarely if ever injured during the act. It *seemed* violent, but he'd learned at a very early age how to perform pratfalls and other stunts without getting hurt. "I learned the tricks so early in life that body control became pure instinct with me," he remembered. Still, the Keatons had to hustle to stay one step ahead of child welfare groups, who kept trying to have the act shut down.

"The law read that a child can't do acrobatics, walk a wire, can't juggle, a lot of those things, but there was nothing in the law that said you can't kick him in the face or throw him through a piece of scenery," Keaton explained. "On that technicality, we were allowed to work, although we'd get called into court every other week."

ON TO HOLLYWOOD

The Three Keatons toured until 1917. By then Joe, drinking heavily, really *was* starting to beat 21-year-old Buster onstage. The act split up and Buster got a job as an actor in film comedian Roscoe "Fatty" Arbuckle's studio.

Say what you will about Buster's "abusive childhood," but when he walked into Arbuckle's studio for the first time at the age of 21, he had more than 17 years of experience performing pratfalls two shows a day, six days a week. He was a master of physical

Six weeks after an aluminum can is recycled, it's back on the shelf in the form of a new can.

comedy and improvisation, someone perfectly suited to make his mark in the movie business.

Arbuckle knew it, too. He let Keaton perform in a movie called *The Butcher Boy* his first day at the studio. And Keaton—already wearing his trademark flat porkpie hat—was such a polished performer that he filmed his scene in just one take.

WHAT GOES UP...

After just two more films, Keaton was promoted to assistant director and soon after that he was writing and co-starring in Arbuckle's films. The pair made 12 short comedies together between 1917 and 1920. When Arbuckle left to work in full-length feature comedies, Keaton inherited his studio, and after making a single introductory feature-length film called *The Saphead,* he began directing and starring in his own movies. These were the films that established Keaton as a star in his own right, and one of Hollywood's most brilliant comedic talents.

He made 19 comedy shorts between 1920 and 1923, including *The Boat* (1921), *Cops* (1922), and *The Electric House* (1922), which are considered some of his finest work. In 1923 he switched to feature films, making 10 in five years, including *Three Ages* (1923), *Sherlock Jr.* (1924), *The Navigator* (1924), and *The General* (1926).

...MUST COME DOWN

Ironically, the film that is now considered his greatest masterpiece and one of the finest comedies ever made, *The General,* ruined Keaton's career as an independent filmmaker. The film was based on an actual incident that took place during the Civil War, when Northern raiders stole a Confederate train called *The General.* Keaton plays the Southern engineer who tried to steal it back.

Keaton shot the film on location in Oregon using real locomotives and more than 400 members of the Oregon National Guard. It was one of the most expensive silent films at the time and though it is now considered a classic, it flopped after its release. So did Keaton's next film, *College* (1927). Those two failures forced his distributor, United Artists, out of the independent film distribution business altogether.

Keaton then made what he would later call "the worst mistake

60% of Americans say they'd be willing to walk barefoot down the streets of New York City.

of my career," when he closed his film studio and signed with Metro-Goldwyn-Mayer in 1928. Keaton, 34, was at the height of his creative powers and had 45 films to his credit. He didn't realize it at the time, but his creative career was largely over.

FROM BAD TO WORSE

Buster's first movie with MGM, *The Cameraman* (1928), is considered the last of his great films. But MGM reneged on its promise to give Keaton creative control and proceeded to stick him in one terrible picture after another.

It was at this point that Keaton's life—both onscreen and off—began to fall apart. As his career plummeted, he began drinking heavily; his long-troubled marriage fell apart and in the subsequent divorce he lost custody of his two sons. By the time he started work on the ironically titled *What, No Beer?* (1933), he was drinking more than a bottle of whiskey a day and was frequently too drunk to show up for work. MGM sent him to alcohol rehabilitation clinics more than once, but he continually relapsed and in February 1933, the studio fired him. He would never star in another major Hollywood film; he was only 37.

AS SEEN ON TV

It took Keaton years to get his drinking under control, but he never gave up. Whenever he was sober enough to work, he did. Between 1934 and 1949, he appeared in 3 foreign films and more than 20 low-budget films he called "cheaters" because they were slapped together in three or four days. They were the worst films of his career.

Still, because the "cheaters" were produced by Columbia Pictures, they got wide distribution, and that helped Keaton get small parts in feature films. And *that* helped him get his first television appearance—on *The Ed Wynn Show* in 1947—at a time when many other film stars were shunning the new medium. He landed his own TV show in Los Angeles the following year, all the while continuing to act in feature films.

NOW PLAYING

Remember, this was before movie channels, VCRs and DVD players made it possible to view old movies, so it may be difficult to imagine how important these TV and film appearances were to reviving Keaton's popularity. He was the only silent film star still working regularly; other greats like Charlie Chaplin and Harold Lloyd were largely unknown to younger audiences because their best films had not been seen in movie theaters for more than 20 years.

Not so with Keaton: by the early 1950s, he was popping up regularly on TV and in films, and this regular exposure helped generate new interest in his old silent films. As they were restored and rereleased they played to huge adoring audiences.

Keaton died from lung cancer in 1966 at the age of 70. By then he'd won an honorary Academy Award and had lived to see his reputation reestablished as one of the legends of the silent screen.

* * *

CAMEO APPEARANCES

Even if you've never seen any of Buster Keaton's silent classics, you may have seen some of his cameo appearances. Look for him in the following films:

• ***Sunset Boulevard* (1950).** Gloria Swanson plays Norma Desmond, a faded silent screen star who takes in a down-on-his-luck screenwriter played by William Holden. Keaton is one of the "wax works"—the old Hollywood stars who play bridge at Desmond's house.

• ***Limelight* (1952).** Charlie Chaplin plays a washed-up music hall clown who tries to revive his career; Keaton is his piano-playing sidekick.

• ***Pajama Party* (1964).** Fourth of the "Beach Party" movies starring Annette Funicello. Keaton plays an indian chief named Rotten Eagle.

• ***A Funny Thing Happened on the Way to the Forum* (1966).** Keaton's last major cameo. His character Erronius spends much of the film going from horse to horse collecting mare's sweat for a love potion.

...than it is to score a perfect 300 game while bowling.

STRANDED!

The Adventures of Robinson Crusoe is a wonderful story, but would you really want to be stranded on a raft in the middle of the ocean? Here are four true stories of shipwrecks and castaways.

L'HERETIQUE

Alain Bombard was a 27-year-old French doctor who thought it strange that shipwreck survivors on life rafts tend to die quickly. A person can live up to six weeks without food and go up to 10 days without water, so why do so many castaways die within days of being set adrift? The common belief was that they drank salt water, which robs their body's tissues of water. Bombard disagreed. He felt sure that the reason people died was because they waited until their bodies were already dehydrated before drinking the seawater out of desperation.

In 1952 Bombard set out to prove that the ocean will support a astaway indefinitely and that drinking seawater is not detrimental to one's health. He decided to cross the Atlantic Ocean alone in a rubber raft without food or water, taking only emergency supplies in a sealed container to be used as a last resort.

Bombard set out from the Strait of Gibraltar in a 15-foot inflatable sailboat dubbed *L'Hérétique*, French for "The Heretic." He sailed first to Casablanca, which took a week, then to the island of Grand Canary, which took 18 days. From there, he set out to cross the Atlantic, leaving on October 19, 1952.

Recipe for Survival

Bombard caught fish, drank seawater, and even ate a bird that landed on his boat. By straining seawater through fabric, he collected plankton, which provided vitamin C and warded off scurvy. Bad weather resulted in constant bailing, but storms brought fresh rainwater, a welcome change after drinking nothing but saltwater for the first 23 days. He lost weight, began to suffer from saltwater boils, got diarrhea, and became depressed.

On December 6, he wrote out his last will and testament. Then, 53 days after leaving Grand Canary, he encountered the freighter *Arakaka*. But instead of asking to be rescued, Bombard

On average, every square meter of the surface of the planet receives 240 watts of sunlight.

only wanted to know where he was—and his location turned out to be 600 miles away from where he thought he was. It meant he had at least another 20 days to go. Bombard was miserable, but he refused all assistance except the offer of a hot shower and fresh batteries for his radio. Then he went back to his rubber raft.

Christmas Present

Two weeks later, he made landfall on Barbados. It was the day before Christmas. After surviving on nothing but fish, seawater, rain (and a bird), Bombard had lost 55 pounds—a little less than a pound per day, typical for castaways. He developed a slight case of anemia, he had diarrhea, weak spells, blurry vision, he'd lost of a few toenails, and had a skin rash. But overall he was in fairly good health. And he proved that a person can indeed survive on salt water (most survival experts still insist that it's better to drink nothing at all).

THE AURALYN

Maurice and Maralyn Bailey were aboard their 31-foot sloop *Auralyn* on their way to the Galapagos Islands on March 4, 1973, when their boat was struck by a wounded sperm whale. The *Auralyn* started sinking—an hour later it was gone. They left the ship in a four-foot inflatable life raft tied to a nine-foot inflatable dinghy. They had all their survival supplies with them with one exception—they forgot the fishing gear. Still, they had a 20-day supply of food and water.

Three hundred miles from the Galapagos Islands, the Baileys spent three nights rowing as hard as they could trying to reach land, but it was futile and they gave up, allowing the current to sweep them farther out to sea. On the eighth day, a ship passed nearby but failed to see them, and they wasted three of their six flares. When food ran out, they survived on sea turtles. Then, using turtle scraps as bait and safety pins as hooks, they were able to catch some fish. To pass the time, they played cards and dominoes.

Don't Pass Me By

On the 25th night, another ship went by without seeing either their flare or their flashlight. On the 37th day, another ship passed, and two days later another one. They set off an improvised smoke

In 1997, 4,824 British people were treated for injuries caused by opening cans of corned beef.

bomb—kerosene-soaked cloth strips in a turtle shell—but weren't spotted. Another ship went by on the 45th day, but they couldn't get their "smoke bomb" to light. One of the main float tubes of their raft collapsed on the 55th day and couldn't be repaired—after that, they needed to pump it up every 20 minutes. Gradually, their health began to fail.

In June torrential rains came, providing fresh water to drink but the deteriorating canopy above their raft failed to keep them dry. By their 100th day afloat, they had to eat the birds that constantly landed on their raft. They even began catching and eating sharks. On June 30, a Korean ship appeared and saw them waving their jackets. Amazingly, after 118 days at sea, they were able to climb aboard under their own power.

THE PETRAL

In August 1985, Gary Mundell set out to sail solo from California to Hawaii aboard his boat *Petral.* Everything went well for the first few days. But then one night, he was jolted awake by a bump. Getting up to investigate, he discovered that the boat had run aground on Caroline Island, one of the most remote pieces of real estate in the Pacific. Mundell had gone to bed thinking the island was at least 15 miles away. Had he miscalculated? It didn't matter now—he was stranded on a deserted island. The island, seven miles long and one mile wide, was completely uninhabited. He couldn't get the boat free and couldn't reach anyone on the radio.

He transferred absolutely everything movable from the boat to the shore using his inflatable raft, and set up camp under a grove of coconut trees. As the days passed, Mundell found plenty of food: coconuts, crabs, and fish. He caught rainwater in his sail and filled the many discarded bottles and jugs that washed up on the beach until he had more than 60 gallons. He never had to ration water—and even filled his raft and had a bath.

Setting Priorities

After the first month passed without spotting a ship or plane, Mundell considered sailing to the nearest inhabited island 460 miles away, but decided to stay put... where at least he had food and water.

On the 50th day, he spotted a ship a few miles away. Taking no chances, he did everything he could to get the crew's attention—flares, smoke signals, and mirror flashes. The ship, the French research vessel *Coriolis*, answered with their searchlight. Rescue! Once aboard the *Coriolis*, he discovered how he had miscalculated his location: he hadn't—Caroline Island was actually 15 miles east of its charted position.

THE SPIRIT

In 1974 Ray and Ellen Jackson, experienced sailors, bought a 42-foot yacht called *Spirit* and spent the next year outfitting her with every safety feature money could buy. They left California in 1975 and cruised 8,000 miles all over the Pacific. But after Ray injured his back in Hawaii, they decided to fly home and asked Ellen's brother, Jim Ahola, to sail the boat back to California.

Ahola had considerable experience with the *Spirit* but still decided to hire more experienced help, Bruce Collins to captain and Durel Miller to crew. His girlfriend, Camilla Arthur, and her friend, Nancy Perry, asked to come along, too. On September 12, 1976, the *Spirit* left Hawaii bound for California.

Sinking Spirit

On the morning of September 27, without warning, there was a huge bang and the ship keeled over. Had the boat been hit by whales? Did it strike floating debris? Had a submarine surfaced beneath them? They never found out. Although the *Spirit* righted itself, there was a hole in the bow and it quickly began to sink. Flying debris had smashed the radio—so no SOS could be sent. There were two life rafts on board, but the survival kits had been washed away. Collins, Ahola, and Arthur got into one raft and Miller and Perry took the other. Five minutes later the *Spirit* was gone. They were 750 miles from land.

The castaways tied the two rafts together and distributed the meager supplies. They had no food, no fishing gear, and little water. Eleven hours later, the tether broke and the two rafts drifted apart. The raft carrying Miller and Perry drifted for 22 days. Miller was an experienced seaman but Perry was a complete stranger to the sea and was debilitated by seasickness. By the 12th day, she was incoherent and helpless. By the time they were rescued, she had lost 43 pounds (she only weighed 113 pounds to start with). Miller lost 55 pounds but cared for her constantly, kept a lookout, and flagged down a ship called the *Oriental Financier* on the 22nd day.

The average American woman thinks about politics 12 min. a day. Average man: 6 min.

Another Survivor

A subsequent search for the second raft covered nearly 200,000 square miles. On the sixth day of the search it was found, but with only one survivor on board, Captain Bruce Collins—Ahola and Arthur were dead. Collins reported that they ran out of fresh water on the 12th day and he had survived by drinking the foul-tasting rainwater he collected from the canopy of the raft. The others had refused to drink it, fearing it was poisonous. Ahola died on the 19th day. His death devastated his girlfriend, and she died two days later.

Camilla's mother sued the Avon life raft company for failing to provide enough survival gear to keep her daughter alive. A court awarded her $70,000, but the company appealed. It was settled out of court.

* * *

PIZZA FACTS

- **First takeout pizza.** In 1889 King Umberto and Queen Margherita of Italy wanted to sample the Neapolitan street food but didn't want to go out. So she asked pizzeria owner Raffaele Esposito to bring the pizzas to her. He made three kinds, including one with tomato paste, fresh basil, and a new ingredient, mozzarella cheese.
- **First pizzeria in the United States.** Opened by Gennaro Lombardi in 1905, on Spring Street in New York's Little Italy.
- **The first mozzarella cheese.** It was made from the milk of water buffaloes, first brought to Italy from India in the seventh century.
- **The first deep-dish pizza.** Invented in the 1940s by Chicago's Pizzeria Uno.
- **The first commercial pizza-pie mix.** Called Roman Pizza Mix, was produced in Worcester, Massachusetts, in 1948 by Frank A. Fiorello.
- **The first frozen pizza.** Marketed by Celentano Brothers in 1957.
- **The first Pizza Hut.** Opened in 1958 by two brothers attending Wichita State University.

DOES YOUR COUCH HAVE HAIRY PAWS?

One of the most fascinating stories of lost treasure is the story of General John Cadwalader's furniture. Seriously. They're among the most valuable antiques on Earth. And who knows—you may be sitting on his couch right now.

STRAIGHT SHOOTER

Revolutionary War general John Cadwalader is famous for two things: defending the honor of George Washington in a duel, and having extremely odd taste in furniture.

Cadwalader fought his duel with General Tom Conway, after Conway schemed to have Washington replaced as commander in chief of the Continental Army. Cadwalader won—he shot Conway in the face and nearly killed him (Conway recovered and moved to France).

HOME IMPROVEMENT

Cadwalader's unique taste in furniture dates back to before the Revolution. In 1769 he and his wife, a Maryland heiress named Elizabeth Lloyd, bought a three-story Georgian house in one of Philadelphia's most exclusive neighborhoods and then spent a fortune refurbishing it and filling it with furniture. They were determined to make their new home the most fashionable address in the city, and by all accounts they succeeded; one member of the Continental Congress who visited the home wrote that it "exceeds anything I have seen in this city or elsewhere."

The most skilled artisans in the city spent months on end crafting hand-carved paneling, ceilings, moldings, and surrounds for the windows, fireplaces, and doorways. Some of the pieces were carved with flowers, others with ribbons, birds, allegorical figures, even dragons.

While this was going on, the Cadwaladers were also ordering furniture. Lots of furniture—the finest in the colonies—also hand-carved by Philadelphia's most skilled craftsmen. They commissioned enough furniture to fill the entire house. For their gilded front parlor alone, they commissioned two card tables, three large sofas, and a huge easy chair that was almost as wide as a loveseat. The furniture was constructed by a master cabinetmaker named Thomas Affleck.

FOOT SOLDIER

The Cadwaladers were fans of the then-modern Rococo style, whose distinguishing feature was bold, elaborate carved ornamentation. One detail appealed to them in particular: "hairy lion's-paw" feet. Have you ever seen an antique chair or table with legs carved to look like animals' feet? It's a common design element in antique furniture, but most people preferred eagle claws or *hairless* lion paws, not "hairy-paws."

In fact, most people considered hairy-paws to be quite ugly—and very few 18th-century examples survive. Not in England, where hairy-paws originated and quickly fell out of favor, and not in the colonies, where they never caught on at all.

In the late 1780s, the ornate Rococo style gave way to the much simpler Neoclassical style, which drew its inspiration from the austerity of Greco-Roman architecture and art. Now the Cadwaladers' furniture wasn't just ugly, it was considered gaudy and passé. And since nobody wanted to buy Rococo furniture anymore—not even the stuff *without* hairy-paws—furniture makers stopped making it. Cadwalader's furniture was unique to begin with; suddenly it became rare.

COLLECTIBLES

Cadwalader's furniture has just about everything that a collector looks for in an antique. It was made of the highest-quality materials. It was fashioned by some of the best-known, most highly skilled master craftsmen of the late 18th century. Its style is both very bold and very rare—it's considered to be some of the finest examples of American Rococo furniture ever made. And it was commissioned by one of the wealthiest and most prominent families in the colonies, a family headed by a Revolutionary War hero, one who defended George Washington in a duel and who entertained the future president and numerous other founding fathers in his home in the very years that the United States of America was being born.

All aboard! Andrew Jackson was the first U.S. president to ride a train.

It's very likely that Washington, Thomas Jefferson, Benjamin Franklin, and other luminaries sat in Cadwalader's hairy-paw chairs, lounged on his hairy-paw sofas, were served tea on his hairy-paw tea tables, and perhaps even played cards at his hairy-paw card tables. Would *you* pay extra for an antique chair if you knew there was a good chance that Washington sat in it? If you said yes, trust us—you aren't alone.

PAPER TRAIL

But there's one more thing that makes the Cadwalader pieces interesting and among the most sought-after antiques: General and Mrs. Cadwalader saved all of their receipts.

It appears that the Cadwaladers saved every single scrap of paper associated with the remodeling and refurnishing of their home—not just receipts but also handwritten letters, bills of sale, inventory lists itemizing each piece of furniture, even day-to-day documentation of the work as it progressed. Everything. Many of these documents survive to this day and have been carefully preserved by the Historical Society of Pennsylvania. How do we know that the Cadwaladers ordered two card tables, three sofas, and a huge easy chair for their front parlor? How do we know that they were made by Philadelphia cabinetmaker Thomas Affleck?

Because it says so on the bill of sale.

MISSING LINK

Saving receipts may not sound like a big deal, but it is in the world of antiques. The Cadwalader suite of furniture "is one of the few extant suites of furniture that has all its documentation in place," says Jack L. Lindsey, curator of American decorative arts at the Philadelphia Museum of Art, which owns a number of pieces of Cadwalader furniture. "There were probably similarly ornate and extensive suites of furniture that were produced for other Philadelphians during the time period that are presently unrecognized because all the documentation is scattered," he says.

Any hairy-paw furniture made in the late 18th century is rare enough to be quite valuable, something worth many thousands of dollars. So if you happen to find one at a yard sale, you're very lucky. But if the piece you find happens to be listed on Cadwalader's receipts and can be definitively linked to the family, the value

The average American will use 2/3 of an acre's worth of trees in wood products this year.

of even a single side chair soars into the *millions* of dollars.

And that's just the side chairs. In the mid-1980s, General Cadwalader's giant easy chair was discovered sitting in the library of a Delaware school, where it was on loan from the owners (who considered it too ugly to keep in their own home). Several months passed before the chair was finally authenticated, but once it was, it sold at auction at Sotheby's for $2.75 million. At the time of the sale—1987—it was the highest price ever paid at auction for a piece of furniture, shattering the record set by an antique French cabinet used at the Palace of Versailles that sold for $1.6 million in 1984.

The general's easy chair was the most valuable chair in the world.

GREAT AMERICAN ANTIQUES

So, would you like to find the rest of the missing furniture? It won't be easy. Mrs. Cadwalader died in 1776, not long after giving birth to her third child; General Cadwalader remarried, had two more children, and then died in 1786. His five surviving children divided his furniture among themselves and rented out his house; it was later sold and then demolished in about 1816.

Over the years the furniture was scattered far and wide as each generation of the Cadwalader family passed on, bequeathing their pieces to friends and relatives. Some pieces are still in the family but many have disappeared and some haven't been seen in more than 200 years. Because the furniture is of such high quality, there's a good chance that many of the missing pieces are still out there, hiding in plain sight, waiting to to be rediscovered. Waiting to make their discoverers rich.

SCAVENGER HUNT

The Cadwaladers' complete set of hairy-paw furniture was huge. Here's just a sample of the items that have already been found, and those that may still be in existence:

- **Side chairs.** Cadwalader commissioned at least 12 side chairs and possibly as many as 20; five of them turned up in Ireland in the early 1970s, apparently having found their way there when Cadwalader's great-grandson moved to that country in 1904. The set of five chairs sold for $207,500 in 1974.

As many as 10,000 bags are lost or "mishandled" by U.S. airlines every day.

Then in 1982 a sixth side chair from the set was discovered, this time in Italy. The Cadwaladers had apparently given the chair to their neighbors the Lewises, who brought it with them to Florence, Italy, and then bequeathed it to a family maid in 1933. Still in the servant's family when it was discovered, the single chair sold at auction for $275,000 that year...and $1.4 million when it came up for auction again in 1999. (A side chair once owned by George Washington sold at the same auction for only $118,000.)

So far, seven hairy-paw side chairs have been discovered, so there may be as many as *13* more still out there.

• **Card tables.** One table surfaced in Canada in 1969 and was acquired by the Philadelphia Museum, which already owned a second identical card table. A third was located at an inn in Maine in 1964, where it had been since Cadwalader's great-great-granddaughter Beatrix Jones Farrand had given it to the innkeeper years before. A collector named G. David Thompson bought it for $640; he apparently never realized what he had, because it wasn't until his widow died in 1982 that it was finally authenticated as a Cadwalader original. In 1983 it sold for $242,000 and was donated to the Philadelphia Museum of Art.

• **Tea tables.** One hairy-paw tea table was found in New England in the summer of 1994, when a Connecticut dealer named William Bartley bought it from an auction gallery that had mislabeled it as an English table. This table is surrounded by more mystery than other Cadwalader pieces that have surfaced. Though it matches the description of a tea table listed in the Cadwaladers' receipts, and its distinctive ribbon-and-flower carved edge is identical to that on other pieces of Cadwalader furniture, it wasn't possible to identify a definitive chain of possession leading back to the Cadwalader family. No matter—the table sold for $695,000 anyway. In 2001 a similar tea table still in the Cadwalader family sold at auction for $1.4 million.

• **Sofas.** Only one of the three sofas listed on Thomas Affleck's bill of sale has been found. "There are still two sofas out there unaccounted for," says John Hays, head of the American furniture department of Christie's auction house. "And they were the most expensive items on the bill: the pair cost Cadwalader £16, four times what the tea table did. They've still got to be out there."

Ready for the million-dollar treasure hunt? Good luck...

Largest city in the United States Confederacy: New Orleans.

SNL PART V: SPARTANS RULE!

We've noticed in writing this long piece about Saturday Night Live *that it probably drops more names than any other article in the BRI's history. Here are some more.* *(Part IV is on page 427.)*

OUT WITH THE OLD

Michaels weathered the latest storm of critical attacks and did yet another shake-up after the disastrous 1995 season. The only surviving cast member was Tim Meadows (against NBC's wishes). And the revolving door kept on bringing in new faces: Impressionist Darrell Hammond; MTV's Colin Quinn; stand-up comics Tracy Morgan and Jim Breuer; and from the Los Angeles-based improv group, The Groundlings, Cheri Oteri, Jimmy Fallon, Chris Kattan, Ana Gasteyer, Chris Parnell, and Will Ferrell.

In the late 1990s, *SNL* entered its fourth golden age. How? By getting back to basics. Tom Shales and James Miller explain the resurgence in their book *Live from New York*:

> In 1996 and again to an even greater degree in 2000, *Saturday Night Live* returned to its richest vein of humor, American politics, and in the process rejuvenated itself for the umpty-umpth time. The cast was prodigious, the writing team witty and self-confident, and the satire biting.

Will Ferrell, according to many critics and cast members, emerged as one of the funniest people in *SNL*'s history. His George W. Bush, along with Darrell Hammond's Bill Clinton and Al Gore, kept the *SNL*'s presidential-bashing alive and well. Even the real Al Gore studied *SNL*'s send-up of the 2000 presidential debates "to help understand where he had gone wrong with his own debate performance."

SATURDAY WHITE LIVE

While *SNL* has been hailed for its no-holds-barred takes on politics and television, it's had less then a stellar track record when it comes to dealing with women and minorities. Many who were there refer to the 17th floor as a "good ole' boys" organization, which is no surprise considering that most of the writers and cast have been white men. And as uneven as the comedy has been over the years, so too has been its take on racial relations.

TOKEN PLAYERS

In the 1970s, Garrett Morris's biggest complaint was that the all-white writing team only gave him stereotypically black roles (he once performed "Proud Mary" dressed as Tina Turner). "I was hired under the terms of the Token Minority Window Dressing Act of 1968," he half-joked. "I get to play all parts darker than Tony Orlando."

But that began to change when Eddie Murphy first got exposure as a commentator on "Weekend Update" in 1981. "There's a different kind of black man on *Saturday Night Live* now," he announced to the world as he held up a photo of Garrett Morris. The next season, Murphy produced and starred in a short film for the show in which he was made up to look like a white man… to see how "the other half" lived. That, along with his portrayals of James Brown and Stevie Wonder, brought the show a black audience.

Damon Wayans joined as a featured player in 1985, thinking that he would take over where Murphy left off. He was wrong. Wayans wanted to improvise his in-your-face brand of racial comedy; the writers wanted him to read his "one line per skit" off of the cue cards. He protested when he purposely flubbed a skit on live television—a cardinal sin according to Michaels—and was fired that night. Wayans would soon get to showcase his talents on Fox's variety show *In Living Color,* which was a huge hit for the fledgeling network. And NBC noticed.

READY TO ROCK

"I got hired because *In Living Color* was on," said Chris Rock, who joined in 1991. "*SNL* hadn't had a black guy on in eight years, and *In Living Color* was hot, so they had to hire a black guy." Rock fared somewhat better than Wayans, most notably with his break-out character, urban talkshow host Nat X: "This week's list—the top five reasons why white people can't dance," he would say wearing a huge afro wig, "Why only five? Because THE MAN won't give me ten!"

That joke hit pretty close to the mark, though, as Rock watched Farley and Sandler each get in twice as many skits. Like Wayans before him, Rock didn't really get to showcase his talents until *after* he left the show.

Tim Meadows has the distinction of being on the show longer than anyone else, and though he had some popular characters (such as the Ladies' Man), the writers never gave him anything too controversial to say. Why? Meadows's heyday fell between the Rodney King riots in 1992 and the O. J. Simpson Trial in 1995—a time when race relations in the United States were tense.

In recent years, Tracy Morgan has added his brand of street comedy to *SNL*. Like Rock and Wayans before him, Morgan was heavily inspired by Eddie Murphy. And like Murphy, he's getting to speak his mind on "Weekend Update" commentaries: "Racial profiling? I'm all for it—if ya' ax me, I say, 'Shake 'em down!'"

BROADENING HORIZONS

While there have been more women then black people on *SNL* (and only two black women, Ellen Cleghorne and Danitra Vance), very few have been given equal footing with the men—and thus very few memorable characters.

But that trend, too, has been changing. The two stand-outs in recent years: Cheri Oteri's cheerleader (with Will Ferrell) and Molly Shannon's neurotic Catholic student Mary Catherine Gallagher. And although she had no breakthrough characters, Ana Gasteyer showed as much impressionistic range and musical talent as anyone on the show since Phil Hartman—a talent that landed her in a lot of sketches.

In 1999 Tina Fey took over as head writer (the first woman to do so). She completely revamped the struggling "Weekend Update" segment by co-anchoring it with Jimmy Fallon, reminding viewers of the chemistry that Dan Aykroyd and Jane Curtin had back in the 1970s. *Saturday Night Live* was as funny and current as ever, but would soon face one of its most daunting tasks.

FROM THE RUBBLE

Only two weeks after the September 11 terrorist attacks in 2001, *Saturday Night Live* began its 27th season on uncharted ground. Lorne Michaels knew that the words "Live from New York" would

The calories in a bagel with cream cheese can run an electric toothbrush for 52 hrs., 20 min.

have a greater resonance than ever before, so he planned the opening very carefully. After an emotional speech by Mayor Rudolph Giuliani, who was surrounded by New York firefighters, longtime *SNL* friend Paul Simon performed a soulful rendition of his song "The Boxer." Then an unsure Lorne Michaels asked the mayor, "Can we be funny?" After a brief pause, Giuliani returned with, "Why start now?" It was perhaps the first good laugh on TV since the tragedy and a sign that life would return to normal.

SIX DEGREES OF SATURDAY NIGHT

After nearly three decades, hundreds of the entertainment industry's biggest names have crossed paths with *Saturday Night Live*, from Robin Williams to Oprah Winfrey to Paul McCartney to Madonna. It's tough to flip through the channels for too long without seeing some evidence of *SNL's* impact: (click) *The Chris Rock Show;* (click) David Spade on *Just Shoot Me;* (click) *Stripes* with Bill Murray; (click) a commercial for *Austin Powers;* (click) "Tonight on *Conan*: Steve Martin, followed by Molly Shannon, with musical guest Elvis Costello" (who made his U.S. television debut on *SNL*).

As *Saturday Night Live* enters its fourth decade, the show continues to collect Emmys and praise from critics, who marvel at the show's longevity. Tom Shales continues to hail *SNL*, calling it a "weekly miracle." When asked how he's kept the show funny in the 21st century, Lorne Michaels answered: "I think that we've got those non-suck devices working again."

* * *

RANDOM *SNL* FACTS

- Youngest host: Drew Barrymore, on Nov. 20, 1982, 7 years old.
- Five hosts cast members most liked working with: Steve Martin, Tom Hanks, John Goodman, Alec Baldwin, Christopher Walken.
- Short list of wanted hosts that have never appeared (so far): Johnny Carson, Tom Cruise, Bill Clinton.
- Other *SNL* alums: Ben Stiller (1989), Janeane Garofalo (1994), Kevin Meaney (1986), Jay Mohr (1993–94), Chris Elliot (1994).

Who figured out that the rings reveal the age of a tree? Leonardo da Vinci.

MICROCARS

One day in the early 1960s, young Uncle John was waiting in line at a Dairy Queen when he happened to see a strange little car pull into the parking lot. It looked like a refrigerator on wheels. That car—the Isetta—was Uncle John's introduction to an unusual class of foreign car known as microcars. If you aren't familiar with them, here's yours:

SIZE MATTERS

In post-World War II Europe, economic realities were forcing car designers to rethink the idea of the automobile. Europeans were already accustomed to smaller cars. More densely populated than America, many of its cities had narrow streets that predated the automobile by centuries. As early as 1923, smaller, more easily maneuverable cars were being built by manufacturers such as Alfa-Romeo and Fiat.

After World War II, fuel was expensive and materials were in short supply. The damaged economy made even these small cars out of reach for most people. In contrast to America's postwar optimism—which was expressed by materialism and a "bigger is better" attitude—Europeans tightened their belts and looked for ways to get by on less. Many people used bicycles or motorcycles for transport, but these left a lot to be desired in inclement weather and were of little use for carrying much more than the driver.

CREATIVE SOLUTIONS

In the late 1940s and early 1950s a number of unconventional inventors began designing vehicles that were a sort of hybrid—more than motorcycles, but not quite cars. Many were designed to use motorcycle engines, particularly the early models. Later versions used more powerful proprietary engines. But one thing all the new cars had in common was size: they were very small. As a group, they became known as "microcars."

Some had four wheels, making them more carlike. But many had just three—usually two in front and one in back—which brought the cost down. According to British law, for example, a vehicle with fewer than four wheels (and without a reverse gear) was considered a motorcycle and was taxed at a lower rate than

Waterfront property: There are more than 30,000 islands in the Pacific Ocean.

regular cars. Another plus: A less-expensive motorcycle license was all that was needed to drive the three-wheelers.

More than 50 different microcar brands were produced in Europe after the war. Some had a great deal of success; others barely got off the drawing board. With names such as Atom, Frisky, Scootacar, Trojan, and Wolf, it was difficult to take some of them seriously. But Europeans seemed to find the names and many of the wacky designs endearing. The vehicles were cheap to buy, economical to operate, and, as one ad said, "Why walk when you can ride?"

SMALL BEGINNINGS

Some of the diminutive vehicles were designed and built by companies with automotive backgrounds, such as British Reliant, which expanded on its prewar line of three-wheeled vans. (Reliant made three-wheelers until early 2001.) But many others were produced by inventive entrepreneurs with little or no experience in vehicle design.

Bavarian businessman Hans Glas manufactured agricultural machinery. When demand for his equipment dropped sharply in the late 1940s, Glas thought there might be a market for a well-built scooter, so he began manufacturing one in 1951. He was right. After the success of the scooter, he went on to design a tiny car, the four-wheeled Goggomobile, first sold in 1955 for about $750. It was as rugged as its agricultural heritage might suggest—one reviewer noted that "the only way to flip a Goggomobile is to drive it over a land mine." With more than 280,000 sold by the end of production in 1969, the Goggomobile became the most successful small car produced in Germany.

LUFTWAFFE CHIC

Another well-known microcar started out as a wheelchair. Shortly after the war, German aeronautical engineer Fritz Fend, a former Luftwaffe technical officer, began experimenting with some ideas he had for a hand-powered tri-cycle for disabled servicemen. His design evolved into a motorized version, with two wheels in front, the single wheel in the rear. When he started producing the vehicles, he was surprised to find that he was swamped by requests for it—not from disabled servicemen, but from ordinary people looking for cheap transportation.

Ulysses S. Grant sometimes smoked as many as 20 cigars a day. (He died of throat cancer.)

Fend was more of an inventor than a businessman, so to meet the demand for the new vehicles, he turned to his aviation contacts at the Messerschmitt aircraft company. The Messerschmitt factory, which had built fighter planes for the Nazis, was closed after the war. They were banned from making aircraft, so it was sitting idle...until it was put back to use making Fend's little cars. The first production model of the eight-foot-long Messerschmitt, which the makers preferred to call the Kabinroller, was introduced to the public in 1953.

With flowing lines and a clear, plastic dome top, it resembled a cockpit on wheels—and some people thought the Cabin-Scooter was made of old fighter plane parts. Reinforcing that misconception, the top opened upward and its two seats were in tandem, one behind the other. With a 191cc engine and a top speed of more than 50 mph, the Cabin-Scooter got 60 to 75 miles per gallon. Some 45,000 were sold by the end of production in 1964. A more powerful sibling, the Messerschmitt Tiger, had four wheels, a 500cc engine, and claimed a top speed of 90 mph.

TINY BUBBLES

Just before World War II, Italian businessman Renzo Rivolta purchased Isothermos, a small company that specialized in making refrigerators. After the war he added scooters and motorcycles to his line, then three-wheeled minitrucks, and then in 1952 his first car, the Isetta ("Little Iso").

Though the Isetta and the Messerschmitt were called "bubble cars" because of their rounded enclosures, the Isetta bore little resemblance to the Messerschmitt—there was no chance anyone could mistake it for a fighter plane. Sometimes called "an Easter egg on roller skates," it was distinctly ovoid, 54 inches wide by 90 inches long.

The *entire* front end of the Isetta served as its single front door, much like a refrigerator door. With the door open, occupants would step into the car, turn around, and sit down on the single seat. The driver closed the door by pulling on the steering wheel, which was attached to the door and would pivot into place. The car had a canvas pullback sunroof, which made motoring around the countryside more pleasant on sunny days, but the real reason for it was that in the event of a front-end collision, passengers

Odds that a thunderstorm will strike Daytona, Florida, in the next four days: 100%.

could use it as an emergency escape.

Though versions of the Isetta were made in Brazil, France, Spain, and Belgium, it was BMW of Germany that refined the little car and contributed most to its success. In the postwar economy, BMW was having trouble selling its more expensive models and was looking for an economy car to manufacture. BMW scouts were impressed by the Isetta's performance in Italy's Mille Miglia (1,000-mile) race. One reportedly finished with an average speed of almost 50 mph and with a fuel efficiency of 60 miles per gallon.

BMW bought the manufacturing rights, replaced the original engine with a more powerful 13-horsepower 247cc motorcycle engine and made several design improvements, such as better suspension and sliding side windows. At a cost of just 20% of its least-expensive luxury cars, BMW sold more than 160,000 Isettas in Germany. Another 30,000 were made in Great Britain under the BMW license. Some critics called it "a death trap," but many historians actually attribute the survival of BMW to the success of the Isetta.

BMW built Isettas until 1962, when competition from sturdier, more carlike microcars, especially the British-built Mini, was making bubblecars obsolete.

MILLIONS OF MINIS

In the late 1950s, microcars enjoyed a second surge of popularity. Egypt had seized the Suez Canal in 1956, and Britain was rationing gasoline. Sir Leonard Lord, head of British Motor Corporation, asked designer Sir Alec Issigonis to come up with something revolutionary—a car to "wipe those blasted bubble cars off the road." And that's exactly what happened.

At roughly 4½ feet by 10 feet, the Mini was only a little larger than most of the earlier microcars, but with proper car-like side doors and a front and rear seat. The engine was in its own compartment, in the front over the drive wheels. But the real revolution was the drive train—by turning the 848cc engine sideways and putting the gearbox underneath it, Issigonis fit all the mechanical parts into just 18 inches. That left plenty of room for four passengers and even luggage.

With its four-cylinder 37-horsepower engine, the Mini could hold its own on the highway among larger cars. The early models had a top speed of 72 mph, but later performance modifications boosted

Look it up (Chuck): Each year, U.S. airlines use more than 20 million airsickness bags.

that figure to over 100 mph, a remarkable speed considering the Mini rode on 10-inch wheels. The combination of size, power, and maneuverability made the car the best in its class, and sales figures reflected its successful design: during the 25 years after its introduc tion in 1959, more than five million Minis were built.

But in spite of its long popularity, the Mini gradually fell victim to the times. It was competing with small but more powerful sports cars and the economical Volkswagon Beetle. By the mid-1980s sales had fallen off dramatically. A new owner, the British auto manufacturer Rover, tried to revive the Mini by offering a number of special editions. Strong sales in Japan helped to keep it going for a while, but as the end of the millennium approached, it looked like the Mini would finally join the Isetta and other legendary little cars on the scrap heap of history.

But history was about to repeat itself.

BACK TO THE FUTURE

In 1994 BMW was seeking to expand its line and bought the four-wheel-drive Land Rover. It turned out to be a bad match. English investors didn't like the idea of a German company owning Rover, and the Rover division cost more money than it made. BMW sold off most of Rover in 2000, but the head of the company was a fan of the Mini...so they kept it.

In 2001 BMW unveiled a new Mini, built in an English factory, sporting BMW styling and engineering. With a motor nearly twice the size of the original and more than twice the horsepower, top speed is estimated at 125 mph. Automotive reviewers think it is both a blast from the past—and a peek at the future.

Though giant SUVs and luxury cars abound today, many car manufacturers with a grasp of history are preparing smaller, more fuel-efficient models. And if the BMW Mini is any indicator, modern microcars will feature high-tech advancements with new designs, materials, and fuels. Meaning: the future may hold mini more surprises.

* * *

"I was hitchhiking the other day and a hearse stopped. I said, 'No thanks—I'm not going that far.'"

—***Steven Wright***

LET'S PLAY NINTENDO!

Today's video game business is less about boing! and crash! than it is about ka-ching! and cash! Here's part V of the story of video games.

NO SALE

As we told you on page 411, back in 1981, Atari was the world leader in video games. In 1983 Nintendo offered to sell Atari the licenses to their Famicom game system, but they couldn't come to an agreement, so Nintendo decided to go it alone. They renamed the American version the Advanced Video System (AVS) and in January 1985, introduced it at the Consumer Electronics Show in Las Vegas, one of the largest such trade shows in the world.

They didn't get a single order.

Nintendo's problem wasn't so much that the AVS was a bad system, but more that the American home video game industry was struggling. After several years of impressive growth, in 1983 sales of video game consoles and cartridges suddenly collapsed without warning. Video game manufacturers, caught completely off guard, lost hundreds of millions of dollars as inventory piled up in warehouses, never to find a buyer. Atari's loss of $536 million prompted Warner Communications to sell the company in 1984. Mattel sold off its version, Intellivision, the same year and shut down their entire video game division. Many other companies went out of business.

GOODBYE VCS, HELLO PC

Meanwhile, computer technology had finally advanced to the point that companies were able to manufacture and sell home computers at prices that families could afford. By 1982 a computer called the Commodore 64 could be bought for as little as $200, which was $100 less than the cost of an Atari 5200.

Why buy just a game system when you could buy a whole computer—which also played video games—for the same price or lower? Just as the video game industry had evolved from dedicated Pong-only games to cartridge-based multigame systems, game systems were

Girl crazy: Dartmouth was the last Ivy League college to go coed. (It held out until 1972.)

giving way to the personal computer. Stand-alone video games were dead...or so most people thought.

Hiroshi Yamauchi, the president of Nintendo, didn't see things that way. His company didn't make personal computers and he didn't know much about the American market. But Famicom game systems were selling like crazy in Japan, and he didn't see any reason why they shouldn't also sell well in the United States. So what if the company didn't receive a single order at the Consumer Electronics Show? He told his American sales team to keep trying.

WORD GAMES

Nintendo's American sales team was headed by Minoru Arakawa, who also happened to be Yamauchi's son-in-law. Arakawa *had* to keep trying. He didn't have any choice—he was a member of the family.

One of the problems the AVS was up against was that retailers had been badly burned by the video game crash of 1983. They weren't about to put any more nonselling video games on their shelves. Arakawa decided that the best way to proceed was to conceal the fact that the AVS was a video game. He couldn't do that while it was still called the Advanced Video System, so he renamed it the Nintendo Entertainment System, NES for short.

He added a light pistol and some shooting games, so that he could say it was a "target game." (Guns and target games still sold well in toy stores.) Then he added the Robot Operating Buddy (ROB), a small plastic "robot" that interacted with a couple of the games played on the NES. "Technologically speaking," Steven Kent writes in *The Ultimate History of Video Games*, "ROB offered very little play value. It was mostly a decoy designed to prove that the Famicom was not just a video game."

DEJA VU

With a new name, a light gun, and a robot, Arakawa was sure the NES would sell. He rented a booth at the Summer Consumer Electronics Show and set the ROB out in front, where everyone could see it.

He didn't get a single order.

Why didn't retailers want to buy? Were consumers turned off too? Arakawa didn't know for sure, so he set up a focus group where he could watch young boys—Nintendo's target market—play NES games. Observing the scene from behind a two-way mirror, Arakawa heard for himself how much the kids disliked the NES. "This is sh*t!" as one kid put it.

ONE MORE TRY

Arakawa was ready to throw in the towel. He called his father-in-law, told him the situation was hopeless, and suggested that Nintendo pull the NES out of the U.S. market. But Yamauchi refused to hear a word of it. He didn't know much about the Consumer Electronics Show and he didn't know much about focus groups. One thing he did know was that the Famicom was *still* selling like crazy in Japan, so why couldn't it sell well in the United States? There was nothing wrong with the NES—he was certain of that.

Yamauchi told Arakawa to test it one more time—in New York City. This time Arakawa left nothing to chance. There were about 500 retailers in the city, and Arakawa and his staff visited every one. They made sales pitches, delivered the game systems, stocked store shelves, and set up Nintendo's in-store displays themselves. They made plans to spend $5 million on advertising during the Christmas shopping season, and—without permission from Yamauchi—promised retailers they would buy back any game systems that didn't sell. And they *never, ever* referred to their video game as a video game. The NES was an "entertainment system."

IS NINTENDO THE NEXT ATARI?

With the buyback guarantee, retailers had nothing to lose, so they agreed to stock Nintendo, even though they didn't think it would sell. They were wrong—more than 50,000 games sold by Christmas, prompting many stores to continue stocking the NES after the holidays. Arakawa launched similar tests in Los Angeles, Chicago, and San Francisco. The NES sold well in each city.

In 1986 Nintendo expanded its U.S. marketing push nationwide and sold 1.8 million game consoles, and from there sales grew astronomically. They sold 5.4 million consoles in 1987 and 9.3 million in 1988. By 1990 American sales of the NES accounted for 10% of the entire U.S./Japan trade deficit.

But if there's one thing that video game makers have learned the hard way, it's that *staying* ahead in the business can be a lot harder

What do baby humans have that baby rattlesnakes don't? Rattles.

than *getting* ahead. For all their successes, Nintendo has made their share of blunders, too. They clung to the NES a few years longer than they should have, on the assumption that its market dominance would allow it to keep ahead of its rivals. They were wrong.

When a rival company called Sega introduced their Genesis system in 1989, Nintendo ignored it, even though the Genesis was twice as powerful as the NES. They shouldn't have—Genesis introduced a character called Sonic the Hedgehog, an edgy, anti-Mario character who appealed to older kids *and* adults the same way that Donkey Kong's Mario had appealed only to kids. In late 1991, Nintendo introduced SuperNintendo, but it was too late. Sonic's appeal, combined with six years of waiting for Nintendo to update their system, helped Sega get a toehold in the market…and outsell Nintendo.

SONY'S PLAYSTATION

But Nintendo's biggest mistake of all came in 1992. The industry was gearing up for yet another generation of game systems—using CD-ROM disks instead of cartridges. CD-ROMs were cheaper to make and stored more than 300 times more information than a Super NES cartridge, allowing for much more sophisticated graphics.

Nintendo had no experience with CD-ROMs, so they made plans to partner with Sony Corporation to make the new system. But there was a problem—Sony had already announced plans to introduce its own game system (Play Station), and Nintendo executives were worried about revealing Nintendo's technological secrets to a competitor as large and powerful as Sony. So what did they do? For some reason, Nintendo waited until the day *after* Sony announced the partnership. Then they made an announcement of their own: they were ditching Sony and partnering with the Dutch electronics giant, Philips.

REVENGE!

Though the company had lost ground to Sega in the U.S. market, Nintendo was still the world leader in video game sales, and many Sony executives were reluctant to challenge Nintendo's dominance. The consensus: scrap the Play Station project because Nintendo will wipe it out. But Sony CEO Norio Ohga was so furious at being humiliated by Nintendo that he almost singlehandedly forced the company to continue work on the project.

The ball that drops in Times Square every New Year's Eve is named the "Star of Hope."

The Sony Play Station was introduced in Japan in 1994 and in the United States in 1995. Nintendo eventually scrapped its CD-ROM–based system and introduced the Nintendo 64, yet another cartridge game system.

BRAVE NEW WORLD

The Nintendo 64 was a blunder of Atari proportions. Compared to the Play Station, it had poor sound, poor graphics...and poor sales. By August 1997, the Play Station had surged past both Sega and Nintendo to become the industry leader. Sega, which spread their resources over too many game systems at once—Genesis, Saturn, and another one called Dreamcast—fell to a distant third and in January 2001 got out of the hardware business altogether. Today they only make game software.

Nintendo's decision to stick with cartridges for the Nintendo 64 continues to haunt them today. When Sony introduced the Play Station 2 in 2000, they were careful to make it "backward compatible," so that virtually all 800 of the Play Station 1 games could be played on the new station. Extra bonus: Because the PlayStation 2 uses a DVD player instead of a CD-ROM player, you can also watch movies on it.

The Nintendo Game Cube, introduced in 2001, is another story. It uses a *mini* DVD-ROM system that doesn't play movies and isn't compatible with Nintendo 64 game cartridges. That means Nintendo 64 owners have no incentive to buy the Game Cube, because their old games will be just as obsolete whether they buy Game Cube or PlayStation 2.

Even worse for Nintendo is the new kid on the block: the Microsoft Xbox. Considered even more technologically advanced than the PlayStation 2, Xbox is giving both Nintendo and Sony a run for their money.

FORTUNE-TELLING

Who will be the next Atari? Will Nintendo's game systems slip to third place behind Sony and Microsoft, or even disappear entirely? Will the PlayStation 2 stay on top, or is the Xbox the new king of the hill? What comes next?

Stay tuned—if there's one thing to be learned from the video game industry, it's that the game is *never* over.

Odds that an American worker won't tell their spouse after they receive a raise: 36%.

BURIED TREASURE

When Uncle John read this article by David Wallechinsky in The People's Almanac, *it immediately made him want to pack his bags and head for the hills to find all the lost loot. But, of course, he's not really going anywhere, so he thought he'd share the info with you. (If you find any treasure, don't forget who told you about it.)*

LOST, BUT NOT FORGOTTEN

There are billions in lost treasure scattered throughout the United States. That's the educated guess of one old treasure hunter, and many of his colleagues think that that's a conservative estimate.

For one, there's loot buried by robbers like Jesse James and Ma Barker "until the heat died down" but never recovered because the robbers were shot or hung before they could retrieve it. There are also gold mines whose owners died without revealing their locations, now hidden by the camouflage provided by the passage of time. And there are misers' hoards, lost caravans, and caches of pirate loot hidden from coast to coast. These bonanzas really exist, and finding one would be the fulfillment of a dream shared by thousands.

TREASURE HUNT

No matter where you live, there's a pretty good chance that some sort of treasure lies lost and forgotten nearby. Getting information about it may involve spending time reading stacks of ancient newspapers to find stories about people who died without revealing where they'd hidden their coins, or legends of old silver mines in the hills that few take seriously anymore. The public library will have listings of books under "Treasure Trove" and "Treasure Hunting" that may offer a lead. Librarians are usually glad to dig up stories about local hoards from their often-overlooked collection of pamphlets and newspaper clippings.

World-famous treasures like the Lost Dutchman Mine or Jim Bowie's lost silver mine are so well known that they've been searched for by untold thousands of people. Since they haven't been found yet, an amateur's chance of finding them is mighty slim. But then again, anyone can be fortunate. All it takes is a little more brains, a little more work, or a little more luck than the rest of the treasure seekers.

BECOMING A TREASURE HUNTER

The most successful treasure hunters have the heart of a Sherlock Holmes but they also carry a metal detector. The less expensive models will find lost coins and watches on a sandy beach, while the better ones can detect masses of metal buried deep under the earth. A detector is a necessity for serious treasure hunting.

Remember—gold, silver, jewels, and money aren't the only valuables lying around waiting to be discovered. Even if that old abandoned mine doesn't have any gold left, it may yield ancient lanterns, vintage guns, or patent medicine bottles. A single old coin can provide a fortune that will last for years. Good luck... and happy hunting.

MONTEZUMA'S LOST TREASURE CARAVAN

More than $10 million in gold and jewels from the Aztec monarch's treasury was buried somewhere north of Mexico City to prevent it from being stolen by the Spanish. Best evidence is that it's near either Taos, New Mexico, or Kanab, Utah.

How It Got There: The Spanish came to the New World to find gold and set about their task with a single-mindedness that would have made Scrooge blush. Rape, pillage, and murder were standard business practices, despite the fact that the vast majority of the Indians they met were friendly and willing to trade huge amounts of gold for small trinkets.

Greed completely conquered common sense, and the Spaniards truly killed the goose that laid the golden egg. Rather than trade peacefully for gold, they enslaved the Indians and forced them to work their own mines, and they stripped sacred temples of their solid-gold ornaments, which they melted down into ingots and shipped back to Spain. (Much of that gold ended up on the ocean floor when the galleons sank in heavy seas.) As a result, the Indians revolted, hid their gold, and fled from their conquerors.

Montezuma's Revenge: In 1520 the Aztec ruler Montezuma learned that Cortés and his gold-crazed troops were heading toward his capital, now Mexico City. Knowing that there was no hope of peaceful coexistence with the Spanish, Montezuma immediately stripped his buildings of their gold, silver, and jewels and sent this treasure by caravan to the north, to be buried until the plague of Spaniards had passed. Unfortunately, Montezuma didn't survive the onslaught. There's no record of the treasure ever having been recovered, so it's likely still hidden where it was buried over 450 years ago. The question, of course, is where.

One account says the caravan went 275 leagues north from Mexico City, then turned west into high mountains, where the gold was hidden in a cave in a huge canyon. There's some question of just how long a league is, but the best guess seems to be that the caravan ended up somewhere in the Sierra Madres.

Other versions say the caravan went much farther north, into present-day Arizona, New Mexico, or Utah.

Previous Searches

• The July 14, 1876, issue of the Taos *Weekly New Mexican* reported that a young Mexican arrived in town to look for the treasure. Some townspeople went out with him because he seemed to have special knowledge of where to look.

Searching among the rocks in the mountains outside town, he scrambled up a cliff ahead of the rest of the party. After a long silence, he called out that he'd found a cave "filled with gold and lit into the blaze of day with precious stones." At that moment, according to the newspaper account, a powerful wind blew him off the cliff. He was dashed against the rocks below and didn't live to reveal the location of the cave. No one else has ever found a trace of it.

• Kanab, Utah, came into the story in 1914, when a prospector named Freddie Crystal rode into town. He told a wealthy rancher named Oscar Robinson that he'd researched the Montezuma legend while in Mexico and found an old book that gave him a solid lead. The book had drawings of symbols that Montezuma's men had supposedly inscribed on the rocks in a canyon near Kanab. Crystal figured he could find the treasure...but he needed money.

It was common for a businessman to outfit a prospector under an agreement to share any wealth discovered, so Robinson agreed to do just that. Crystal and his string of packhorses trailed off into the mountains and weren't seen again for eight years.

By 1922 the town had almost forgotten about the prospector.

Bullish: When the stock market dips in Pakistan, people sacrifice goats to bring it back up.

So they were surprised and excited when he came ambling back out of the mountains saying he'd found the treasure. They got even more excited when he said he needed a lot of help to get it out.

The citizens of Kanab migrated en masse into the mountains with Crystal. There, in a canyon on White Mountain, they found strange symbols carved into the cliffs that matched those found in the book. Nearby was a giant tunnel that had been carefully sealed long ago. The townspeople attacked the tunnel with a zeal that matched that of the original *conquistadors*, but day after day they found nothing. After three months, everyone gave up. Crystal was never seen again.

How to Get There: Taos is in northern New Mexico, about 60 miles northeast of Santa Fe. Ask local residents to point out Taos Peak. Kanab, Utah, is just north of the Arizona border, on Highway 89, about 90 miles east of Interstate 15. Ask local residents for White Mountain and the canyon with the symbols carved in the rocks.

MAXIMILIAN'S MILLIONS

Emperor Maximilian of Mexico (1864–1867) sent at least $5 million in gold, silver, and jewels out of the country when he learned that he was about to be deposed. His men were robbed and killed, and most of the treasure was buried in Castle Gap, Texas.

How It Got There: During the Civil War, France had ideas about regaining some of its lost New World empire, and as a first step, Napoleon III placed Maximilian, the Austrian archduke, on the Mexican throne. Maximilian had delusions of grandeur, though, and arriving with his entire Austrian fortune, used his position to amass even more.

The foreign ruler was despised by the Mexican peasants, and plots for his overthrow began almost before he arrived. The emperor realized that if he wanted to live, he'd need to find a more agreeable climate. First, though, he wanted to get his wealth out of the country.

It's not easy to be inconspicuous when you're moving gold and jewelry through rural Mexico, but Maximilian had a plan. He had four trusted aides pack all his valuables in 45 flour barrels and sprinkle a layer of flour on top. His aides and faithful peons set out in a caravan for the north and crossed into Texas near El Paso. The caravan now had to contend with the bandits that roamed the lawless

In a typical year, 11,000 Americans seek medical aid after "trying out new sexual positions."

Texas border country. A band of former Confederate soldiers warned the travelers just how dangerous the area was, so Maximilian's men hired the soldiers on the spot as guides and guards.

A few nights later, curiosity got the better of one of the guards. He had to know why a caravan of flour needed so much protection. So while the rest of the camp slept, he discovered the secret. Maximilian's men didn't live to see daylight.

The soldiers knew they'd never get all that gold past the other bandits in the area, so they stuffed their saddlebags with as much as they could carry and buried the rest. There are various versions of just how many soldiers there were and just how they died. It is agreed, however, that none lived to recover their hidden treasure.

Previous Searches: As one of the men died with a doctor in attendance, he gasped out the story of the buried millions at Castle Gap. The doctor went to search for it many years later but found nothing. None of the landmarks on the map drawn by the dying outlaw matched anything that he could find. Yet it's certain that Maximilian's men were escorting a fabulous treasure and that the treasure has never been seen again.

How to Get There: By all accounts, the treasure is still hidden somewhere around Castle Gap, high in the King Mountains north of El Paso. Ask in El Paso how to find the gap. Be prepared for hot, dry, dusty mountain country.

VERMONT'S CIVIL WAR BANK ROBBERY

A band of Confederate raiders robbed three banks in St. Albans, Vermont, and buried $114,522 in gold and currency somewhere near the Canadian border.

How It Got There: St. Albans was a sleepy village on October 18, 1864; the townsfolk didn't pay much attention to all the strangers that had appeared during the previous few days. There was a war on and strangers were always coming and going. But that war was much closer than anyone suspected.

As the afternoon wore on, the strangers began moseying over to the village green. Suddenly they formed into three separate groups and converged on the three banks fronting the square. While some of them held the townspeople at gunpoint, the rest cleaned out the banks. In minutes the task was complete, and they

Traditionally, Tibetans disposed of their dead by hacking them up and feeding them to birds.

galloped out of town.

Fourteen of the twenty-two were soon arrested in Canada, and St. Albans was amazed to learn that they were Confederate soldiers who had planned to use the loot to stage similar raids on other New England towns. The arrested men had some of the money with them, but $114,522 was missing. The banks offered $10,000 to anyone who could locate the missing gold. There were no takers.

Previous Searches: After the war, one of the soldiers came back to St. Albans. He didn't say much, but a local farmer secretly followed him as he wandered along the Vermont side of the Canadian border. He was obviously searching for something but seemed confused. At length he left, empty-handed, and was never seen again.

How to Get There: St. Albans is about 20 miles north of Burlington, Vermont, near Lake Champlain. The soldier's search seems to place the treasure somewhere along the Vermont side of the border near there.

MUD LAKE GOLD

Gold bullion and money totaling $180,000—stolen from a Wells Fargo stagecoach—was thrown into Mud Lake in Idaho by escaping bandits.

How It Got There: In 1865 a stagecoach bound for Salt Lake City was attacked by the notorious Updike and Guiness gang. Four passengers were killed and the driver knocked unconscious. At least $100,000 in valuables was taken from the wealthy passengers, along with $80,000 in gold bullion from the stage's strongbox.

The driver and the surviving passengers made it to McCammon, Idaho, where they told their story. A posse quickly formed to track the gang. The outlaws got trapped in the murky waters of Mud Lake and knew that they'd never escape with the heavy gold weighing them down. While the posse was still in the rocks above, they saw the robbers throw heavy sacks into the water.

The gang escaped but never returned to the area for the treasure. The posse couldn't pinpoint the exact spot where they had seen the gold dumped, and there's no record that it was ever found.

Previous Searches: A treasure hunter named B. C. Nettleson and his partner, Orba Duncan, searched the lake for 20 years without

Sesame Street update: Oscar the Grouch has a pet—a worm named Slimey.

finding a clue. Then in 1901 Duncan came up with three bars of solid gold, which he sold in a nearby town for $25,000. He kept searching but found nothing more. That's all that has ever been found, but local residents are convinced that the gold is still on the muddy lake bottom.

How to Get There: Mud Lake is in east-central Idaho, in Jefferson County, about 30 miles northwest of Idaho Falls, and about 60 miles north of Pocatello.

RENO GANG TRAIN ROBBERY

Gold coins, bars, and currency worth more than $80,000 were stolen from a train in Marshfield, Indiana. The robbers apparently stashed it nearby and were hanged before they could retrieve it.

How It Got There: In 1868 a passenger train of the Jefferson, Madison, and Indianapolis Railroad stopped for wood and water at a station in Marshfield. As the crew left the train, some men hidden behind a woodpile leaped out, knocked the fireman and engineer unconscious, uncoupled the passenger cars, and took off with the engine and the baggage car. The empty safes from the baggage car were found in a wooded area 20 miles from Marshfield, but there was no sign of the contents.

A short time later, four members of the same gang were arrested for killing three of their companions. The four prisoners were taken to nearby New Albany for safekeeping, but that night 50 vigilantes rode into town with red bandannas on their faces and demanded to know where the loot was hidden.

With the sheriff and prison guards tied up, they dragged the gang members one by one out of their cells. They were given a choice—their money or their lives. One by one they refused to tell where the gold was buried, and one by one they were hanged. The last man spit defiantly and said, "You'd hang me anyway, so why should I tell?" He was probably right.

How to Get There: Marshfield, Indiana, is in Warren County, near the Illinois border in the west-central part of the state. The gold is probably somewhere in the vicinity, hidden under Indiana farmland.

JESSE JAMES'S MEXICAN GOLD

Jesse James's gang stole gold bars worth more than $1 million and buried them in the Wichita Mountains near Lawton, Oklahoma.

How It Got There: During the 1870s, the gang staged a series of raids along the Texas–Mexican border, and in one of them took a caravan of gold bullion belonging to a Mexican general. The gang headed north into Indian territory with its loot and buried it in the Wichita Mountains.

Previous Searches: Years later, with brother Jesse dead, Frank James bought a farm and settled down near Lawton, Oklahoma. He made no secret of the fact that he was using the farm as a base from which to search for that gold. He'd helped bury it, but the intervening years of dodging the law had dimmed his memory. He knew that they'd left a marker of pick heads and a code scratched on a bucket, but he couldn't find these clues. He was convinced that this fortune was within a few miles of his farm but after years of searching, found nothing.

In the 1950s, a man named Hunter Pennick dug up a brass bucket, two old pick heads, and an iron wedge. On the bucket was scratched an undecipherable code. Pennick dug numerous holes in all directions around his find, but discovered nothing more.

How to Get There: Lawton is located in southwestern Oklahoma, about 80 miles from Oklahoma City. Ask local residents for the site of Frank James's old farm.

GOLDEN WASHTUB

An old prospector apparently hid a washtub half full of gold dust and nuggets worth over $1 million near Hill City, in the Black Hills of South Dakota.

How It Got There: In 1879 two prospectors named Shafer and Humphry picked out a claim in the Black Hills near Tigreville and began panning. They struck it rich and worked the 20-acre claim for years. One hole alone is said to have yielded 17 pounds of gold, while another hole—16 feet square in size—yielded over a pound a day. They put all their dust and nuggets in a big washtub, using a few pinches now and then to buy provisions. They agreed to split everything 50-50.

By the time the claim played out, their washtub was full and Humphry decided to return to his wife and kids in Ohio. He took his half and left, but Shafer stayed on. A confirmed prospector, he

Don't bet on it: 76% of Americans say they have never participated in illegal gambling.

staked out another claim farther down Newton Fork and worked it until the day he died.

Shafer had no known relatives, nor any friends. He spent his time alone working his claim, didn't drink or use tobacco, and never gambled. Townspeople said that his fortune must have been hidden somewhere near his claim. All traces of his old cabin are gone, but old-timers remember seeing its rotting remains along the road to Deerfield. Not a single nugget has ever turned up.

How to Get There: Hill City is in southwestern South Dakota, about 30 miles southwest of Rapid City, not far from Mount Rushmore. Ask old-timers or the local librarian where Shafer's cabin was, along Newton Fork.

TREASURE MOUNTAIN, COLORADO

Gold worth anywhere from $5 million to $40 million was buried by French miners in the San Juan Mountains of southwestern Colorado in the late 18th century.

How It Got There: Tales of incredibly rich gold mines being worked by the Spanish began to drift out of the West with the French fur traders in the late 18th century. Since the French felt that they had a claim on the area, they sent a party from New Orleans to find out what all the excitement was about.

The French traders finally reached the San Juan Mountains and were amazed to find them even richer than they were rumored to be. They set up camp and began working their first rich strike—without bothering to look up the Spanish.

The size of the French party and the amount of gold its members mined is in dispute, but everyone seems to agree that they buried the gold to keep it from falling into Spanish or Indian hands. The fields were so rich that the French stayed on through the first winter, even though it got so cold and the snow got so deep that mining was impossible. They wintered in what is now Taos, New Mexico, and returned to their mines in the spring. They continued this pattern for several years.

But trouble came in the form of American Indian raids. Perhaps the Arapaho began their raids because the French were friendly with the Utes, traditional enemies of the Arapaho. Perhaps the Spanish put them up to it because of complaints from the señoritas in Taos about the Frenchmen's "love 'em and leave 'em" ways. Perhaps it was because the Spaniards had learned just how rich the French mines were and had decided that they didn't want anyone else to have all that gold. Whatever the reason, the French forces were soon decimated.

Lone Survivor: Some accounts claim that the surviving French men had three hiding places for their gold. Others say that they dug a single shaft into the bedrock of Treasure Mountain, a tunnel full of death traps. They also dug a well nearby, according to this tale, and put a map showing the gold's location in a bottle, and dropped it to the bottom of the well. Trees in the area were marked with arrows pointing to the shaft concealing the gold.

The small French party suffered more attacks during their flight, and only one man—Remy Ledoux, the party's leader—survived. When he straggled into a French trading post on the Missouri River and spilled out his tale of fantastic riches in the mountains to the west, his countrymen scoffed. It was too much to believe. The treasure was soon forgotten.

Previous Searches: In 1842 Ledoux's grandson, who had a map that he said came from his grandfather, organized an expedition of 40 men to search for the buried gold. The map, unfortunately, wasn't drawn to scale, and all the mountains in the San Juan range looked alike to the searchers. Worse, Grandpère Ledoux included false landmarks to throw off interlopers. The search party did find a fleur-de-lis scratched on a rock with an arrow underneath it and searched for days nearby with no luck.

Young Ledoux returned the following spring to continue his quest but drowned in the process. His body was recovered by a William Yule, who, many years later—while drinking—admitted he had Ledoux's map.

Another man, Asa Poor, obtained the map and eventually claimed that he had deciphered an inscription in one corner, which supposedly said: "Stand on grave at foot of mountain at six on a September morning, face east, where the shadow of your head falls you'll find the gold."

Although these directions seem a little strange—your shadow falls the same way whether you face east, west, or stand on your head—Poor said that he found a grave that fit the map's descrip-

Doctors in ancient India closed wounds with the pincers of giant ants. (They bit them shut.)

tion and nearby found a sealed shaft that seemed to be a worked-out gold mine. Snowslides and avalanches had greatly changed the mountainside over the years, and no traces of the hidden gold could be found.

How to Get There: Treasure Mountain is located in the San Juan Mountains of southwestern Colorado, in Rio Grande County, between Summitville and Wolf Creek Pass. It's about 100 miles east and a little north of Durango, the nearest sizable town, off Highway 160.

CAPTAIN T. M.'S OKLAHOMA TREASURE

A copper box full of at least $80,000 in gold coins is buried in the Kiamichi Mountains near the present community of Cloudy, Oklahoma.

How It Got There: Captain T. M. (name unknown) and his Indian wife lived in the Seven Devils Mountains (now the Kiamichis) around the turn of the 20th century. Over the years, the captain had hoarded $80,000 worth of gold coins and in his old age he decided to put them in a safe place.

He put his money in a large copper box and buried it somewhere near his cabin. A few years later, he died. He hadn't told his wife exactly where the box was hidden, but she had watched him whenever he went to fetch money from it. She said that he sometimes would head north and return from the east, and sometimes he'd head east and return from the north.

Unfortunately, in her old age the captain's wife couldn't remember exactly where their cabin had been. Or perhaps she was reluctant to discuss the gold with other people. At any rate, she said that the cabin had stood on a low hill a half mile west of a certain rocky ledge. Local residents say that there used to be a cave near this cliff, but it has never been found.

How to Get There: Cloudy, Oklahoma, is near the Texas-Arkansas-Oklahoma border, in Pushmataha County. Ask local residents where Captain T. M.'s old settler's cabin used to stand, or try the library's newspaper clipping file.

* * *

"As long as you're thinking anyway, think big." —**Donald Trump**

Nose-art: Mozart wrote a piano piece that required the player to use both hands *and* his nose.

The Back Side

You're not done yet:

Here are the answers to the quizzes found on pages 168, 250, and 416...

...And info about how to be a part of the Bathroom Readers' Institute

BRI BRAINTEASERS

(Answers from page 168)

1. The third. Lions that haven't eaten in three years would already be dead.

2. Sure you can: yesterday, today, and tomorrow!

3. It's a wolf pack.

4. It's a game of Monopoly.

5. Freeze them first. Take the ice blocks out of the jugs and put them in the barrel. You will be able to tell which (frozen) water came from which jug.

6. The letter *e*, the most common letter in the English language, does not appear once in the entire paragraph.

7. They're the remains of a melted snowman.

8. The woman was a photographer. She shot a picture of her husband, developed it, and hung it up to dry.

9. Charcoal.

10. He is born in room number 1972 of a hospital and dies in room number 1952.

THE GRANNY QUIZ

(Answers from page 416)

1. b) Mandell was involved in a car accident in which she rear-ended another car. Arresting officer Tyrone Davis claimed she refused to sign the ticket he gave her and then "punched him in the arm and chest." She said she was "just reaching for her dead husband's pen," which she claimed the officer had stolen. She was handcuffed and, after refusing to walk, was carried to the police car. Mandell, who is five feet tall and weighs 90 pounds, later said, "It was very stressful, but the ladies in the cell with me were nice."

2. c) Mrs. Meckel actually shot two bucks that winter, one of them being the eight-point prizewinner, and won a hunting rifle

"Q" is the only letter of the alphabet that doesn't occur in the name of any state.

for her accomplishment. She had been watching them sneak around her backyard for weeks and kept a rifle handy just in case. When asked if she was known as a good shot, a local man said, "Oh yeah, you don't want to get on her bad side while you're within fifty yards of her."

3. a) After Barber's home was robbed four times in 18 months she surrounded the house with razor wire. Incredibly, police told her she had to take it down because of the danger to anyone trying to rob her. She refused. The police finally relented, but insisted that she at least put up signs warning intruders of the potential danger.

4. a) Hulmes quit smoking at 84, lived without hot water until she was 94, lived alone until she was 98, and swore by her four daily pints of Guinness stout.

5. b) Michetti was arrested, along with her 56-year-old boyfriend, for smuggling Ecstacy. She told airport police that she knew the pills were there, but she thought they were Viagra.

WHAT AM I?

(Answers from page 250)

1. A butterfly
2. Few
3. Candle
4. Glove
5. The letter M
6. Deck of cards
7. Pair of eyes
8. Dictionary
9. Anchor
10. Postage stamp
11. Your breath
12. Cloud
13. Drum
14. Rainbow
15. Road
16. An hourglass

* * *

"If you can't read this, please ask a flight attendant for assistance."

—***United Airlines Flight Safety Brochure***

Uncle John's "Classic" Bathroom Readers

Uncle John's ***Unstoppable*** *Bathroom Reader*
Copyright © 2003. 504 pages. $16.95

Uncle John's ***Ahh-Inspiring*** *Bathroom Reader*
Copyright © 2002. 522 pages. $16.95

Uncle John's ***Supremely Satisfying*** *Bathroom Reader*
Copyright © 2001. 522 pages, $16.95

Uncle John's ***All-Purpose Extra Strength*** *Bathroom Reader*
Copyright © 2000. 504 pages, $16.95

Uncle John's ***Absolutely Absorbing*** *Bathroom Reader*
Copyright © 1999. 522 pages, $16.95

Uncle John's ***Great Big*** *Bathroom Reader*
Copyright © 1998. 468 pages, $16.95

Uncle John's ***Giant 10th Anniversary*** *Bathroom Reader*
Copyright © 1997. 504 pages, $16.95

Uncle John's ***Ultimate*** *Bathroom Reader*
Copyright © 1996. $12.95

The ***Best of*** *Uncle John's Bathroom Reader*
Our favorite articles from BRs #1 – 7.
Copyright © 1995. 522 pages, $16.95

Uncle John's ***Legendary Lost*** *Bathroom Reader*
BRs #5, #6, & #7 bound together in one big book
Copyright © 1999. 684 pages, $18.95

****

Uncle John's Bathroom Reader ***For Kids Only***
Copyright © 2002. $12.95

Uncle John's ***Electrifying*** *Bathroom Reader For Kids Only*
Copyright © 2003. $12.95

To Order

Contact:
Bathroom Readers' Press
P.O. Box 1117
Ashland, OR 97520
Phone: 541-488-4642
Fax: 541-482-6159
orders@bathroomreader.com
www.bathroomreader.com

Shipping & Handling rates:
- 1 book: $3.50
- 2 – 3 books: $4.50
- 4 – 5 books: $5.50
- 5 + books: $1.00/book

Priority Shipping also available.
We accept checks & credit card orders.
Order on-line or via fax, mail, email, or call us.

• Wholesale Distributors •
Publishers Group West (U.S.):
800-788-3123
Raincoast Books (Canada):
800-663-5714

More *Bathroom Reader* titles

Uncle John's Bathroom Readers *are soooo good, others have joined the effort to entertain the growing number of bathroom reader enthusiasts accross the globe. Here is a list of Bathroom Reader titles available on our website www.unclejohn.com*

The **"Uncle John Plunges Into..."** series
Published by Portable Press San Diego, CA

Uncle John's Bathroom Reader
Plunges Into History
Copyright © 2001. 490 pages, $16.95

Uncle John's Bathroom Reader
Plunges Into the Universe
Copyright © 2002. 494 pages, $16.95

****

The **"Uncle John Presents..."** series
Published by Portable Press
Necessary Numbers: An Everyday Guide to Sizes, Measures, and More
Copyright © 2002. 250 pages, $12.95

Uncle John's Presents
Blame It on the Weather: Amazing Weather Facts
Copyright © 2002. 250 pages, $12.95

Uncle John's Bathroom Reader, © 1988, 224 pages $9.95
Uncle John's Second Bathroom Reader, © 1989, 224 pages $9.95
Uncle John's Third Bathroom Reader, © 1990, 224 pages $9.95
Uncle John's Fourth Bathroom Reader, © 1991, 224 pages $9.95
Published by St. Martin's Press, New York.

THE LAST PAGE

FELLOW BATHROOM READERS:

The fight for good bathroom reading should never be taken loosely—we must do our duty and sit firmly for what we believe in, even while the rest of the world is taking pot shots at us.

We'll be brief: now that we've proven we're not simply a flush-in-the-pan, we invite you to take the plunge: Sit Down and Be Counted! Become a member of the Bathroom Readers' Institute. Send a self-addressed, stamped envelope to: BRI, PO Box 1117, Ashland, Oregon 97520. Or visit our website at: *www.bathroom-reader.com*. You'll receive your attractive free membership card and a copy of the BRI newsletter (sent out irregularly via email), receive discounts when ordering directly through the BRI, and earn a permanent spot on the BRI honor roll!

UNCLE JOHN'S NEXT BATHROOM READER IS IN THE WORKS!

Fear not—there's more on the way. In fact, there are a few ways you can contribute to the next volume:

• Is there a subject you'd like to see us research? Write to us or contact us through our website (*www.bathroomreader.com*) and let us know. We aim to please.

• Have you seen or read an article you'd recommend as quintessential bathroom reading? Or is there a passage in a book or website that you want to share with us and other BRI members? Don't let it go to waste—tell us how to find it. If you're the first to suggest it and we publish it in the next volume, there's a free book in it for you.

Well, we're out of space, and when you've gotta go, you've gotta go. Tanks for your support. Hope to hear from you soon. Meanwhile, remember:

Keep on flushin'!